KISSINGER'S YEAR: 1973

KISSINGER'S YEAR: 1973

Alistair Horne

Weidenfeld & Nicolson
LONDON

First published in Great Britain in 2009
by Weidenfeld & Nicolson

Originally published in the USA in 2009
by Simon & Schuster

1 3 5 7 9 10 8 6 4 2

A CIP catalogue record for this book
is available from the British Library.

ISBN: 978 0 297 85091 5 (hardback)
ISBN: 978 0 297 85908 6 (trade paperback)

Printed in Great Britain by Mackays, Chatham, Kent

The Orion Publishing Group's policy is to use papers that
are natural, renewable and recyclable products and made
from wood grown in sustainable forests. The logging and
manufacturing processes are expected to conform to
environmental regulations of the country of origin.

Weidenfeld & Nicolson

Orion Publishing Group Ltd
Orion House
5 Upper Saint Martin's Lane
London, WC2H 9EA

An Hachette UK Company

www.orionbooks.co.uk.

*To the memory of WFB Jr., oldest and dearest of friends,
and a constant encouragement in writing this book. RIP.*

Contents

FOREWORD

"The statesman has not to make history, but if ever in the events around him he hears the sweep of the mantle of God, then he must jump up and catch at its hem."

— Otto von Bismarck, *Memoirs*

AT THE RISK OF burdening readers with fragments from an autobiography, I feel I owe it to them to explain the rather unusual provenance of this book. How does a British writer, fundamentally committed to works on the history of France, suddenly find himself writing about a German-Jewish-American professor, who became for a time—in 1973—the single most powerful man in the world?

I first met Henry Kissinger in November 1980. He was out of office, as of the four Jimmy Carter years, yet hoping for a call from the recently elected president, Ronald Reagan; it never came. The occasion was an evening reception for my then subject, former British prime minister Harold Macmillan,* at the Woodrow Wilson Center in Washington's old Smithsonian Building. Currently working on the papers of presidents John F. Kennedy and Dwight D. Eisenhower relevant to the Macmillan years, I had been invited to act as a supernumerary host to Macmillan. All the Great-and-the-Good of Washington were there. A photograph shows me sitting next to Kissinger and two seats away from Averell Harriman, with Kissinger appearing to blow

---

* I had been appointed his official biographer.

through his rolled-up order papers like some portly cherub. Macmillan, then eighty-six, looked terrible. He had been visiting the United States, not—as he stressed—as a former prime minister, but as a very active publisher, selling *The New Grove Dictionary of Music and Musicians* for the family firm. But that night he was once again the elder statesman. After dinners, lunches, and speeches every day for two weeks, his pace had been killing. So, understandably, Kissinger turned to me and whispered: "Do you think the old man will die before he speaks?"

Optimistically, but with experience, I replied: "No, he always looks like that. Once he's spoken he'll be completely rejuvenated and keep us up all night!"

And so indeed it came to pass. The old "actor-manager's" wit and erudition, his ability to evoke tears when speaking of the lost generation of 1914–18, held this hardened audience of *le tout* Washington spellbound, and rocked them with laughter, when, inter alia—in answer to a rather crass question as to what was the purpose of the Soviet invasion of Afghanistan—he replied, "Well, I don't suppose they've come for the winter sports, do you?" At the end, Kissinger turned to me, with fresh respect, remarked "You vere right," and invited me to one of his famous breakfast rendezvous. (In the event, breakfast was canceled because Washington became covered overnight in a perilous skin of ice; Kissinger's security guards wouldn't let him out of the house; so instead the invitation was transformed into a rather more relaxed dinner at one of the city's top Italian restaurants, accompanied by his delightful wife, Nancy.) There began a friendship, spasmodic but never close.

Little could I have foreseen that, two decades after that first meeting in Washington, I would be sitting in that same center writing a book about my host.

Early in 2004, I had just completed a run of three books on France, *Seven Ages of Paris, Friend or Foe** (a short history of France from Caesar to Chirac), and *The Age of Napoleon,* and was sitting back in a

---

* Titled in the United States, *La Belle France.*

state of depleted afterbirth. The telephone rang. It was my publisher, George Weidenfeld, with a proposition—out of the blue—that I should write the official life of Kissinger. It was a hugely flattering, and tempting, proposition. I had reservations about my expertise on the U.S. scene, but—more important—I felt I had now reached an age to be deterred by the mass of material that the work would involve (it was rumored that, whereas most eminent figures measure their archives in feet, Kissinger's totaled *thirty-three tons*!). Gracefully, but feeling much honored, I declined. Immediately I regretted the decision; how could any person turn down an offer to write about one of the most pre-eminent men of our times?

I flew to New York to see Kissinger and came up with a counter-proposal. Perhaps I could write just one year in his life, one key year in history?

"Which year?"

"Nineteen seventy-three?"

To my surprise, his response was immediate: "I think that's a great idea."

So a deal was struck. At about the same time, the brilliant Oxford-based, and *young*, historian, Niall Ferguson, contracted to do the much longer-term project, the whole official life. Niall and I talked over the two projects between ourselves and decided there need be no conflict of interest. But why 1973? It was *the* "big year": the year of the signing of the pact to end the Vietnam War, the year of détente with the Soviet Union, but also the year when all hopes were undermined by Watergate. It was the year that Kissinger won the Nobel Peace Prize, and became secretary of state, buttressing an increasingly debilitated president, under threat of impending impeachment. That October the world was rocked by the surprise Yom Kippur War in the Middle East; the previous month, in far-off Chile, Salvador Allende had been overthrown in a brutal coup by General Augusto Pinochet. On both these last subjects I had myself written extensively, the latter in a book called *Small Earthquake in Chile*.* In both I retained a lively interest (dur-

---

* Later I was to discover that an earlier book of mine, *To Lose a Battle: France 1940*, had been of benefit to General Ariel Sharon in his successful crossing of the Suez Canal, which clinched the Yom Kippur War.

ing the Yom Kippur War I had actually been at work in Algeria on a book, *A Savage War of Peace*).

At least I felt I shared one thing with Henry Kissinger; we had both been refugees from Hitler—though in rather different senses.* Perhaps, however, it would give me an insight into one of the most puzzling aspects, among many, of the man: how someone who had reached the very pinnacles of power and success could be so hypersensitive to how the world saw him? About his place in history? This essential insecurity was, in many ways, an endearing attribute; but it was also, as I said, puzzling—and it continued to puzzle me throughout my work on the book. While he had his many admirers, and many friends still from his years in office who remained deeply loyal, even devoted, to him, he also had—I was to discover—a massive weight of detractors and critics, from all colors of the spectrum, ranging from far left to far right, and in varying degrees of passion. Nobody was neutral about Henry Kissinger. Some of his critics were well informed, some not so. One bright American woman remarked to me that "he was an evil man, because he got America into Vietnam." (Not so; America was embroiled in Vietnam many years before Kissinger came on the scene.) Members of both the Cambodian and Chilean human rights lobbies declared that he should be indicted and brought to justice—like ex-President Pinochet. Perhaps here were indeed some reasons for that excessive sensitivity?

But was I, as a foreigner, a Brit, qualified to write a biography about this exceptionally complex American statesman—even just one year in a remarkable life? I had had some unexpected success in writing about the Algerian War, still a raw wound to many in France; to my surprise I found Frenchmen willing to tell me things, as an outsider, that they would not discuss with their fellow countrymen. Could I find similar openings in the United States? I had written much about European military commanders. The interplay of powerful men and events in the making of history, and their being created by history, had always fas-

---

* Unlike my subject, I was a "Bundle from Britain," sent to the United States aged fourteen after the fall of France in the summer of 1940. I returned to Britain in 1943, to fight the remainder of the war in British uniform, and never changed my nationality. See *A Bundle from Britain*, 1992.

cinated me. The challenge to write about Kissinger was irresistible; for here was an opportunity to study at closest hand one of the most interesting, and influential, men of power of our age. I was driven with curiosity, and was to be granted unique, unparalleled, and unqualified access to him personally and his copious archives. Over a period of more than three years I had many hours of prolonged meetings with him, in Washington, New York, London, and Paris, and up at his house in Kent, Connecticut. We exchanged scores of calls and e-mails. Many issues remain controversial—but I was not there to argue, but to question. It was, altogether, a thrilling opportunity for any historian. Brent Scowcroft, a longtime colleague of Kissinger's, did warn me: "Henry could tell the same story ten different ways to ten different people and never fib!" Maybe, but of course it's finally the role of the historian to decide which one he should take on board as history.

From my early, wartime days at school in Millbrook, New York, under an inspired history teacher, I had always been equally fascinated by the romantic part of the American past with its persistent "can do" ethos. But was this enough? There may be chasms in my attunedness to recent U.S. history, those remain entirely my fault, but I deemed myself free from that congenital anti-Americanism which besets some of my countrymen; possibly I could be accused of erring too much in the opposite direction. Certainly I admit to entering the ring with a predisposed respect for the magnitude of what Kissinger had attempted to achieve while in office. At the same time, I have always set my teeth against that other sin besetting us contemporary historians—the tendency to judge events with 20/20 hindsight, too much in the light of today's knowledge and mores. Already there is a growing school which holds the Cold War to have been "unnecessary," the Western stand against Sovietization excessive. To those I would simply urge they spend two hours to see that remarkable German movie, *The Lives of Others*, which more than any words demonstrates why the Cold War had to be waged—and won. Henry Kissinger was both a product of, and a combatant in, the Cold War.

Did I like my subject, many people inquire? Well, frankly, I would never take on a book about someone I disliked in the first place. But, with Kissinger, as with Harold Macmillan, unashamedly I came to like him, as a person, more over the years as work progressed—rather than the converse. (It proved to be a labor which would take nearly five years of my life to that one of his—which, as much as a critique of sloth on the part of the biographer, not to mention the misadventure of three serious illnesses, may say more about the scale of the man and his works.)

One danger of which I was grateful to have been warned—among others, by the Cambridge historian David Reynolds—was that given the weight of Kissinger's own three lengthy volumes of memoirs and his powerful personality, there was a danger of their becoming the standard texts for the period, putting his spin on events—much as, for a generation, Winston Churchill's massive *The Second World War* had become regarded as something like gospel. For all their herculean scale, never dull, always illuminating, the Kissinger memoirs make marvelous reading, and his skill in depiction of characters is, surprisingly, something any novelist of talent might envy, but, inevitably, they constitute one man's version of the history he lived through. Fortunately, although burdensome, declassified releases of the underlying documents have recently assisted the diligent historian's researches. They constitute the core of that alleged thirty-three tons of archives, making the life of Henry Kissinger in office the most documented that ever has been—or, for that matter, because of today's political and technical circumstances, almost certainly ever will be. In consequence I consider myself fortunate not only for having had Dr. Kissinger give me full access to all his private and state documents, as well as the invaluable assistance of Rosemary Niehuss, his archivist of thirty years standing, whom I nicknamed Miss Moneypenny and who helped me find my way through the mountain, in addition to access to files available through the Library of Congress.

Unquestionably the most valuable—and, indeed, enjoyable—factor in the course of the many months of research was the unstinting access to the subject himself that I was granted. Often I came back to that first connecting link through the person of Harold Macmillan, without which I would probably never have met Henry Kissinger. The terms of engagement were similar, but with one important difference: with both Macmillan and Kissinger I was promised full access plus an affidavit of "noninterference," neither requiring to read my manuscript; with Macmillan, then well into his eighties when we started, there was attached the additional proviso that the biography was not to be published in his lifetime ("that will make it easier for both you and me, dear boy!" he said). Kissinger, however, wished to be able to read in print what anyone was to write about him.

In contrast to Harold Macmillan, Kissinger rigidly eschewed the use of a tape recorder; perhaps the dread memories of Nixon and Watergate were too vividly in his mind. So I had to rely on my handwritten notes, transcribed—on tape—later in the day. After our evening work sessions, the Connecticut house would often be filled for dinner by an intriguing miscellany of locals, writers, eminent doctors, New York gallery directors, and the Oscar de la Rentas, he the famous fashion designer. It was always convivial; Kissinger loves good conversation, and the social life—the gracious and elegant Nancy provides it. Sometimes, rather sadly, I would recall in contrast the final, lonely, and austere years of Harold Macmillan. Though he would have been the last to admit it, his seemed to me always a life of tragedy—the last act being the medical error which had persuaded him to resign in 1963, leaving him to face another twenty-three years of what he called "life after death," i.e., political death. After Kissinger's retirement in 1976 with the fall of the Republicans and the advent of Jimmy Carter, Kissinger too seemed condemned, with all its bitter frustrations, to a "life after death" which lasted for nearly thirty years up to the time of writing. But it was crammed with interest, and action. Even under the administration of George W. Bush, he would be invited almost monthly to the White House, or State Department, where the president or National Security Adviser, later Secretary of State Condoleezza Rice would listen attentively to his accrued wisdom, while his professional and social life thrived on a multiplicity of levels. While I always saw in Macmillan that essentially tragic side, there was nothing tragic in Kissinger's makeup. Had there been he would always have been saved by the bon viveur bursting to escape—and by Nancy. Richard Nixon, yes—truly the definitive player of classical tragedy—but that remains to be spelled out in later chapters.

Apart from the hours of his time Kissinger was so unstinting with, I had the good fortune to talk to many protagonists who played a role

in that key year of 1973, both in the United States and elsewhere. When
I started the two-volume Macmillan biography in 1978, the time span
from his leaving office in 1963 added up to only fifteen years, yet many
of his contemporaries were already dead. In contrast, the interval between 1973 and the time of this writing adds up to more than twice
that—thirty-two years. Yet I found many of the players alive, and indeed kicking. Men like the late Peter Rodman, for instance, were still
actively employed as assistant secretary to Donald Rumsfeld in the
Pentagon; while the secretary himself had been one of Kissinger's team.
It speaks for the relative youth of that team—or do Americans in
power tend to live longer than their British counterparts? In my
months of research in the United States, I was extremely fortunate in
the access I was able to have with all whom I wanted to see, or speak
to, with that wonderful American readiness to open up to a stranger.

CHAPTER I

A VERY ODD COUPLE

"The loneliest and saddest Christmas I can ever remember."
— Richard Nixon to David Frost

"If you want a friend in Washington, buy a dog."
— Harry S. Truman

NINETEEN SEVENTY-TWO was a year Henry Kissinger was glad to see come to a close. After twelve months of turbulent activity, and nail-biting negotiations with the North Vietnamese, it had ended on an upbeat note of considerable optimism — insofar as the global position of the United States was concerned — yet one of some uncertainty in terms of his own private ambitions. A triumph in which Kissinger could claim to have played some little part, in the presidential elections that November President Richard Nixon had won the second greatest landslide in American history. Forty-seven million Americans had voted for him — and for his and Kissinger's policies — representing more than 60 percent of all the votes cast. It was an impressive endorsement of his strategy of opening the door to China the previous year, and détente with the Soviet Union. Moreover, despite the huge underswell of opposition to the ever-rumbling Vietnam War, it surely indicated that a majority also supported Kissinger's tireless trips to Paris in 1972, endeavoring to wrestle a "peace with honor" out of the granite-faced, unyielding men from North Vietnam.

Yet that strange human being, Richard Milhous Nixon, the strangest—and perhaps the most fascinating if not egregious—of all U.S. presidents, had celebrated his triumph, not with oysters and champagne as had British prime minister Harold Macmillan in a comparable triumph on coming to power in 1957, but with a demand for the resignation of his entire staff.

Christmas 1972 was a lonely time, for Kissinger as well as for his boss, and a period of serious reflection. Kissinger was then a bachelor, enamored of the tall, elegant, but elusive WASP Nancy Maginnes, but still very much a bachelor—Washington's most sought-after bachelor. Each Christmas he would "ask her to marry me; every year she refused—said she 'wasn't ready'—and yet she wasn't seeing anybody else."[1] So he continued to live in a cramped bachelor house, two up, two down—one bedroom of which he used as an office—on Waterside, a small road running up from Rock Creek.

Originally he was to have spent Christmas with Nixon in his Florida hideout at Key Biscayne.[2] But the invitation had been withdrawn, or rather curtailed to a two-day working visit from December 20 to 22, to debrief General Alexander Haig (then White House chief of staff) on his recent Saigon trip to see the prickly President Nguyen Van Thieu. The two most powerful men in the United States were undergoing a patch of strained relations. There were various reasons: the Christmas Bombing of Hanoi had led to disagreements among the two over its public image; and, on a more personal level, Nixon had been sorely piqued by a recent interview with the attractive Italian female journalist Oriana Fallaci, where Kissinger had rashly let his hair down. Coupled with *Time* magazine bracketing the president, and his adviser, as their Man of the Year, it had caused the highly sensitive president, ever seeking a slight, to feel grievously sidelined by his ebullient subordinate.[3] So Nixon spent a solitary Christmas ("the loneliest and saddest Christmas I can ever remember," he told David Frost,[4] "much sadder and much lonelier than the one in the Pacific during the war").[5]

Certainly these glum reflections were not shared by his national security adviser; he had his own.

For Kissinger the business year (as recorded in his immaculate

"Record of Schedule"＊) ended on December 23 with visits from Admiral Thomas Moorer, the browbeaten chairman of the Joint Chiefs of Staff, Chief of Staff Al Haig, to discuss the effect of the Christmas Bombing, a session with his close associate, Peter Rodman,† in the Map Room, a lunch date with the journalist William Safire, currently a presidential speechwriter; then, at 3:22 P.M., Nancy arrived to collect him from his office. It was a familiar mix, though less intensive than his habitual workday. Christmas Day was spent lunching with Joseph Alsop, his favorite and most trusted among the Washington journalists, at 2720 Dumbarton Avenue in Georgetown, and then dining with Evangeline Bruce‡ in her grand abode nearby.

Though Washington had closed down for the holidays, the next day, December 26, a key message from Hanoi brought Kissinger racing back to his office. It was the signal the White House had anxiously been awaiting; it was also the day of one of the biggest raids by the giant B-52s. The North Vietnamese had agreed to a resumption of the Paris peace talks as soon as the U.S. bombing stopped, and registered its willingness to settle "the remaining questions with the U.S. side." It looked like the ultimate climb-down by Hanoi. Kissinger observed in his memoirs, "We had not heard such a polite tone from the North Vietnamese since the middle of October."[6] He signaled back suggesting a resumption of talks on January 8 (ultimately deferred to the 23rd). The bombing was ceased forthwith. A visit from the White House barber, and at 2:50 P.M. Kissinger took off—alone§—on a well-earned six-day holiday to Palm Springs in the Southern California desert.

For a man whose mind was never still, it was a time for serious reflection. While strolling down the beach near the San Clemente White House, the weekend before the elections in November 1972, Kissinger

---

＊ One of the many sets of records that Kissinger kept.

† Rodman, then in his thirties, remained one of Kissinger's closest associates to the end. At the time of writing he was assistant secretary of defense to Donald Rumsfeld.

‡ Wife of Ambassador David Bruce.

§ When I checked with him (at our meeting in Paris in 2006) whether Nancy had accompanied him to Palm Springs, he roared with laughter: "Certainly not! We weren't married then. And—imagine—what the media would have said: 'We're bombing Hanoi, the world's against us, and Kissinger's gone off with *a woman*'!"

had mused gloomily to author Theodore "Teddy" White: "How do you withdraw? How do you get out of a situation where every single crisis around the world gets dumped on us?"

Not since conversing with grandees like George Marshall and Dean Acheson could White recall "the use of American power so carefully explained" as in that conversation. A passerby shook Kissinger by the hand, thanking him "for peace." Kissinger seemed taken aback, exclaiming, "Where else could it happen but in a country like this. . . . To let a foreigner make peace for you, to accept a man like me—I even have a foreign accent!"[7]

Events had taken a distinctly encouraging upturn since that November stroll, but similar thoughts were not far from the forefront of Kissinger's mind over the Christmas break. The prospects for the coming year looked good, certainly better than they had at the same time twelve months ago. As he apostrophized the coming year of 1973 in his memoirs, it was to begin "with glittering promise; rarely had a Presidential term started with such bright foreign policy prospects."[8]

As his close associate on most of his ventures at that time, Winston Lord, adumbrated these heady days to the author, "U.S. foreign policy was at an absolute peak," with the Nixon-Kissinger team looking "poised to continue to build a structure of peace." Nixon had been reelected in a landslide, the Vietnam War was (or looked to be) over; the Middle East seemed stable; there was the opening to China to build on; and major progress in détente with the Soviet Union. "Now they could continue progress on those fronts while turning to issues that needed more attention; relations with Europe and Japan (especially after the shock of China), Middle East, other regions including our own backyard, 'newer' issues like energy, North-South relations, etc. Congress buoyed by an end to Vietnam War and dramatic summits and progress with two Communist giants."[9]

There was just one small, one very small, blip. It was called Watergate.

Back in the idyllic European peacetime summer of 1870, British foreign minister Lord Granville had been able to discern, justly so it seemed at the time, not "a cloud in the sky." Yet three months later

Emperor Louis-Napoleon's Third Empire had collapsed, crushed by a triumphant Prussia, the emperor himself forced to abdicate; the whole European order had been turned upside down. In 1870 the whole balance of power in Europe had changed overnight. In America, though the skies were perhaps not so cloudless, there was certainly no sense of the drama that lay ahead: a major war in the Middle East, but—with far profounder significance—the leader of the free world, successor to Abraham Lincoln and Franklin Delano Roosevelt, disgraced and disabled. But, perhaps less than a cloud on the horizon, Watergate was more like a shark circling, as of January 1973 at a respectful distance, still—but slowly out there moving in. Whether, that lonely Christmas of 1972, the ripples in the water figured yet anywhere near the forefront of the mysterious, dark reflections—brooding on thoughts of revenge against his many foes—of Richard Milhous Nixon, will never be known. There were rumblings over the break-in at the Watergate complex the previous summer; but that probably caused the least of disturbance to the slumbers of this secretive man. We'll never know. Yet there was no reason to think they did. Had he not just won one of the most spectacular reelection victories of all time? So why the dark thoughts, the sadness?

Certainly they were unlikely to have featured in those of his national security adviser (he of course had his own worries, but not such torments). In his memoirs Kissinger wrote, "We had begun Nixon's second term imagining that we were on the threshold of a creative new era in international affairs; seldom, if ever, had so many elements of foreign policy appeared malleable simultaneously."

Malleable. However, "Within months we confronted a nightmarish collapse of authority at home and a desperate struggle to keep foreign adversaries from transforming it into an assault on our nation's security." Whereas, from a diplomat's point of view, he saw Nixon's first term having formed "in a sense an adolescence. . . . Diplomacy in the second term, which ended abruptly in the late summer of 1974, was a rude accession of maturity." As far as his own role was concerned, he summarized, it was to fall "to me to attempt to insulate foreign policy as much as possible from the domestic catastrophe." But "all our calculations were soon to be overwhelmed by the elemental catastrophe of Watergate."[10]

With the full impact of that foolish break-in still imperceptible to him, Kissinger could not help but look toward 1973 in a "mood compounded of elation and relief." This was not, however, how he regarded his own future. "I thought we were then in a superb governmental position—everything seemed to be running well," he told me. "But I had really made up my mind to have left by the latest by the end of 1973. I was thinking of going to Oxford, to All Souls. I had had talks with Isaiah Berlin (the famous philosopher) . . . the international situation was very strong and I thought, personally, my relations with Nixon could not go on much longer. We had just been made Joint Men of the Year by *Time*—now this was something impossible for a president to share with another." This surely said something about the curiously insecure jealousy of the most powerful man in the Western world. "Also," continued Kissinger, "I was having a lot of nagging from [Chief of Staff Bob] Haldeman about how many times I was meeting Nixon. I didn't think I could go on juggling the NSC with State." [11] There lurked too the steadily worsening relationship between him and his office and the worthy but unimpressive secretary of state, William P. Rogers, a Washington lawyer—a lame, if not a dead, duck secretary of state. Repeatedly Kissinger had urged Nixon to let him take over at State. [12] He was addressing deaf ears. To Kissinger's chagrin, Nixon had consistently refused.

What did Kissinger plan to do among those dreaming spires of Oxford? "Maybe work on my memoirs . . ." He continued: "David Bruce, whom I hugely admired, also felt I should leave*—so by the end of 1972 I had a period of expecting to leave by the end of '73, and a conviction that Nixon and I had left foreign policy in extremely good shape." As he outlined it in his memoirs, "I intended to stay on long enough in 1973 to see the peace in Indochina established; to launch the new initiative toward the industrial democracies that came to be known as the Year of Europe; and to consolidate the new Moscow-Washington-Peking triangle." [13]

But was he being entirely sincere? There was always something compulsively irresistible about Washington to any outsider who had

---

* Kissinger had dined with the Bruces on Christmas night.

once sampled its heady embrace; power, Kissinger himself was once quoted as saying, was the "ultimate aphrodisiac."

So, after the Christmas break, the working year of 1973 began on January 3, with a fairly quiet day in the life of the president's national security adviser:

WEDNESDAY, JANUARY 3, 1973

8:30	Arrive Office
8:50	General Scowcroft/Col. Kennedy (9:00)
9:05	JCS Briefing (Situation Room) (9:15)
9:30	Ron Ziegler (9:42)
9:45	Christine Nadeau—Interviewee (10:26)
	(HAK went to President at 10:00; Julie talked to CN)
10:00	The President—Oval Office (10:50)
10:57	John Ehrlichman/Bob Haldeman—Ehrlichman's office (11:35)
11:40	Ambassador Phuong (12:25)
12:28	Arthur Burns (12:45)
1:20	Lunch—Ambassador Dobrynin (Soviet Embassy) (3:50)
3:58	Larry Eagleburger (4:15)
4:17	The President—Oval Office (5:10)
5:13	Dr. Riland (5:43)
6:20	Depart Office—New York[14]

On the 7th he set off to Paris, once more, on his seventeenth trip to negotiate with the North Vietnamese.

Any which way you looked at it, by any criterion—and this was not peculiarly related to Henry Kissinger's role in it—1973 was not an ordinary year. Whole books have been written about it. One most recently, by Andreas Killen, identifies it, for the United States at any rate, as "the decade's pivotal year . . . a year of shattering political crisis and of remarkable cultural ferment." In it[15] Killen saw three major shocks to the United States:

1. Defeat in Vietnam (though it may not have quite seemed so at the time).
2. Watergate, calling, by the year's end, for presidential impeachment.
3. A collapsing economy, caused by Arab oil embargo.

All three were to occur on Henry Kissinger's watch.

Though it may have marked a low point in U.S. history, it was a bountiful year for moviemakers, especially those catering to violent and to pornographic tastes. *Last Tango in Paris*, *Deep Throat*, *The Exorcist*, and *The Godfather* all contributed to make 1972–74 box office record years. In the fall of 1973, Erica Jong assaulted the last surviving bastions of old-fashioned modesty with her *Fear of Flying*. Assisted by the new technology, lightweight cameras, and abandon of all inhibition, U.S. TV scored a runaway success through a twelve-part series called *An American Family*. In a precursor of the horrors of "reality television" three decades later, week by week the American public would hunker down to watch as the Loud family lived their daily lives, and tore themselves apart in Santa Barbara—all for the benefit of the eager media. Amazingly the Louds had actually volunteered for the purgatory that they were submitted to. By the year's end the couple had gotten divorced. Their son, Lance, had been outed as a transvestite. During the series he became successively the darling then the hate-object of the gay community, and was to admit "television swallowed my family."[16] An identical sentiment might just as well have been voiced by the first lady, Pat Nixon. By a curious stroke of fate, the premiere of the Loud family crucifixion took place the very day that Senate Democrats first voted to investigate Watergate—January 11, 1973, while the taping equipment for both the White House and the Loud house had evidently also been installed at about the same time. Equally, in the course of the series, Pat Loud—with extraordinary parallelism to the Plumbers of Watergate—is seen rifling her husband's files for evidence of his infidelity.

Each series was to rival the other for prime time watching as the year went on.[17]

But was 1973 worse than any other year?—or did it just establish a benchmark for the future?

Certainly the media was coming to assume an increasingly dominant role in American public life. As Abigail McCarthy, the wife of defeated presidential candidate Eugene McCarthy, bemoaned: "In public life one learns very quickly that everyone wants to be on television. There are very few private people left."[18] Looking back from the no less agitated vantage point of 2008, some might even see 1973 as the year the media burst out of Pandora's Box, never to be recaptured, as an unelected power took over from the legitimately elected democratic rulers. Doubtless this was how Richard Nixon saw it.

To an outsider, Washington, D.C., often seems a bizarre place to plant the capital of the world's most powerful nation. With all its mind-boggling beauty, cultural *richesse*, and the vibrant political buzz, over many months spent there I personally have come to love it second only to Paris. But it's still a crazy place to have a capital, and maybe this fundamental craziness has something also to do with the events of 1973. Built in a swamp as a compromise between the mutually hostile North and South, Washington freezes you in winter, and boils you in summer—where its humidity can make you feel hotter than Cairo can. In the good old days the affluent Founding Fathers could take off to run the country from the relative coolness of their estates in Virginia, but even by 1973 the advent of air-conditioning did little more than take the edge off Washington's oppressive summer heat. Tempers fray, judgment wanders. Feeling that modern Turkey was lopsided, in the 1920s Kemal Ataturk moved his capital from Istanbul to Ankara in the dusty heartland of Anatolia; Lenin, in one of his few acts of wisdom, moved from Peter the Great's old capital back to centrally located Moscow (which probably saved the country in 1941). But both St. Petersburg and Istanbul were at least major hubs, great seaports. You could barely ever get a pleasure cruiser up the Potomac to Washington. As the capital of fifty states reaching from Florida to Hawaii, with the decisive fulcrum of voters well to its west, by the late twentieth century, Washington did seem to give the country a politically lopsided appearance.

As of 1973, this lopsidedness received an additional spin (certainly in the eyes of Richard Nixon) within the city from the apparent pre-eminence of Georgetown, and everything it stood for. An elderly, indigenous, black cabdriver (if you can find one) will reminisce today how his father lived in a worker's house, in the 1920s, off what is now plush 34th Street. Streetcars still clanked down the middle of O Street. Particularly since World War II, Georgetown became progressively gentrified into a tightly packed village. In charming, cozy little Georgian houses of brick surrounded by box hedging, its denizens would gossip and conspire politely in elegant and engaging little dinner parties. The Muffies lived next door to the Buffies, all were the best possible friends (for the most part). They took in, but literally, each other's washing. The trouble is that, all too good friends, they know precisely what you do, and with whom, almost from the moment you think about doing it. No secrets in Georgetown. But that also applies to Washington as a whole, for the city dominated by a regime often known as "government by leak." As of 1973—and it hasn't changed much—almost everybody in Georgetown is a "liberal," in the old-fashioned sense of the word. They could afford to be. In 1973 you would be hard-pressed to meet a right-wing Republican there, or what later emerged as a neocon.

The collective influence of Georgetown was—and is—immense; though perhaps never quite as much as Nixon believed. But it was a world he hated, and distrusted. In contrast Henry Kissinger loved Georgetown, and envied it, and felt comfortable in the company of its denizens. For Richard Nixon, the Californian who would flee to the farthest reaches of Florida for his time off, this overall geographical lopsidedness may also have had a bearing on the personal issues that were ultimately to destroy him.

Much admired for his statecraft by Kissinger, that supreme opportunist Bismarck once remarked of a statesman: "if ever in the events around him he hears the sweep of the mantle of God, then he must jump up and catch at its hem." Paraphrasing the same thought, while I was writing his official biography, Harold Macmillan once remarked to me of his own life: "Things never turn out quite how you expect, dear boy—but never miss an opportunity."[19] It was an aphorism that came to mark his own upward path, from unpromising backbench member of Parliament to prime minister in the space of twenty years. The same might have been said of Henry Kissinger, from being a lonely German refugee, a humble PFC in the U.S. Army of World War II, to the most powerful man in the world in thirty years. Kissinger was certainly never one to pass up an opportunity.

Henry Kissinger was born Heinz, in May 1923 in the prosperous Franconian town of Fürth in southern Germany. He and his younger brother, Walter, were blessed with two loving parents, to whom they owed not only their genes but their survival through the Holocaust that lay ahead. Fürth had been a thriving community where Jews had traditionally lived in equanimity, and distinction—until Hitler came along. Kissinger's father, Louis, was a much respected schoolteacher, but removed by the Nazis. He never quite got over the indignities and persecution experienced under them. As with Harold Macmillan, it was Henry's mother, Paula, who seems to have been the stronger of the two parents, urging their flight from Germany to the United States in 1938. He was naturalized a United States citizen in 1943, while in military training at Spartanburg, South Carolina. But he would never lose his accent despite all his later years teaching at Harvard. (He used to joke that his brother "learned American as a street vendor, but I kept my accent because I went to Harvard instead!" Walter's riposte was that "I listened to others, Henry did not.")[20]

World War II took Henry back to Europe as an infantry PFC, seeing action in the Battle of the Bulge of 1944, where he came uncomfortably close to the front line, able to hear tracks of the German panzers "grinding out the foxholes of my buddies up front."[21] With that heavy Bavarian accent, he remained more at home with Europeans like Metternich and Kant than Americans like Benjamin Franklin and Mark Twain; however, he would never pause in his gratitude for what America meant to him, and what he owed to it. In those formative years, apart from his parents, Kissinger had essentially two—two very disparate—influences.

In the earliest days, it was fellow PFC Fritz Kraemer, and—much later—Nelson Rockefeller. Kraemer was an unusual person, certainly not your run-of-the-mill GI. They met at an army training camp in the sweltering Louisiana summer of 1944. Kissinger had just emerged from boot camp, after he had been naturalized the previous year. Beaten into shape like most recruits, he had done his best to remain inconspicuous, giving this excellent fraternal advice to his younger brother, Walter: "Always stand in the middle because details are always picked from the end. Always remain inconspicuous because as long as they don't know you, they can't pick on you." [22] Yet he was conspicuous to his buddies for always having a book at hand, or a copy of *Time* in his knapsack on marches—if not for his accent.

Fifteen years older than Kissinger, Kraemer was a German refugee too, but non-Jewish, son of an affluent Prussian family who had fled Hitler on account of their deeply conservative political beliefs. He boasted two Ph.D.'s. That summer of 1944 he too was a simple private, but—eschewing any urge to remain inconspicuous—sported a Teutonic monocle and riding crop. Under instructions from an inspired general to bring home to the troops what the war, morally, was all about, he appeared in front of Kissinger's company, clad in Wehrmacht uniform, and berated it. "For the first time in my life—and perhaps the only one," Kissinger recalled, "I wrote [to tell] a speaker how much he had moved me." [23] Kraemer responded by inviting him to eat in a GI club. "Out of this encounter," Kissinger continued, "grew a relationship that changed my life."

Reaching Europe for the final push on Germany, Kraemer managed to arrange for both to be transferred to G-2, the intelligence section, in which capacity Kissinger reentered the country his family had fled seven years previously. Promoted to sergeant, there he reputedly earned brownie points rounding up former members of the Gestapo, by the simple ruse of advertising in the local press for applicants with "police experience." It seems an extraordinary indictment of the U.S. Army at war that, because of their knowledge of German and intellectual ability, the two had not instantly been picked out for intelligence work. After the war, and for the next few decades, Kraemer, said Kissinger, "shaped my reading and thinking, influenced my choice of college, awakened my interest in political philosophy and history, inspired both my undergraduate and graduate theses." [24] He was profoundly influenced by the way his fellow German "dedicated his life to fighting against the triumph of the expedient over the principled." Kraemer in return modestly denied that he had been "the man who discovered Kissinger." His role, he declared, had simply been "getting Kissinger to discover himself!"[25]

Kraemer became an increasingly ascetic prophet, and prophet-without-honor—an absolutist about the Cold War, divorced from the world of nowism. When Kissinger entered government, the two men split, on a matter of principle; said Kissinger, "He would lecture me on the evils of Communism. It was probably a mistake that I didn't see him more when I was in office. But he wanted constantly to go at me to be tougher with the Russians. *It came down to nuclear warfare* [author's italics]."[26]

They did not meet, nor would Kraemer speak to him, for thirty years. Kraemer died in 2003.

The army helped toughen Kissinger, gave him an American identity and a hard shell (thought Walter Isaacson).[27] On release from the army, following Kraemer's advice that "a Gentleman does not go to a local New York school,"[28] Kissinger applied to Harvard. There he read deeply on German philosophers. He became fascinated by the statescraft of those great nineteenth-century exponents of realpolitik, Metternich, Castlereagh, and Bismarck—who were to become subjects of his two finest books.[29] The European quest for an acceptable and workable balance of power, the status quo as opposed to revolution and disorder, struck a strong chord in an intrinsically conservative mind. As the Cold War grew ever more menacing, Kissinger came increasingly to abhor the potential alternative to status quoism: nuclear warfare. Here he was instinctively at one with Nixon, who, as Dwight Eisenhower's vice president, had been up there on the coal face. His studies at Harvard did not lead him to agree with General Robert E. Lee's "It is History that teaches us to hope." The essential, pessimistic sense of the tragic of the Central European was too strong in him.

Kissinger's was "a quest for a realpolitik devoid of moral homilies," observed his rather more left-wing Harvard colleague, Stanley Hoffmann.[30] Putting into practice, while in office, that principle of realpolitik would earn Kissinger critics and enemies on both sides of the political spectrum. Thoughtful articles in *Foreign Affairs* and books such as *Nuclear Weapons and Foreign Policy* (1957) earned him respect—but in a world of limited frontiers. Until the late 1950s and early 1960s, few outside the world of academe had heard of him. Ronnie Grierson, one of his oldest friends, observed how in those days when he came to England "he knew only two people—me and Wayland Young—and was free for every meal!"[31] And not all attendants at his lectures were entranced; a successor at the National Security Council, Zbigniew Brzezinski, was one. New at Harvard in 1950 as a first-year graduate student, he heard Kissinger give an introductory seminar on political theory. Though initially impressed, after one session of hearing his voice Brzezinski decided to give up the course. "That heavy German accent, the stretching out of Nietzsche—and Spengler, I couldn't take it!"[32]

Allegedly their mutual animosity stemmed from Harvard.*

One of those who *could* listen to, or read, Kissinger was Nelson Rockefeller, then an assistant for international affairs to President Eisenhower. In 1956, the essentially liberal Rockefeller took Kissinger on board as director of a "Special Studies Project." He was to become described as Rockefeller's closest intellectual associate. Through Rockefeller, Kissinger now discovered Washington, and vice versa. For the next twelve years he remained a part-time consultant for Rockefeller, and close to the man, but still teaching at Harvard—though, for reasons of personality, he encountered difficulties in obtaining tenure. He married, and divorced (in 1964), Anneliese Fleischer, a fellow Jewish refugee from Bavaria, by whom he had two children. Loyal to Rockefeller, in the 1960s Kissinger expressed many misgivings about Nixon, once calling him "a hollow man, and evil."[33] In 1968, Rockefeller ran for the Republican nomination in the presidential race. A generous and talented man, but lacking the killer instinct, he lost to Nixon. Kissinger felt at the time that, with Lyndon Johnson withdrawn from the race, Rockefeller was the only candidate "who could unite the country," torn apart as it was by Vietnam, and could not disguise his despair. Then came the call from Nixon's office for Kissinger

---

* Another perhaps more fundamental reason: hostility of the dispossessed Pole to Kissinger's acceptance of the status quo, which threatened to perpetuate the Soviet subjection of Poland?

to come and serve as a foreign policy adviser. Kissinger was unable to refuse, but observed at the time that maybe he could help more "if I work behind the scenes." As of the first Nixon election, Kissinger had met him only once. Following the election, Nixon sent for him to become his national security adviser at the White House, no less. His old mentor, Fritz Kraemer, was horrified; he didn't see how Kissinger could trust Nixon: "the Right will call you the Jew who lost Southeast Asia, and the Left will call you a traitor to the cause."[34] Kissinger was astonished by Nixon's offer, but—after he had outlined his foreign policy views, came away "struck by his perceptiveness and knowledge so at variance with my previous image of him."[35]

And so the waters divided, and would remain divided—rendering Kissinger the most controversial of all Washington public servants. The world then looked more uncertain, if not dangerous, than ever before. The USSR had, for the first time, attained parity with the United States in the arms race, especially rocketry. Its new preeminence had enabled Soviet leader Leonid Brezhnev to invade Czechoslovakia and crush Alexander Dubček's brave Prague Spring with impunity earlier that year. The war in Vietnam dragged on, apparently unwinnable, having destroyed Nixon's predecessor, Lyndon Johnson. Splitting Americans increasingly, it would reach the horrendous point of National Guardsmen shooting down American students at Kent State University in May 1970. Until Vietnam was resolved, the United States was paralyzed in the world at large. Nixon seemed faced with the same conundrum that had faced France's Charles de Gaulle over the Algerian War at the beginning of the decade; France then had to get out of Algeria in order to "marry her age." Nixon determined upon the same course, not to scuttle as de Gaulle had, but to exit Vietnam in a "peace with honor." According to his memoirs, however, Nixon told Kissinger at this first meeting that he was "determined to avoid the trap Johnson had fallen into, of devoting virtually all my foreign policy time and energy to Vietnam, which was really a short term problem." Instead there were "longer-term problems"—such as "the vitality of the NATO alliance," the Middle East, the Soviet Union, and Japan. "Finally," he mentioned "the need to re-evaluate our policy toward Communist China."[36]

Nevertheless, headed by Kissinger, in the utmost secrecy peace talks began with the North Vietnamese in Paris in August 1969, half a year after Nixon's first inauguration, and they would take some twenty more meetings and nearly four years before they would finally come to fruition, as will be seen in a subsequent chapter. At the same time Nixon embarked on an even bolder rethink of basic U.S. foreign policy, and radical deviation from the past. Instead of the principle of aggressive containment of the Soviets and China, such as had ruled since John Foster Dulles and the early days of the Cold War, Washington would seek to persuade Moscow and Beijing that they should no longer regard themselves as revolutionary, expansionist powers. More could be attained through "linkage," the carrot of commercial benefits their ailing economies needed, in return for good behavior. A moratorium by agreement must be sought in nuclear escalation. Most dramatic of all, Nixon would open the door to the unmentionable Chinese, who only two decades earlier had been killing Americans—many of them—in Korea, to bring Beijing into play as a counterbalance to Moscow. These were the themes which would dominate White House policy from 1969 through to the end of the Nixon era—and beyond. But more, in detail, later. It was perhaps no coincidence that this radical Grand Design, the pursuit of a new global balance of power, echoed thoughts put forward by the new national security adviser in his masterly study of how Metternich and Castlereagh achieved a balance of power, resulting in a hundred years of European peace, in *A World Restored*. One can be sure that this was a book Nixon had read most carefully. From 1969 onward Kissinger would become the chief activist of Nixon's Grand Design. The subtle and discreet backchannel diplomacy that it involved was admirably suited to both his and Nixon's secretive personas. But it would certainly not be likely to suit the secretary of state, Nixon's old friend William Rogers.

Washington's National Security Council is a strange anomaly, both a duplication of, and a rival to, the U.S. State Department. What is its purpose? The anomaly was to become particularly pronounced during the Kissinger-Rogers era, and it still remains unresolved to this day. Historically, it was all to do with the management of U.S. foreign policy. During World War II, issues were clear-cut, and there was never any question of where control resided—in the White House, and the strong hands of FDR personally. Harry Truman, less sure of himself and less trustful of a State Department shaken by leakages and scandals connected with the Alger Hiss revelations, first created the National Security Council in July 1947, at a time when the Soviet threat became manifest. Chaired by the president, with the secretaries of state and defense as its key members, and the director of the newly formed CIA its intelligence adviser, the council was designed to be the president's principal forum for considering national and security problems, and to help formulate speedy decisions. It was in effect a cabinet within a cabinet. Reorganized in 1949, the NSC was then placed firmly inside the executive office of the president, operating from within the heart of the White House, but strongly influenced by Truman's powerful secretary of state, Dean Acheson. Each successive incumbent modified it to meet his own requirements. Because of his training as a soldier, Eisenhower reshaped it along the lines of a military staff system. At the heart of it he appointed Robert "Bobbie" Cutler to be the assistant to the President for national security affairs (1953–55). A Boston lawyer with no political background, but a close personal friend, trusted implicitly, Bobbie* came to act as Ike's "whiskers," and voice.

With the advent of John F. Kennedy, the debacle at the Bay of Pigs in early 1961†, laying both the State Department and the CIA open to much criticism, led to a series of measures aimed at ensuring that the president received better independent advice. Under the vigorous McGeorge Bundy, with incremented powers, the NSC also reentered the arena of monitoring policy implementation. Under Lyndon Johnson, the NSC was allowed to atrophy once more, with the president relying more on the advice of individuals rather than institutional staffs. While within the Eisenhower administration the NSC had the essence of military structure, under Kennedy and Johnson it became chaotic; under Nixon-Kissinger between 1969 and 1974 it once more became highly structured. With the NSC's numbers expanded from twelve to

---

* Whom I remember well as a child growing up in the wartime United States as a most convivial and witty individual.

† His famous comment at the time, as quoted to the author by the late Professor John Kenneth Galbraith, was "I learned then never to trust the experts."

thirty-four, the national security adviser (Kissinger) was appointed
chairman of the key Review Group, which was empowered to screen
all papers, as well as all outgoing policy signals, before they were presented to the full NSC, chaired by the president. Thus from the very
moment of the 1969 inauguration, Kissinger was swiftly able to establish his ascendancy. At the same time, Rogers, Nixon's secretary of
state, a not very thrustful New York lawyer, was progressively to lose
his. Within the embrace of the NSC were six powerful subcommittees,
such as the 40 Committee (charged with clandestine operations) and
the Washington Special Action Group (WSAG), summoned to deal
with specific crises. Each was chaired by Kissinger.

From the beginning Nixon made it clear that he wanted his national security adviser (Kissinger) to conduct important matters of foreign, and security, policy directly out of his own office in the White
House. As Nixon wrote in his memoirs, "From the outset of my administration, [I] planned to direct foreign policy from the White
House. Therefore I regarded my choice of a National Security Adviser
as crucial."[37] Deeply distrustful of the State Department to deal with
sensitive negotiations in a leakproof fashion, Nixon gave Kissinger
fullest range for his very special skills as a backchannel operator. In
other nations with presidential structures, Kissinger's function would
have come close to filling that of prime minister—except that he would
not be directly answerable to the floor of the legislature. Special aircraft of the White House Communications Agency would be set at his
beck and call. Throughout the first term, it was only Kissinger who
took part in Nixon's important discussions with foreign dignitaries.

As of January 1969 onward, the U.S. secretary of state had been
William Pierce Rogers. His middle Christian name may well have
come from Franklin Pierce, a president not acclaimed with distinction.
In the way of the American system, Rogers was a political appointee
who had never previously served in any foreign, or State Department,
post. He was a decent and respectable East Coast establishment figure,
Cornell Law School, etc.—everything that Nixon and Kissinger were
not—a lawyer who had started off life prosecuting organized crime in
New York City. Ending his wartime career as a navy lieutenant commander in the Pacific, he had advised Nixon on the Hiss case, and had
served Eisenhower as attorney general. In this capacity he had helped

Nixon out over his "little local difficulty" of the Checkers affair.* He would terminate his public career investigating the disaster of the space shuttle *Challenger*.

Secretary Rogers was also not accountable to the House of Representatives. (Nor, for that matter, would Kissinger be, either in his NSC capacity, or later as secretary of state.) A leading conservative journalist declared acidly that Rogers could not, so it was said, "find the State Department in broad daylight with a flashlight,"[38] while Nixon's opinion of the State Department was roughly summed up in his remark: "If the Department of State has had a new idea in the last 25 years, it is not known to me."[39] He had "given" Rogers the State Department partly as a "grace-and-favor" job, for his unquestioning loyalty, and partly because he reckoned that, with Rogers, he could run his own foreign policy without let or hindrance. From 1969, progressively and systematically the honorable, but unhappy, Rogers found himself sidelined, indeed humiliated, with Kissinger repeatedly pressing Nixon for his job. The "special relationship" which sprang up between Kissinger and Soviet ambassador Anatoly Dobrynin completely bypassed Rogers; he was kept out of the loop on the sensitive negotiations with the Chinese, which preceded Nixon's world-shaking visit there in 1971, and — pointedly — was not even allowed to appear on TV being greeted by the welcoming Chinese. As Kissinger once remarked, he was left "dealing with Ghana and suchlike important affairs of State!"[40] It remains a puzzle why, in view of his studied downgrading by Nixon and Kissinger — which redounded to the credit of neither — Rogers did not resign before he was pushed. His loyalty was probably the answer.

As suggested earlier, to those habituated to other political systems, it may seem a strange way to run a railroad: to have one huge, cumbersome, and expensive apparatus, the State Department, operating out of its oft derided base in Washington's Foggy Bottom; then duplicate it with another vast apparatus, the National Security Council — with neither always singing from the same hymn sheet. But this is all part of the fabric of checks and balances inherent in the American system.

---

* In the 1952 election campaign Nixon answered charges that he had accepted an illegal slush fund payment of $18,000, declaring that the only gift he had kept had been Checkers, a cocker spaniel. The slogan "We're keeping the dog" gained widespread sympathy for Nixon, and may have saved his political career.

To a remarkable extent, Nixon's genius operated by instinct. It was one of the features that drew the two odd bedfellows together, with the historian's training of Kissinger complementing the sometimes erratic, but frequently brilliant, instinct in foreign affairs of the president. When he summoned Kissinger in 1968 he admitted that he had been "uncharacteristically impulsive," and had "a strong intuition about Henry Kissinger"[41]—perhaps surprisingly so, given that he would almost certainly have been aware of Kissinger declaring repeatedly, while he was working with Rockefeller in committed opposition to the drafting of Nixon during the primaries, that "The man is unfit to be president."[42] But here Nixon had not been acting out of pure impulse; he knew more about his man. Three works by Kissinger would have made a powerful impact on the well-read president, striking as they did chords with his own thinking. The first, written while Kissinger was still a little known academic at Harvard, was his 450-page *Nuclear Weapons and Foreign Policy*, which, for all its density, had—quite surprisingly—become a best-seller when published in 1957. In it he expressed most strongly his abhorrence of the notion of nuclear war with the Soviet Union, and the necessity of exploring every possibility of limited warfare, and all other diplomatic options. (Kissinger himself was astonished by his success, remarking with that self-deprecating sense of humor that it had to be "the most unread best-seller since Toynbee.") But, no, Nixon had certainly read it, and digested its message. That same year of 1957 Kissinger had also published a refined version of his doctoral thesis for Harvard, under the ponderous title of *A World Restored: Metternich, Castlereagh and the Problems of Peace, 1812–1822.* It was a fascinating book, the arguments superbly presented, but not something to be digested at a sitting. Most important, a careful reading discloses a remarkable blueprint of how Kissinger would conduct policy once empowered to do so. "Under the impact of Napoleon," wrote Kissinger in *A World Restored,* "there disintegrated not only the system of legitimacy of the 18th century, but with it the physical safeguards which, to contemporaries at least, seemed the prerequisite of stability."[43]

In prevailing mid-twentieth-century terms, the same might almost have been written about Mao Zedong or Joseph Stalin. Diplomacy, the essence of commerce between civilized nations, Kissinger saw as being "possible only in 'legitimate' international orders." After the upheaval produced by Napoleon, "what is surprising is not how imperfect the settlement emerged, but how sane . . . the period of stability which ensued was the best proof that a 'legitimate' order had been constructed." The two most important words in Kissinger's vocabulary were "legitimacy" and "stability." With Metternich he agreed that "No peace is possible with a revolutionary system, whether with a Robespierre who declares war on chateaux or a Napoleon who declares war on Powers." [44]

In contemporary terms, what was essential was to impose "legitimacy" on systems such as the USSR's and Red China's, which considered themselves "revolutionary." * Then you could do business with them, via diplomacy. As regards techniques of diplomacy, he thoroughly endorsed the wily Metternich's view that "to show one's purpose is to court disaster; to succeed completely is to invite disintegration." [45] Here was backchannel diplomacy. At the same time, and this would be a helpful hint when dealing with a president like Nixon, "A man who has been used to command finds it almost impossible to learn to negotiate, because negotiation is an admission of finite power." [46]

Writing admiringly of his subjects, Metternich and Castlereagh,† Kissinger summed up: "Their goal was stability, not perfection, and the balance of power is the classic expression of the lesson of history that no order is safe without physical safeguards against aggression." He cautioned: "The statesman is inevitably confronted by the inertia of his material, by the fact that other powers are not factors to be manipulated but forces to be reconciled"; then continuing in what reads almost like a forecast of events a decade and a half in the offing: "The requirements of security differ with the geographical location and the domestic structure of the powers. His instrument is diplomacy, the art

---

* Kissinger qualifies this meaningfully later on: " 'A legitimate' order, as long as it is not stagnant, achieves its transformations through acceptance . . . a revolutionary order having destroyed existing structure of obligations, must impose its measures by force . . . the legitimate order confronts the problem of creating a structure which does not make change impossible; a revolutionary order faces the dilemma that change may become an end in itself" (*A World Restored*, p. 172).

† He had originally planned to include Bismarck in his thesis, but—in the way familiar to authors—Bismarck ran off the page, and was kept for a subsequent blockbuster, *Diplomacy* (1994). The original, 1957, text of *A World Restored* was republished unaltered in 2000.

of relating states to each other by agreement rather than by exercise of force by the representation of a ground of action which reconciles particular aspirations with a general consensus."[47]

If read carefully, the young Kissinger's treatise of 1957 comprises a revealing blueprint of how his thought processes would operate when in office a decade and a half later. Then, toward the end of 1968, and thus well *before* the announcement of Kissinger's first appointment to the NSC, a distinguished British foreign official, Robert Wade-Gery*, recalled being excited by Kissinger's delivery of a lecture on U.S. Vietnam policy.[48] In it he laid out with astonishing precision, and openness, exactly how he would handle negotiations if, by any remote chance, he were to find himself in a position of power in Washington (which, at the time, he was certainly not expecting, since he was still working with Rockefeller). The lecture was closely based on a major article in *Foreign Affairs*, which, although dated January 1969, had been written the previous August, and actually appeared in print at the beginning of November; i.e., before Nixon's election, and well before Kissinger could have had any intimation of the call which was to come. He began with remarking how the peace negotiations then underway in Paris "had been marked by the classic Vietnamese syndrome; optimism alternating with bewilderment; euphoria giving way to frustration," and continuing "we must realize that a civil war which has torn a society for twenty years and which has involved the great powers is unlikely to be settled by a single dramatic stroke."[49]

He then went on to explore past U.S. failures in seeking a purely military solution in Vietnam, and the political problems facing both North and South regimes, and how the Tet Offensive of 1968 had overthrown all "assumptions of American strategy": "The choreography of how one enters negotiations, what is settled first and in what manner is inseparable from the substance of the issues." He torpedoed any thoughts of realizing a coalition government between "parties that have been murdering and betraying each other for 25 years," while at the same time hinting at the importance of backchannel diplomacy with the other main, outside players—Russia and China. He closed

---

* Later to become British high commissioner in India, retiring as Sir Robert Wade-Gery.

with the recommendation "We should continue to strengthen the Vietnamese army to permit a gradual withdrawal of *some* American forces" while giving strong emphasis to the key words, "*ending the war honorably* [author's italics]." Even the *Washington Post* praised it as a "remarkable analysis . . . free from the myths and prejudices of the past."[50]

Thus, in marked contrast to Secretary of State Rogers, with Kissinger at the helm of the rival NSC, Nixon could rest well assured that "his" foreign policy would be executed, with maximum efficiency. For all the contrast in their backgrounds and personalities, on essentials of policy — as well as technique — they spoke the same language, a fact that manifested itself very soon after the 1969 inauguration and Kissinger's arrival at the White House. Yet, in all the history of U.S. government, could there ever have been an odder couple, a more contrasting couple, than Richard Milhous Nixon and Dr. Henry Alfred Kissinger? Aged respectively sixty and not quite fifty as of January 1973, the Quaker and the Jewish refugee. One, the poor California boy, son of a grocer, whose parents couldn't afford to fulfill his dreams by sending him to a chic Eastern college, but to unsmart local Whittier instead. There followed a World War II career as a naval officer of no great distinction in the Pacific, then to Washington, where as a young lawyer on the Hill he made his name, and earned the hatred of many good liberals, for his prosecution of Alger Hiss*. Then came a lifetime in politics; defeated for the presidency in 1960, by JFK, by the narrowest of margins. Finally, becoming president in 1969.

If Kissinger and Nixon were drawn together by shared doctrine in foreign policy, and ambition — the desire to establish a place in history — there was also one human characteristic that bound the two together. That was a certain, extraordinary insecurity — or so it seemed to me. Given that here was a man who had scaled every summit, received every blessing life can bestow, Henry Kissinger's own insecurity never ceased to surprise me. Not least, it manifested itself, repeatedly, in his anxiety as to what his biographer might be proposing to say about him! Once, over the whiskey in his lair at Kent, Connecticut, when he had been expounding at length on this deep insecurity of

---

* The State Department official accused of having been a traitor.

Richard Nixon, I dared venture to observe on his own, unexpected, sense of insecurity: "But aren't you too very insecure?" With the gentlest of smiles, he replied: "Well, you can say that, I can't!"

Nixon's insecurity, largely socially based, was apparent in almost everything he did or said; Kissinger's, as defined by his longtime friend Arthur Schlesinger, was "his refugee's desire for approval."[51] It was an aspect that was also affirmed by Lawrence Eagleburger, one of Kissinger's close associates and friends, himself Jewish too, who observed: "You can't understand Henry unless you understand his insecurity—his *Jewishness*—the anti-anti-Semitism of the Jew—and the background of Germany."[52]

If there were contradictions between Nixon and Kissinger, they were as nothing compared with those residing in the bosom of the president himself. Many books have been written analyzing them. To John Freeman, British ambassador (1969–71) under Harold Wilson, who had many meetings with Nixon, and possibly knew him better than most of his own entourage, he remains America's "greatest undiscovered U.S. president."[53] Passionately, pathetically, Nixon wanted to be loved; but even more than that, he wanted to remain undiscovered. This was one of the many paradoxes about Nixon. While Kissinger was gregarious to a fault, loving the hubbub of social life, cultivating friendships in all walks of life, Nixon was a paid-up misanthrope. He had, it seems, only two close friends, Bebe Rebozo, a Cuban exile who had made a fortune banking in Florida, and Bob Abplanalp, who had made a killing in aerosols. Inseparable from and totally loyal to Nixon, they were curious soul-mates for a president. Their intellectual, and political, input was virtually nil. With Abplanalp, renowned for his foul language, the dirty—often anti-Semitic—jokes would flow. Vacationing in their Key Biscayne hideout, Rebozo would often sit with Nixon in total silence for hours on end.[54] Kissinger, however, could understand, and sympathize with, Nixon's need for such comrades: "It was that terrible claustrophobia induced by the White House—impossible to have normal friends; and neither of them had any demands to impose on Nixon."[55] Like Kissinger, Nixon was not averse to hearing gossip; but it had to be political—he was not interested in the social and sexual tidbits that amused the man of Harvard. He would talk meaningfully, but in grandiose abstractions, about the working class—yet he cherished absolutely no contact with men-of-toil. The arm-pressing, backslapping hail-fellow-well-met manner essential to your average American politician was completely alien to Richard Nixon.

Meanwhile, as part and parcel with his misanthropy went an obsession for secrecy, to an extent shared with no other previous U.S. president, and which would provide the fatal flaw, destroying Nixon in the end. Another curious flaw, of notable relevance to 1973, was that he could not take any measure of alcohol. Even loyal colleagues such as Al Haig would assert that "one drink, and he'd slur . . . two and he was out. But he was very disciplined."[56] "Two martinis, and he'd change . . . he couldn't hold his liquor," confirmed Brent Scowcroft.[57] It was a phenomenon that would manifest itself at various times, and to varying degrees, under the pressures of Watergate. John Freeman continued: "If he trusted you, you were in forever; and Henry was one of those."* Like his old boss, Eisenhower, Nixon found it hard to sack anyone—but not easy to work with them either. Said Peter Rodman, who worked with both Nixon and Kissinger in the 1970s, "He basically hated people. He would much rather communicate by written memos than in any kind of discussion. A loner, but his comebacks after one defeat after another—right to the end—were truly amazing."[58] Stephen Ambrose comments on how Nixon's "mind never rested," and how, even at sixty (on January 9, 1973), his formula for living remained—"never slow down."[59]

Back in 1968, Nixon was determined that, if reelected, he intended to run foreign policy from the White House, and not through the State Department. From study of the underlying documents, it is abundantly clear that the original thinking, the initiatives, notably the opening to China† and détente with Russia, came from the unceasingly restless brain of Richard Nixon, and not from Henry Kissinger. Though he never resisted others doing so over the years, Kissinger did

---

* This may have been only partially true; otherwise, how equate it with Nixon's precipitate sacking of Bob Haldeman and John Ehrlichman under the pressures of Watergate?

† Freeman noted that Nixon had "been thinking about it for many years before" (interview, 1/19/06).

not aver it was otherwise. The joint chord that Nixon struck with Kissinger was a bold belief in realpolitik, which he felt a great power like the United States could enter into in *reality*, and not just contemplate from the pages of historians—like Kissinger's fellow eggheads at Harvard. When asked during the 1968 election how he would most like to be remembered, Nixon answered, revealingly: "as having made some contribution to the kind of a world in which we can have peace in the last third of this century . . . the greatest honor history can bestow is the title of peacemaker." [60]

With all those years of experience wrangling on the Hill, Nixon had achieved the reputation of being an unsurpassable political operator. Haig, who served under seven presidents and was himself subsequently a secretary of state, could declare also that "Nixon had no peer in foreign affairs." [61] Certainly one should never try to take away the brilliance, the essential greatness of Nixon. Some lapidary words of advice given to me, before embarking on this project, by friend and neighbor Lord Carrington, former foreign secretary, was: "Never underrate Richard Nixon." [62] Advice I would never forget, nor ever find wanting.

From a dramatist's point of view, Nixon might well seem the more interesting character than Kissinger. He conformed so closely to the principles of tragedy as defined by Aristotle: the human being of great stature who plunges from the highest position to the very depths, and essentially through a fatal flaw in his own character. Kissinger was never a tragic figure; he never fell from a great height. As Brent Scowcroft observed, Nixon was "a very complex, tortured figure, always playing roles." [63] To author Garry Wills, he was "the least authentic man alive." [64] And who could tell which was the real Nixon? Certainly no more complex, tortured, and fascinating human being ever sat in the Oval Office. What most tortured him was his list of hates. It comprised the whole bureaucracy, especially those of the State Department, and the CIA (which he would knock at every turn—a recurrent theme). In his own memoirs, Kissinger observed: "He felt it imperative to exclude the CIA from the formulation of policy; it was staffed by Ivy League liberals. . . . They had always opposed him politically." [65] The long list continued: East Coast intellectuals and college professors, all Republicans east of the Ohio, all Democrats who were not from the

South, and most members of his own cabinet. High on the list came the collectivity of Georgetown. But above them all stood the media. It was an astonishingly long list. "Nixon hated them all," concludes Stephen Ambrose.[66] He might have added the Jews, if one were to judge from the anti-Semitic* tone of much of Nixon's table talk.†

The U.S. media responded by giving Nixon the worst press of any president in the twentieth century. Widely he was regarded as "Tricky Dick," with even his best motives constantly under suspicion. Well before the election of 1972, the battle lines were drawn. Nixon declared that October that he would not hesitate to "give the knife"[67] to journals and journalists that had been proved unfriendly. Many times he was recorded in his desire to "destroy" or "kill" his enemies. Progressively a kind of "stockade mentality"—a stockade "in the midst of rebellion and siege" as David Frost in his Nixon interviews saw it[68]—grew up around the White House. Since Lyndon Johnson, Vietnam above all had drawn a line between the media and the executive. Hostilities were supported, on both sides, by a new art form—the calculated leak. On one side there were the Pentagon Papers leaked to the media; on the other, the "reliable journalists" to whom the White House would leak tidbits beneficial to its policy. This latter was an art form of which Kissinger would prove himself a master.

It was all part of Nixon's distrust of the world which distrusted him, and his urge for "revenge" against it that lay behind his extraordinary decision to celebrate his landslide electoral victory of November 1972 by requesting the resignation of his entire cabinet.

Within a very short space of time, certainly well before the new term began in 1973, Nixon and Kissinger had achieved a remarkable degree of symbiosis. As Nixon himself admitted, "The combination was unlikely—the grocer's son from Whittier and the refugee from Hitler's Germany, the politician and the academic. But our differences made the partnership work."[69] Rarely meeting socially, their worlds did not overlap. Leonard Garment, a White House aide and himself

---

* What Jean-Paul Sartre once defined as "a poor man's snobbery."

† Of course other presidents have had their private hate lists; FDR, for instance, apart from the Anglo-Saxon elite who had *not* attended Groton, distrusted the State Department; and, in particular, those he felt impeded his policy of cultivating Stalin.

Jewish, noted how Kissinger was treated "as an exotic *wunderkind* — a character, an outsider." His colleagues laughed at his thick *Mitteleuropa* accent. He had to endure, said Garment, "the railings against Jewish power which were part of the casual conversation among Nixon's inner circle."[70] As Stephen Ambrose quotes Garment: "You can't begin to imagine how much anti-Semitism there is at the top of this government—and I mean at the top."[71]

David Frost agreed: "Henry must have heard him [Nixon] on more than one occasion say something like 'those Yids.' "[72] Probably he turned a deaf ear.

Scanning the style, rather than content, of the telcoms of Kissinger telephone conversations, the casual reader gains the impression of obsequiousness, almost to excess. "When I'd be talking to Henry," a friend of Nixon's remembered, "and the President would telephone, his voice would shake; the whole tone of his voice would change."*[73] "It was not a pretty scene," Ambassador Arthur Hartman remarked, referring to the grosser side of Nixon, "to see HK and RN together, RN known for his anti-Semitism, and yet HK would nod assent, not protest."[74] In her excellent book, *Nixon and Mao: The Week That Changed the World,* Professor Margaret MacMillan observes how Kissinger "was prepared to sit for hours, if necessary, while Nixon, as was his way, worked out his ideas in rambling conversations. As he told a journalist, 'If I'm not in there talking to the President, then someone else is.' In Kissinger, Nixon had found someone who was his intellectual equal, who understood his policies and who could carry them out."[75]

Yet was this excessive deference to the president really egregious? One has to recall the relations between Franklin Roosevelt and George Marshall, close associates over many years, but always on a basis of "Mr. President." There is something unique about the freezing formality of the White House, whoever the occupant, that reminds you immediately on entry that here is the office of the most powerful man on earth, a monarch as well as a mere prime minister, like the court of the Great Mogul, or Kublai Khan; it is a combination of Buckingham

---

* I am much indebted to Professor Margaret MacMillan for drawing my attention to relevant points made in her book *Nixon and Mao.*

Palace and No. 10—but also the Temple whence orders go out that affect the entire world. Even the fearless Bob Woodward was struck by "awe" when he first visited it. When I was received by President George W. Bush in the Oval Office in 2007, I noted that even in the outer lobby people whisper. The sheer grandeur of White House protocol forbids anything less; and Henry Kissinger, had he himself not once been subject to the hierarchical discipline of the U.S. Army? Was he not, after all, a junior officer in the presence of a general, and the highest-ranking general of them all? There was also something about Nixon too that repulsed any degree of informal chumminess. As Kissinger once remarked to Peregrine Worsthorne, "Only professors think that Presidential aides ever flatly contradict Presidents. That is not how it happens in the real world."[76]

Though Kissinger came around to finding Nixon "a good, warm-hearted man," he never shared such generous views about the White House staff. In the early days, to John Freeman, Harold Wilson's ambassador in Washington, he confided that, though he found the JFK entourage "unattractively narcissistic, they were idealists. [But] these people are real heels," and "I have never met such a gang of self-seeking bastards in my life."[77] He was presumably referring to John Ehrlichman and Bob Haldeman.

Under Nixon-Kissinger, cabinet meetings would be rare. Richard Helms, director of the CIA, was startled to be informed by Kissinger that all intelligence reports were henceforth to be passed through the national security adviser. So it was across the board, with Kissinger the essential sieve for all matters that went up to the president. Many in the executive entourage, not least the discountenanced and sidelined Rogers, did not like at all what they encountered. Between Nixon and Kissinger, in their own separate "degrees of paranoia," so Lawrence Eagleburger, a close associate of Kissinger's who later became secretary of state under President George H. W. Bush (1992–93), observed to Walter Isaacson, "They developed a conspiratorial approach to foreign policy management."[78] Out of hearing (and often not very far) Nixon would frequently make opprobrious remarks*. But Kissinger's

---

* "I don't trust Henry, but I can use him," Isaacson quotes Nixon as saying at the outset of his administration (*Kissinger*, p. 142).

input, however, was to become invaluable to Nixon—so much so that it would be hard for historians subsequently to distinguish whether the original input was Nixon's or Kissinger's. What truly bonded Kissinger and Nixon, thought Kissinger's biographer, Walter Isaacson, was "an appetite and affection and feel for foreign policy." [79] And by the application of covert means, rather than State Department–style diplomacy, it was the kind of realpolitik diplomacy that Bismarck would have understood.

Inside his own office (initially in the basement of the White House, then upgraded to be down the hall from the president in 1970)[80], Kissinger had acquired a reputation as something of a slave-driver. Certainly he was a perfectionist. "He stretched everyone beyond what they thought was their limit," said Al Haig. "In the process he sharpened their wits on assessments, and in underlings brought out ideas that they thought they would never have . . . he was first and foremost a teacher." [81] To Brent Scowcroft, national security adviser to both Gerald Ford and the first Bush, Kissinger had "the finest strategic mind I have ever come across. He could balance a whole lot of disparate issues and interrelate them all a year or two on. That was very rare. Several years later all the strands would come together." In dealing with equals, as well as with his staff, "He would play on each person's characteristics . . . often telling the same story quite differently to each person—not lying, but just deploying what was most suited to his interlocutor."

With his staff, "He thought he got the best out of people by *terrorizing* them . . . some ran in terror, or in disgust. There were those who didn't appreciate his manner of operating, but there were those who stayed and became lifelong friends and supporters." [82]

"Devious?" I asked Lawrence Eagleburger.

"No, but very close-mouthed. He doesn't let everybody know what he is doing." [83]

Arthur Hartman, former ambassador in Moscow, was rather more forthright: "He could be hugely dishonest," he said with a chuckle. "He will look at a person he is talking to, and tailor to him what he said—then he would say some pretty dreadful things! . . . But it was a very good team—*and, I love him!* [author's italics]" [84]

Jan Lodal, keeper of the memcons and expert on figures, found Kissinger's "short fuse and secrecy" irritating; he had to have "watertight compartments . . . he didn't trust Nixon and the 'Germans'—therefore he wanted everything recorded, demanding that his staff also keep verbatim notes of conversations." But he was "the most amazing man; there was not a subject he did not know a lot about."[85]

Taping, as the president was to discover to his cost in 1973, was strictly illegal; so Kissinger introduced batteries of slave-driven secretaries, transcribing conversations and meetings, thus providing an unprecedented bonus both for posterity, and his biographers—and those who had the staying power to wade through the yards, and tons, of documentation.

Rosemary Niehuss, Kissinger's archivist of thirty years, recalled his meticulous standards of drafting: "He would alter a letter, even if it was just 'the' to 'a,' as a matter of principle."[86] This was confirmed by Jan Lodal: "As a university professor, he insisted that these accounts would be absolutely accurate. He probably expected that they would never be released. So I would lock myself up immediately after the meeting . . . lock the door, let no one in, and write the report absolutely verbatim . . . It then went straight to the president and was never doctored. Thus they are totally reliable."[87] "He pushed you very hard, but he knew which skills to push," commented Winston Lord. Lord went on to confirm an often told story of how he had been ordered by Kissinger to redraft a document no fewer than eight times. Each time Kissinger said "Is that the best you can do?"

Finally, the eighth time, a despairing and exhausted Lord said yes. Then Kissinger said "Now, if that really is the best you can do, I will read it!"

Once Lord tried to test Kissinger by putting a sentence in the middle of a paper that made no sense, containing a list of all the titles of his books; Kissinger picked it out, and roared with laughter at the joke. "He pushed me hard—but I was very grateful . . . We were very loyal. . . . We all recognized the pressures on him. Yes, there was an element of brutality—then he would make up for it, not apologizing, but making up."[88] Another very close collaborator, Lawrence Eagleburger, who remained an "ardent admirer, a friend" of Kissinger's, endorsed this: "Hell to work with? Yes. But, he trusted you. . . . He could be unpleasantly hard to work with. . . . I quit five times—we got mad at each other, but I had huge respect, and came away with great affection."[89]

Perhaps surprising, considering the brutality, almost all of Kissinger's team, like Winston Lord and Peter Rodman, from the 1970s remained loyal friends; some, like Rosemary Niehuss, as we have seen, worked for him for three decades and more.

As Walter Isaacson shrewdly notes in his massive biography: "Kissinger was acutely aware of the world around him and self-aware of his role in it. Nixon was not."[90] While Nixon, continues Isaacson, when attacked by critics, withdrew "into Walter Mitty–like fantasies and pretended to be impervious to what others thought," Kissinger was painfully sensitive, endeavoring to "coopt his enemies and ingratiate himself with his critics." Brent Scowcroft saw the insecurity that underlay both Nixon and Kissinger as having led to a strange, "constant rivalry." Though it didn't come across in the telcons, Scowcroft "saw it all the time—they were always trying to be one up on the other—in this brilliant partnership."[91]

It was, all through his life, a curious facet of this immensely gifted man that—having achieved almost everything life and fame could offer, every post with the exception of (and only just) president of the United States—Kissinger should remain so sensitive to the opinions of others, and of far lesser mortals. When engaged in researching this book, I sensed him constantly worrying about what I was going to say, questioning friends as to whom I was seeing in Washington, worrying (often unnecessarily) over how I saw his image over specific issues. He was furious when the State Department thirty years later decided to publish (without consulting him) conversations with Nixon about Indira Gandhi during the 1971 Indo-Pakistan War, in which he was quoted as having castigated her as "a witch" and "a bitch."

As of 1973, his reputation stood at a high peak. Yes, there were stern critics who attacked him for the bombing of Cambodia, but it was no accident that *Time* had selected him for its Man of the Year. Victoria Legge-Bourke, as a twenty-one-year-old social secretary to the British ambassador Lord Cromer in 1971, recalled the news on TV of Kissinger's visit to China being "shatteringly exciting," so much so that when he came into the room she felt "quite gob-smacked."[92] At the beginning of 1972, a columnist in the *New York Times* expressed widely felt views when he lauded Kissinger as "Mister Professident of the United States." The secret missions into "Deepest Unrecognized

China . . . Mysterious flights in and out of Paris—in dead of night, presumably; certainly in disguise; false beard, smoked glasses" made of him a latter-day Scarlet Pimpernel. "One can imagine Leslie Howard playing this damned elusive Professident. . . . He has made a lot of red-blooded American boys want to be professors when they grow up."[93]

At the year's end, the same journalist (Russell Baker) was jesting how (in an article headed "Public Celebrity Number One"), by sharp contrast to his somber boss, "unapt for capering to the public lute, and hence despair of editors," "Henry" suddenly appeared, "as though in fulfillment of ancient prophecy that a successor to Jackie would one day come, another great public star whom America could address, as its passion, by first name.

" 'Henry.' . . ."[94]

How the owlish professor, ever eager for public approbation, must have loved all this—as much as the brooding genius in the Oval Office resented it—yet knowing there was no price at which he could do without "Henry"!

In sharp contrast to Nixon, with his obsessive loathing of journalists, Kissinger made a point of currying favor with them. He had his preferences and also his dislikes. Nixon, for instance, would never have had a real friend, like Joe Alsop*, among the media with whom he could relax and let his hair down. But with all of them Kissinger would go to immense trouble to see they got a story right, catering skillfully to their own characteristics, strengths, and vulnerabilities, what in more modern terms would be described as spin; or swiftly put them right, should they get it wrong. When one reads the list of his daily calls, how he found the time to do all the personal telephoning he did is a mystery, and a miracle. Those in favor at the time were led to believe they were being fed special treats; often they were not. The treats might vary subtly; but always there was a clear purpose behind each one. It was a subject at which Henry Kissinger was a master ahead of his day. Wrote the *New York Times* some three decades later: "He schmoozed, spun and lectured his way into the heart of Washington's media establishment, and that transformed him into Super-K, escort of starlets, perennial

* Kissinger regarded Alsop as "a great influence. A great moral support to me. He was one of the few *serious* people" (interview, 10/28/05).

magazine cover story and master of foreign affairs." [95] The schmoozing was also something of a two-way traffic. Many Washington journalists of the day could have competed for *Private Eye*'s "Order of the Brown Nose": "Despite all appearances to the contrary," veteran CBS correspondent Marvin Kalb is quoted as remarking (during a chaotic period in 1975, the year after Nixon's downfall), "you still have some friends." [96] While Ted Koppel of ABC News about the same time told Kissinger, "We are lucky to have had you."

On the other hand Kissinger would not hesitate to try to block publication of pieces he did not like. There were also ugly rumors, prior to Watergate, of Kissinger's involvement in the wiretapping of a number of eminent journalists in 1969–70. One of those concerned was the august correspondent of the London *Sunday Times*, Henry Brandon, a Czech refugee by origin—and himself a strangely opaque figure. While even close members of the Kennedy administration thought the issue exaggerated ("Every president did it"),[97] Kissinger sidestepped the accusations, laying responsibility entirely at FBI director J. Edgar Hoover's door. Nevertheless, it was a long time before the Brandons would speak to Henry Kissinger. Walter Isaacson raises the query here: "Did Kissinger reinforce Nixon's dark side by catering to it?" though he comes up with an ambivalent conclusion.[98]

Again, however, in sharpest contrast to the misanthropic Nixon, Kissinger actually derived pleasure from the media. At its most frivolous level he placed them in the category of "court jesters." He also loved the high, and not so high, life of Tinsel Town and Broadway; in between calls from the president, the Soviet ambassador, etc., his telcons abound with social calls from Frank Sinatra, Jill St. John, and Danny Kaye. All would find an open door when they came to Washington. "Yes, that's a good description," he remarked to me, when I had suggested the notion of the court jester.

"Well, that's just what they were, in a way—my court jesters. It was relaxation. They made no demands. Of course I never asked them for advice on foreign policy! Washington then was a very compressed city, compared with now. You were always on display. People had no other interests. They were obsessed by what the columnists said—the columnists were obsessed by themselves—whereas nobody in the rest of the country gave a damn." [99]

CHAPTER 2

THE BLACK HOLE: VIETNAM

"A balanced judgment on Vietnam continues to elude us—and therefore the ability to draw lessons from the national tragedy which America inflicted on itself. As a result, Vietnam has become the black hole of American historical memory."

—Henry Kissinger[1]

"We won't wait a hundred years."

—General Vo Nguyen Giap[2]

As KISSINGER PUT IT (in his *Ending the Vietnam War*), for America, Vietnam was, quite simply, "the defining experience of the second half of the twentieth century." For him it also constantly remained "the black hole of American historical memory."[3] Yet, for a writer whose country, rightly or wrongly, stood aside from the United States during the agony of Vietnam, it is not easy to engage in a discussion of the war without treading on the holy face of America's dead, and of American misery, with however much of a bounty of innate sympathy for the history of this great nation. It is peeping through a very intimate keyhole. One can only write with the most extreme diffidence. Yet maybe a little distance—distance of na-

35

tionality as well as time—helps over an issue where passions still remain unresolved even thirty years on. Of all the war memorials I have visited as a military historian, two remain etched in my mind: the soaring white twin columns at Vimy Ridge to the Canadians, to sixty thousand dead in each of two world wars, all volunteers from a tiny population who came to fight for a far-off "mother country," and the somber Ossuaire at Verdun, where lie the unidentified bones of hundreds of thousands of French, and German, dead, who died in 1916 in the most hideous battle fought by mankind. But equally moving to me, in its very different way, is the Vietnam Memorial Wall in Washington, D.C., erected amid bitterest controversy.

It lies, buried—decently, or indecently—out of sight, tucked away in an artificial ravine on the edge of the city's monumental Mall. Only a couple of hundred yards away stands the superb World War II monument, as triumphantly magnificent as the great obelisk to George Washington or the Lincoln Memorial, between which it stands halfway—proclaiming in pride the sacrifice of the last conflict where America stood undivided. In sad, but eloquent contrast, the Vietnam memorial lurks hidden away, as if in shame for a war which half of America still believes should never have happened, and where the other half deplores a shameful exit, and the dumping of an ally. In its ravine, it consists simply of a long, dark granite wall with the names of the 58,000 who never made it home alive. What is so moving is the daily spectacle of family, or buddies, who come solemnly and in silence, or sometimes in tears, looking for the names of loved ones.

It also takes a trip to Vietnam, to the dread tunnels of Cu Chi, to have reinforced the full horrors of that war, of a war which draftee farm boys from Iowa were simply not educated to fight; a nightmare world of jungle ambushes by an unseen enemy, of inhuman tiger traps where an incautious GI could lie, impaled and screaming for death. Then the lucky ones would return home, not as the feted heroes from the Pacific in World War II, but shunned—and even spat upon—by a populace that simply did not want to know about *that* war. To be in America in those years, as an outsider looking in, was an experience agonizing to watch, and to remember.

In its silent eloquence, that tucked-away granite wall states the simple fact—America today still does want to recall the Vietnam War, to come to terms with it. (Will it, one wonders, come to treat involvement in Iraq the same way?)

By 1973, the U.S. commitment to South Vietnam had existed for the best part of twenty years. Four, if not five presidents had wrestled with its intractability. "It all began with high aspirations," remarked Kissinger when quoting Truman's address of January 20, 1949, with its high moral commitment to the principle: " 'All nations and all people are free to govern themselves as they see fit.' "[4] In fact, the grim saga of Vietnam which Nixon and Kissinger finally had to resolve had begun back in World War II. Then, after France had capitulated to Hitler in 1940, her rich empire in Indochina, comprising Laos, Cambodia, and Vietnam, progressively fell to being a puppet of Japan. After the capitulation of Japan, the most powerful emergent force was the Communist Party, under Ho Chi Minh, the former pastry cook who had witnessed the Versailles Treaty, with its revelation of how European Great Powers could be brought low. By 1945, France seemed as weak relatively as the kaiser's Germany in 1919. But, almost as a gauge of survival, and virility, successive French governments showed themselves prepared to sacrifice a class of Saint-Cyr officers almost every year to hang on to *Indochine*. And, by 1952, one-third of all French expenditures in Vietnam were in fact subsidized by the United States. Finally, to the accompaniment of the immortal slogans of Verdun, *"ils ne passeront pas!,"* the generals allowed themselves to be cornered at Dien Bien Phu—a remote outpost uncomfortably close to the Chinese border. Upon it poured artillery (most of it American, supplied to the vanquished Chinese warlord, Chiang Kai-shek). Rather than see an ally humiliated yet again, President Eisenhower's secretary of state, John Foster Dulles, threatened a nuclear strike to save Indochina, but was dissuaded by Deputy Prime Minister Anthony Eden of Britain.

After a heroic, costly defense of fifty-seven days, on May 7, 1954, Dien Bien Phu fell to General Vo Nguyen Giap's forces. One of history's decisive battles, it marked the first post-1945 defeat of a Western power by "colonial forces"; among those who witnessed it were regiments from French Algeria. At the end of that year revolt broke out in Algeria. Meanwhile in Geneva, "Accords" ending the war created neutralist independent states in Cambodia and Laos, and divided Vietnam into a Communist North and "free" South.

Almost immediately Ho Chi Minh and General Giap showed their determination to take over the soft South, which, divided between Christian and Buddhist factions, and riddled with corruption, clearly could not survive unsupported. Eisenhower, then Kennedy, found themselves committed by the Truman Doctrine of rallying to the help of a people desiring to be "free to govern themselves." From then on, from the Tonkin Gulf Incident of 1964 onward, the United States would find itself committed—committed, among other things, by fear of the Domino Theory, the prevailing wisdom that, if Vietnam was allowed to fall, all the rest of Southeast Asia would collapse as well. It was, remarks Kissinger, "The precise reverse of the famous dictum of the British prime minister Lord Palmerston that Great Britain had no permanent friends, only permanent interests."[5]

Dollars by the millions, arms, then men, flowed into South Vietnam in ever increasing numbers. Each new U.S. commander, like France's General Robert Nivelle in World War I, indeed the mantra of army commanders across the ages, in 2006 as well as 1966 or 1916—felt that they "had the answer . . . one more push. . . . Each new administration obliged to deal with Indochina felt compelled to take another step into the morass."[6] With a commitment risen to 500,000 men and total air cover, still the United States could not achieve a result that would free Saigon from the fear of invasion from the North, and the ubiquitous menace of the Viet Cong guerrillas.[7] President Johnson ordered one bombing pause after another, then canceled them—giving Hanoi "every incentive to make the price of peace as high as possible."[8] By way of celebrating the Lunar New Year—Tet—at the end of January 1968, the diminutive General Giap launched a concerted, surprise offensive all over the south. The ancient capital of Hue was captured. But, though caught on the wrong foot, with utmost courage the U.S. Marines fought back, recapturing Hue (though destroying it in the process—a Catch-22 replayed throughout Vietnam). Though a military victory for the United States, such were the losses that it proved to be politically decisive for Hanoi.*

With some similarity to the French-Algerian War of less than ten

---

* North Vietnamese casualties were estimated as high as 100,000, to 1,536 U.S. dead.

years previously, the *real* battle however was fought and lost "neither on the battlefield nor in our diplomacy, but at home," wrote Kissinger in *Ending the Vietnam War*.[9] Tet was to prove the turning point. It might have been a good time to do a peace deal with the battered North—but who can rewrite history? Although American public opinion polls went on showing a majority supporting the war, this support continued to deteriorate and the nation became increasingly polarized as "mounting self-doubt . . . compounded the despair caused by Kennedy's assassination."[10] It was, Kissinger declared angrily of the Jane Fonda and Mary McCarthy lobby, in his foreword to *Ending the Vietnam War*, "the only war in which well-known Americans traveled to the enemy's capital to express solidarity."[11] Pessimism, if not defeatism, struck deep into the heart of President Johnson, who saw his popularity fall sharply. In March of 1968 he withdrew as a candidate for reelection that November (leaving the way open for Richard Nixon) and passing on the problem of extrication from Vietnam, which he had never been able to resolve. Tet was indeed a triumph in the art of propaganda, media influence, and popular opinion in the pursuit of military objectives.

By 1973, the U.S. commitment to South Vietnam had existed for the best part of twenty years. When Nixon took over from Johnson in 1969, there were 536,000 U.S. troops in Vietnam, and two hundred Americans were being killed every week. The trouble was, as the French had discovered in Algeria, in this kind of guerrilla warfare there were no front lines; success depended on whose forces controlled a given area at what time of day.[12] The war was costing America billions of dollars a year. Kissinger himself was already convinced that the war was unwinnable; yet the objective that Nixon and Kissinger would pursue over the next four years—Nixon, particularly—was an exit formula ensuring "peace with honor." In essence this meant: getting back safely all the American POWs (almost entirely shot-down aircrews), and not abandoning the Saigon government of Washington's South Vietnamese ally—for whom the war had notionally been fought. There were generals in the Pentagon who still harbored notions of outright military victory—"one more push." Kissinger, though instinctively pessimistic by nature, lay somewhere in between, feeling that Hanoi would only agree to terms after it had been made to realize—by the process of short, sharp shocks—that it too could not win. For this reason he supported the much criticized policy of bombing neutral Cambodia and Laos, as well as the military installations at Hanoi and Haiphong—actions which were much to be attacked by his critics in future. The overlay of extreme secrecy with which the Cambodian bombing was surrounded was perhaps a reflection of Kissinger's own tenets of secret diplomacy.

In his extraordinarily foresighted article published before his appointment in 1969, discussed earlier, Kissinger made it clear that ending the war honorably was essential to maintaining U.S. "credibility," which had to be maintained at all costs. This "credibility" extended, naturally, to the U.S. position in Europe and elsewhere. It was a mantra he would be repeating three decades later over Iraq. At the same time, at moments of extreme pessimism, even in the early period of his tenure of office, he was to be heard observing that after a "decent interval" of two to three years, following a settlement, the Communists would probably take over. He saw the "asymmetry" of guerrilla warfare with painful clarity; it was all about control of the population, not occupation of the land, and "if you don't win, you lose." By both of these yardsticks, the situation inherited in South Vietnam was hardly encouraging.

Although at their first meeting, Nixon had insisted to Kissinger how he was determined to avoid the Vietnam "trap" Johnson had fallen into, almost immediately it was brought home most brutally to him, and to Kissinger, that it was not going to work out that way. All through his two tenures of office Vietnam would continue to dominate, as it had done with Johnson. On February 22, 1969, the day before Nixon left on his first tour of Europe, North Vietnam launched an offensive across the board. Saigon came under shell fire. Nixon responded with an order to proceed with the (already planned) bombing by B-52s of the Ho Chi Minh Trail supply routes, and North Vietnamese command centers in the South. These supply routes lay across the border in Cambodia. Continuing for fourteen months, and temporarily effective, the bombings slowed the Communist attacks; American deaths dropped by nearly a half—then, swiftly, the route, a primitive affair based on manpower and bicycles and no Western-style transport, simply moved a few miles away. That U.S. planes were regularly bombing neutral Cambodia was kept a closely preserved secret; when it leaked out the outrage was immense. Once the bombing campaign proved unsuccessful, Nixon ordered a full-scale ground incursion into Cambodia. Again, secrecy surrounding the operation was almost obsessive—held to be especially a hallmark of Kissinger's influence. Almost equally obsessive as the planning proceeded was Nixon's showing and reshowing of *Patton* (Kissinger claims to have seen it twice before being able "to escape for an hour in the middle of it to plan for next day's NSC meeting"[13]). (It was an interesting insight into the passion of men at the top for showing their important guests movies—generally old ones—to while away the evenings. Winston Churchill was prone to this. Macmillan dreaded his visits to Eisenhower because of the endless replay of cowboy movies—"Galloping hooves once again.") Nixon's decision on Cambodia was "not appealable"—one of his favorite expressions, to summarize a decisive action which veiled, however, a good deal of indecision.

In February 1970, USAF B-52s bombed Laos to counter a North Vietnamese invasion of that neutral state. In May, 31,000 U.S. troops—this time backed by 43,000 South Vietnamese—moved into two Cambodian enclaves known as Fish Hook and Parrot's Beak. Campuses across the United States erupted. There was the tragedy of Kent State, Ohio, when nervous National Guardsmen fired into an unarmed crowd of demonstrators, killing four students. Under threat from the demonstrators, estimated at 100,000 strong, Kissinger had to move from his Georgetown house to sleep in the basement of the White House.[14] During this period Kissinger was himself (according to the FBI) even under threat of being kidnapped by a group of nuns and priests.* Nevertheless, Kissinger concluded that, militarily, the Cambodian incursion was a success. It was claimed the campaign had captured up to 40 percent of the North Vietnamese weaponry stockpiled across the border, resulting in a two-year "breather" in threats to the border area, and Saigon itself. But, if it bought time for Vietnamization, the passing to the South Vietnamese responsibility for their own defense, as far as U.S. public opinion was concerned many felt that the

---

* Director Hoover claimed the ecclesiastics intended holding Kissinger until the United States agreed to end the war.

Cambodian incursion was to prove Hanoi's greatest moral victory since Tet two years previously.

In 1975 I recall a young journalist named William Shawcross leaping to his feet at an international conference in Germany, and vigorously denouncing Kissinger as "the greatest enemy of peace." A few years later he followed this with his damning book *Sideshow* in which he blamed the spreading of the war to Cambodia for having led directly to the genocidal nightmare of Pol Pot's Killing Fields of Cambodia five years later. He singled out Kissinger as his principal target.[15]* Kissinger hit back with a vigorous point-by-point rebuttal in his memoirs, *Years of Upheaval*. Shawcross later recanted (becoming an arch-hawk on Iraq—perhaps a war too late?) and Kissinger gracefully accepted his proffered handshake at a reception.† On the other hand, I know at least one distinguished *New York Times* journalist who, to this day, considers Kissinger indictable for crimes against humanity for his responsibility in the Cambodian operation.[16] Either way it could surely be argued with equal force that the Congress of the United States was ultimately to blame, through withdrawing all responsibility for Indochina in the course of 1973 and 1974. It could equally be argued that the Cambodian bombing campaign was ineffectual, given the North Vietnamese ability to shift the primitive Ho Chi Minh Trail a few miles farther into the jungle each time it was disrupted.

Because of troop withdrawals, the end of 1970 to early 1971 saw the last time U.S. combat troops would be available for offensive ground operations. Kissinger thought it the best time and place for a dry season offensive into Cambodia and Laos. It was also the first major blooding of South Vietnam's army. But, at best, it was regarded as a limited, passing success. On paper, it looked like a "splendid project" but, observed Kissinger, "South Vietnamese divisions had never conducted major offensive operations against a determined enemy outside Vietnam and only rarely inside."[17]

---

* His often critical biographer, Walter Isaacson, was supportive of Kissinger's defense, placing the blame for the subsequent genocide of the Killing Fields firmly on the shoulders of the Khmer Rouge (*Kissinger*, pp. 272–75).

† Kissinger joked at the time: "I will accept your apology—I only fight thirty-year wars, but my wife won't—she fights hundred-year wars!" (interview, 12/7/07).

One additional, endemic problem was that each ARVN—Army of the Republic of Vietnam, i.e., South Vietnam—division was tied to the military region from which it came—so that when a division was moved out of its home region it lost morale. On top of this, President Nguyen Van Thieu ordered his commanders to stop as soon as they had suffered three thousand casualties. It was a bit like the French army in the Phony War of 1939–40. And the opposition frequently had prior intelligence. Was it then surprising that, in Kissinger's words, "the operation, conceived in ambivalence and assailed by skepticism, proceeded in confusion."[18] Worst of all, Hanoi would have gained both a good idea of how fundamentally flawed was the new ARVN, and—from their good friends the media in Washington, not least the leaking of the ten thousand classified documents of the Pentagon Papers—that this would assuredly be the last American ground effort.

Kissinger exculpated the Laos bombing as having been inherited from the Johnson regime, and over an area that was largely "unpopulated except for some 60,000 Vietnamese troops."[19] The Ho Chi Minh Trail had been used to "infiltrate at least 630,000 North Vietnamese troops"[20] as well as huge amounts of weapons and ammunition into the South. But, following the Laos offensive of 1971, pressures in Washington, media and congressional, escalated. Under U.S. persuasion, Thieu held elections; only marginally corrupt—but by Communist standards free—they returned huge support for Thieu, in contrast to the 35 percent with which he had scraped home in 1967. Yet still Kissinger's negotiating partners in Paris at that time would persist in scorning Saigon as U.S. "puppets." Then, on March 30, 1972, the North launched a powerful, all-out spring offensive with four full divisions and Soviet heavy tanks. Not since 1968 had they moved so openly. The key stronghold of Quang Tri was captured, dealing a staggering blow to Saigon—and Nixon's hopes for Vietnamization. Kissinger, however, was convinced that this was "Hanoi's last throw of the dice," but the trouble was that with many ARVN units "retreat had become an end in itself."[21]

On April 1, Nixon ordered a heavy bombing attack on the North, but limited to within twenty-five miles of the demilitarized zone—largely to minimize danger of hitting Soviet personnel. In Paris the peace talks seemed bogged down; in South Vietnam, near the DMZ and in the Central Highlands, the ARVN showed signs of faltering; the United States built up its attack force of B-52s in Guam. Meanwhile the U.S. withdrawals continued to the point where, by July 1, over 90 percent of the numbers there in 1969 would have left. There remained the overwhelming airpower of the United States, with its great lumbering force of wildly inaccurate B-52s.* At the beginning of May 1972, Nixon followed up with a massive two-day strike on Hanoi itself, eventually spreading to the port of Haiphong—essential to the shipment of munitions from the Soviet Union. Kissinger did not believe in a "one-shot operation" and wanted something more sustained, persuaded that in the bombing of the Hanoi delta lay the key to success. But Nixon's order was "unappealable."

The military chiefs in the Pentagon were delighted; it was what they had been urging for years. For Nixon great risks were attached; Moscow might cancel the imminently forthcoming summit between himself and Brezhnev. This would have been humiliating, and politically disastrous. It was a period of great nervousness in the White House, as Kissinger pressed every button both with the North Vietnamese negotiators in Paris, his good friend Soviet ambassador Anatoly Dobrynin in Washington—and his new friends in Beijing. In Haiphong, Soviet ships had been hit. There was an angry exchange. The Chinese seemed less perturbed. Nixon gave a powerful TV address to the nation. Media reaction was predictably hostile. The *New York Times* spoke of Nixon's "desperate gamble."

Meanwhile, in conjunction with the stick of the Cambodia and Laos operations, Nixon demonstrated his determination to exit Vietnam by pressing ahead with Vietnamization and, at the same time, swiftly incremental withdrawals of U.S. ground troops: the carrot for North Vietnam. At a meeting on Midway Island, scene of the great battle of 1942 which changed the course of the Pacific War against Japan, already in June 1969, Nixon, accompanied by Kissinger, had laid out the principles that would require South Vietnam to assume the burden of the fighting. For a start, 25,000 U.S. combat troops would be with-

---

* Well might one speculate on the course of the Vietnam War had the United States Air Force then possessed the armory of smart missiles with which it defeated both the Serbs and Saddam's forces in each of two Gulf wars, almost without loss.

drawn. Kissinger recalls how it was "painful to see" the discomfiture of General Creighton "Abe" Abrams, probably the best U.S. commander sent to Vietnam (and after whom a main battle tank was later named), when confronted by the realization "that he was doomed to a rearguard action, that the purpose of his command would increasingly become logistic redeployment and not success in battle." [22]

This at a time when Abrams remained convinced that military success still lay within reach. But Centurions in far-flung outposts were seldom aware of the mood in Rome. It had then remained for Nixon to put the new policy, and its timetables, to President Thieu. Because of U.S. domestic pressures, Thieu, "for whose country 36,000 Americans had now died but who was not allowed to visit the soil of his powerful ally," had been required to fly to Midway aboard a chartered Pan Am plane; wrote Kissinger: "I felt sorry for him." [23] Was it any way to treat an ally? This way lay trouble, but—recorded Kissinger, "we had crossed a fateful dividing line."

Hand in hand with all this activity proceeded negotiations conducted in deepest secrecy by Henry Kissinger. The groundwork had already been laid under Johnson. But with consummate skill, the men from Hanoi had then fought a procrastinating action, arguing endlessly over the size and shape of the conference table, followed by who should sit where; repeating their tactics from the Geneva Conference of 1954. Shortly after the vital Midway talks, on August 4, 1969, Kissinger made his initial—the first of fourteen—secret trip to Paris, under cover of an open visit to meet President Georges Pompidou, to open negotiations with his North Vietnamese interlocutor, Xuan Thuy. They met secretly in an apartment on the Rue de Rivoli belonging to a French friend and pupil of Kissinger's, Jean Sainteny, a former French diplomat in Hanoi.[24] The rendezvous had been set up through General Vernon Walters, currently serving as U.S. military attaché in Paris.

Walters was a kind of American Richard Hannay, or Ashenden.* Though he was born in New York City, his father was a British immigrant and insurance salesman. From age six, Walters lived in Britain and France with his family. His formal education included a few years

---

* The author knew, and admired, him in Washington in 1980; a charming, cultivated man—anything but a 007 spook.

at Stonyhurst College, the Jesuit secondary school in Lancashire, England, but he never attended university. He joined the army in 1941, serving in Africa and Italy, earning medals for distinguished military and intelligence achievements, and rising to the rank of lieutenant general. He came to speak six West European languages fluently, learned Portuguese in two months during the war so as to interpret with the Brazilian contingent with the U.S. Fifth Army in Italy, and was familiar with several others. He was fluent in Chinese and Russian. His language skills helped him win President Truman's confidence, serving as a key aide in Truman's unsuccessful effort to reach a reconciliation with the insubordinate General Douglas MacArthur in Korea. In Europe in the 1950s, he served Eisenhower and other top U.S. officials as a translator and aide at a series of NATO summit conferences, and helped set up its military headquarters. He was with Vice President Nixon in 1958 when an anti-American crowd stoned their car in Caracas, Venezuela. Walters suffered facial cuts from flying glass. Nixon avoided injury.

In Paris during the Nixon years, Walters's simultaneous translation of a speech by Nixon once prompted Charles de Gaulle to say to Nixon, "You gave a magnificent speech, but your interpreter was eloquent."[25] It was also Walters who acted as intermediary transmitting a letter from Ho Chi Minh to Nixon. Later, 1972, appointed deputy director of CIA, he reappears in various undercover missions, whether brokering with the Chinese in Paris, in the Yom Kippur War, or the subsequent oil crisis, and he played an important role in keeping the CIA out of the Watergate scandal.* To Kissinger he was known simply as "Mr. Fixit." He thoroughly deserved it. Secrecy was such that, with Secretary of State Rogers kept out of the loop, the Paris military attaché could divulge nothing to his own ambassador. When Kissinger came to Paris he was installed in the Walters bedroom, his two aides in the guest room, the general on the sofa. When Kissinger had gone, Walters found himself spending nights decoding top secret messages: "the

---

* Despite numerous importunings from on high, Walters flatly refused to cast a cloak of national security over the guilty parties. At the critical moment, he declined to involve the Agency, and bluntly informed the highest levels of the executive that further insistence from that quarter would result in his immediate resignation.

highest paid clerk in the U.S. government service!" was how he described himself.[26]

It was Walters's suggestion to bring Pompidou into the plot, so as to facilitate Kissinger's secret trips in and out of France. On one occasion there was an element of hilarity, almost of Feydeau farce, when Air Force One with Kissinger on board became stuck in Frankfurt with technical problems. At 9:30, Walters called the Elysée, and Pompidou personally put at his disposal the presidential fighter-bomber Mystère. To satisfy the curiosity of the air force colonel piloting the plane, with an appeal to his French sense of gallantry, he told him "it involves a woman."

"But what if Madame Pompidou finds out?"

Walters gave him his word of honor that "if that happened, I would tell her that it was Henry Kissinger."

Walters had instructed the owl-like, hardly feminine emissary to take off his glasses and roll up his collar as they transferred to the fighter-jet.[27] Cover was preserved.

On a joint visit to Paris with Kissinger in May 2006, I persuaded him to revisit his memories of those endlessly protracted secret talks, which he did, vividly recalling that flight: "That first time I flew in Air Force One, described as a training run to Frankfurt; then we flew on it to a provincial French airport. From there, very secretly, by French plane to Villacoublay. I slept in Mr. Fixit's bedroom. I was so little known then that Walters told the housekeeper I was a General Kirchner."[28]

The efforts of the Hanoi delegation to spin out the talks exasperated Kissinger and the rest of the Americans. Walters found himself interpreting from the French into English, but "Why we used three languages instead of two I never understood." While the Vietnamese provided a "superb interpreter," he was "not a pleasant person [and] always translated unpleasant statements with an expression that made it clear that he was enjoying what he was saying."[29] As an initial impression, Kissinger found the men from Hanoi "subtle, disciplined, and infinitely patient." He was "impressed by their dignity and quiet self-assurance," unexpected for such men of violence and guerrilla leaders. "Patient, disciplined, superbly skillful in nuances of formulation, they had earned their place at the conference table by ruthless struggle . . . it was our misfortune to stand in the way of Hanoi's obsessive drive for hegemony in Indochina."[30] Throughout the long spell of meetings, they remained "always courteous"—until 1972, when ("carried away by the early success of the spring offensive") they "turned insolent."[31] They were utterly inflexible, deviating "from their quest for victory only after the collapse" of that offensive left them totally exhausted." Throughout, as Kissinger wrote, "There were four or five feet of space and eons of perception separating us."[32]

In 1970 Kissinger flew to Paris for three further secret meetings, this time with Le Duc Tho, a key member of the Hanoi Politburo, who was to become Kissinger's negotiating partner over the next four stormy years. They first met "in a worker's house in the suburbs—very discreet, picked by the Vietnamese. Very narrow space between us— no room. No food—no lunches, no drink. Four to five hours discussions at a time. Their strategy was to break our spirit, show us that they were in no hurry. A deputy would open; like a picador—make incredibly interminable statements about the 'heroic struggle.' "[33] In Kissinger's own vivid description, this new interlocutor was "grayhaired, dignified, rather short, invariably wore a black or brown Mao suit. His large luminous eyes only rarely revealed the fanaticism that had induced him as a boy of sixteen to join the anti-French Communist guerrillas. He was always composed; his manners, except on one or two occasions, were impeccable. He knew what he was about and served his cause with dedication and skill."[34] (Peter Rodman, on Kissinger's staff, saw Le Duc Tho as "incredibly arrogant, tough when they were winning—but gave way when they were losing."[35]) A committed Marxist from a country with almost as long a history of wars and oppression as his Chinese neighbors, Le Duc Tho also knew that time was on his side; especially as the unraveling of the U.S. domestic scene began to pick up momentum in 1973. As a veteran of many years of guerrilla warfare, to him the negotiations were just another battle.

Already wedded to the art of diplomatic negotiation, Kissinger had picked useful practical experience during his long sessions with the brilliant and supple Zhou Enlai* in 1971; his acquaintance with the

---

* Zhou Enlai, 1898–1974, Mao's long-surviving premier and foreign minister of the People's Republic of China.

Oriental mind encouraged him further in his already ingrained instinct for that almost obsessive secrecy. On the other hand, apart from his own Marxist training and discipline, coupled with deep nationalist convictions, Le Duc Tho had also had the advantage of studying how the previous occupiers of Vietnam, the French, had been defeated by the Algerian nationalists in 1962. After nearly eight years of war and three of negotiations, through giving not one point away, the Algerians defeated de Gaulle utterly, causing the expulsion of one million Pieds-Noirs and the abandonment of all French claims.* How much more vulnerable to protracted attrition was the United States, with presidential elections every four years and an increasingly embattled president? And what was four years to a people who claimed to have been fighting for their independence for two thousand years? (When I interviewed Giap in March 1998, the legendary and undefeatable general recalled how at about this time Mao had tried to encourage him by saying "Within one hundred years the U.S. will be withdrawing from the south," to which Giap claimed to have replied, "We will consider this, but we won't wait a hundred years!")[36]

Thus Le Duc Tho was a most redoubtable interlocutor and adversary, even for Kissinger, the heir to Metternich, delighting as he did in what he called the balletlike "choreography of diplomacy." In 1971 there followed four more secret meetings in Paris; and in 1972 a further six, leading to the breakthrough of October 1972; finally, in January 1973, Kissinger flew to Paris to initial the Vietnam agreement. By this time Kissinger was given to nicknaming Le Duc Tho (strictly behind his back) "Ducky"; a singularly inappropriate sobriquet that doubtless provided a private chuckle to sustain his team over the tedium of the endless talks.[37] "He was there to wear me down," wrote Kissinger many years later.[38] That October, Le Duc Tho and Kissinger were awarded the Nobel Peace Prize for their joint efforts, and in December Kissinger met him in Paris for one last time that year.

Considering that Kissinger, somewhat resentfully, always consid-

---

* In retrospect (*Ending the Vietnam War*, pp. 72, 100; interview, 12/7/07), Kissinger concluded that de Gaulle had been in a stronger position than Nixon, through the "nature of [de Gaulle's] opposition . . . who wanted victory and thought he was conceding too much," in marked contrast to Nixon's domestic opposition on the left who demanded a quick out.

INDOCHINA, 1954-1975

CHINA

Nanning

DEMOCRATIC
REPUBLIC OF VIETNAM
(NORTH VIETNAM)

BURMA

Dien Bien Phu

Hanoi

Red River

Haiphong

Red River

N

LAOS

*PLAIN
OF JARS*

*Gulf of
Tonkin*

HAINAN

Vientiane

Vinh

Mekong River

Dong Hoi

DMZ (1954)

Udorn (Udon Thani)

Khe Sanh

Tchepone

Quang Tri

Hue

Mekong River

Da Nang

THAILAND

Ho Chi Minh Trail

Kontum

Pleiku

Bangkok

CAMBODIA
(KAMPUCHEA)

Banmethout

U Tapao

REPUBLIC OF VIETNAM
(SOUTH VIETNAM)

FISH HOOK

An Loc

Gulf of Siam

Phnom Penh

PARROT'S BEAK

Cam
Ranh Bay

Sihanoukville
(Kompong Som)

Mekong River

Saigon

Mekong Delta

Area of Detail

*South
China Sea*

Saigon

Mekong River

My Tho

Vinh Long

Ben Tri

Vung Tau

Cantho

Mekong Delta

N

0 Miles   50   100

0 Kilometers   150

0 Miles   100   200   300

0 Kilometers   300

© 2009 Jeffrey L. Ward

ered the Vietnam negotiations a sideshow to the mainstream of his objectives on the world scene, his stamina throughout the Paris talks surely deserves recognition. Few men would have possessed comparable staying power, sustained over so long a period; and against so discouraging a backdrop—not least the backdrop of mounting dissent at home. Walters recorded that—though he had disagreed with him on a number of occasions—"every time I tried to think of who could have done the job better, no name came to mind." There was Kissinger's "uncanny skill in debating and rapier-like ironic repartee." What particularly impressed itself on Walters's memory was a day in September 1971, with Le Duc Tho standing at the top of the villa steps, "smiling triumphantly down at Kissinger and [he] said 'I really don't know why I am negotiating anything with you. I have just spent several hours with Senator [George] McGovern and your opposition will force you to give me what I want . . . ' The note of triumph in his voice was grinding." [39]

Like lightning, Kissinger riposted sharply: "You are the representative of one of the most tyrannical governments on this planet. You have always crushed any opposition that raises its head in your country. Do not talk about things about which you know nothing such as an opposition. Leave that to those of us who tolerate an opposition." In the words of Vernon Walters: "Never again did they make such a direct reference to internal US affairs." [40] Marveling at Kissinger's "patience with these thugs," Walters judged it "one of Kissinger's great days." At the same time "there was never any doubt in my mind that the ultimate authority as far as he was concerned was President Nixon." Not one for lavishing vain praise, Walters concluded—with a touch of acidity—"he really was nearly as good as he thought he was." [41]

Kissinger and Nixon have often been criticized for not accepting terms that might have been available in 1969, instead delaying a settlement till 1972; a period in which a further nearly 15,000 U.S. servicemen were killed and more than 100,000 wounded. The criticism does not really hold water. During that period the North consistently rejected American overtures, or riposted with their own offensives. Often it seems that Washington was not fully aware of Hanoi's endgame. Occasionally a kind of intellectual isolation from history dulls its thought processes. For instance, it might have helped had the administration properly studied the lessons of the French-Algerian War as closely as had Hanoi. In Algeria the rebel FLN leaders, even through times of crushing military defeat, persisted over *eight years*— or the sum of two U.S. presidential terms—in their determination to accept only *total* victory. Thus negotiation became almost meaningless, and even so skilled a negotiator as Kissinger had to discover that. The Algerian leaders never gave up one inch of ground; with the result that, after eight years, they forced de Gaulle to abandon every single point in his position. Similarly, Hanoi—where the Algerian War was studied most closely—never really budged from its basic, rocklike position. It consistently rejected American overtures, or countered with their own offensives.

What caused protraction of the talks were terms proposed that were unacceptable to either side. Back in 1969, the North Vietnamese peace proposals (which remained essentially the same until October 1972) called, primarily, for a dumping of the Saigon government, and its replacement by a tripartite coalition government comprised of the Hanoi National Liberation Front, various neutralists standing for "peace and freedom," and members of the existing structure. Secondarily, they would only accept negotiations between Hanoi and Washington over the fate of the U.S. POWs—once the peace agreements were settled, and total U.S. withdrawal effected. Both of these points were totally unacceptable to both Washington and Saigon, a fact ignored by peace factions within the United States who nevertheless— stirred up by Hanoi's skillful propaganda—continued to claim that terms could have been reached back in 1969. It was these two issues, plus prohibition against future North Vietnamese infiltration into the South, which caused Kissinger to fly back and forth for all those secret meetings with the unmovable Ducky.

Finally, following the damage caused by the May bombings of Hanoi and Haiphong, a chink of light appeared. It came swiftly after what Kissinger described bleakly as "The worst moment of the talks, with the apparent success of the North Vietnam spring offensive in 1972. Le Duc Tho just read out articles from the U.S. press about our domestic problems. Very humiliating."[42] But it was the bombing offensive which "brought them back to the table." Militarily, on the ground, the bombing campaign of May 1972 seemed to have the effects hoped for by the Pentagon. After moments of great danger for the embattled ARVN troops, fighting now without U.S. soldiers at their side, the Hanoi offensive petered out. Stalemate left the balance of forces roughly where they had been after Tet years previously. "If Hanoi did not soon accept our proposals," recorded Kissinger gloomily, "the new Congress would force us to settle on worse terms."[43] Then, in September, by recapturing the key position of Quang Tri, the South Vietnamese gained the "strongest bargaining position of the war." After five more secret trips to Paris by Kissinger (one in July, two in August, two more in September), between October 7 and 12 a breakthrough seemed to occur. It was only just in time for the White House, with a presidential election in a matter of weeks. In Kissinger's view, the United States could be in a far weaker negotiating position after the elections—especially if Democrat George McGovern, the "peacenik," were to win. The press was becoming ever more restive. Whereas in July the *New York Times* had been flattering Kissinger as the "inscrutable occidental," praising his "dazzling intellect, fancy footwork, beguiling aplomb and it sometimes seems, mirrors,"[44] by October 1 it was accusing him of conducting "the most highly publicized secret missions in history, accomplishing nothing so far except to set off politically useful rumors that peace is near. As his smiling, bespectacled round face pops out of yet another airplane door, one is prompted to the melancholy thought that peace might have come a long time ago if he and Mr. Nixon did less flying and better thinking."[45]

This was offensive talk. The pressure on Kissinger was peaking.

Then, at the end of a nonstop session lasting sixteen hours on October 11, hours of "excruciating tension"[46] for Kissinger, Le Duc Tho at last modified his stance to accept the minimum U.S. terms. Hanoi would drop its demand that Thieu immediately be replaced by a coalition government; on the other hand, and this was to prove "the devil in the detail," the United States conceded that North Vietnam not be required to withdraw its troops from the South.[47] In the meantime, U.S. forces had been whittled down from 543,000 in 1969 to an insignificant 27,000. Thus henceforth only U.S. airpower and munitions could play a role in support of Saigon.

Kissinger was ecstatic at the results achieved. In Paris, he and his assistant, Winston Lord, "shook hands and said to each other: 'We have done it.' "* Haig, who had served in Vietnam, declared with emotion that "we had saved the honor of the military men who had served, suffered, and died there." Kissinger continued in his account: "I have participated in many dramatic events . . . But the moment that moved me most deeply has to be that cool autumn Sunday afternoon, while the shadows were falling over the serene French landscape and that large quiet room, hung with abstract paintings, was illuminated only at the green baize table across which the two delegations were facing each other. At last, we thought, there would be an end to the bloodletting in Indochina." [48]

Years later Kissinger would resist fiercely those charges that what was settled in 1972 could have been available in 1969. Never before, he insisted, had "Hanoi agreed to abandon its demand for the overthrow of the Saigon governmental structure," [49] nor an immediate cease-fire, and the simultaneous return of the U.S. POWs. After those nearly four hard years of grinding talks, his emotions perhaps got the better of him. Back in Washington on October 12, as Kissinger reported to the president, according to Nixon, he smiled "the broadest smile I had ever seen. 'Well, Mr. President, it looks like we have got a three out of three!' " [50] Nixon ordered steak and a bottle of Château Lafite to celebrate; no champagne—he was less exultant, and remained more skeptical, than his jubilant negotiator. Al Haig also seemed "rather subdued," having just returned from Saigon. There he had found Thieu "visibly shaken. He was suspicious of the motives behind the North Vietnamese proposal and unsettled by our willingness to accept them even as a basis for negotiations." [51]

Thieu had every reason to be suspicious. On October 22, Kissinger flew to Hanoi to wrap things up. Returning on the 26th, he proclaimed at a televised press conference: "Peace is at hand." It was, he admitted later, "a phrase that was to haunt me from then on." [52] Opponents of Nixon were to denounce it as a cheap shot in the election. Nixon himself was furious: "This was going considerably further than I would have gone." [53] For there were two ghosts at the feast: one was President

---

* To the cynical mind, the wording, as well as the circumstances, make it difficult not to be reminded of Professor 'Enry 'Iggins in *My Fair Lady*.

Thieu in Saigon, the other—though still only an all but invisible small cloud far off on the horizon—was Watergate. Thieu had not been kept fully informed of the Paris negotiations. This was a direct consequence of Kissinger's residual insistence on secret diplomacy. It may have been rash, if not deceitful, to keep out of the loop the key ally—the country most immediately affected by the agreements, into which in less than two years' time the Communist hordes would come pouring down from the North. Critics of Kissinger castigated the agreement as typifying the dangers inherent in his obsession with secret diplomacy. Kissinger himself would always insist vigorously that there could never have been any agreement with Hanoi had Thieu been kept fully in the picture. Even Haig, upon whom the brunt of dealing with Thieu now fell, largely agreed: "No, he shouldn't have been brought in—as it was he knew everything . . . he trusted me, as a soldier. He did not trust Kissinger."[54] But now, forewarned of the full gravamen of the talks, first by intercepted intelligence, then through a brilliant, but indiscreet, scoop from Hanoi by the ace journalist Arnaud de Borchgrave, Thieu exploded, declaring to Kissinger: "For us it isn't a question of choosing between Moscow and Peking. It is a question of choosing between life and death."[55] Haig, the "trusted" soldier, now made fifteen trips to Saigon—as many as Kissinger had made to Paris—to get Thieu on side.

In the United States a Harris poll asked if the only way to get peace was to have Thieu resign; 60 percent replied yes. In Saigon, every distrust of America surged to the fore. The flames were fanned by Nixon's adversary, McGovern, who, in the final run-up to the November election proclaimed that he would bring an immediate halt to all bombing, and an immediate withdrawal of all American troops and equipment, and close down U.S. bases in neighboring Thailand. Occasionally reduced to tears, Thieu in Saigon dug his toes in. Temperatures escalated; so did the language. By the end of October, Thieu was rejecting the entire plan, and Kissinger was referring to the South Vietnamese allies as "the worst shits." He warned Thieu, "We have fought for four years, have mortgaged our whole foreign policy to the defense of one country," while to Nixon he reported that "there was no possibility that we could come near anything that would satisfy all of Thieu's requirements."[56]

Meanwhile, Nixon had won the election with a landslide; but now Ducky came back and categorically rejected every modification, sixty-nine in all, which Kissinger had submitted to meet South Vietnamese objections. In addition, he "introduced several new and unacceptable demands of his own."[57] Everything seemed in ruins. On the 6th, another six-hour session with Ducky ended without progress. According to Nixon's diary, "The North Vietnamese surprised him by slapping him in the face with a wet fish."

"Tawdry, filthy shits. They make the Russians look good"[58] was how Kissinger now rated Ducky and his team; though it could be argued that he had brought much of the trouble on himself.

In early October, all had at last looked so rosy; now, between North and South "there was no doubt we were caught in a vise," admitted Kissinger.[59] To put maximum, final pressure on both sides, before the agreements totally collapsed, Nixon ordered a renewed all-out bombing operation on North Vietnam—the Christmas Bombing of 1972. At the same time, Haig was dispatched once more to Saigon to take the toughest line with Thieu: "The time has come," Nixon wrote Thieu, in his own hand, "you must decide now whether you desire to continue the alliance or whether you want me to seek a settlement with the enemy which serves U.S. interests alone."[60] Did ever an embattled ally receive a direr threat?

There was disagreement between Kissinger and Nixon over presentation of the bombing to the public at home. Kissinger urged that the president make on television "a stirring and convincing case" to "rally the American people." But Nixon disagreed. "I preferred an unannounced stepping up of the bombing," explaining in his diary: "What Henry does not understand is what I tried to get across to him yesterday before he left, that is that rallying the people as we did on November 3 on Cambodia, and then May 8, has now reached the point of no return."[61] In Saigon anti-U.S. feelings plunged to new depths; anti-Semitism raised its head, with Thieu allegedly declaring: "The Jew professor comes to Saigon to try to win a Nobel Peace Prize."[62] Kissinger, according to Nixon, came close to resigning.

Certainly no one knew better than both Nixon and Kissinger how little patience, how little belly for this terrible war, which had consumed so many young American lives, now existed in the nation and the Congress. Meanwhile, cynically waiting for the ripe fruits to fall into their patient laps, Le Duc Tho and his bosses in Hanoi all this time just "stood at the sidelines, coldly observing how America was negotiating not with its adversary but with itself."[63] Those patriotic Americans who vociferously called for an end to the interminable war at any cost would not have seen it that way, but—in World War II terms—it was almost as if the enemy had an invaluable built-in fifth column working away in the heart of America; at least that is how Hanoi would have seen it.

On December 18, the Christmas Bombing blasted the North for twelve days. Nixon raged at the Pentagon's inability to throw in enough B-52s, threatening the respected chairman of the Joint Chiefs of Staff, Admiral Thomas Moorer, "I don't want any more of this crap about the fact that we couldn't hit this target or that one. This is your chance to use military power effectively to win this war, and if you don't I will consider you responsible."[64] Again rejecting Kissinger's advice, Nixon refused to go on TV to explain his motives behind the bombing. Kissinger pleaded, but Nixon was "not appealable." (One of Kissinger's close aides at the time, Peter Rodman, however, thought that Nixon was "absolutely right—he was really quite magnificent. He just carried out the bombing without any appeal to the public—as if to say to the Vietnamese 'There you are—see what I can do—I don't need public support.' ")[65] Nevertheless, liberal (and, now, not only liberal) opinion in the United States raged: Joe Kraft: "an action of senseless terror which stains the good name of America."[66] James Reston: "war by tantrum."[67]

Moral indignation rose daily. "Terror Bombing in the Name of Peace," declared the *Washington Post*.[68] "No foreign policy of the Nixon Presidency evoked such outrage as the Christmas bombing. On no issue was he more unjustly treated . . . his decision speeded the end of the war," declared Kissinger; even in retrospect, he could think "of no other measure that would have."[69] Nixon steadfastly refused to be deflected. Losses to the powerfully reinforced (and Soviet-supplied) North Vietnamese missile batteries were heavy. So were civilian casualties—over 1,600, claimed Hanoi. On December 20, the third day, six B-52s were lost, and two more out of thirty planes the next day; by the end of the bombing, fifteen of the B-52s had been lost, and with them ninety-three American airmen.[70]

Following the embarrassment of Kissinger's overhasty exultation of "Peace is at hand," relations with Nixon had taken a further downturn early in the winter, and shortly after the election of 1972 with the publication of Oriana Fallaci's interview. Editing if not actually doctoring her tapes with some ruthlessness, the Italian man-eater in her interview portrayed Kissinger most unflatteringly as an arrogant egotist, and a philandering playboy. He was quoted as having referred to China as "my success," and to himself as the "cowboy who leads the wagon train by riding ahead alone on his horse . . . [an] amazing, romantic character." Subsequently he tossed his playboy flirtations aside as being "only a diversion, a hobby." Published in *The New Republic* that December, while the controversial Christmas Bombing was underway, the article, infuriating to the feminist lobby, provoked a cruel riposte in the *Washington Post* of Kissinger emerging "not as a skilled student of foreign affairs, but as a girl-crazed happy hamster."[71]*

Deeply embarrassing to Kissinger, it sent Nixon into a fury. Already since the election he had been saying he was "going to fire the son of a bitch."[72] Finally, that Christmas there had come the additional blow to Nixon's spirit, in the shape of the shared billing, with his aide, of *Time*'s Man of the Year. According to John Ehrlichman, it provoked in Nixon a "white-lipped anger," seeing it as "another self-serving grab for publicity by Henry."[73] Thus, at this critical moment in the Vietnam negotiations, relations between Nixon and his NSC adviser, and chief

---

* The press was loath to leave the "playboy" theme alone. A few weeks later, Kissinger was being needled by Barbara Walters of NBC.

> MISS WALTERS: Some serious people have been concerned that the man who goes out with beautiful women and dates movie starlets, also negotiates with Chou-En-lai and Le Duc Tho, do you see any conflict between these two aspects of your life?
> KISSINGER: I find there is no conflict. One has to do with my social life and the other has to do with my professional life and I don't let my social life interfere with my professional life. (NBC transcript, 2/23/73).

negotiator, had never been worse. Should Kissinger be sacked? Wrote James "Scotty" Reston in the *New York Times* of December 30: "The capital is buzzing these days with rumors about a split between President Nixon and his security adviser Henry Kissinger. . . . Mr. Kissinger would be more willing than the President to take a chance on signing the ambiguous truce terms of October 26. But Mr. Kissinger is too much of a scholar, with too good a sense of humor and history, to put his own thoughts ahead of the President's."[74]

That sense of humor was running a bit thin; but the bombing had worked—or so it seemed. (Or had the canny North Vietnamese seen something else in the tea leaves?) On December 26, Hanoi capitulated and declared it would accept the U.S. terms. It was the day Harry Truman died. The bombing ceased on the 30th; it had been, Kissinger stressed to the author, "essential to getting Hanoi to sign."[75] He agreed to meet Le Duc Tho once again in Paris, on January 8.

Meanwhile, as a threatening pointer to the way ahead, on January 2, 1973, the majority House Democratic caucus voted 154–75 to cut off all funds for military operations in Vietnam. It was the beginning of the end. Nothing would have indicated more clearly to Ducky and his colleagues that time was on their side, that all they had to do was wait. On January 8, Kissinger was back in France, this time at "a French businessman's house. Now they started to serve us food—we had had no real food until 1972. Le Duc Tho was charming. He wasn't so monolithic as [Soviet foreign minister Andrei] Gromyko."[76] But it was all a bit "like a movie that had been restarted after the film had broken."[77] It was the eve of Nixon's sixtieth birthday. Kissinger flew back to Washington for Nixon's second inaugural, the day "cold and clear and blustery." Aboard the plane he heard, on the 22nd, that Lyndon Johnson, a casualty of Vietnam, had died. Nixon thought he had died of "a broken heart."[78] In February, Kissinger flew to Hanoi to sign the final deeds. It was, he said, like "stepping onto the moon." The airport was "pockmarked from our B-52 bombing that had destroyed most of the buildings and cratered the runways, though they had been patched up well enough to permit the plane to come to a bouncing stop. Le Duc Tho greeted me almost affectionately. That dour, dedicated revolutionary and I had developed a curious relationship over the nearly four years of secret meetings in Paris."[79]

But the premier, Pham Van Dong, when Kissinger met him "dropped an ominous hint of renewed warfare." [80]

There was one last curtain call in Paris with Ducky. On that definitive occasion, Le Duc Tho even managed "to make himself obnoxious by insisting on ironclad assurances of American economic aid." [81]

But—wrote Kissinger—"America's Vietnam war was over." [82] It had cost 58,000 American lives and 350,000 casualties overall. He lauded, in retrospect, with generosity the beleaguered president: "This man, so loathed in his hour of triumph, so ungenerous in some of his motivations, had navigated our nation through one of the most anguishing periods of its history . . . yet with all his insecurities and flaws, he had brought America by a tremendous act of will to an extraordinary moment when dreams and possibilities can join." [83] He felt "an odd tenderness" toward him. "At peace with myself, neither elated nor sad," was how he ended *White House Years.* [84] The rift with Nixon had peaked. At the time, Kissinger believed, "and I believe now that the agreement [with North Vietnam] could have worked." [85] But would Congress "support us"? While Kissinger was actually speaking at the White House briefing on the Paris agreements, he "did not realize that Watergate, the extent to which I was still unaware of, was foreclosing the hopes for the healing of the United States." [86]

On January 15, the Watergate burglars pleaded guilty. On the 20th, Nixon was sworn in, for his second term, as thirty-seventh president of the United States. Five days later, Nixon's chief of staff, H. R. Haldeman (nicknamed "the Brush" on account of his haircut), was passing Kissinger instructions from the president on how to comport himself with Congress: "When you go to the Capitol you must at all cost give no quarter to the doves. . . .

". . . We must emphasize these points. Among them:

"(a) This is a peace with honor which achieved the major goals for which the war was waged." [87]

But within a matter of weeks, the North Vietnamese were already beginning to cheat.

On February 15, Nixon gave a pep talk in the Pentagon to the Joint Chiefs of Staff. He explained how Vietnam had been "important not for itself but because of what it demonstrated in terms of support for our friends and allies and in terms of showing our will to our enemies. We had to see it through. I could have 'bugged out' free after the '68 election, but we had to see it through. . . . I understand what vilification you, the military, have gone through over Vietnam, but you should remember that the big issue in the war was the American spirit."[88] Words that George W. Bush might well have mimicked thirty-three years later.

That same February the first of 591 POWs released under the Vietnam Paris Peace Accords began to return. Except for the immediate kith-and-kin, it was a sad, muted homecoming, unlike VJ Day, or Korea. Many, like John McCain, came back wounded; some had suffered as long as eight years under terrible conditions, often in solitary confinement. And then there were 200,000 more wounded still in VA hospitals; not to mention an even larger number listed as deserters or draft resisters. The returning prisoners seemed like men "stuck in a time warp"[89]; they were taken aback by the change in hairstyles, by the sexual revolution, by the role played in the war by women like Jane Fonda—and by movies like *Deep Throat*. One North Vietnamese warder had told Admiral James Stockdale, the senior POW: "We will win this war on the streets of New York,"[90] and certainly this is how it must have seemed to many a returnee. It was a strange, unfriendly America. There were certainly no celebrations on Times Square. The men were welcomed more with shame than as heroes; most had been bomber pilots, and therefore regarded by the Fonda faction as war criminals. In the presence of the author in September 2008, General David Petraeus, currently head of the U.S. Central Command, recalled how recently he had encountered a demonstration against the Iraq War in Cambridge, Massachusetts, flying banners saying "HATE THE WAR, BUT LOVE THE BOYS."[91] How different attitudes to the returning POWs had been in 1973. Vietnam was a war America wanted, and in many ways continues to want, to forget as quickly as possible. Certainly the future of the South Vietnam ally was swiftly placed on the back burner.

Nixon, however, determined to turn it into a triumphal occasion, marking the immediate dividend of all Kissinger's arduous negotiations. He "personally bought more than 600 orchid corsages and had one sent to each of the wives or mothers" of the repatriates. On the advice of Sammy Davis Jr., on May 24, Nixon with all the personal razzmatazz, and emotional display of which he was normally so ineptly bad, threw the party of the year at the White House, for the POWs. One thousand three hundred invitations were sent out for a sit-down dinner, a thousand more than for the previous record for 231 senior citizens at Thanksgiving 1969. Ominously it rained all day and most of the evening; ladies' long dresses were spattered with mud. Nevertheless spirits were undaunted. Eloquently the president toasted the "brave wives and mothers." In return a senior officer declared that on December 18, "when we heard heavy bombs impacting in Hanoi, we started to go and pack our bags, because we knew we were going home, and we were going home with honor." Nixon was presented with a plaque inscribed: "Our leader—our comrade, Richard the Lion-Hearted."

The irrepressible Bob Hope opened the entertainment. John Wayne got a standing ovation as he told the POWs, "I'll ride into the sunset with you anytime." [92] Then, an eighty-five-year-old Irving Berlin, frail and in failing health, got up and sang his "God Bless America." Many wept. The show and the dancing went on till after 2 A.M., when Nixon and Pat crept upstairs; he kissed her good night, then sat in the Lincoln Room as the sounds of revelry faded below. "I felt," he recorded, "that this was one of the greatest nights in my life. There were no words then, and there are really none now, that could describe the joy and satisfaction that I felt at the thought that I had played a role in bringing these men back home, and that they . . . genuinely seemed to consider the decisions I had made about the war to have been courageous and admirable ones." [93] Certainly there would be few more such nights before the chasm opened the following year.

There was no reference, however, to the man whose hard-slogging at the coal face, through all those grinding meetings with Ducky in Paris (and whom Nixon had come close to sacking only weeks earlier), had made "peace at hand," then—finally—"peace with honor" achievable. Now peace seemed indeed in the hand: the prisoners were home; Vietnam could be forgotten. Time to move on. In April, President Thieu had been allowed to creep into Washington; it was the first time he had been permitted on U.S. soil, but only the about-to-be-disgraced vice president, Spiro Agnew, was there to welcome him. Kissinger would record it as "one of the saddest experiences of my period in office."[94] Meanwhile, for the White House, that evening in May must have seemed like one last flicker of triumph, as the evil-smelling, oily floodtide of Watergate, still only barely visible to Kissinger, continued to rise around Nixon. Kissinger, who was at the POW dinner quietly in the background, reckoned, "Yes, you could say it was Nixon's last hurrah—but Watergate was already biting."[95]

CHAPTER 3

THE OPENING TO CHINA

"That place [Taiwan] is no great use for you . . . but a great wound for us."

— Zhou Enlai to Henry Kissinger[1]

"Take care, the Polar Bear is going to punish you."

— Mao Zedong to Henry Kissinger[2]

AT 5:45 P.M., Eastern Daylight Saving Time, on July 15, 1971, the American public heard a "cryptic announcement" from Nixon's Western White House that the president was to make a "major statement" to the nation on all TV and radio networks exactly five hours later. What could it be? Americans waited with bated breath. Just two years previously Nixon had been able to announce the successful flight of Apollo 11 to the moon and back, fruit of the Kennedy administration, but what news under the moon could that strange, unloved, and unknowable president have left to startle folk with? Peace in Vietnam? That was all most Americans concerned themselves about; and that seemed unlikely. Then, from NBC television studios in Burbank, California, Nixon delivered a brief, three-and-a-half-minute speech. "Good evening: I have requested this television time tonight to announce a major development in our efforts to build a lasting peace in the world . . . In pursuance of that goal, I sent

Dr. Kissinger, my Assistant for National Security Affairs, to Peking . . ." Like John the Baptist, Kissinger's visit was to make way for an official visit by the president himself the following year.

As Nixon left the studios, Kissinger recalled a small group greeting him with chants of "Get out of Vietnam." But otherwise the impact on American society was electric. Because of the total, habitual secrecy of Kissinger's movements, the shock wave had been all the more overwhelming. Many Americans, battered by constant bad tidings from Vietnam, or the apparently superior power of Communism across the board, or the wilting U.S. economy, felt the same. For the past two decades, ever since those bugle-blowing Chinese hordes had dealt Douglas MacArthur's troops a humiliating blow on Korea's Yalu River, China had been a pariah, a dangerous enemy, a land as "forbidden" and unknown as Tibet in a previous era. It is hard to recall just how powerful were the emotions unleashed by that brief announcement. They rivaled even the reactions to Neil Armstrong on the moon.

As Nixon himself recorded, "The first months of 1971 were the lowest point of my first term as President. The problems we confronted were so overwhelming and so apparently impervious to anything we could do to change them that it seemed possible that I might not even be nominated for re-election in 1972."[3] Only the previous month, joy at his daughter Tricia's wedding had been marred by the earthshaking release of the Pentagon Papers, a seven-thousand-page, top secret study of U.S. involvement in Vietnam, rated by Nixon as "the most massive leak of classified documents in American history."[4] Now, at a stroke, news of the Kissinger visit to Beijing—hardly less historic than that of Marco Polo to the Great Khan five centuries previously—changed everything. If Neil Armstrong had taken "one giant leap for mankind" on the moon, Kissinger's trip to Beijing—given all the historic circumstances—was little less for Nixon's America.

The story of the Kissinger-Nixon visits to China has been well trodden; even an opera has been written about it. Chronologically too it hardly belongs in this account. Yet it forms a backdrop of essential relevance to all that was to happen in 1973, to the fruition of relations opened in 1971 and 1972. Also, in the combination of high drama, adventure, and snatches of downright hilarity which accompanied the two men on their historic pilgrimage to the Great Khan, it has its own irresistible fascination to this recorder of history.

To all but a small coterie of fanatical Kissinger-worshippers, there can be little doubt (indeed Kissinger himself has none*) that the initiative for the opening to China came from Nixon, not Kissinger. Nevertheless, both may have begun thinking on parallel lines, and as the project developed, their strategic views came closely to coincide—and hard to differentiate. Back in October 1967, thus well before the White House seemed to be within his reach, Nixon had started the ball rolling with an article in *Foreign Affairs* in which, assisted by William Safire, he wrote: "We simply cannot afford to leave China forever outside the family of nations."[5] With Mao's China currently locked into its savagely atavistic Cultural Revolution, Nixon then favored, however, a policy of "firm restraint": "The world cannot be safe until China changes." His reputation, after all, had been founded—as the lawyer prosecuting Alger Hiss—on doctrinaire anti-Communism. At the same time, as a Californian he had grown up with his eyes trained on China beyond the Pacific, in contrast to the Europe-oriented men of Washington's Foggy Bottom. Nixon's starting point was visionary, almost—one might say—romantic, and messianic. Kissinger, true to Metternichian principles and realpolitik, saw the opening to China in terms of "global equilibrium"—world balance of power. As he later explained, "It was not to collude against the Soviet Union but to give us a balancing position to use for constructive ends—to give each Communist power a stake in better relations with us."[6] Or, as he put it elsewhere, it was "not to expiate liberal guilt over our China policies of the late 1940s, but to shape a global equilibrium."[7] To him the overriding importance of the China card lay in how it could affect relations with Moscow—not in China per se.

Perhaps there were unspoken recollections of how the Tito card of rebel Yugoslavia had been played against Stalin with success twenty years previously. Most immediately, both men conceived that some-

---

* If, over the years, by default Kissinger seems to have acquired most of the glory for the China opening, it came from his allies rather than himself—though he may have done little to dispel the limelight (interviews, Paul Delaney, 10/23/05; Strobe Talbott, 5/23/05).

how the China card could be used to break the logjam over Vietnam. Then, with the United States seemingly outgunned by the huge margin of missile superiority of the Soviets, coupled with Brezhnev's new display of aggressive tendencies culminating in the invasion of Czechoslovakia in 1968, the charm of deploying Beijing as a counterweight to Moscow grew. It assumed more momentum as, in the course of 1969, news came out of serious border conflicts between the two Communist, nuclear behemoths, up on the Ussuri River, and the language between the two capitals became more that of hostile than fraternal states. That same year, China tested two nuclear devices—a warning to the Soviets? There was even alarm in Washington that the Soviet Union might be contemplating a sudden nuclear strike on China. Soviet forces on the Chinese border had expanded from fifteen to over forty divisions—roughly equal to the whole strength of NATO.

But, how to put out a first hand—when Beijing and Washington had not spoken to each other in a generation? It was clear from the beginning that Mao would be hard to get. There was an anecdote that Zhou Enlai, when asked by a British diplomat for his views on the French Revolution, had remarked that it was "too soon to tell." With their centuries-old experience in "Cycles of Cathay," * the Chinese knew how to play it long, and were in no hurry to be "opened" to the West. Thus the process of turning the knob of the door, let alone inserting a foot in it, was going to test even the kind of patience Kissinger would so remarkably show in the long-protracted Paris talks over Vietnam. Kissinger himself was skeptical; early in 1969 when Haldeman remarked that Nixon was deadly serious about visiting China before the end of a second term, Kissinger was said to have exclaimed: "Fat chance!"[8]

A variety of back channels was deployed. One contact made in Warsaw via the U.S. ambassador, Walter Stoessel, led to 136 meetings, and little progress. Not for the first or last time, Nixon and Kissinger were in agreement that William Rogers and the State Department with its cumbersome procedures should be cut out. "Let us see that State does not drag its feet on this," Nixon scrawled in longhand on one of

---

* "Better fifty years of Europe than a cycle of Cathay," Tennyson.

Kissinger's memoranda.[9] Meanwhile Kissinger had opened up another channel via the long-suffering Vernon Walters in Paris (who had "proved so adept at arranging my secret meetings with Le Duc Tho").[10] His instructions, in the summer of 1970, were to pass word to the Chinese embassy in Paris that the United States was prepared to hold secret talks. On one occasion when Walters attempted to deliver a letter to his opposite number, the Chinese military attaché, "his mouth dropped open."[11] Throwing the letter back he leapt into his Mercedes and sped off. Nevertheless, despite the initial rebuffs, there followed forty-five meetings between Walters and the Chinese in Paris. Though Walters had served in the Korean War against the Chinese, he seems to have established cordial relations with them in Paris. By comparison, "dealing with the North Vietnamese was nowhere near as interesting as dealing with the Chinese. I had to carry on both relationships and maintain the fiction that neither knew about the other. Sometimes I felt like a juggler with three balls in the air." But "At least with the Chinese I could see some progress."[12]

Kissinger, in his memoirs, describes the wooing of Beijing as "an intricate minuet . . . so delicately arranged that both sides could always maintain that they were not in contact."[13] Carrots were judiciously thrown out, in the shape of concessions on trade and travel. But still the inscrutable men of Beijing declined to react, playing it cool, and long. Finally, by sheer happenstance Nixon and Kissinger suddenly found the most bizarre of allies—the American Ping-Pong team, teenagers, who—in the spring of 1971—were playing in a tournament in Japan. A warm bond was struck up between the U.S. and Chinese teams; T-shirts were exchanged, and suddenly an invitation came for them to visit Beijing the very next week. Zhou Enlai told the young Americans: "You have opened a new chapter in the relations of the American and Chinese people."[14]

The expression "Ping-Pong diplomacy" entered the lexicon.

It at once became big news in the world media, and the come-on was unmistakable. Nixon suddenly found himself in possession of a potential conduit to the Forbidden City. On April 21, a direct invitation came through for a "special envoy of the president" to visit Beijing. Kissinger's name was specifically mentioned. To Nixon, Kissinger, for obvious, personal reasons—jealousy, for instance, lurked never far below the surface—was not the president's immediate choice. There was a long list of others, including Nixon himself, without any preliminary emissary. (Pointedly omitted was the name of the obvious candidate: Rogers, the hard-treated secretary of state.) For several days Kissinger was kept in an agony of suspense; Walter Isaacson claims that Nixon was "merciless in toying with him."[15] Much of Kissinger's *Weltanschauung* depended on his being the man chosen to make the historic trip. He admitted that this period was "the most maddening of the entire tortuous process."[16] Finally, after several days on tenterhooks, Nixon told Kissinger: "Henry, I think you will have to do it," with the somewhat backhanded compliment: "I am confident that a man who can come and go undetected in Paris can get in and out of Peking before anyone finds out."[17]

As Nixon read out the Chinese final letter of confirmation, Kissinger observed solemnly: "This is the most important communication that has come to an American President since the end of World War II."[18]

Nixon walked down to the small family kitchen in the White House and came back with a bottle of Courvoisier that he had been given for Christmas. "Let us drink," he intoned portentously, "to generations to come who may have a better chance to live in peace because of what we have done." As he explained in his memoirs, the words may have sounded "rather formal"; however, "the moment was one not just of high personal elation, but of a profound mutual understanding that this truly was a moment of historical significance."[19]

At the same time, as Kissinger saw, it was also a moment of immense danger—what if things went wrong, if the modern-age Marco Polo(s) had met with a steely rebuff in the court of the Great Khan? For, after all, Nixon—at a time when the United States perceived itself to be in a position of great danger in the world—was authorizing "a mission that, had it failed, would surely have produced a political catastrophe for him and an international catastrophe for his country."[20] Given his leader's innate loneliness, Kissinger thought "it took a resolute man to walk along the edge of a precipice with only a single associate." Alexander Haig, then Kissinger's deputy, also agreed that the whole operation, through any awkward chance move, could have been "squashed before it was ever born"; hence the importance of total secrecy.

But this was something, in the words of Margaret MacMillan, for which both Kissinger and Nixon had "a natural bent." [21]

There still remained the highly complex logistical problem, that somehow the high-profile doctor could make the long trip unbeknown to the whole of the world. America's best friend in South Asia, President Yahya Khan of Pakistan, was now brought into play. The mission, appropriately (though rather transparently) dubbed "Polo I" would, at the beginning of July 1970, fly Kissinger to Vietnam for "consultations," then on to Pakistan for more talks. In Islamabad he would then develop a "stomachache," which would require him to rest for three days in a mountain station. During those lost three days, he would in fact be flying to Beijing on a Pakistani jet. With him went three aides, including Winston Lord, but no representatives from State—and a bagful of books, on Chinese philosophy, etc. (The cat nearly crept out of the bag, twice; once when a junior American diplomat observed how strange it was that Kissinger had consumed a healthy dinner just before "disappearing" sick; and second when a dedicated Pakistani stringer for the London *Daily Telegraph*, M. F. H. Beg, happened to be at the airstrip as Kissinger embarked—for China, an indiscreet official disclosed to him. But when Beg breathlessly telephoned the news to London, his editor assumed he was drunk and spiked the story—thereby depriving the unfortunate journalist of the scoop of a lifetime.) Otherwise the world press was totally fooled, with the *New York Times* printing one small paragraph reporting, on July 10: "Fleeing the hot, humid air of the plains around Rawalpindi, Henry A. Kissinger, President Nixon's national security adviser, spent the day at Nathiagali in the cool hills of northern Pakistan. He was described as feeling slightly indisposed." [22]

As a further hitch, Kissinger discovered an assistant had forgotten to pack his shirts. He flew into a rage, and had to borrow from a much taller aide (a six foot two West Pointer); using elastic bands to shorten the sleeves, it made his boss—thought Winston Lord—look "rather like a penguin" whenever he took off his jacket in the summer heat of Beijing. (Well might one speculate on what the faultlessly elegant Zhou might have construed as "loss of face"; did he think this was just normal attire for this alien from outer space? His thoughts, alas, were not recorded.) Also, rather undiplomatically, the shirts bore labels "Made in Taiwan."* On top of all this, Kissinger failed with chopsticks, remaining "hopelessly clumsy." The mere smell of shrimp in Chinese cuisine nauseated him, and when he tried to wash the fishy taste away with mao-tai rice wine, the fiery liquid seared his throat, and made him fearful of getting drunk: "There was long chit chat about Chinese cooking at those moments when I could speak,"[23] he recorded in his notes for Nixon.

Oh, the perils and horrors of high-level diplomacy!

Nevertheless, superbly described in Margaret MacMillan's *Nixon and Mao*, Polo I proved to be as great a success as could have been anticipated. On being greeted by Premier Zhou Enlai, Kissinger remembered John Foster Dulles's never-to-be-forgotten snub when he had refused to shake hands with Zhou at the Geneva Conference of 1954, and "ostentatiously" stuck out his hand. It was, he claimed, "the first step in putting the legacy of the past behind us."[24] Out of forty-nine hours in China, Kissinger spent seventeen of them in tête-à-tête with Zhou alone. Modern scholarship today indicates the elegant sophisticate Zhou as having been almost as brutal a villain as his master, Mao,[25] but at the time, in the wake of the crassly inhuman horrors of the Cultural Revolution, he appeared as the civilized face of ancient China. To me Kissinger described him as "one of the most impressive minds I had ever met"; "indeed one of the two or three most outstanding men I have ever met"; "He moved gracefully and with dignity, filling a room not by his physical dominance (as did Mao or de Gaulle)† but by his air of controlled tension, steely discipline, and self-control, as if he

---

* With one of his not infrequent flashes of humor, Kissinger remarks in his memoirs, how when remarking to the Chinese that Taiwan was "a matter close to me" he was telling the literal truth (*White House Years*, p. 753).

† Once, when talking about baseball, Kissinger, up at Kent, surprised me by likening the legendary Joe DiMaggio to Mao; they were, he said, the only two men he had ever met who "filled a room" with sheer power of personality. Would DiMaggio have been pleased by the comparison? (HAK interview 10/28/05.)

were a coiled spring." In the course of their protracted conversations, Kissinger found in Zhou "an inner serenity" that gave him a distinct advantage over fellow Communists at the negotiating table.[26] Kissinger became genuinely attached to him: "The Chinese," he wrote in his memoirs, "were cold-blooded practitioners of power politics,* a far cry from the romantic humanitarians imagined in Western intellectual circles. And yet when Chou died, I felt a great sadness. The world would be less vibrant, the prospects less clearly seen."[27]

On the other side, Zhou is quoted as having commented—with a typically Chinese compliment—that he found Kissinger very "intelligent . . . he could talk for an hour without giving one substantive answer!"[28]

Those first encounters of Polo I were far from plain sailing. Kissinger assiduously steered clear of any reproaches on human rights, or the excesses of the Cultural Revolution, and unlike Ducky and the North Vietnamese, or indeed Brezhnev, Zhou "never bargained to score petty points." Yet, though the tenor of the talks would be "philosophical, humorous, and illuminating,"[29] when it came to first principles there were moments when the two threatened to walk away from each other. Kissinger was surprised to discover how Taiwan assumed such supreme importance to the Chinese, regarded as an integral part of China, and he was disappointed that the Chinese were not prepared to act as "brokers" over Vietnam, or apply any kind of pressure upon Hanoi. There had been an "intoxicating" brief period when Kissinger hoped that there might be a simultaneous breakthrough toward peace in Vietnam. Nevertheless, they parted having mutually—according to Kissinger—agreed upon "a comprehension by each side of the fundamental purposes of the other."[30] But what was surely most important of all was that the trip had been made, that the door was now open for the first U.S. president ever to visit China.

One can share the elation Kissinger and his staff all experienced on the seemingly shorter flight back to Pakistan; perhaps rather as Pinkerton might have felt after that first encounter with Madame Butterfly. On the way to Tehran, homeward-bound, with the secret remarkably

---

* Thus, men after Kissinger's own heart.

still preserved, Kissinger signaled Nixon with one jubilant code word: "Eureka!"[31] It must have seemed like the greatest moment in his career to date; Archimedes could hardly have been more excited as he overflowed his bath. With an element of self-praise which, in the context, was hardly excessive, he exulted to U.S. ambassador to Pakistan Joseph Farland, "I did a beautiful job."[32] On the plane he prepared a forty-page report for Nixon, culminating with the dramatic words: "We have laid the groundwork for you and Mao to turn a page in history."[33] Finally, on his twelve-day round-the-world flight, he stopped over in Paris for one of his secret meetings with Ducky. Without giving away his big secret, he optimistically felt that three-hour session to be "the most hopeful I had had. . . . For some intoxicating weeks we thought that we might have simultaneous breakthroughs towards peace in Vietnam and towards China."[34]

Returning to the United States, Kissinger was summoned to San Clemente to brief the president—over a period of two hours. Looking out across the Pacific from the window of Nixon's "modest study," he found it tempting to imagine the "far shore of China, thousands of miles distant." One of Nixon's first concerns was that only a "sanitized" account of Kissinger's exploits should go to the secretary of state—a small revelation that, even in triumph, Nixon could still indulge in petty warfare. So on that July 15, Nixon appeared before the massed TV cameras to launch his thunderbolt: that he had now accepted an invitation "to visit China at an appropriate date before May 1972." He and his entourage then moved on to a dinner of crab and Château Lafite (a curious mix) at Perino's restaurant in Los Angeles, where the president "reveled in an unchallengeable triumph."[35]

Following the broadcast, it was—quite justly—Kissinger's reputation that soared. His face was on the cover of every newsmagazine. *Time*: "At the height of a brilliant career, he enjoys a global spotlight and an influence that most professors only read about in libraries." Such "spotlights" for his assistant were hardly a delight for Nixon's ears, and via Haldeman, he sent an order for Kissinger to put up "an *absolute* wall around himself—he must not on *any* basis speak to the *New York Times*, the *Washington Post*."[36] Even if Kissinger had been of a more retiring nature, such was his public image now that Nixon's edict would have been almost impossible to obey. Coming at a time of universal bad news, Americans with their instinctive appreciation for derring-do escapades and for grandiose, Hollywood-style gestures, the outpouring of admiration was coupled now with some affection—but all of it directed toward Henry Kissinger. In this context, secrecy had helped, insofar as it enhanced the blitz factor. Overnight (in the opinion of biographer Walter Isaacson) Kissinger was transformed "into an international celebrity."[37] But few of the hyperboles would spill over to the genius behind the whole story; which was perhaps one good reason the tantalizing prize of secretary of state would remain beyond Kissinger's reach for another two years. The whole episode speaks volumes about the minefield concealed within the relationship between the president and his "assistant."

Kissinger now followed up his secret success of the summer with a public but low-key return to China that October—Polo II—to set the stage and prepare an official agenda for the presidential advent in February. Two glitches preceded the trip, however. Bad timing for Kissinger, his second visit coincided with a vote in the United Nations to seat the People's Republic of China and expel Taiwan as representative of 750 million Chinese. Taiwan lost 76–35. It was a serious setback for the Nixon-Kissinger armory. Nixon was outraged. But much more menacing to the whole project was war which broke out, suddenly, in November between India and Pakistan—America's close ally, and essential partner in the China gambit. Washington was caught badly on the back foot, and found itself having to back Pakistan—a country which, though provoked by India, was morally in the wrong for the war. Passions escalated, with Nixon and Kissinger both recorded as lambasting India's forceful prime minister, Indira Gandhi, alternately as a "witch" and "an old bitch."[38] Kissinger particularly noted how Nixon "cut me down to size" over the war.[39]

Under powerful U.S. pressure, the war ended in December. Pakistan lost its important territory in the east, which became independent Bangladesh. President Yahya, Kissinger's friend and essential accomplice in Polo I, fell from office. Recalling their hours as co-conspirators, Kissinger wrote that "I was probably responsible for the last pleasant day Yahya had before he was overthrown."[40] Both countries were left with a sense of grievance toward the United States. The brief war represented a serious setback for the Nixon-Kissinger global policy and a growth in the perception that Kissinger was insensitive to human rights. But at least Nixon's visit to China, now scheduled for February 1972, was safe. Haig for one was fearful that the whole project might have to be called off. Had the war continued into the new year, certainly it was hard to see how Nixon could have made the trip with all that would imply—not least for the presidential election the following autumn. Timing was everything; and everything hung together.[41]

Performing a dress rehearsal for Nixon, this time in the comfort of Air Force One, in Beijing, Kissinger flew into trouble. Between the two Polos there had been a strange hiatus, when the White House suddenly became aware that all China's leaders "had disappeared from public view for five days." In fact, what had transpired was the—still mysterious—flight and death of the pro-Soviet Lin Biao, Mao's presumed heir.* After all the sweet talk of the summer, and amid the tension of the Lin Biao affair, Zhou now declared the U.S. formula for the February agenda "unacceptable." Kissinger was handed a "counterdraft that took his breath away."[42] But, according to Nixon, Kissinger replied "calmly"—and toughly: "We cannot have an American President sign a document which says that revolution has become the irresistible trend of history, or that the 'people's revolutionary struggles' are just!" Kissinger became restless as the Chinese came up with proposals, and counterproposals. Time hung heavy, filled in with moments of "stupefying boredom" at a "revolutionary" opera. The main problem was to find a formula over Taiwan which would be acceptable to Congress as well as Beijing. "It turned into a contest of physical endurance," recorded Kissinger, averaging three hours of sleep a night: a specific kind of Chinese torture.[43] Eventually, over the course of an arduous six-day visit, an acceptable compromise was reached. The key words, which were to be accepted as the basic communiqué for Nixon's visit, read: "The United States acknowledges that all Chinese

---

* The story of Lin Biao's flight and ensuing death remains cloaked in some mystery. The assumption is that he was defecting to the Soviets—in protest against China's rapprochement with the United States?

on either side of the Taiwan Strait maintain there is but one China. The United States Government does not challenge that position."[44] Nixon's epoch-making visit, only two months away, could now go ahead.

Starting, as per schedule, on February 21, 1972,[45] the visit had taken three years to arrange, through the kind of "intricate minuet" that would have been familiar to Kissinger's hero, Metternich.[46] Though Kissinger's trip the previous summer had inevitably taken some of the cream off the bun, it was still an internationally earth-moving event, well trumpeted by the abundant presence of the media; though, true to form, Nixon had insisted that his pet pariahs be excluded—thereby perpetuating, if not exacerbating, existing animosities, and possibly missing an admirable PR opportunity for healing wounds. Equally no opportunity was missed to sideline, humiliatingly, the secretary of state. As the plane landed, Nixon (also bearing in mind Dulles's slight in 1954) marched out with arm extended almost like a weapon of martial combat; but, under Haldeman's instructions, a "burly aide" prevented Rogers (and Kissinger too) from being seen until the president was well onto the red carpet and had shaken hands ceremoniously with Zhou on the windswept tarmac. The hosts were left briefly puzzled as to what had happened to the rest of the huge delegation aboard Air Force One.[47] But, with supreme tact, a Chinese band blasted out a brave rendition of "The Star-Spangled Banner."

The Nixon visit, written up in relentless detail by the attendant world press, and more recently described in detail by Margaret MacMillan, was in fact more form than substance; the substance having largely been beaten out by Kissinger and Zhou in their Polos I and II meetings of the previous year. It was manifestly Nixon's show. There were incidental moments of hilarity (generally at the expense of the unloved media), as when members of the American party suffered from "baboon bottom" from lavatory seats overzealously varnished by the hosts; and when Walter Cronkite had to be rescued from the Great Wall with burnt calves caused by a malfunction of his electric socks, which had been specifically designed to meet the North China winter. There was also appalling banality, in the public talks, as the culturally limited president swiftly succumbed to boredom with an excess of the wonders of Chinese civilization—or at least those left still undestroyed by Mao. On the Great Wall he was driven, by sheer battle fatigue, to remark, "Imagine climbing all these mountains carrying stones," and ultimately proclaiming that it was indeed "a great wall, and that it had to be built by a great people."[48]

On that first day, the Nixon motorcade swept on through Tiananmen Square up to the northwest of the city, to the Diaoyutai, a Forbidden City within the Forbidden City, a heavily guarded compound created by Mao at the end of the 1950s for the celebrations of the tenth anniversary of the founding of the People's Republic. Most of its villas were new but the site itself was very old. In the bad old days, generations of Chinese scholars had loved its lakes and groves. A famous Chinese poem talked of its weeping willows against the darkening hills to the west: "Peach blossoms float on the water at sunset." Emperors and noblemen built their pavilions there and fished from its terraces.[49] The president and staff (including Kissinger and his team) were housed in a large villa*, filled with overstuffed armchairs and sofas, each with its antimacassar, in the favored Communist style. Rogers and State were conspicuously housed in a lesser residence down the hill a few hundred yards away; separate dining rooms guaranteed that they remained more or less sealed off.

After their welcome, the hosts gave the visitors a lavish lunch and left them to settle in. There was nervousness as they awaited a message from Mao, whom Kissinger had still not yet encountered. Kissinger wandered about aimlessly. Abruptly a summons came for an immediate interview. Similar to experiences visitors have had with that other dictator, Fidel Castro, it was always Mao's way of doing things; it must also have been calculated for its putting-down effect on envoys to the Court of the Great Khan. The Americans were shocked to find Mao swollen with edema, and manifestly sicker than they had anticipated. Nixon noted how a girl secretary had to help him to his feet, and he complained "I can't talk very well."[50] "He could move only with difficulty," recorded Kissinger, "and speak but considerable effort. Words seemed to leave his bulk as if with great reluctance."[51]†

---

* Today, in the new China it can be rented for $50,000 a night (*Nixon and Mao*, p. 45).

† According to Jung Chang and Jon Halliday, nine days previously "Mao passed out, and came very close to death" (*Mao*, p. 606).

Nevertheless, Kissinger (accompanied by Winston Lord as note-taker), was stunned by the impact Mao made. He described that first meeting at length, as well as emotively, in his memoirs,[52] stressing to the author that he was one of the few men he had ever met who instantly "filled the room with his presence."[53] In their reaction to Mao, Nixon and Kissinger have been accused in the monumental biography of Mao by Jung Chang and Jon Halliday* of "fawning" upon the chairman ("Mao was especially careful not to pay Nixon any compliments, while Nixon and Kissinger both flattered Mao fulsomely"[54]). One questions whether the charge is a fair one. Like Marco Polo, the Americans too had arrived as honored guests, with all that that signifies to the Oriental mind, at their own initiative. It would have been disastrous to have blasted in à la Dulles; or to have evoked human rights qua the Cultural Revolution; and one can only recall Churchill's words when confronted, in June 1941, with the horrendously unpalatable prospect of finding himself an ally of Joseph Stalin: "If Hitler invaded Hell, I would surely give the Devil a good reference."[55]

There was some badinage (which the authors of *Mao* found "revolting"[56]), mainly at the expense of Nixon versus Kissinger. For Kissinger, the content of that first of five meetings with Mao was essentially banal,[57] his utterances "elliptical." "Later on, as I comprehended better the many-layered design of Mao's conversation, I understood that it was like the courtyards in the Forbidden City, each leading to a deeper recess distinguished from the others only by slight changes of proportion, with ultimate meaning residing in a totality that only long reflection could grasp."[58] Definitely a worthy challenge for a former Harvard professor! In contrast to Zhou and his fixation upon Taiwan, Mao concentrated on his security fears about the former blood brother, Soviet Russia—the predatory "polar bear" as he described it. Dovetailing with Kissinger's own priorities of "equilibrium," this was to provide the focus of their successive meetings.

Meanwhile, the media pursued the sledgehammer itinerary laid down by the hosts. There were the endless banquets, the repetitive

---

* A monumental achievement, ten years in writing, which has nevertheless been criticized by some scholars as having allowed its objectivity to be excessively influenced by the authors' passionate, and understandable, loathing of Mao—given, particularly, the sufferings personally suffered by Jung Chang's own family—viz. *Wild Swans.*

rounds of toasts ("that deadly brew" [59] mao-tai a fearful tiger trap for the light-headed Nixon to eschew*), to the accompaniment of Chinese military renditions of "America the Beautiful," † and the relentless sightseeing. Preoccupied with preparing notes for the final communiqué, Kissinger admitted to participating in none of it. Only once was he lured onto the Great Wall (where Nixon made his grandiloquent declaration to the assembled world press, "This is a great wall" ‡), when the vista was somewhat impaired by the illustrious Walter Cronkite, who "staggered" into the picture, singed by his malfunctioning socks, and "a little the worse for wear, dressed in heavy furs more appropriate for a polar expedition and weighed down by a spectacular assortment of photographic gear around his neck . . . the scene lost some of its serenity." [60]

Such discomforts meted out to the unloved media doubtless afforded Nixon a little holiday in his heart. But, as the days wore on, a man always with a low threshold of boredom, he was swiftly becoming jaded. He had heard "She'll Be Coming 'Round the Mountain" whistled by Chinese musicians once too often. Nevertheless, obliged to do yet more sightseeing, at the last round he fell to remarking "I never saw goldfish that big." [61] Even conversations with Zhou had now become perfunctory. To one journalist, Nixon and Zhou had "the look of men who for the moment have had more than enough of one another." [62]§ Nixon's mood was growing dark, as he grumbled increasingly how fed up he was with the unfortunate Rogers.

As the final communiqué came up for formulation, like the diminished triangle-player in the school band, Rogers and his beaten-down

---

* The thoughtful and bossy Haig had issued instructions: "Under no circumstances should the President actually drink from his glass" (*Nixon and Mao*, p. 149).

† Kissinger confesses to having been "deeply moved" at this being played by an army "with which two decades before we had been at war" (*White House Years*, p. 1070).

‡ Rather more meaningfully, when shown a pair of ear plugs worn by an emperor to screen out criticism, Nixon exclaimed for the benefit of the assembled U.S. press corps: "Give me a pair of those!" (*Nixon and Mao*, p. 284).

§ As the festivities in China drew to an exhausted close, this historian cannot help be reminded somewhat of Louis-Napoleon's extravaganza at the Great Exhibition of 1867, when he threw Paris open to the rulers of Europe; only, on this occasion, roles of host and guest were inverted, the course of subsequent events less dire. At least no one tried to assassinate Nixon in Beijing—as befell the Czar of Russia in 1867 Paris.

State Department contingent insisted on their involvement. Kissinger accused them of nitpicking, Nixon stormed about in his underwear, and both threatened to deal with this "mutinous bureaucracy" once and for all.[63] The bureaucrats snapped back, accusing Kissinger of sloppy drafting on Taiwan. It was embarrassing, if not pronouncedly bad form in China, that the battle of White House versus Foggy Bottom had been allowed to spill out into the Forbidden City. Though he did little to discourage it, in fact generally aiding and abetting, Kissinger was in a difficult bind: he wanted Rogers's job, and strongly felt he merited it; while Nixon constantly seemed to be offering it, then taking it away. Why he did not sack Rogers after the election of 1972 remains open to speculation; equally, why didn't Rogers resign after Beijing? Yet when it came to the plunge, Nixon was like Shakespeare's jealous Turk, "who bears no brother near the throne." That nagging jealousy of his ambitious assistant would never leave him. Kissinger notes how, throughout the 1972 China visit, Rogers and his accompanying assistant secretary, Marshall Green, were deliberately excluded from talks with Mao. Nixon had expressly wanted them to be "occupied elsewhere";[64] humiliatingly, washing dirty linen in public, to the shocked Chinese, he explained to Zhou: "Our State Department leaks like a sieve."[65] Zhou laughed. Mao would surely have known how to handle such a problem. For the treatment of Rogers, Kissinger eventually apologized in his memoirs: "The neglect was technically unassailable but fundamentally unworthy. The Secretary of State should not have been excluded from this historic encounter."[66]

Finally, after many sleep-deprived nights, and frayed tempers, Kissinger, Winston Lord and his team—plus the State Department team, once Rogers had finally put his foot down—had a communiqué, the Shanghai Communiqué, acceptable to both sides. It was a most carefully crafted document. As foreseen, to the last the future of Taiwan had been the stumbling block. To the end the Chinese had insisted that it was an "internal matter." As Zhou had remarked explicitly: "That place is no great use for you . . . but a great wound for us."[67] Throughout his three visits to China, Taiwan had also been of lesser interest to Kissinger, his view—as the historian—steadfastly being that history would take care of it. But he had warned Zhou not to press too hard for concessions on Taiwan, pointedly observing that "Other political leaders" might be "destroyed by what is called the China lobby in the U.S." [68] if they went too far. So, modifying the formula that had emerged from Polo I somewhat in the favor of Beijing, this most carefully crafted document now read: "The U.S. side declared: The United States acknowledges that all Chinese on either side of the Taiwan Strait maintain there is but one China and that Taiwan is a part of China. The United States Government does not challenge that position. It reaffirms its interest in a peaceful settlement of the Taiwan question by the Chinese themselves. With this prospect in mind, it affirms the ultimate objective of the withdrawal of all U.S. forces and military installations from Taiwan. In the meantime, it will progressively reduce its forces and military installations on Taiwan as the tension in the area diminishes." * [69]

As Nixon departed via Shanghai, utterly exhausted by yet one more bout of sightseeing — this time to the Shanghai Industrial Exhibition, where he had remarked lamely "we don't see many pictures of Engels in America" — the U.S. party was confronted by a giant billboard: "WE WILL CERTAINLY LIBERATE TAIWAN." [70] At 3 A.M. on the last night of the trip, Kissinger recorded being summoned to Nixon's room, Haldeman joining them, where Nixon "talked about his accomplishments, asking for confirmation and reassurance. And we gave him both, moved in part by an odd tenderness for this lonely, tortured and insecure man." [71]

It was, one felt, Kissinger speaking from the heart.

Immediately the brickbats greeted Nixon's return. On February 28, the *Detroit Free Press* headlined: "They Got Taiwan; We Got Egg Rolls." Nevertheless, as Kissinger pointed out in his memoirs, the "negative stories" were "overwhelmed by the visual impact of Nixon's visit to Peking." [72] Almost every family in America had watched it, 98 percent — glued to their TV sets as they had been, in not dissimilar contexts, to the return of Armstrong from the moon three years previously. A triumphal result in the presidential election eight months

---

* This recalls an interview the author had with President Chiang Ching-kuo in Taipei in 1979, after Russia had invaded Afghanistan. If the People's Republic were also attacked, he insisted vehemently that tiny Taiwan would fly to its assistance: "All Chinese, one people," he asseverated.

later was now a certainty. But what had been achieved, what given away? Severe critics like Jung Chang and Jon Halliday, writing three decades later, thought that the monster Mao had been "given a lot, and on a platter." "For his own electoral ends," they charged, "Nixon de-demonized Mao for mainstream opinion in the West."[73] He and Kissinger had made excessive concessions on Vietnam, and got nothing in return; the subsequent outflow of funds from the West had only helped Mao fund his wild and costly schemes in the Third World, at the cost of famine at home for his wretched subjects.* They had enabled him to consolidate his evil grip domestically. Refining their position on this charge, Halliday specified to the author: "It was not blame, but *fallout*. What happened was the opening of floodgates of recognition, persuading China into these absurd loans to the Third World, notably [Zaire's] Mobutu"[74]—and Taiwan had been "cut loose." To this particular charge, inter alia, Kissinger responded to the author in June 2005 acidly: "Some cutting loose. Here we are, thirty-four years later. We have navigated a tricky situation for a generation, maintaining friendly relations with China while Taiwan has remained, with our help, strong and democratic—all this based on documents negotiated in 1971 and 1972."[75]

Equally robust was Kissinger's riposte on Vietnam; and here he was to find support from another critic, Margaret MacMillan, who reckoned: "The mere fact that Nixon went to China, though, did help the United States. The North Vietnamese were obliged to recognize that China placed a high priority on enhancing its new relationship with the United States. . . . The Americans did indeed hit hard that spring; in retaliation for the North Vietnamese attack in the south, American planes bombed the north and mined Hanoi's harbor of

---

* Here it could be countered that, rightly or wrongly, human rights and welfare within China had never been, could never have been, part of the Nixon-Kissinger brief. Otherwise, the visit would have ended on Day One. Kissinger would argue that, in the long run, one consequence of the trip eventually was to pave the way for the more humane face of Chairman Deng Xiaoping.

As a marginal sideline on today's world, in 2007 the French Socialist presidential candidate, Ségolène Royal, went on her official visit to China equipped with a sixty-five-page booklet put out by the French Ministry of Tourism which urged the avoidance of "talking about Chinese politics: for example, events at Tiananmen or strategic questions about Taiwan or Tibet" (*Sunday Telegraph*, 1/7/07). *Plus ça change!*

Haiphong."[76] Beijing complained, but went no further. As far as the "triangular relationship" with Moscow was concerned, it "contributed to breaking the Soviet back and winning the Cold War. China had achieved some reassurance against the 42 Soviet divisions on its borders. I will let others decide who gained more. When an arrangement lasts 35 years, usually both sides gain something."[77]

When Nixon and Kissinger reached Washington at the end of February, they were treated to a hero's welcome—everything short of a ticker tape acclaim. *Life* magazine likened it to the "arrival of a king."[78] Nixon's popularity rose to the highest for many a month, 56 percent, and Kissinger shared in it to the full. But not everyone rejoiced. Japan was shocked to the core. As a further ricochet of the White House's Byzantine obsession with secrecy, America's closest ally in the Pacific since 1945 had been told absolutely nothing of the talks. Prime Minister Eisaku Sato walked out of a press conference, "mumbling angrily at Nixon."[79] A serious part of Kissinger's diplomatic endeavors over the next years would be spent in restoring relations with Tokyo. That most prickly of leaders, Britain's prime minister, Edward Heath, though he had preceded Nixon to China, took deep umbrage— because he had been kept out of the loop. He had prided himself on the excellence of his personal relationship with Nixon. According to an American diplomat quoted by Margaret MacMillan, "He never really recovered."[80] From this point on he began to invest his energies elsewhere—to improving Britain's relations with Europe. (Possibly it was in the light of this pique that Heath recorded in his memoirs the highly unflattering, and out-of-character, comment allegedly made to him by Mao at their first meeting of Kissinger being "just a funny little man. He is shuddering all over with nerves every time he comes to see me." *[81])

If Japan was shocked, the Taiwanese were hit as if by a tsunami. Despite much mollification, Taiwan was convinced that the big sellout was underway. As far as Hanoi was concerned, nevertheless within a month North Vietnam would be violently attacking the South. Soviet

---

* On the other hand, to Heath, Mao declared "immense respect for Richard Nixon. '*There* is a man who knows what he stands for, as well as what he wants, and has the strength of mind to get it'" (MacMillan, *Nixon and Mao*, 288–89).

and Chinese arms supplies continued. Then when Nixon bombed and blockaded Haiphong, neither country would do more than raise complaints on behalf of their ally. The impact on the Soviets was striking; clearly even the omniscient KGB had failed to keep Moscow abreast of events. At a reception in Washington's Soviet embassy during Peking Week, the journalist Joe Kraft recalled: "A sadder party there never was."[82] On his return, Kissinger immediately called his close buddy, Ambassador Dobrynin; he replied "almost plaintively," and was "almost beside himself with protestations of goodwill," so Kissinger told Nixon.[83] Moscow swiftly began to modify its earlier attitude of procrastination toward a summit—as will be seen in a subsequent chapter. Kissinger remained emphatic that the China card had brought the Soviet Union to a more accommodating frame of mind. Certainly when Nixon went to Moscow in May 1972, he was to encounter an atmosphere that was far friendlier than expected.[84]

Was the China trip, three years in the most complex of preparation, justified? Margaret MacMillan, for one, in the summing up of her book, concludes soberly that in general it was "good for both countries, and their new relationship had great potential—which still remains—to act as a stabilizing force in world politics. It is possible though, to ask whether the U.S. was too eager and whether it gave away too much. Should, for example, Nixon have visited China first without knowing whether or not he would see Mao, and without a firm agreement on the Shanghai communiqué? Should the Americans have handed over quite so much confidential material about the Soviets and, moreover, given the impression that the United States was eager to have an alliance with China against the Soviet Union?"[85] She closes with a quote from Zhou relaying to Kissinger the useful philosophy of an old Chinese proverb: "The helmsman who knows how to guide the boat will guide it well through the waves. Otherwise he will be submerged by the waves. A farsighted man will know how to till the helm."[86]

So, with the advent of spring 1973, the light filtering in through Eastern windows looked much, much brighter than it had for a very long time. In February, Kissinger was back in the Middle Kingdom on his way home from signing the Vietnam peace treaty in Hanoi. Except for China, "Whenever I left a Communist country," he recorded (perhaps somewhat euphorically) that he experienced "an overwhelming sense of relief. When one breaks free of the monochrome drabness, the stifling conformity, the indifference to the uniqueness of the human personality, the result is a sudden easing of tensions, a feeling akin to exhilaration." We have perhaps all sensed this on some visit or other; passengers used to be given to cheering as their plane took off from Moscow. On February 15, 1973, he found arriving in Beijing "a warmth to our welcome that the settlement of the Vietnam war had clearly released. . . . Our hosts stood at the bottom of the steps and applauded as my colleagues and I disembarked from the aircraft." This time there were, he noted, special concessions for the more than thrice honored visitor. He was spared the statutory presentations of revolutionary opera, "whose stupefying simplemindedness one could escape only by a discreet doze." [87] (The risk was being caught out when the lights came on. With some *Schadenfreude* he retailed how his good friend, West German chancellor Helmut Schmidt, who once undid his belt to be more comfortable, missed his cue and "awakened only when the applause was well started, and had trouble hitching up his trousers and applauding at the same time.") [88]

Drollery aside, it was, he and Winston Lord both thought, "the best trip ever." [*] [89] With Zhou he had by now "developed an easy camaraderie not untinged with affection"; to Lord, who sat in on most of the talks (there were no State Department officials included in the party), "it was as though the two of them were resuming a seamless conversation." [90] At the same time, with Nixon reelected by a landslide, the Chinese now counted on dealing with a strong leader for the next four years. There were no further menaces toward Taiwan. Over matters of discord such as Vietnam, and the imperiled regime in Cambodia, he and Zhou largely agreed to disagree. Zhou was too sophisticated to insist, for instance, on removal of Thieu's regime in Saigon. On this occasion, the talks focused on the Soviet threat. The number of Soviet divisions on the Chinese border had risen from twenty-one in 1969, to

---

[*] It was also Lord's last trip for a while, as—burnt out—he decided that May it was time he "left government to spend more time with the family and recover from an exhausting four years. It was a good time to move, because foreign policy was in very good shape, especially issues I had worked on—relations with China and Russia" (interview, 10/30/05).

thirty-three in 1971 to forty-five in 1973. Here Kissinger found a clear sense of common danger; equally he harbored an ever-latent fear that "clumsy American diplomacy" might drive the two Communist superpowers together again. He wooed the Chinese by giving them extensive, secret information from CIA sources on the state of Soviet arms. This apparent indiscretion, a paradox at odds with his normal oh-so-secret approach, was clearly done with a purpose; these were not lapses of security, careless slips, but all part of the triangular game. Nevertheless, he would be hotly attacked for it. In their powerful book, Jung Chang and Jon Halliday, however, go further to suggest that the Nixon visit "also opened up for Mao the possibility of laying his hands on American nuclear weapons."[91] Kissinger, as well as all his entourage, including Winston Lord, vigorously refute this. There was never any proposition from the United States to help China expand its "nuclear deterrent," and definitely not the alleged scenario of "airlifting American nuclear artillery shells and battlefield nuclear missiles to Chinese forces in the event of war. . . . This opened up the prospect of U.S. nuclear weapons on Chinese soil."[92] Never any such suggestion, snorted Kissinger—staunchly supported by Lord;[93] that would have been too incredibly dangerous to contemplate.[94] Nevertheless, in *Mao* the authors go on to conclude that, though "one ostensible purpose of Nixon's journey to Peking had been to lessen the danger of war. . . . thanks to Mao, this danger had if anything increased."*[95]

The Chinese feared seriously that as their economic and military power base grew, so the Kremlin would be tempted toward a preemptive strike. Kissinger reassured his host by stressing that, were Moscow to prevail, "the impact on the world balance of power would be scarcely less catastrophic than a Soviet conquest of Europe."[96] In consequence, the United States would clearly have no other option than to

---

* Summing up on *Mao*, one distinguished American sinologist, Jonathan Spence, in a lengthy review for *The New York Review of Books* (11/3/05), comments: "By focusing so tightly on Mao's vileness—to the exclusion of other factors—the authors undermine much of the power their story might have had . . . As I was reading this book, I kept asking myself why historians should feel that they ought to be fair even to pathological monsters, if that is truly what Mao was. The most salient answer is perhaps structural as much as conceptual. Without some attempt at fairness there is no nuance, no sense of light and dark. The monster, acute and deadly, just shambles on down some monstrous path of his own devising."

"help China resist." Kissinger records that he put all this to Zhou "in one of the most candid and comprehensive accounts of our foreign policy that I ever made to any foreign leader." There were, he postulated, two theoretical possibilities ahead: one was that the Soviet leaders genuinely wanted détente. That was "in our common interest." But the second possibility, and to him the evidence pointed more strongly in that direction, was that the Kremlin had decided upon "a more flexible strategy" so as to "demoralize Western Europe by creating the illusion of peace: to use American technology to overcome the imbalance between its military and economic capability."

Therefore, the United States had a vital interest in "new propositions," "in the global balance of power in general and in China's territorial integrity in particular."[97]

One can imagine Zhou, a supreme student of the balance of power principle, listening raptly, as raptly as Kissinger's former students at Harvard, to this disquisition, and nodding his approval. However, one should also note that Kissinger's stern caveats about Moscow's aggressive instincts came before either his forthcoming May trip to the Soviet Union or Brezhnev's return engagement to the United States that June; and they would be modified as he formed the opinion that, after all, he could "do business" with the old men in the Kremlin. Zhou appeared to share extensively Kissinger's fears of February 1973; as indeed he shared his misgivings about the vulnerability of the weaker European brethren, notably Chancellor Willy Brandt and his Ostpolitik gambling with the Soviet Union. But, says Kissinger plaintively, "The question was never finally resolved either in our dialogue with the Chinese leaders or in our domestic debate because Watergate was soon to impose its own imperatives."[98]

Suddenly, at 11 P.M. on February 17—his second day—as was the wont of the old tyrant, Kissinger was summoned to attend Mao in his "modest house" within the old Imperial Forbidden City. Once more Kissinger noted how Mao, sick as he was, still "dominated the room as I have never seen any person do except Charles de Gaulle." "I don't look bad," observed Mao as if reading Kissinger's thoughts, "but God has sent me an invitation."[99] (Kissinger found it somehow incongruous that this arch-atheist should invoke the deity.) In an "almost jocular manner," the two reviewed the world situation until almost 1:30 A.M.

Mao reiterated Zhou's fears about a fake détente with the Soviet Union, which could only sap resistance to Soviet expansionism; then stressed that the United States and China had to cooperate.

On this concern Kissinger flew home. It was, he noted at the time, with some false cheer, his "first foreign trip free of the incubus of the Vietnam War." Compared with the breathtaking events of 1971–72, and the staggering breakthrough made in Sino-U.S. relations then, the 1973 visit was relatively quiet—a time of consolidation. To Nixon he reported enthusiastically, and with just a touch of cynicism: "With conscientious attention to both capitals we should be able to continue to have our mao tai and drink our vodka too." Now for Moscow, and Brezhnev—the "Polar Bear," of whom Mao had left Kissinger with the stern warning: "Take care, the Polar Bear is going to punish you."[100]

As one immediate, tangible result of the trip, it was agreed to exchange diplomatic missions, at first known as liaison staffs, subsequently assuming full ambassadorial weight. To Beijing went the remarkable David Bruce. Hugely experienced, with Paris, Bonn, and London behind him, Bruce was a wealthy Virginian aristocrat of great, almost unique, distinction, but also a hard-eyed, unsentimental realist like Kissinger himself.[101] To Washington, the Chinese reciprocated by sending Huang Zhen, the ambassador to Paris, who had been Vernon Walters's interlocutor in the early stages of setting up Polo I. Kissinger came to see him as a warm and sensitive man, whose hobby was painting. Nevertheless, "Like all Chinese diplomats he was rigidly disciplined." This did not prevent the gourmet in Kissinger from ribbing him on his first appearance in Washington that May: "I am eager for your cook to arrive!"[102]

That last trip to China had, Kissinger concluded at the time, "marked a great step forward . . . It became the last normal diplomatic enterprise before Watergate engulfed us."[103]

CHAPTER 4

A FEATHER-BRAINED CRIME

"This feather-brained crime . . . as nutty an episode as I can recall."
—Richard Helms[1]

"I will be known for two things. Watergate and the opening to China. . . . I don't mean to be pessimistic, but Watergate, that silly, silly thing is going to rank up there historically with what I did here."
—Richard Nixon, on his last trip to China, in 1993[2]

O N APRIL 14, 1973, Kissinger had a visit from Leonard Garment, special consultant to the president on domestic issues, and particularly Jewish affairs. Garment was a talented clarinet player,* a gentle soul, and—by Nixon standards—a liberal Republican. He was not in the inner ring of the White House. However—for the first time—Garment filled Kissinger in on Watergate, and the full extent of its ramifications. Both until that moment, and afterward, Kissinger had—he claimed—not been involved in any capacity, or even been aware of the gravity of the situation. He must have been one of the few of the Nixon entourage who was not; which

---

* I remember him on a visit to Switzerland, it would have been prior to Watergate, charming us all with his haunting rendition of "The Shadow of Your Smile."

fact was to clad him with a cloak of probity without which his preeminent role in the administration would have been impossible. Yet it threatened to cast a strangling web around everything he had set out to do from 1969. What Garment had to tell him would, in effect, fundamentally alter the course of Henry Kissinger's life and career—as well as much else. It would bring him the job he had coveted, as secretary of state—but it would also endanger the whole structure of his foreign policy.

As Kissinger recalls that fateful weekend of 1973 in his memoirs,[3] on the Friday night (ominously the 13th) he had delivered a speech to the Federal City Club in Washington, which was honoring him with an award. He had concluded his remarks with a plea for national reconciliation; now there was peace in Vietnam, it was "time," he declared, to end "our civil war"—given that a semblance of peace in Vietnam had been achieved. It had been a friendly occasion, and his remarks had been well received. He left feeling pleased with the evening.

But the next day came the rude awakening, with Garment's visit. "What he told me shattered everything."[4] The events were, for him, "precisely charted." Not one to beat around the bush, Garment—so Kissinger noted—launched in by exclaiming: "Have you lost your mind?"[5] Now, he said, was not the time to speak of "national reconciliation." At this point, Kissinger knew the bare details of the Watergate break-in of the previous June, but neither much more, nor less, than the newspaper-reading populace of Georgetown. He had either been too busy to inquire further, or closed his mind to what was going on in other departments of the White House. Garment now told him that crisis was about to "blow up," and it would implicate "the highest levels of the Administration." The ramifications went far beyond the original break-in at Democratic National Committee headquarters in the Watergate complex. The finger of congressional accusations was pointing closer and closer to the president himself. Particularly in the line of fire now were his two closest associates, Bob Haldeman and John Ehrlichman (whom Kissinger privately dubbed "the Germans," perhaps as much on account of their crew cut hair as their names, and somewhat Teutonic manner). The knives were out for the mistrusted, indeed hated, Nixon. In Garment's view, "we are in deep trouble," and only "radical surgery and the fullest admission of error could avert catastrophe."

Kissinger says (in his memoirs[6]) that he was "stunned" by Garment's revelations. Hitherto he had dismissed the Watergate affair as "juvenile" shenanigans. Perhaps he—like others further removed—had been taken in by Nixon's own lighthearted handling of the issue: only a month previously, for instance, when greeting the Soviet Women's Gymnastic Team (which included the redoubtable Olga Korbut) in the White House, he had joked how, watching the Olympics on television, he had "noticed you always land on your feet. That is what our politicians always try to do—not always with success."[7]

Could a politician on the edge of the precipice really have made a remark like that?

Kissinger suddenly saw Watergate setting at risk not only social cohesion in America, but the foreign policy he and Nixon had so laboriously constructed. After four hard years of striving for a solution in Vietnam, he claims in some of the most eloquent passages in his memoirs that he "felt like a swimmer who had survived dangerous currents only to be plucked from apparent safety by unexpected and even more violent riptides toward uncharted seas."[8]

How had it all begun? So many million words have been written about Watergate (FBI files alone were said to run to 16,000 pages)* over the years that the mind becomes numbed, yet—given that it all happened now more than three decades ago, and was so complicated at the time—it may be worth revisiting some of the key dates and events, particularly where they most impinged on Henry Kissinger and the world of foreign policy.

On June 13, 1971, the *New York Times* and the *Washington Post*

---

* "A cottage industry," Kissinger described it in *Years of Upheaval*, p. 81; see also Richard Helms, *A Look over My Shoulder*, p. 7.

began publishing the Pentagon Papers—the Defense Department's secret history of the Vietnam War, leaked by Daniel Ellsberg.*

September 3, 1971: The Plumbers, so called because of their orders to prevent leaks in the administration† burgled a psychiatrist's office to find damaging files on his client, Daniel Ellsberg.

June 17, 1972: Five men of the Plumbers unit, with close links to a body with the appropriate acronym of CREEP (Committee to Reelect the President) were arrested at 2:30 A.M., burgling the offices of the Democratic National Committee at the Watergate complex in downtown Washington. They were found to have a suspiciously large amount of money on them.

Nixon records that, at the time, when local headlines first gave him the news, down in Key Biscayne, proclaiming "MIAMIANS HELD IN DC TRY TO BUG DEMO HEADQUARTERS," he was engrossed in reading the last volume of Churchill's war memoirs, *Triumph and Tragedy*. He then took time off to congratulate Jack Nicklaus on winning the U.S. Open at Pebble Beach.[9] Could he possibly have foreseen how closely the title of Churchill's tome would resemble what fate now had in store for him?

At first the news made papers across the United States, but only as a relatively minor item. Any political significance was not immediately apparent. After the initial furor, Watergate not only failed to make the headlines, it did not even reach the front pages; the *Washington Post*, which subsequently was to claim so much of the glory, carried only three minor stories.[10] A Gallup poll found that 48 percent of the populace had never heard of Watergate. It was really not until Deep Throat came along that the *Post* got anywhere close to the true story.

---

* No trendy liberal, Ellsberg had served as a company commander in the Marines for two years, and then became an analyst at the RAND Corporation. A committed Cold Warrior, he served in the Pentagon in 1964 under Secretary of Defense Robert McNamara. He then served for two years in Vietnam as a civilian in the State Department, and became convinced that the Vietnam War was unwinnable. He further believed that nearly everyone in the Defense and State Departments felt, as he did, that the United States had no realistic chance of achieving victory in Vietnam, but that political considerations prevented them from saying so publicly.

† Given Washington's longtime reputation as "government by leak," one would have thought that any Plumbers unit confronted a problem on a scale with plugging the Hoover Dam.

At this point, enter Bob Woodward and Carl Bernstein, supported by their redoubtable editor, Ben Bradlee. Woodward and Bernstein were both junior reporters in their twenties; Woodward had only been on the *Post* a few months; Bernstein was rated on the paper as "the house misfit." Yet within months the two were to become the most famous, and probably the richest, journalists in the United States. Over Watergate, undeniably, the industry and the resourcefulness of the *Washington Post* duo proved phenomenal. Certainly, like Bismarck, they too recognized opportunity when it passed by. They also enjoyed phenomenal good luck, happening to be in the right place at the right time—but most of all, with the right source, the mysterious Deep Throat. It was Deep Throat who handed Woodward the essential clues* that the trail of gunpowder would lead all the way to the Oval Office. For years practically every name in the Washington establishment was dragged out as a candidate for the mystery source: they ranged from General Al Haig, to Ehrlichman and Ron Ziegler, Nixon's press secretary, William Colby (director of the CIA), Supreme Court Justice William Rehnquist, to George Bush Sr., to Henry Kissinger, and—even, with a twist worthy of John Le Carré, to the embattled president himself. There were people who, like one writer, Adrian Havill,[11] suspected Deep Throat was pure invention; others, including Henry Kissinger (and his biographer, Walter Isaacson), continued to believe that he was a composite figure. Kissinger retained this belief even after the self-outing of Mark Felt.[12]

Certainly, when the first *Washington Post* accusations were published, implicating the White House, even some of Woodward and Bernstein's fellow pressmen were deeply skeptical. At a press conference shortly before the election, a respected Pulitzer Prize–winning journalist, Clark Mollenhoff of the *Des Moines Register*, got up and lambasted Bernstein for irresponsible journalism.[13] When George McGovern was already trailing 26 points behind Nixon, why ever would the Republicans need to resort to dirty tricks? Why, why, why? The eternal mystery that still prevails. Why did Nixon order, or be ac-

---

* One may ask oneself why Deep Throat didn't come straight out with one full installment; was it to protect himself? Or sell copies of the *Washington Post*? He finally revealed himself, in May 2005, as Mark Felt, a disgruntled FBI man.

cessory to, the Watergate break-in, when he really didn't need to? What did he possibly have to gain? Was it simply Nixon's fatal attraction to dirty politics? Historians will still be asking the same, utterly mystifying, question in a hundred years' time.

August 1, 1972: A $25,000 check, apparently earmarked for the Nixon election campaign, was discovered in the bank account of one of the Watergate burglars.

September 15, 1972: E. Howard Hunt, G. Gordon Liddy, and the five Watergate burglars were indicted by a federal grand jury. Nixon congratulated John W. Dean III, then counsel to the president, on his handling of the matter.

October 10, 1972: The FBI established that the break-in was traced back to a massive operation of spying and sabotage conducted on behalf of Nixon's reelection campaign.

November 7, 1972: Nixon was reelected in one of the largest landslides in American history, with more than 60 percent of the votes.

January 30, 1973: With Judge John Sirica presiding (nicknamed "Maximum John" for his tough sentences), the seven former Nixon aides, including John McCord, were convicted of conspiracy, burglary, and wiretapping in the Watergate incident. That same day Nixon wrote down on one of his yellow memo pads: "Restore respect for office."

It was the week after Kissinger had signed the Vietnam peace accords.

February 7, 1973: The Senate Watergate Committee was established, under veteran senator Sam Ervin.

Ervin, a shrewd Southern politician already seventy-six at the time of the hearings, had made his reputation in the early 1950s when his robust Southern humor helped bring down Senator Joe McCarthy. Said the *Washington Post* at the time of his death in 1985, he came across in 1973 "as a stern father figure who wasn't confused about what was right and wrong," at a time when Americans were buffeted by Vietnam. With his "arching eyebrows and flapping jowls that signaled his moral indignation at much of the testimony before his committee," he swiftly became a kind of folk hero, and a major figure in the downfall of Nixon. His opening remarks put it immediately on the line: "If the many allegations made to this date are true, then the burglars who broke into the headquarters of the Democratic National Committee at the Watergate were in effect breaking into the home of every citizen of the United States, and if these allegations prove to be true, what they were seeking to steal was not the jewels, money or other precious property of American citizens, but something much more valuable— their most precious heritage: the right to vote in a free election." [14]

He declared that the perpetrators of Watergate showed "the same mentality as the Gestapo." By then it was clear that the White House was in for a rough ride.*

March 19, 1973: John McCord wrote to Judge Sirica stating the defendants had pleaded guilty under pressure, admitting that perjury had been committed, and expressing "fear for my life." [15]

April 6, 1973: John Dean, White House counsel, began to cooperate with Watergate prosecutors.

Of the five miscreants apprehended at Watergate in the early hours of June 17, 1972, one, James McCord, Jr., was found to be both a former CIA employee and currently a security man working for CREEP. In another's address book was found the telephone number of E. Howard Hunt, whose name was also accompanied by the incriminating inscriptions "W. House" and "W. H." The trail to the White House now began. Deep Throat informed Woodward that senior aides of President Richard Nixon had paid the burglars to obtain information about his political opponents.

Six days after the break-in, on June 23, 1972, Richard Helms, the much respected director of the CIA[†], was summoned to the White House by John Ehrlichman, assistant to the president for domestic affairs. With him went General Vernon Walters, of the Paris peace talks, now deputy director of the CIA as of only seven weeks. They were ushered into Ehrlichman's tiny conference room, which Helms took to be only an antechamber, and joined in this compressed space by Bob

---

* When Nixon refused to allow his aides to testify before the Ervin committee, Ervin made one of his classic judgments: "Divine Right went out with the American Revolution and doesn't belong to White House aides. What meat do they eat that makes them grow so great? . . . I don't think we have any such thing as royalty or nobility that exempts them . . . That is not executive privilege. That is executive poppycock" (*Washington Post*, 4/24/85).

† Kissinger remarked of him: "There was no public servant I trusted more . . . [or] respected more" (Preface to Helms's autobiography, *A Look over My Shoulder*, p. x).

Haldeman, Nixon's chief of staff. Rather menacingly, Haldeman asked Helms—"very formally"—what connection the CIA might have had over the Watergate break-in. He went on to say that the FBI investigation "of certain Mexican leads" might jeopardize CIA activity there, and he was going to ask Walters to visit the FBI to call off its investigations. Toward the end of this "increasingly baffling session," [16] Haldeman took on a "rather threatening tone," to claim that, if the FBI didn't suspend investigations, "it would lead to an unraveling of the [1961] Bay of Pigs activity." Helms exploded, remarking that "the Bay of Pigs hasn't got a damned thing to do with this." He refused to comply with Haldeman's request; though he noted how he "complemented his chief by issuing the commands and orders which the President, for whatever reason, declined to express himself. . . . It was a clear case of the president attempting to obstruct justice, and led directly to Nixon's resignation." [17] Nixon was thereby calling on the CIA to commit an illegal act (the original charter forbade the CIA from any domestic operations). It was one of his worst mistakes.

Three days later (June 26), John Dean*, then still counsel for the White House, came to see General Walters, with a fresh plea for the CIA to intervene and pressure the FBI to drop Watergate charges. Walters was profoundly shocked as a thoroughly rattled Dean "told me that those arrested were looking for help and wondered if there was anything we could do. I said there was nothing. Director Helms was correctly determined to keep the Agency out of this business." Walters went on, "Mr. Dean, the President should be protected from his would be protectors. If you go ahead with this idea, you will have a political thermonuclear explosion." Dean then said almost desperately, "What can we do?" Walters replied bluntly, "Fire everyone connected to this affair." [18]

As it turned out, it was the best possible advice; if only Nixon had taken it.

In common with many Americans at the time, Walters was one who at first simply could not conceive of Nixon's involvement in Wa-

---

* In his testimony before the Senate committee, Dean claimed Nixon knew about the 1972 break-in at the national headquarters of the Democratic National Committee and had helped to cover it up. Dean's supporters saw him as courageous and truthful; his detractors saw him as self-serving and disloyal.

tergate. "I was sure," he wrote, "that the break-in had been a crackpot idea of some middle-level figure at the White House . . . those who cooked up this crazy idea, when it was clear that President Nixon would overwhelm Senator McGovern, were simply not in touch with reality." He went on to note that Nixon was "not the first president to do things against the law. Lincoln suspended Habeas Corpus, Roosevelt, Johnson and Kennedy had all bugged people; but when they did it, it was only a venial sin. When Nixon did it, it became a mortal sin, a grave threat to our Constitution and democratic freedoms—or that is the way it was presented." * [19]

In the aftermath of Len Garment's revelations, Kissinger, deeply disturbed by its implications, "pondered Nixon's options." [20] In what is one of the most readable, and illuminating, chapters in his voluminous memoirs, as well as to the author, he recalled how, when the previous summer he had quizzed Haldeman what Watergate was all about, Nixon's chief of staff had said "I wish I knew," and then immediately changed the subject. With hindsight, he admitted that he should perhaps have been alerted earlier in 1973—by "the behavior of Nixon himself." There had been moments when he found it "difficult to get Nixon to focus on foreign policy, to a degree that should have disquieted me. In the past, even in calm periods, he had immersed himself in foreign policy to enliven the job of managing the government, which ultimately bored him. Now it was difficult to get him to address memoranda. They came back without the plethora of marginal comments to indicate they had been carefully read." Now, considering Garment's proposed solution of "radical surgery, and the fullest admission of error" on Nixon's part, he had grave doubts. "The vision of Nixon's putting himself at the head of a reform movement to clean up his own Administration stretched credulity." [21] It simply did not fit in with the president's self-isolated character. (Years later, he would reflect that, as far as his own personal position was concerned, on hearing Garment's exposé, "if I had acted wisely, I suppose I should have accepted David Bruce's suggestion back at Christmastime to retire." [22])

---

* Walters recalled how de Gaulle had once remarked to him: "The Puritanism of the Americans does not prevent them from sinning, it just prevents them from enjoying their sins" (*The Mighty and the Meek*, p. 39).

Then again, in response to suggestions that he had contemplated resigning at that point, he insisted to me, "I *had* to stay on, after Garment's revelation: I was the glue that held it all together in 1973— and I'm not being boastful." [23]

The night of Garment's fateful visit, April 14, Kissinger attended the annual dinner staged by the White House correspondents. (It would be hard to imagine a less welcome occasion.) To Kissinger's surprise, Nixon showed up at what must have been a tense gathering. As the gathering broke up, Kissinger was called to the telephone by a "highly agitated" president, who put a surprise, if not weird, question to him: "Do you agree," he asked, "that we should draw the wagons around the White House?" [24]

Kissinger was "stunned," but admitted that few advisers would have had the "fortitude" to tell their president "that they did not know what he is talking about." So Kissinger "mumbled something noncommittal," then urged him to "do what you will have to do ultimately *now*." [25] This Nixon "construed as assent."

"All right . . . we will draw the wagons around the White House."

He recognized then that "Clearly, the President was severely wounded." He was probably also under the influence of one too many. Attempting to confront the crisis, Kissinger set up a meeting on the Sunday with George Shultz and Arthur Burns*, two government figures of unquestionable probity. The meeting achieved little. Like Kissinger himself, both Shultz and Burns "were at first unbelieving. But we all shared a sense of impotence. We did not know the dimensions of the looming scandal. We agreed to keep each other informed of whatever we learned." [26]

Two days later, on the afternoon of April 17, Nixon made a statement at a White House press conference in which, referring to the Ervin Committee, he expressed the sanguine belief that "an agreement has been reached which is satisfactory to both sides." [27] It was a pious hope. He continued, noting that: "On March 21, as a result of serious charges which came to my attention, some of which were publicly reported, I began intensive new inquiries into this whole matter. . . . I

---

* Shultz was Nixon's secretary of the treasury (and later secretary of state under Ronald Reagan); Burns was chairman of the Federal Reserve.

can report today that there have been major developments in the case."
Refusing to elucidate further, he ended—on a vigorous note: "I con-
demn any attempts to cover up in this case, no matter who is involved.
Thank you."[28]

That evening there was a state dinner at the White House for Prime
Minister Giulio Andreotti of Italy. Kissinger's friend Frank Sinatra
performed. Later, Kissinger observed caustically how the milestones
of Watergate always seemed to be marked by state banquets. Though
the Andreotti dinner was "festive and relaxed," it made Kissinger
think, evocatively, of the *Titanic*, where "one part of this ship was
flooding but no one else was aware, or affected to be aware, of the danger. The band played on. It was, as it happened, the last 'normal' dinner of Nixon's term." Later, the irrepressible playboy streak in
Kissinger emerging, he joined Sinatra at a small party. It was also attended by Vice President Spiro Agnew—a man of whom Nixon
(rightly, as it turned out) had the lowest possible opinion.* In the
course of the party, Nixon rang to ask Kissinger what he thought about
the "Watergate announcement"; then astonished him by asking
whether he should now fire Haldeman and Ehrlichman. Kissinger's
"dumbfounded" reaction was that "it was one thing for Garment to
speculate along these lines; if Nixon himself held that view, he must be
in mortal peril."

Agnew came in at this juncture, and remarked acidly, in a "somewhat contemptuous, unfeeling manner . . . that Nixon was kidding
himself if he thought he could avoid firing Haldeman and Ehrlichman.
He would be lucky if he could save himself."[29] To Kissinger, Agnew's
"icy detachment" from his chief's travail "brought a premonition of
imminent disaster."

April 30, 1973: Nixon sacked his top White House staff members
Bob Haldeman and John Ehrlichman. Attorney General Richard
Kleindienst resigned, and White House counsel John Dean was also

---

* Born Spiros Anagnostopoulos, of Greek emigrant parents, Agnew started off his political life as a Democrat, but switched to the Republicans to become governor of Maryland. He was forced to resign in October 1973 after being charged with tax evasion and
money laundering. Though it was Nixon who had selected this relatively unknown figure as his running mate, this profoundly insecure man came to rate Agnew as his "best
insurance against assassination" (*Years of Upheaval*, p. 92).

fired. Two days later J. Edgar Hoover died, hands-on czar to the day of his death of the FBI, which—to Nixon's fury—had initiated, and relentlessly pursued, the Watergate inquiries. As Nixon admitted to David Frost, unlike Mr. Gladstone, he was "not a good butcher," and with the sacking of the "Germans," the buck had now come about as close as it ever could to the president himself.

Kissinger's relations with the "Germans" were mixed; almost certainly cooler than he allows in his memoirs with little love lost on either side. Of Ehrlichman, the more liberal-inclined of the two, he writes that "Towards me Ehrlichman showed a mixture of comradely good will and testy jealousy," while Haldeman "was made of sterner stuff . . . at bottom uninterested in policy. Genuinely admiring of Nixon, he considered it his paramount duty to smooth out the roller coaster of Nixon's emotions."[30] A man of "chilly discipline," with Kissinger his relations "had ingredients for friction. He was a conservative middle class Californian, with all the sentiments, suspicions, and secret envy of that breed." In general, he found that Haldeman's attitude to him reflected Nixon's; when Kissinger felt himself being harassed by Haldeman's comportment, "I could be sure that it was to carry out some design of the President." The attitude of the White House staff to the president he found "resembled that of an advertising agency—from whence indeed most came—to an exclusive, temperamental client."[31]

By the end of April, Kissinger records that he was convinced that Haldeman and Ehrlichman would not survive. Spending that weekend with his future wife, Nancy, he recalled a call from Nixon at Camp David "nearly incoherent with grief," having called for the resignations of Haldeman and Ehrlichman. As Kissinger states, he interpreted that they had, with a fair degree of honor, "not thought of their conduct as a 'cover up' but as a means to protect an elected Administration that still had much left to accomplish from opponents working against the national interest as they conceived it."[32] And yet Nixon was about to throw them into the fiery furnace. Years later Kissinger would reflect that it was "always a mistake to fire your chief of staff when in trouble. I think [George W.] Bush may have made the same mistake this time. But Haldeman and Ehrlichman simply couldn't stay. They were just too visible, and too involved." It had been Nixon's "fundamental mistake," he thought, to bring the whole Watergate issue "inside the White House office. He should have kept it outside, and almost immediately he should have consulted an eminent Washington lawyer—instead of trying to bring in the CIA. That was his serious mistake. I was out of the country, but I would have told him he was crazy to bring in the CIA."[33]

In their separate recollections of events in this dramatic month of April 1973, there seem to be important differences in those of Kissinger and Nixon. Yet both men kept meticulous accounts, to the mortal damage of the latter. For instance, as of April 5, Nixon claims that *he* had already intimated to Kissinger the necessity of sacking Haldeman—to which Kissinger had allegedly responded: "Even if he is guilty in part they are after him because they know he is the strong man in the administration. He is the most selfless, able person you've got, and you have got to have him."[34] Apart from this standing somewhat at variance with his known views of Haldeman, was Kissinger therefore being somewhat disingenuous about being "stunned" by Garment's revelations on the 14th, and "dumbfounded" by Nixon's call on the night of the 17th? As biographer one has to ask oneself, did he know more about Watergate, and earlier on, than he declared in his memoirs? And if so, why did he not do more about it, by way of intervening to forestall the appalling avalanche that was about to descend on the Nixon administration?

When one thinks of the close proximity of offices within the White House confines (those of the Plumbers were only a matter of yards from the NSC), plus the propensity of Washington officialdom to gossip, plus the acuteness of the Kissinger antennae, it may seem puzzling that he didn't know more. To this, in his published recollections, he explains: "In the Nixon White House there was an almost total separation between the domestic and the foreign policy sides. The relations of the various Nixon aides to one another was like that of prisoners in adjoining cells. They might hear something about the scale of the activity: proximity did not invite participation or intimate knowledge. To all practical purposes I was excluded from domestic issues and Ehrlichman, who handled domestic policy, from foreign policy discussions."[35] And again, later: "The White House is both a goldfish bowl and an isolation ward; the fish swim in a vessel whose walls are opaque one way. They can be observed if not necessarily understood; they themselves see nothing."[36] On the other hand, of the two officials first to smell something of Nixon's involvement, already back in June 1972, there was Dick Helms, the director of the CIA, sitting in ex officio on NSC meetings—and therefore in regular close contact with Kissinger—and his deputy, Vernon Walters, with whom Kissinger had bonded closely over the endless Vietnam talks in Paris. Would they not have discussed the implications of Watergate together? Then there were the accusations of his own, questionable, involvement in taping, and wiretapping in the past.

If one were to apply the worst interpretation, Kissinger could be seen as one of those Wehrmacht generals who insisted "we didn't know." But one should set against this his own involvement, amounting to almost total commitment and distraction, in foreign affairs. Running in parallel during all the Watergate story were Vietnam, China, Russia, and détente, the Year of Europe, and—later—the Middle East.[37] Add on top of this the extraordinary nature of Nixon himself, his self-isolation and unapproachable personality, and the very definition of Kissinger's complex relationship with him. Kissinger notes that "Throughout the Watergate crisis, not once did Nixon tell me his version of events. He maintained in private the same posture he had adopted in public, every revelation was new to him."[38]

More recently he adumbrated this to say, "Luckily for me there was an impenetrable Chinese wall between foreign and domestic affairs in the White House—so I was never brought in. No way that Nixon would have consulted me." He admitted, "It was very fortunate that I did not get brought into Watergate—I would have been destroyed."[39]

Should he, however, could he, have pressed Nixon to be more forthcoming? (On the other hand, if he had, what could he, Kissinger, have done about it?) Again, later in the same chapter of his memoirs, he explains how "My attitude towards Nixon had always been ambivalent, compounded of aloofness and respect, of distrust and admiration. I was convinced that he was at the heart of the Watergate scandal even if he did not know all of its manifestations. He had set the tone and evoked the attitudes that made it inevitable. And yet . . . I was touched by the vulnerability of a man who lived out a Walter Mitty dream of toughness that did not come naturally and who resisted his very real streak of gentleness."[40]

As noted earlier, Kissinger's relationship with the president was at best precarious. His critics could accuse him of being obsequious; yet there was always something about the office, particularly under Richard Nixon, that invited awe, formality, and distance. Head-on confrontation was not the agile doctor's technique for dealing with his prickly boss; on issues with which he dissented, he employed instead a strategy of the indirect approach. Anyway, would Richard Nixon have listened?*

Given the almost boundless quantity of dissimulation cloaking the whole Watergate affair, a certain amount of modification of memory might be understandable—but how much does it affect Kissinger's reputation? Could he have done more? Could he have persuaded Nixon where others closer to him failed? Surely, as events were to prove over the remainder of the crumbling presidency, he was right to maintain a distance. In the critical days that lay ahead, Kissinger would remain the only key member of the administration who would be unblemished by Watergate. Had it been otherwise, the consequences to the world role of America would have been incalculably horrendous. Perhaps Kissinger's blind eye during Watergate will come to be rated almost his finest hour?

To replace Haldeman as Nixon's chief of staff, General Haig moved in, up from the basement of the White House, which he had tenanted as Kissinger's deputy. Decorated as a battalion commander in Vietnam, Haig was a highly ambitious, political general, the kind of soldier who could be malleably subservient to his superiors, but overbearing to subordinates. He caused merriment among Americans with his inventive syntax and "Haigisms" such as "That's not a lie. It is a ter-

---

* Woodward claimed that during the summer of 1973 Kissinger endeavored to persuade the president to disavow his former aides publicly, and accept a measure of responsibility for Watergate. The suggestion was angrily rejected by Ron Ziegler, the White House press chief: "Contrition is bullshit" (*All the President's Men*, 335).

minological inexactitude."* Kissinger saw him in May 1973 as having been appointed by Nixon as "keeper of the gate," the strongman who would help "draw up the wagons" in the mounting crisis. But Kissinger was not entirely happy with the choice. He had known Haig for four years, admired his efficiency and skill at "bureaucratic in-fighting—and his capacity for ruthlessness"; yet he disliked and mistrusted Haig's technique of "squeezing to the sidelines potential competitors for my attention. He was not averse to restricting the staff's direct access to me or at least making himself the principal intermediary to the outside world."[42] He questioned Haig's personal loyalty, suspected his driving ambition, and indeed potential rivalry. For Nixon, however, what was "Equally important was that he understood Henry." At first Kissinger resisted the appointment, even threatening—allegedly—to resign.[43] Eventually the direness of Nixon's position prevailed on him: "I therefore decided to put the best face on the situation."[44] It proved, he later wrote, a choice that was "fortunate for the nation," and—aside from the "occasional petty squabble over status . . . For the next fifteen months Haig and I worked in closest harmony . . . we sought to hold the ship of state steady even while its captain was gradually being pushed from the bridge."[45]

In the opinion of Kissinger's assistant, Peter Rodman, in terms notably of Vietnam, April 1973 was "the pivotal moment when Nixon lost his nerve. Watergate was on top of him. He refused to bomb the Ho Chi Minh Trail in Laos, which could have been decisive. Instead, the North Vietnamese realized that Nixon had lost his will; and it followed that Congress would not support any further intervention. A really decisive time—April–June."[46]

Certainly, after the sackings of Haldeman and Ehrlichman, the collapse of the isolated Nixon, and the disintegration of his administration, assumed an unmistakable new momentum. On May 8, the Senate Watergate Committee began its nationally televised hearings. On May 18, the formidable Archibald Cox was appointed special prosecutor.

---

* Merriment turned to shock and suspicion when, in 1981 with President Reagan narrowly escaping assassination, Haig as secretary of state emotionally declared on TV: "I am in control here." In fact, the order of succession places the secretary of state below the vice president, the speaker of the House, and the Senate majority leader.

Later that month, Kissinger celebrated his fiftieth birthday. Given the circumstances, it was a cheerful occasion, attended by some eighty guests, and organized for him at New York's Colony Club by Nancy Maginnes.[47] It was the moment when Nancy accepted to marry him — at last. The Gallup poll now rated him number one among the "most admired Americans," and his birthday provided the occasion for some effusive tributes — even from those of his friends who recently had felt betrayed by the wiretapping scandal. William Safire saluted "an authentic American hero midpoint in his first century," while Joseph Kraft ranked his diplomatic achievements with the USSR and China as "comparable in magnitude to the feats of Castlereagh and Bismarck."[48] That must have pleased him, casting his mind back over that first academic success, at Harvard, all those many years ago. Joe Alsop, his closest friend in the media, a man of modest height, toasted Nancy: "She's a great girl . . . even if she is taller than God."

For Richard Nixon, however, as that terrible summer began it all began to seem "as if a convulsion had hit Washington."[49] At the beginning of June, he admitted that he was beginning to feel "discouraged, drained, and pressured."[50] It showed.

CHAPTER 5

THE YEAR OF EUROPE

"I must honestly tell you that I find it astonishing that an endeavor whose purpose was to create a new spirit of Atlantic solidarity . . . should now be turned almost into a European-American confrontation."
— Richard Nixon to Chancellor Willy Brandt, 1973[1]

DON'T YOU THINK you were rather *cheeky*," remarked Lord Carrington, former British secretary for foreign affairs, provocatively to his onetime counterpart and good friend, Henry Kissinger, across the lunch table, "to label 1973 the Year of Europe?"

We were lunching *à trois* in November 2006 in London's posh Wiltons Restaurant. I felt privileged to be included with a distinguished former U.S. secretary of state and an equally distinguished foreign secretary of Britain. The last time we had met like this was on a very different occasion, in 1982 at a dinner given by my publisher, George Weidenfeld—which had the aim of cheering up Carrington, who had just resigned his post at the Foreign Office over the Argentine attack on the Falklands. I never saw a man more miserable; Kissinger was there to distract him. Now, in London at the end of 2006, the situation was somewhat reversed. On this occasion, it was Kissinger who was deeply unhappy over the dire situation in Iraq, and—more personally—at the way in which he was being accused in Washington of having been a hawk in his advice to President George W. Bush. So Carrington's provocative remark on the Year of Europe was targeted at distracting his guest. Kissinger, however, jibbed at the very English schoolboy slang, "cheeky"; the connotation was obviously not familiar to him. I translated.

Carrington was right; the Year of Europe, as it was dubbed, with singular infelicity, was rather cheeky. It was most certainly not to be Kissinger's finest hour. But it also showed up weaknesses in the European Union system which would bedevil U.S.-European relations thirty years on, when Europe—grown fat, greedy, and flabby on an excess of good living, health care, and so forth, and eventually no longer fearful of the Polar Bear to the east—would perennially expect the United States to be there to save it in case of Soviet attack; so that, in 2006, it couldn't even send one battalion of troops to Afghanistan to take on the Jihadist Taliban, the greatest threat to Western values since the Cold War. All that Europe's leaders could see, predominantly, was Yankee arrogance—the nanny super-state.

As a student a priori of Metternich and Castlereagh, to Henry Kissinger, Europe, and the European order, was of prime consequence. Yet barely had he returned from his testing trip to Hanoi and Beijing, let alone the signing of the Vietnam peace treaty in Paris, than he had to launch himself full tilt into the Year of Europe. Had he really given himself time to think it all through? If the opening to China was Nixon's show, rather than Kissinger's, and Vietnam had been forced upon him by events, détente with the Soviet Union was very much Kissinger's—and even more so was the Year of Europe. Europe was not an area where Nixon felt at ease, or even a paramount interest in its affairs. But to Kissinger, as of 1973, it had represented almost the totality of his academic input, in addition to which there was the German background he was never quite able to shrug off. He would, however, find dealing with America's allies of three decades' standing considerably more fatiguing, and irritating, even than negotiations with adversaries like the nimble Zhou or the bearish Brezhnev. At their worst he would find them almost on a par with North Vietnam's Ducky. He would certainly not be the last American statesman to be driven to the brink of dementia by the Europeans. The Year of Europe was intimately connected to his, and to Nixon's Grand Design, driven notably by fear of the mounting power, seemingly, of the Soviet Union in the Cold War—memories of the invasion of Czechoslovakia in 1968 were all too fresh. And now there was the Kremlin's apparent edge in rocketry. It had left Western Europe, and therein America's principal bastion in the West, looking extremely vulnerable. The bastion had to be refortified. Meanwhile, New Year's Day had greeted three new members joining the European Economic Community: Ireland, Denmark—and, at last, Britain, despite the long protracted resistance of Gaullist France.

So now the Six became Nine. On paper, the economic and *potential* military power of the European bloc was now larger than that of any other world region. But was it so, in fact? What did this power of NATO (plus the unpredictable French) add up to, if one were to subtract the American, nuclear component? Not a great deal, the White House thought—when it looked at the alarming array of conventional gun power on the Soviet side of the Iron Curtain, still only a couple of leisurely days' drive from the Rhine.

On April 23, Kissinger made a formal speech at the annual meeting of the editors of the Associated Press, meeting in the Waldorf-Astoria, where he expounded his theme on the Year of Europe. It was his first public speech on such a major subject; indeed, under another administration it was the kind of speech that might have been expected from a secretary of state. Explaining the reason for choosing 1973 as the anchor year, he began by stressing how, disquietingly, "The East-West strategic military balance has shifted from American preponderance to near-equality, bringing with it the necessity for a new understanding of the requirements of our common security." Meanwhile, he noted, in Europe "a new generation to whom war and its dislocations are not personal experiences takes stability for granted. But it is less committed to the unity that made peace possible and to the effort required to maintain it." He went on: "We are prepared to work cooperatively on new common problems we face. Energy, for example, raised the challenging issues of assurance of supply. . . . This could be an area of competition; it should be an area of collaboration."[2]

Kissinger's reasoning was sound, but, to most Europeans, notably in post–de Gaulle France, this was the voice of nanny speaking—and they did not like it. Press coverage in the States was poor, with only a few of the more serious newspapers giving it space, let alone editorial attention. Typically the *Washington Post*, currently with its eyes obsessively on that other, more profitable target menacing to the administration devoted most of its coverage to Kissinger's "few remarks" to Watergate. It "muffled," complained Kissinger, "the thrust of our initiative."[3] Nevertheless, despite what Watergate was shortly going to do to it, as well as to almost every other foreign initiative of the Nixon administration, the Year of Europe was to fall stonily upon the worst possible timing, as well as the most unpromising constellation of European recipient statesmen. It even began inauspiciously in the portentous British embassy on Massachusetts Avenue. Victoria Legge-Bourke recalled how, at her first awestruck encounter with Henry Kissinger when he called to discuss the Year of Europe, with Ambassador Cromer, her small shih tzu (known in the embassy as "Who-Flung-Dung"), contrived to deposit a large turd between the two great men.[4] It was perhaps fortunate that the hypersensitive Prime Minister Edward Heath was not there that day; though possibly even Who-Flung-Dung's contribution to the dialogue might have done little to modify Heath's frigidity toward the Nixon administration in general.

To begin with, if not the date, the personalities were undoubtedly out of joint. In France, President Georges Pompidou, successor to de Gaulle (*"le grand Charles"*), had been on good terms with Kissinger since his generously given aid over the secret Vietnam talks in Paris encouraging him with the enigmatic words: "In my view you are condemned to succeed."[5] He was the first European leader to be let in on the new program, and seemed receptive. Subsequently, Kissinger thought it ironic that, though "born in the office of the President of the French Republic," the Year of Europe was also to die there.[6] It suggested that, at that moment, Kissinger could have been better informed about the vagaries of the Gallic character. Pompidou had been personally offended when, on a state visit to the United States in 1970, he and Madame Pompidou had been rudely jostled by pro-Israel demonstrators in Chicago, protesting about France arming Libya. A naturally courteous man, but as unfamiliar with American ways as Kissinger was of the French, Pompidou was left with an unpleasant taste. At the same time, he had a Frenchman's natural, atavistic distrust of Germany—

and of any hint of recrudescent nationalism. The old, remarkable honeymoon of de Gaulle and Dr. Konrad Adenauer had passed with them. Instead, now leading West Germany there was something of a wild card, the Socialist Willy Brandt, former playboy, former and much loved *Oberbürgermeister* of Berlin, who seemed to want to play his own game with the Soviets—as, indeed, had de Gaulle. But de Gaulle was de Gaulle. Brandt's game was called Ostpolitik, and it was aimed at finding a solution to the division of Germany—and ending the Soviet occupation of the East—by direct talks between the two German regimes.

Nevertheless, when—in December 1972—Kissinger had bruited the project to Pompidou, he found him "avuncularly encouraging,"[7] certainly not initially hostile. The following month, that great Frenchman Jean Monnet, true father of the European Community, was quite positive about the need to bind the United States and Europe into a more coherent system, on both economic and defense issues. On April 13, Kissinger had received in his Washington office a firm friend of the United States of many years standing, Dr. Joseph Luns of Holland, now secretary general of NATO.* The conversation had been amicable, with some teasing banter about the modern art in his office— whether it resembled a Rorschach test, or a naked lady (in fact, Kissinger explained, it was the organization chart of his NSC office). Kissinger put it to Luns that, although the West was in danger of finding the Soviet reaching nuclear parity, "every Ally is conducting some kind of relations with the Russians." Consequently, "we have to put the whole Atlantic relations on a fresh basis." He warned of the growing mood of isolationism in the United States; and, "If our troops leave Europe they will most definitely be demobilized." He added pessimistically that he thought the Germans under Brandt were "really insane. They have nothing to offer the Russians. The only thing they have left to offer the Russians is to wreck NATO. After that is done they will have nothing to offer them. The Russians will never permit a powerful bloc in Central Europe led by Germany. Only if Bonn becomes like Helsinki."[8]

---

* Attended, incidentally, by a young Donald Rumsfeld, at the time ambassador to NATO.

In Britain, by tradition America's closest ally, Nixon was up against Prime Minister Ted Heath. *"Ah, ce pauvre 'eath!"* as President Valéry Giscard d'Estaing once lamented to this author. Heath was the prickliest human ever to inhabit No. 10 Downing Street. Never, probably, had the "special relationship" been in worse shape than with Heath at the helm in London. Bizarrely for a right-wing Republican administration and a left-of-center Labour one in London, prior to Heath, Harold Wilson in his first (1964–70) government had got on famously with Nixon. Few British ambassadors had enjoyed closer relations with the White House than Wilson's popular envoy, John Freeman (1969–71). But it was all very different when Heath was in power from 1970 to 1974. As already noted in the previous chapter, Heath had been upset by being kept out of the loop over the China gambit; he didn't really like Americans, and certainly didn't try to understand them; and his number one priority was to cement Britain's relations with Europe. Little else counted. He had no sentimentality whatever for the mystical "special relationship."

Heath was a strange man, not given to warm or generous impulses, cold and monolithic in his interests, and with a chip on each shoulder big enough to break the bank at Monte Carlo. His political fortunes had prospered under Harold Macmillan, to whom he had been chief whip — and who had put him in charge of the calamitous offensive to get Britain into the EEC in 1963. This had failed in the face of de Gaulle's icy *"NON!"* A passionate sailor and musician, it was hard to know what else stirred this cold fish, and Heath could be a stunningly boring man. Given to sweeps of historical imagery, Macmillan (to the author) once circumscribed Heath as follows: "Now, as you know, Hengist and Horsa were very dull men. . . . They colonized Kent; and ever since then the men of Kent have been very slightly — well, you know . . . ? But Ted was an excellent chief whip . . . a first-class staff officer, but no army commander."[9] Perhaps history will one day suggest that the fortunes of the Tory Party might have been better served had Ted Heath limited his ambitions to the whip's office, and nothing higher. Unmistakably his old-maidish crusty, chippy misogyny made life for his successor, Margaret Thatcher, about as difficult as it could have been.

In *Nixon and Mao*, Margaret MacMillan, drawing attention to the

out-of-character comment on Kissinger by Chairman Mao, comments
pointedly on Heath's lasting pique at not having been informed by
Nixon in advance of the China gambit. He was particularly hurt, because he had hitherto assumed that Nixon and he had a good relationship. "He never really recovered." [10] Dr. MacMillan goes on to suggest
this may have been the starting point for Heath to concentrate his energy into the EU. Here his monolithic dedication was total; and he
would ever remain foremost among Britain's "Europhiles." * As
Kissinger saw it, Heath "preferred a leading position in Europe to an
honored advisory role in Washington, and he did not consider the two
functions compatible." [11] He thought that in many ways Heath and
Nixon shared the same complexes.

When Heath had come to power, unexpectedly, in 1970, Nixon had
been filled with optimism, but swiftly found it "tough going" in their
personal exchanges. Kissinger saw in Ted Heath, not without a certain
admiration, "a stubborn, almost heroic, streak" [12] in his single-minded
policy over Europe. It was a view not shared by Nixon, though
Heath's suave and pro-American foreign secretary, Sir Alec Douglas-
Home (he had also served under Macmillan, and had briefly been his
predecessor as prime minister), did his best to rub down the sharp cor-
ners. Nevertheless, the *froideur* that developed between the two,
Heath and Nixon, was to be mirrored most pointedly in the tenor of
communications (now released) between the White House and the
British embassy (ruled then by that lofty oligarch Lord Cromer), and
Whitehall. When the going got particularly rough, Kissinger would urgently invite over from London an old friend, the subtly diplomatic
secretary to the British cabinet, Sir Burke Trend.

The third leg of the European tripod, or triumvirate, was Willy
Brandt, West Germany's first Socialist *Bundeskanzler*, or chancellor,
since its inception in 1948. Brandt had had an extraordinary wartime
career, fleeing to Norway after Hitler's seizure of power, and then—
following the Nazi occupation of Norway in 1940—joining the Nor-

---

* And yet, Heath could manage even to make Britain's momentous decision sound drab;
the author was present at a dinner at which Heath first announced the success of the
complex EU negotiations, this stunning news—in a monotone, deadpan voice evocative
of the returning officer announcing results at an election.

wegian resistance against his fellow countrymen under his real name of
Frahm ("Willy Brandt" was in fact his nom de guerre, which he later
adopted). Conservative Germans would never allow Brandt to forget
his wartime role, referring to him scathingly as "that *Herr Frahm*." As
a young foreign correspondent in Bonn, I got to know Willy quite
well; he was a boisterous, uninhibited, and rather lovable personality
with a colossal appetite for boozing and wenching. We shared some
carefree exploits together. Many in Germany were surprised that this
"Prince Hal–like" figure should become, first, mayor (a role with immense powers in a divided Germany) of Berlin, and then successor
leader of the SPD, the Social Democrats, opposition. Until Brandt
came along in 1969, in the wake of revolts of 1968, U.S. foreign policymakers had had an easy time with a federal Germany ruled either by
the veteran, seemingly immortal, Dr. Konrad Adenauer, firmly supportive of the anti-Soviet views of John Foster Dulles, or his Christian
Democrat successors. To his critics, under Adenauer, the Federal Republic had become an almost totally compliant satellite of the United
States.

Brandt was to upset all this by his pronouncement of Ostpolitik,
which would attempt to wrest concessions from the Soviets by a more
independent West German policy. Its aim would be to bring the divided halves of Germany together. World opinion was powerfully affected by the image of a West German chancellor visiting Poland, to
kneel down before the victims of the Warsaw Uprising; but, at the same
time, Washington was suspicious that Brandt would end by giving
away too much. For, in the long run, it was only through a collapse
of Soviet power—or an accommodation with it—that Brandt could
achieve the one goal of transcendent value to a truncated West
Germany—reunification with the East. Though a later Socialist West
German chancellor, Helmut Schmidt, was to become one of Kissinger's
closest personal friends, Kissinger never seemed to get the measure of
Willy Brandt. In the opinion of Strobe Talbott, director of the Brookings Institution, and a deputy secretary of state under Bill Clinton,
Kissinger was always "distinctly uncomfortable" with Willy. He
viewed his Ostpolitik as "parochial"[13]—"if you sup with the devil, you
need a long spoon." Also, it threatened to lead further down the path
of fragmentation of NATO Soviet divisions, once Czechoslovakia had

comfortably been redigested. Nixon and Kissinger were both deeply apprehensive about Brandt's Ostpolitik. Kissinger's particular fear was that it could only end up strengthening the Soviet position. He was not reassured by Brandt's confidant, Egon Bahr, an unprepossessing and chilly personality who was the intellectual driving force behind Ostpolitik. A much more shadowy figure in the Brandt pack of cards was Herbert Wehner, the SPD party chairman, whom I also knew well in 1950s Bonn (and who, I still suspect, was a KGB operative). As it was, Brandt, remaining unruly in his private life, was eventually brought down and destroyed, rather tragically, in 1974 by the revelation that one of his closest aides was a paid-up Stasi agent.

Brandt's first meeting with Nixon, in Washington on May 1, was hardly auspicious, coming as it did the day after Nixon had been forced to announce the resignation, over Watergate, of his two right-hand men, Haldeman and Ehrlichman. It was with some difficulty that he managed to master his growing distraction in his talks with the German leader; it was a prickly meeting, with Nixon at his most remote, while Brandt had come with a brief clearly to settle nothing.

From the word go, Nixon, in that part of his mind which was shaped by bureaucratic procedure, became infuriated by the conundrum posed by the "New Europeans": "When I speak to Europe, I don't know whom I'm speaking to."[14] The meeting with Brandt had sharpened the problem. To Kissinger, Nixon intimated that he could not now officially receive his old friend, Alec Douglas-Home,* former prime minister, but now Heath's foreign secretary—because he did not know whether he was representing Britain, or the EU. Otherwise Nixon, as U.S. head of state, might find himself besieged with requests for audiences with the prime minister or foreign secretary of Luxembourg, wearing his European hat.

In Pompidou's representative in Washington, the French ambassador, Jacques Kosciusko-Morizet, Kissinger came up against a product of the *grandes écoles* of whose alumni another French leader, Marshal Pétain, had once remarked: "They know everything. Unfortunately they do not know anything else."[15] Kosciusko had one of those bril-

---

* Fairly described by Kissinger as "one of the wisest and most decent men I have had the privilege to meet" (*Years of Upheaval*, p. 721).

liant, analytical French brains which tend to focus only on French national interest. Meanwhile, at the Quai d'Orsay the bonhomous and voluble Maurice Schumann had been replaced by the "precise and austere" Michel Jobert, a "Gaullist of the Left," as foreign secretary. He was to show himself progressively less and less pro-American, or sympathetic to the idea of the year of Europe. On Jobert's shoulders Kissinger would lay the burden chiefly for the failure of the Year of Europe. The two men were almost immediately antipathetic. To Hal Sonnenfeldt, Kissinger's aide on most of the Europe talks (and, like him, born in Germany), Jobert "seemed to make a point of getting under Henry's skin; he studied his technique and set out to irritate him . . . and it was all built up by the media."[16] All Jobert asked, said Kissinger, "was that he be permitted to play the leading role," and that France be left to shape events.[17] A very French position; but Jobert, in Kissinger's eyes, contrived to carry Gaullism to new heights of confrontation. Though on paper both Kissinger and Nixon liked the tidy ideal of the EEC, they became less and less drawn to the reality of it in practice, as it evolved.

It was difficult enough to get the U.S. press to interest itself in such abstract concepts as "Europe," but by now Watergate had come to dominate both headlines and column inches. At a White House press conference on May 29, Kissinger presented the objectives of the Year of Europe, namely "to see whether we can define where the nations bordering the Atlantic want to go over the next ten years in the field of economics, the field of defense, the field of foreign policy." The questions that followed were lackluster and halfhearted, the first noting that Heath and Pompidou had both recently made it clear that they were "not particularly interested in the so-called European summit meeting." The focus swiftly switched from Europe to the course of the Vietnam talks, then ended with the more parochial but immediate issue of wiretapping in Washington; finally, to whether Dr. Kissinger disapproved of "burglaries in offices," and did he believe his credibility had been "tainted." At that point, he closed down the questioning.[18]

So, at the end of May, Kissinger's earthshaking pronouncement on the Year of Europe had fallen a bit like the proverbial pregnant pole-vaulter. It was effectively drowned out by the noise generated by the resignation from the White House of Haldeman and Ehrlichman. Already Kissinger was finding that Nixon's attention span on foreign affairs, previously his forte, was deteriorating as Watergate progressively came to obsess him. Reluctant to go to Europe for a new European summit, Nixon got the cogs of protocol grinding for an acceptable venue. Finally Iceland, at the end of May, was settled on. The auspices were not promising in this "hard land of rockstrewn tundra and stark mountains."[19] Iceland, though a marginal member of NATO, was as far from Europe as you can get; but its halfway position may have seemed symbolic. The hosts were themselves chiefly concerned with the forthcoming "Cod War" with Britain. The French had grabbed the best villa on the island; they were, from the beginning, noncommittal; Heath adopted the unhelpful stance of a "pained bystander at an incipient family quarrel";[20] while Nixon showed himself increasingly distracted by events nearer home. Kissinger was shocked by the physical change he found in Pompidou—bloated by massive dosages of cortisone to mitigate the effects of his cancer. Normally the soul of courtesy, occasionally he would let signs of irascibility slip through. Panegyrics by Nixon, though meant with all honesty, on his late predecessor, Charles de Gaulle, just seemed to irritate Pompidou. At one point he was to remark, with true Gallic acidity, that only Americans could invoke *a* Year of Europe; for a Frenchman, surely every year was *the* Year of Europe.[21]

The Americans had wanted to depart Reykjavik with some kind of "Atlantic Declaration" in their pocket of joint solidarity, with which they could face Brezhnev on his state visit to Washington in less than a month's time. But they came away empty-handed, with Jobert hinting that it was France's interest to hedge until that summit was past, and warning the Americans not to use Atlantic cooperation to exact concessions to their own advantage. Altogether Iceland for Kissinger proved to be about as frigid as its climate—bizarrely in contrast to the almost cozy jocularity that had prevailed only so recently with the Soviet team outside Moscow or, indeed, with Zhou and Mao in Beijing the previous year. And in Iceland the Americans had been among allies of three decades standing! With its attention fixed on a bigger story, back in Washington the press—once again—gave the conference minimum space. On June 8, Kissinger was in Paris for the stalled Vietnam talks. There he found that his relations with Jobert had sunk to the level of "a duel."[22] To his extreme irritation, he admitted falling into a diplomatic "honey-trap," set by Jobert, of rival drafting of communiqués—finding at the same time a waning degree of support from America's former "best friends" among the other Europeans.

At the end of the month, however, Kissinger would get his modicum of revenge on the aggravating Frenchman in an unattended fashion. Jobert had been invited to visit him at Nixon's Pacific White House at San Clemente. Kissinger gave what he describes in his memoirs as a "disastrous dinner" for him in Los Angeles—disastrous, though he recounts the story today accompanied with gales of laughter, almost to the point of causing him to roll off his chair in merriment. To that dinner Kissinger had also rashly invited his close friend, the famous performer—but "unpredictable genius"—Danny Kaye. Jobert had arrived late, and insisted on speaking in French (though his English was excellent). Hardly had he sat down, and before an interpreter could be engaged, the "unpredictable genius" was on his feet, delivering a hilarious performance—in his own nonsensical double-talk representation of a "Frog-speaking Frog." Kissinger observed that "Jobert seemed not amused"—though, as he pointed out, it was a true case of art imitating life in that his and Jobert's own dialogue was beginning to approach Kaye's "elegant gibberish." The other guests must have sat dumbfounded. It would be hard to think of a greater diplomatic insult; in past centuries, wars have been fought for less—for instance, over an insult not much greater, in 1830 France itself seized the whole of Algeria.[23]

Jobert, however—at least in Kissinger's view—had not fired his last shot. Through intricate wheeling and dealing, by July he had managed to sour American relations with PM Heath; Kissinger noted: "During the climactic part of the negotiations, Whitehall, feeling itself discriminated against, treated us more aloofly than even in the previous period of the Heath Government."[24] On July 23, the foreign ministers of the European Community met in Copenhagen to discuss Kissinger's Year of Europe speech—three months to the day, he noted sourly, after he had made it. "Once again our allies took refuge in procedure." Nothing was decided; except that the Danish foreign minister, who would be in the chair for the remainder of 1973, would formally present a draft of the proceedings to the United States, "then report back to the other foreign ministers, who would consider our views at the next monthly meeting."[25]

It was none of it very encouraging. Meanwhile, his close friend at court in Britain, Burke Trend, made it painfully clear that—on Heath's instructions—he no longer had authority to consult Washington bilaterally. It made a nonsense of the "special relationship" which leaders going back to Churchill and Roosevelt, Kennedy and Macmillan, had fought so hard to enshrine. Europe now "had responded to the Year of Europe initiative with a procedure in which those who talked with us were not empowered to negotiate, while those who could have negotiated with us no longer had the authority to talk."[26] Kissinger blamed Jobert and his "ruthless" manipulation of Heath.

Accordingly, Nixon sent off a presidential letter to Heath of "unusual coolness"; it ended plaintively: "I find puzzling what you say about the exploitation of our private bilateral contacts by the country [i.e., France] that had initially insisted on them." On July 30, Nixon was putting his feelings even more forcefully in a letter to Brandt: "I must honestly tell you that I find it astonishing that an endeavor whose purpose was to create a new spirit of Atlantic solidarity and whose essence should have been that it was collaborative at all stages should now be turned almost into a European-American confrontation." He went on: "Let me say now, however . . . I will not come to Europe unless there is a result commensurate with the need for strengthening Atlantic relationships."[27] Nixon would now never make his official, presidential, visit to Europe.

On the day Nixon dispatched his tough letter to Brandt, "the wise and gentle" Sir Burke Trend arrived in Washington. But, in the light of Copenhagen and Heath's edict, he had "nothing to talk about."[28] It was, Kissinger recorded, a "painful session. . . . We both realized . . . that we were at a turning point in Atlantic relations." The old, cherished form of Anglo-American intangibles of trust and relaxed mutual consultation were now being "put into a straitjacket of legalistic formalisms." Harbingers of the apparatus of Brussels three decades later had arrived! Trend showed his distress as closely as "the code of discipline of the British Civil Service" would permit. So by the end of July, shortly before his promotion to be secretary of state, Kissinger felt gloomily that: "Though bureaucratic inertia and Watergate despair impelled us to continue to go through the motions, the Year of Europe had lost its meaning."[29]

Now promoted secretary of state, Kissinger vented his frustrations on the hapless Knud Borge Andersen, Danish foreign secretary, when he came to see him wearing his European Community hat on September 25. Kissinger started, acidly: "As you may know from my comments, we recognize the importance of the development that Europe is speaking with one voice, although it is surprising that we read this in the *New York Times.*" Kissinger continued, brusquely: "For the U.S. it is a new and extraordinary phenomenon, in that Europe speaks with one voice which we welcome but that in its preparations we were not consulted; then a document is presented to us by a representative that is not empowered to negotiate but only to receive comments and take back to the Nine our comments. We seem to be talking to those who can't negotiate and those who can negotiate won't talk to us. Frankly, I must tell you that this is not a procedure we can accept as a permanent arrangement. . . . You seem to be dealing with us as you would deal with the Russians."

The chastised Dane was given little chance of response. Finally, Kissinger issued this stern warning: "Europe must decide if it intends to build Europe or also to build Atlantic relations. If the decision [is] to build Europe when the Atlantic relationship is collapsing, then the European achievement will be at the expense of Atlantic relations."

Andersen responded manfully: "We can have a dialogue."[30]

About the same time Kissinger confided to Douglas Dillon*, who thought the dialogue with Andersen had been "ridiculous," that Europe "now bothers me not because of any problem but the leaders of the 1950s and 1960s are gone and now they are run like a bunch of state governments. . . . I think we made a mistake with the British in pushing them into the Common Market. Now they seem to be pursuing a Gaullist policy with vigor." What the Europeans now wanted "is for the president to go and meet with a group of foreign ministers in Eu-

---

* Former ambassador to Paris and John F. Kennedy's secretary of the treasury.

rope. [But] the president will never meet with anyone lower than the heads of state."[31]

Irritability over the Year of Europe was certainly not all one way, however. One distinguished French diplomat, who later became ambassador to London, Gérard Errera, was a young first secretary in Washington in 1973, dealing with internal U.S. politics. He and his colleagues found that Kissinger "could be very arrogant—very rude; he had to show he had power." At one conference with Jobert, he recalled Kissinger being "really tough," and threatening: "If you don't play we'll do terrible things—we'll hit you in Wall Street and we'll side with Mitterrand at the next election." With Jobert at the time, Errera concluded that Kissinger's "big mistake" had been "to patronize Europe." His view was "as long as the U.S. and the Soviets had an agreement, then all the other pawns were in place . . . the real issues were Vietnam. . . . One had to reckon that he had all the pressures of Vietnam, and Watergate—and Nixon's incapacity—on his shoulders at the time."[32]

In the meantime, however, much was happening on the international, "out-of-area" scene that would fundamentally affect Atlantic relations. The Yom Kippur War had been fought, and peace restored. But the Saudi-initiated oil crisis had shaken European regimes to the core, introducing a new, unintended, dependence on America. A fresh and rather less acerbic and overweening tone entered the transatlantic dialogue. The Year of Europe, as Kissinger had conceived it, was over—a dead duck. Close colleagues of Kissinger's, like Secretary of Defense James Schlesinger, felt that it had "definitely left scars on Henry; the idealist in him was justifiably upset . . . for a 'good European' like him—and in some ways he was *very European*—the Europeans were quite antagonistic."[33] Brent Scowcroft, Kissinger's successor on the NSC, agreed: "Yes. It bothered him a lot."[34]

Among the last epitaphs on the abortive Year was perhaps Nixon's, at a staff meeting in the Oval Office on November 12, 1973, as the jaws of Watergate were closing down on him: "Whatever we planned to do with respect to Europe has been delayed by the Middle East. We'll be meeting probably early next year. What we desperately need is new ideas. We can't keep going to Congress to keep the troops, get offset, etc. You know it's getting tougher each year."[35]

Within the year Pompidou was dead, Heath out of office, Brandt had resigned—and Nixon had been replaced by Gerald Ford. The Year of Europe would prove to be Kissinger's least successful initiative—even though, with his special European interests, it was one closest to his heart. It was also one that would break the spirits of other, subsequent, U.S. leaders.

CHAPTER 6

STORM CLOUDS OVER THE MIDDLE EAST

"A cloud no larger than a man's hand . . ."

—I Kings 18:44

A S OF THE BEGINNING of summer 1973, Kissinger was occupied with Vietnam, Cambodia, the Soviets, China, Europe—and now, most recently Watergate, coupled with the mounting truculence of a hostile Congress. Two areas which were not then on his crisis map were the Middle East and Chile. One was to present him with his biggest test in office; the second, a sore which would deepen many years after he left office.

Since Israel's astonishing David and Goliath triumph in the Six Day War in June 1967, a kind of uneasy stability seemed to have descended on the Middle East. When I was in Israel shortly after the war, I vividly recall an unpleasant exchange with the architect of the air victory, General Ezer Weizman, a huge, dominating figure and an ultra-hawk, regarded as the father of the Israeli Air Force.* In a display of nationalist

---

* Weizman later became president of Israel (1993–2000). In the subsequent War of Attrition on the Suez Canal, his son suffered appalling injuries, which reduced him to vegetable state, and Weizman swung from being ultra-hawk to ultra-dove.

self-confidence that was frankly disturbing, he boasted to me one evening—in bluntly racist terms—how Israel now could "lick any combination of Arabs that come at us." Those six days changed both the character of Israel and its manifestation in the world setting. Before 1967, it was an infant state menaced by neighbors on all sides, rent by economic problems and internal tensions between Sephardim and Ashkenazim, of little significance to the outside world. The war turned it into a major military power, brimming with self-confidence.

Jokes like the following would flash through the Israeli centers of power: "What does the Israeli army need in order to occupy Damascus, Moscow, or Vladivostok?—to receive an order."

Moshe Dayan, Israel's minister of defense from 1967 to 1974, was quoted as cracking: "There is nothing to do . . . What about invading another Arab country?

"But then what would we do in the afternoon?"[1]

Orientations changed; prior to 1967, Israel's main arms supplier was France, but the war caused General de Gaulle—fearful of France's prestige in the Arab world—to cut supplies at what could have been a critical moment in the battle. The United States now moved in to supplant France as the armorer of Israel; and, for the first time, became closely involved as its political guarantor. Israel now became a greater presence in the life of the American Jewish community than it had heretofore—and with a proportionately growing influence on U.S. policy.

By 1973 the mood in Israel had altered little since 1967; the feeling widespread was that, for the first time in its stormy history, the territorial gains made in 1967 now ensured its security. It could sit back, free from fear of attack by its enemies, and wait for them to come up with acceptable peace proposals. One analyst speaks of the "impertinent sense of invulnerability"[2] prevalent in Israel. Some might call the mood hubris. It was dangerous; and it had become accepted all too readily in Washington, D.C. The sum of intelligence reports from the Middle East was that so long as Israel enjoyed its current military superiority, there was no *reasonable* likelihood of either Egypt or Syria, the principal among potential combatants, launching a *serious* attack. The stress was upon the words *reasonable* and *serious*. In 1970 there had been an ugly threat of a renewed Middle East war when the Syrians moved into Jordan, and Israel poised itself to intervene. Under heavy U.S. pressure, however, the crisis resolved itself and from then until the autumn of 1973 a deceptive calm ensued.[3] The Washington intelligence community, which, with its SIGINT spies miles up in the skies, was to prove incapable of predicting the Iraq-Iran War of 1980 from the millions of men mobilizing down below, equally, in 1973, would write off the massive movements of Anwar al-Sadat's* Egyptian army near the Suez Canal as nothing more than maneuvers.

Both Nixon and Kissinger wanted the deadlock in the Middle East to remain undisturbed, at least until after the Israeli elections in the autumn at the end of October. Then there would be a new, concerted U.S. initiative; so Nixon promised President Sadat of Egypt. And first, of course, Vietnam had to be moved off the front burner. Nixon's own philosophy toward Israel remained somewhat ambivalent, tinctured by his innate anti-Semitism. Unlike the norm of U.S. political leaders in their ritual wooing of the domestic Jewish lobby, AIPAC, the American Israel Public Affairs Committee, Nixon felt that he owed the Jews no favors; relatively few had voted for him, so their opinion was of little importance. And that was what counted with Richard Nixon. He had no problem in putting his signature to a memorandum chiding America's Jewish community for "putting Jewish interests above US concerns,"[4] something few U.S. politicians would dare risk today. Kissinger would comment: "I did not keep track of how often I was told to cut off all aid to Israel in retaliation for the actions of some wayward Jewish members of Congress; Senator Jacob Javits† seemed to have a special ability to get under Nixon's skin."[5] Nixon had little personal affection for the Milwaukee-educated Prime Minister Golda Meir, whose down-to-earth toughness perhaps reminded him of the Jewish voters with whom he had to deal at home. (Equally her robust plainness as a woman appealed little to Kissinger.) On the other hand, always one to respect courage, Nixon greatly admired Israel for its performance in 1967, and was determined to see it topped up sufficiently

---

* Sadat had taken over on the death of Gamal Abdel Nasser in September 1970 as a relatively junior officer in the Egyptian army; as of 1973 he remained an unknown quantity.

† Republican senator from New York.

with U.S. arms to deprive any renewed Arab attack of success. His ignorance of, and lack of interest in, the Arab world was profound; just
as long as it remained moderately tranquil and went on producing oil
for the Western world, its machinery and arms.

As of early 1973, Kissinger would not claim to be much more
closely involved in Middle Eastern affairs than Nixon. His "starting
point" on Israel was simply, and rather movingly, stated in his memoirs: he could never forget "that thirteen members of my family had
died in Nazi concentration camps. I had no stomach for encouraging
another holocaust by well intentioned policies that might get out of
control. Most Israeli leaders were personal friends. And yet, like
Nixon, I had to subordinate my emotional preferences to my perception of the national interest. Indeed, given the historical suspicions towards my religion, I had a special obligation to do so. It was not always
easy; occasionally it proved painful."[6] To the author he once spelled it
out: "I could not conceive of being responsible for the foreign affairs
of any regime which might preside over the demise of the state of
Israel"[7] however pessimistic he might feel about its long-term future.
On the other hand, over the years he found few emotional ties that
would attach him to Israel, or the Israelis—whom he regarded as "ungenerous people."[8] The Arab world did not form any major part of his
intellectual equipment—preoccupied with the Cold War, he had never
met Sadat and knew little about him. As part of the world chessboard,
his principal objective was to see Soviet influence squeezed out of an
area where—since Nasser—it had been so strong and menacing to U.S.
interests.

To some extent U.S. Middle East policy could only blame itself for
the powerful Soviet presence there, harking back to the Suez Crisis of
1956, when Britain and France had attacked Nasser's Egypt, and John
Foster Dulles, compounding Franco-British folly, had helped create
the vacuum in Egypt into which Soviet premier Nikita Khrushchev
happily moved. Over the ensuing fifty years, that U.S. intervention on
the side of an Arab country was to gain it little more kudos or friends
in the Muslim world than Britain or France. Now, under his first term,
in the early 1970s, Nixon encouraged William Rogers to launch a
United Nations–based peace plan, coupled with the name of Gunnar
Jarring of the U.N. This was as much to keep Rogers and the State

Department occupied over issues, and an area, Nixon cynically thought could do no harm. At the same time he may have been influenced by a desire to keep Kissinger's hands off Middle East policy, because of his Jewish background. In 1971, Rogers became the first U.S. secretary of state to visit the Middle East since Dulles in 1953. But, largely as a result of Israeli opposition, coupled with its low priority in the White House, the "Rogers Plan" got nowhere. The famous U.N. Resolution 242* became the accepted symbol of stalemate; it did not, as of spring 1973, seem to involve any threat to oil supplies to the Western world.

State Department policy on the Middle East under Rogers, with all the hallmarks of traditional diplomacy, favored a more evenhanded approach to the Arabs vis-à-vis Israel. Within Foggy Bottom, Michael Sterner, a future ambassador†, then in charge of the Egypt desk, thought there was "too much bilateralism in State," and welcomed Kissinger's global approach. To Sterner, Kissinger regarded the Middle East as an "empty chessboard, where the Soviets and the U.S. were moving the pieces."9 Kissinger himself was critical of Rogers's diplomacy as being carried out too much in the glare of publicity. He believed that the United States should not become involved too early in the *substance* of any negotiations. He also doubted whether U.S. restraint in supplies of arms to Israel would do anything to encourage the Arabs toward greater malleability. The Israelis detected this, and began to bypass Rogers in favor of direct dealings with the White House. It is difficult to see what possible advantage accrued to U.S. government policy here from this twin-track technique: yet one more indication of the underlying dangers in the duality that lay between the two machines, State and the NSC. But soon Kissinger and foreign minister Yitzhak Rabin (later Simcha Dinitz) were establishing a back channel, under Nixon's encouragement. And there was a third "special channel" in play, between Kissinger and Soviet ambassador Anatoly Dobrynin, that was scouting the possibility of a joint Soviet-U.S. *com-*

---

* Which called upon Israeli "withdrawal from territories conquered" (subtly, as opposed to "from *the* territories conquered") in 1967.

† Ambassador to United Arab Emirates (1974–1976); director of Egyptian Affairs at the Department of State (1970).

binazione in the Middle East. Only Kissinger was aware of all three channels. It must have been all very confusing for the other spiders in the web.

Yet, if the Americans were hamfisted in their dealings with Egypt and the Arab world in 1973, it seems to have been paralleled by the crassness of the Soviets; as of the 1950s, Ivan Serov, the KGB boss, we are told, "knew so little about Egypt that he believed Egyptians were black Africans rather than Arabs." [10] In July 1972, Washington was stunned by the news that—of his own accord—Sadat had expelled Egypt's Soviet advisers, some 25,000 in all. Washington, in the midst of Vietnam negotiations and the run-up to the presidential election, did not then venture to seize what might have seemed like an opportunity; nor did its intelligence analysts consider whether the Egyptians were clearing the decks for a potential military offensive. Meanwhile, Egypt continued to rely on the Soviets for its military hardware (notably in SAMs, surface-to-air missiles, that were to prove lethal to the Israeli Air Force in October 1973), while Moscow stepped up its supplies to Hafez al-Asad's Syria—a country and a regime far more adamantly hostile to Israel even than Egypt.[11] But, as Kissinger analyzed it, the Soviets had put themselves in the position of being able to "stoke the embers of the crisis, but once they exploded into conflagration it could use them for its own ends only by risking a great power confrontation . . . it acted as the Arabs' lawyer but could not advance their case." [12] As a Cold War position it was not an unappealing one for the United States. At the same time, Moscow had its own sensible motives for not wanting to rock the Middle East boat excessively; currently it was desperately anxious for a vast grain deal with the United States to go through—as will be seen shortly.

In the fall of 1972, there had been efforts between Cairo and Washington to arrange a meeting between Kissinger and Hafez Ismail, Sadat's own national security adviser—known as the "Egyptian Kissinger." This had been postponed because of the U.S. elections and Kissinger's deep involvement in the Vietnam talks; while the waters had been muddied by the brutal murder, that "Black September," of Israeli athletes at the Munich Olympics; which in turn had led to retaliatory raids against Lebanon and Syria. Finally the meeting with Ismail took place in Washington, in February 1973, under cover of great secrecy. The State Department was not informed. Ismail's visit came close upon the heels of Jordan's King Hussein, America's loyalest and most reliable ally in the Arab world, and he was followed in turn by Golda Meir. As so often, the Arab allies were not seen to be singing from the same hymn sheet: Sadat did not like Hussein, or for that matter kings in general. Hussein was prepared to deal directly with Israel about the West Bank, and felt that there would perhaps be two or three years of peace still in which to achieve this. But he was pessimistic about the motives behind Sadat's expulsion of the Soviet advisers.

Drawn into its labyrinthine diplomacy somewhat against his will, Kissinger made it plain that he was "certainly not" going to turn "my primary attention to the Middle East";[13] nevertheless these talks constituted his first real introduction to Middle East peacemaking, and would hone the skills that he would be called upon to deploy, formidably, at the end of the year. Like the first-class university lecturer that he was, in a key exposition in his memoirs he expounds how "The opening of a complicated negotiation was like the beginning of an arranged marriage. The partners know that the formalities will soon be stripped away as they discover each other's real attributes. . . . The future being mercifully veiled, the parties attempt what they might not dare did they know what was ahead."[14] Yet he would always endeavor, he once explained to the author,[15] to outline early the objectives he sought to achieve in the endgame. He would, he continued, spend the first session of a new negotiation "educating myself. I almost never put forward a proposal. Rather, I sought to understand the intangibles in the position of my interlocutor and to gauge the scope as well as the limits of probable concessions. And I made a considerable effort to leave no doubt about our fundamental approach." "The art of diplomacy," he continued in his memoirs, "is not to outsmart the other side but to convince it either of common interests or of penalties if an impasse continues."[16]

To Ismail, Kissinger began by trying to explain "the strange ways of our government," its "two-channel system."[17] He imparted no particular urgency, repeating that little could be achieved before the Israeli elections scheduled for late October. But Ismail, clearly under considerable pressure from Sadat, insisted there *had* to be a Middle East settlement in the course of 1973. Meeting on February 25 and 26, outside

New York in the Connecticut mansion of the ubiquitous Pepsi-Cola magnate Don Kendall, a friend of Nixon's who had formed an early (commercial) link with Sadat,[18] Kissinger says he found Ismail disappointingly noncommittal, hoping merely that "heads of agreement" could be achieved by September. He would not agree to any interim agreement, such as a disengagement on the Suez Canal front. It had to be all or nothing. As a precondition Israel would have to agree to return to its pre-1967 frontiers; which it would clearly not accept, without provision of unattainable guarantees. It may well have been that Ismail, who still had the erect bearing of the army officer he had once been, was confused by the various tracks of diplomacy then afoot in Washington: State, NSC, White House. "Within the space of forty-eight hours," Kissinger writes, the bemused Egyptian encountered "the American President uttering generalities, the State Department pushing an interim agreement without White House backing, and Nixon's national security adviser discussing principalities of an overall settlement at a secret meeting without State Department participation."[19] (Or, already, he may have gleaned that Sadat's thinking had by now gone beyond the stage of talks?) Kissinger sensed no particular urgency. It was also unlikely that anything Ismail had offered would be acceptable to Mrs. Meir. Nixon, on the other hand, with his extraordinary intuitiveness, frequently referring to the Balkans analogy of pre–World War I, sensed that "This thing is getting ready to blow." He wanted to press on with negotiations for a peace settlement, and was "determined to move off dead center" with the Israelis. He noted with irritation that "I have yet to see *one iota* of give on their part." The time "has come to quit pandering to Israel's intransigent position."[20] The tragedy was that domestic circumstances were rapidly eroding his power to take this kind of initiative.

Then, at the beginning of March, Golda Meir and her team of Israeli military men arrived in town. "Shrewd, earthy, elemental, she felt herself to be the mother of her people"[21] was how Kissinger saw the redoubtable Israeli leader then. One of the founders of the state of Israel, Golda Meir was among the most outstanding and forceful women of her era, giving coinage to the expression "Iron Lady" well before Margaret Thatcher entered the arena. She was renowned for her inflexible, black-and-white view of the world. David Ben-Gurion, Israel's first president, regarded her as "the only man in the Cabinet." A French friend of mine, Francis Huré, was sent by de Gaulle as ambassador to Israel, to repair relations after France had cut off supplies of aircraft during the Six Day War; when delivering his credentials, Prime Minister Meir cut him off by saying, "Yes, I know. If Israel went under, your president would be the first to offer her an *enterrement de première classe*."[22] Kissinger held her in respectful awe, frequently admixed with extreme irritation; he was not beyond teasing, according her homely appearance with the nickname "Miss Israel." Born Golda Mabovitch on May 3, 1898, in Ukraine, her earliest memories were of her father boarding up the house as precaution against a pogrom. Such memories, reinforced by the dreadful history of generations of Russian brutality, left an imprint upon those fleeing from it that was as ineradicable as the briefer but more absolute Final Solution of Germany, a nation where prior to Hitler Jews had enjoyed relative harmony. It was something that Golda would take with her to America, and then on to Israel, accounting in part for her residual distrust of any dealings with the Russia of Brezhnev. Such deep distrust would be reinforced by the Soviets' refusal to "let my people go," in the persons of dissidents like Anatoly Sharansky in the 1970s; and it would not make relations any easier with America's first Jewish secretary of state—dedicated as he was to détente with Moscow.

In 1906, Golda emigrated with her family to Milwaukee, Wisconsin, where her father worked as a carpenter. With her husband, Morris Myerson, a sign-painter, she moved to what was then British-mandated Palestine in 1921, changing her name to Meir—which means in Hebrew "to illuminate." As the mandate collapsed, she became the principal negotiator with the British, renowned for her unyielding stance. In 1948, with independence approaching, King Abdullah of Jordan urged her not to hurry to proclaim the new state, to which she is alleged to have replied: "We've been waiting for two thousand years. Is that hurrying?"[23]

Although already diagnosed with cancer (lymphoma) and suffering from exhaustion, when Israel's prime minister, Levi Eshkol, died suddenly in 1969, she took over at the head of a shaky coalition government. She earned the sobriquet "Mother of Israel" in the truest sense, in that she regarded the death of every single Israeli soldier like the personal loss of a son. It was she who, after the Black September massacres of Israeli athletes in Munich in 1972, outraged by lack of worldwide support, ordered Mossad to hunt down and kill those responsible. From the Yom Kippur War, her reputation would emerge severely tarnished by the Agranat Commission report, but she would win the elections of December 1973, then bow to the "will of the people" and resign the following April. She would die, of cancer, in December 1978—aged eighty. Of her many memorable quotations, she was alleged to have said: "The Muslims can fight and lose, then come back and fight again. But Israel can only lose once," and "The Arabs will stop fighting us when they love their children more than they hate Jews." Rabin, her successor, like Sadat, and Abdullah of Jordan, was murdered by extremists for seeming to give up too much in the quest of Middle East peace.

As of her visit to Washington in March 1973, she saw no imminent danger of war, as Israel was now militarily impregnable. She declared "we've never had it so good." [24] Israel could live with a stalemate indefinitely. The nation had nothing to fear. But she wanted a new delivery of Phantom jets. While this was being considered, two top American diplomats were taken and brutally murdered in Khartoum, Sudan, by Palestinian terrorists. Nixon agreed to the sale of the forty-eight jets to Israel. On the news being leaked from Washington, Sadat erupted in fury. But a further meeting was fixed, at the Egyptian Dr. Kissinger's insistence, for May 20, in Paris.

Over the past two years there had been a variety of warnings that "things" were "getting ready to blow" in the Middle East. As early as 1971, Sadat himself had made direct threats of war, and repeated them through 1972. As it was considered inconceivable that Egypt could confront Israel militarily, Washington assumed that Sadat was thinking in terms of a stepping up of *fedayin*, guerrilla-style, raids: nothing more serious—as Kissinger himself would admit many years later.[25] Several times nothing happened, and Foggy Bottom went back to sleep, writing off such warnings as nothing more than bombast on the part of the Egyptians. Sadat repeated his threats in 1972; troops concentrated for maneuvers on the Suez Canal, and then dispersed again. Then, in April

1973, Arnaud de Borchgrave, the ace roving editor of *Newsweek*, who had caused embarrassment with his well-informed scoops from Vietnam, published a brilliant exposé of an interview with Sadat, entitled "The Battle Is Now Inevitable." To de Borchgrave Sadat declared that "the time has come for a shock."[26] It was in fact a careful plant, designed once again to lull the Israelis, and the United States, into a false sense of security. Israel mobilized its reservists—at a cost of $35 million, a sum the Israel Defense Forces budget could not readily spare. But the maneuvering Egyptian troops dispersed back home. Once more it seemed like "wolf, wolf!" As Kissinger recorded the threat "seemed to refer to commando raids and renewed shelling," and, he admitted, "We still considered this psychological warfare, however, rather than serious preparation for war."[27]

There was no shortage of further serious warnings coming from visitors to Saudi Arabia that spring. The well-placed CIA station chief, Raymond Close, had picked up a fairly direct threat from King Faisal himself that, "under pressure from our Arab brothers," in the event of war, his country would use the "oil weapon"—something hitherto unimaginable.[28] The king felt "constantly rebuffed by the State Department—who would not link oil with foreign policy. They didn't want to know." To Close, he passed on how Sadat, "in despair," had concluded: "No one in the West respects us [Arabs]. We have to show them; start a war only to prove that we can."[29] To the end, however, the Saudis thought that Sadat's idea of war was "madness."

Close found his own reports stifled, at whatever level of the CIA, in the Langley headquarters. On April 20, the CIA submitted to Kissinger an enigmatic—and unhelpful—assessment to the effect that Sadat "may have begun to take his own talk more seriously, but . . . the CIA concluded that there were no indications of planning for any specific operation at a specific time."[30] An editorial in the *Washington Post* that same day criticized the Saudis for threatening an oil boycott, and added: "It is to yield to hysteria to take such threats as Saudi Arabia's seriously."[31] This deaf ear to Arab cries in Washington so disturbed Faisal that, for the first time in his life, he went on U.S. TV to issue an unmistakable warning: "America's complete support for Zionism against the Arabs makes it extremely difficult for us to continue to supply U.S. petroleum needs." This was promptly pooh-poohed by

Israel's illustrious foreign minister, Abba Eban, renowned as a moderate, declaring that "the Arab states have no alternative but to sell their oil because they have no other resources at all."[32] It was the kind of arrogant challenge almost guaranteed to provoke a proud nation, however hopeless the cause.

On April 18, however, an even more meaningful consultation had taken place in the heart of Israel's government—around Golda Meir's kitchen table. It was, as she put it, a place "where we could consider things over a cup of coffee or during a light meal." Present were Defense Minister Moshe Dayan; the director of Military Intelligence, Major General Eli Zeira; Mossad chief Zvi Zamir; chief of staff General David "Dado" Elazar; Israel Galili, minister without portfolio and éminence grise in Meir's office; plus assorted aides. The larger cabinet was excluded. Minutes (published years later) of this meeting show this inner group mistrustful of revealing the true state of affairs, as they knew it, to the Americans. No one there that day wanted to consider returning the Arab territories taken in 1967, but—so it was reckoned—if they were to reveal to the Americans a pessimistic view, "that things were reaching the boiling point, then the Americans would say: Let's go to Camp David, we'll talk and reach a compromise."[33] This, as of April 1973, was the last thing Golda Meir and her kitchen cabinet wanted. So the Israelis themselves were not prepared to pass on to Washington any fears, however slight, of the possibility of war. The report of a bright young officer, Benjamin Tov, analyzing the Egyptian movements as clearly presaging war, was pigeonholed—along with all the rest.[34]

Ally was not speaking the whole truth to ally. As Dayan had once remarked in what represented a fairly perennial, and derogatory, Israeli viewpoint: "Our American friends offer us money, arms and advice. We take the money, we take the arms and we decline the advice."[35]

The following month, at the celebrations of Israel's twenty-fifth Independence Day, the mood of that kitchen meeting was reechoed in exultant messages from the great and the good of the nation. Dayan proclaimed to *Time* magazine that Israel was out of danger for the next ten years, while Golda Meir declared in an interview in Israel's *Ma'ariv* about Sadat—"Let him stew." Already planning large-scale Jewish settlement on the West Bank, on July 30, Dayan told *Time*: "There is no more Palestine. Finished." General Elazar, the man who was to carry the blame for the blow that was about to befall Israel, alone seems to have believed that war was possible, and that "everything should be done to deter, to prevent a war." Thus it should be made plain to the Egyptians that Israel was prepared and would not be taken by surprise. But no such deterrent posture was adopted.[36]

That same May in Saudi Arabia, King Faisal summoned in first the chairman of Aramco, Frank Jungers, then later four other leading U.S. oilmen, to warn them: "You may lose everything. Time is running out." But when they tried to relay the warning to Washington no one in government would take it seriously; allegedly Kissinger refused to see them; while an explosion of protest from the Washington Israeli lobby threatened a boycott of Standard Oil of California.[37] Close remains highly critical of Kissinger's attempts to "muzzle" the grumbles coming out of Riyadh. Finally, in a most unorthodox manner (as will be revealed in the following chapter), one further warning of an impending attack would come direct to Nixon from Brezhnev, at the end of his June visit to the San Clemente White House.

Kissinger held a second secret meeting with Hafez Ismail at a pleasant house outside Paris on May 20, 1973. He found the Egyptian less interested in substance than he had been during the February talks, concentrating his questions on the role the United States intended to play. He pressed, however, the predominant importance in any settlement of a solution to the Palestinian problem. According to Ismail's account, when he begged Kissinger to put pressure on the Israelis to open the Suez Canal, which had been closed since 1967, he "pounded the table," declaring: "In Vietnam we could obliterate Hanoi—but we are still losing. The Israelis are on the Canal. So what can we do with Israel?" Issues unresolved in February remained unresolved. The tone of the negotiations seemed much less encouraging than those of three months previously. Kissinger recalled how, at the end of the French encounter, the Egyptian, "visibly dispirited and glum, had sat alone in the garden for a long time contemplating the waterfall behind the house, head cupped in hands."[38] Kissinger suggested further talks; Ismail promised an early reply—but when it came (on June 3) it was "guarded and unenthusiastic.[39] With hindsight we now know that Ismail, the former soldier, had by then realized that the die was cast, that Sadat had already decided to throw Egypt's forces into a battle that would be costly, and uncertain.

Observers on the spot, like Raymond Close and the late Archie Roosevelt (grandson of Teddy), also an expert on the Middle East, felt bitterly that Kissinger—for whatever reason—had missed a prime opportunity with Hafez Ismail in those two meetings in early 1973. He could have opened a door. Some eminent Egyptians, like the leading journalist Mohamed Heikal, even entertained a suspicion at one time that Kissinger was actually enticing Sadat into an act of war.[40] The question, which has been debated ever since 1973, and remains open: could Nixon and (notably) Kissinger have done anything to avert the pending catastrophe of October 1973—had they been better informed on Egyptian intentions? Certainly by that spring, like the trains that had already left their stations in 1914, Sadat's—and Asad's—plans were already too far advanced. To have achieved anything earlier would have involved a monumental recasting of U.S. Middle East policy, of which it was probably no more capable than was the case thirty years later, at the time of Saddam Hussein and George W. Bush. Yet, secure with such an electoral majority, plus the will, for once, to "sit on" the Jewish lobby, *pro bonum publicum*, almost unique in recent U.S. history, did the Nixon administration pass up a unique opportunity for world statesmanship? Was Watergate, once again, to blame for a paralysis in Washington over the Middle East?

Chapter 7

Coming to Grips with the Polar Bear

"Stalin, Khrushchev, and Brezhnev are on a train. Train breaks down. Stalin says, 'Shoot the driver!' Khrushchev says, 'Raise the driver's wages!' Brezhnev says, 'Let's all get underneath the train, and rock it, and pretend that it's moving!'"

—Soviet anecdote of 1973,
illustrative of the nation's economic stagnation[1]

"America must commit itself to a moral opposition to Communism, not just geopolitical opposition to Soviet encroachment, or its policy will be based on quicksand. But while I sympathize with this point of view, a statesman must relate general theorems to concrete circumstances."

—Henry Kissinger[2]

"The major, *long term question is whether the Soviets can hold their own bloc together while waiting for the West to succumb to a long period of relaxation* and to the temptations of economic competition.

"... If the West saw to containment, I was convinced that it would win its historical bet. The Soviet Union's economic system was glaringly weak."

—Henry Kissinger[3]

FOR ALL THE excitement over the breakthrough to China, and the earthshaking significance of the Nixon-Kissinger visit, nevertheless in 1973 relations with the "Polar Bear" remained, and always would remain, number one among Kissinger's priorities. It was after all the Cold War; he and Nixon and all American statesmen of the post-1945 generation had grown up with it, and were profoundly conditioned by it. As a World War II soldier too, Kissinger had seen at first hand the devastation that could be caused just by conventional bombing. He would never forget the scenes of total destruction he witnessed in 1945 Germany. And, one has to recall, Nixon's reelection in 1972 had come only ten years, almost to the day, from that episode of ultimate terror—the Cuban Missile Crisis of October 1962 when John F. Kennedy and Nikita Khrushchev had indeed come alarmingly close to the brink. Ever since, Western statesmen had dedicated their efforts to finding ways of moving back from it—and Kissinger was foremost. Indeed, the USSR was seldom out of his thoughts.[4]

The Nixon-Kissinger strategic philosophy toward Mao's Polar Bear was fraught with contradictions, irrationalities, and risks. The risks were very great. A generation which has grown up in the two decades since the fall of the Berlin Wall might well ask itself, and its elders, Did the Cold War have to be fought? Was it all worth the risk? A historian's answer might be that, anyone who doubts that the basic evil of the "Evil Empire" (in the phrase conjured up subsequently by Ronald Reagan) had to be combated should simply go and see that most remarkable German movie, *The Lives of Others*, with its unembellished exposure of how the Stasi secret police invaded and corrupted the lives of every single citizen in Sovietized East Germany. Over the intervening years, information seeping out of post-Soviet Russia suggests that Brezhnev's USSR was not poised to commit aggression outside its own sphere, and that it was militarily and economically far weaker than it seemed. But that was not how it appeared to Henry Kissinger, or Nixon, in 1973; it was just five years since Soviet tanks had rolled into Czechoslovakia, and it would be only another five years after the fall of Nixon in 1974 that they would roll into Afghanistan, to the deep shock of the whole world. (That they would meet their nemesis there was not then on the cards—which were far from readable anyway.) Kissinger's perceptions were little aided by CIA intelligence, which was at best patchy ever since the execution of the West's star double agent, Colonel Oleg Penkovsky, following the Cuban Missile Crisis.

Underlying all Kissinger's perceptions was the alarming awareness that—whereas in the days of the unpredictable Khrushchev, the United States could operate from a position of relative superiority in rocketry—by the 1970s the gap had been closed, if not the proportions actually reversed. Therefore, the name of the game had to be coexistence via détente. For this caution, Kissinger would come under regular fire from the conservative wing of the Republican Party, Sovietologists like Professor Richard Pipes, and even those like Zbigniew Brzezinski. To become secretary of state under the liberal Jimmy Carter, Brzezinski would castigate the doctrine which countenanced the status quo, permitting the Soviets to keep a brutal foot firmly on a great swath of Eastern Europe. Their argument was—and to a large extent, remains—that what Ronald Reagan achieved in the 1980s, the collapse of the "Evil Empire," could, with a little more firmness, have been achieved in the 1970s. Too much had been given away for too little in exchange? It is a view that Kissinger rigorously disputes.

There was also something of a dual purpose in the quest for détente; as well as "a need to educate the Russians on arms control," there was "a need in America to split the peace movement."[5]

One of the apparent contradictions of the U.S. practice of détente was that on the one hand it came with an olive branch, while on the other it was prepared to use every available lever to remove the Soviets from the Middle East, a prime interest of the Kremlin. In *Diplomacy,* Kissinger insists "Nixon and his advisors saw no contradiction in treating the communist world as both adversary and collaborator."[6] And they were playing the China card hard, to the manifest discomfort, and disadvantage, of Brezhnev. Here was a grave, latent danger; on several occasions Brezhnev, expressing a thoroughly racist, passionate loathing of the Chinese, would seem to be seeking U.S. endorsement of a preemptive nuclear strike on his immense neighbor.* This would have run up against the fundamental gospel of whatever U.S. administration was in power; yet, given a crazed dictator like Hitler, or maybe even an unstable Khrushchev, or some Machiavellian Dr. Strangelove, the danger always existed. And what if Moscow perceived a Chinese threat on Russia's frontiers, or vice versa, via Afghanistan? At the same time, there was a certain cynicism on the Soviet side toward its client state Vietnam. Disappointingly, Moscow, like the Chinese, would not lift a hand to help the U.S. peace moves; on the other hand, neither would it challenge the bombing of Hanoi and Haiphong, where it had—so it might have been thought—serious commitments in the form of vast deliveries of arms, as well as the presence of Soviet shipping in the harbor. Had Kissinger and Nixon appreciated this apathy on the part of the Soviets, they might have been tempted to make more use of this bombing weapon against North Vietnam, which had proved to be the most effective lever in the U.S.-Hanoi peace talks, a great deal earlier. One can only speculate. Kissinger certainly favored it, in retrospect.

So what Kissinger aimed for in his negotiations with the Soviets was, first, peace via détente, and, second, a reduction in the towering menace of Soviet rocketry; what Brezhnev sought was abolition of the anti-ballistic missile (ABM) programs of the United States, and nonaggression treaties which could hamstring American relations with her key allies—in Europe as in the Middle East. In all these ambitions of Kissinger, the skies would be constantly overcast by the thunderous twin clouds of Vietnam and Watergate.

In the pursuit of détente, at home Kissinger cultivated an extraordinary friendship with the long-term Soviet ambassador in Washington, Anatoly Fyodorovich Dobrynin, aged fifty-three in 1973. Their copious telephone conversations, now released, sometimes read more like the gossipy chat of two old college roommates than representa-

---

* At the time of the conflicts on the Ussuri River in 1969 and China's explosion of two nuclear devices, there was talk in Moscow about Maoism being "a criminal racist theory," and "we'll kill those yellow sons of bitches" (Margaret MacMillan, *Nixon and Mao*, p. 136). There were serious fears in Washington that the Soviets might launch a preemptive nuclear strike. It all made conversations with Brezhnev that much more immediate.

tives of potentially hostile states. For example, on May 25, here are the two buddies discussing a subject that comes up very often during the backchannel conversations they held almost daily: Dobrynin notes that Kissinger was seen with an attractive young woman previously pictured in the *Playboy* calendar. Kissinger calls Dobrynin a "dirty old man." The following day, before leaving for New York, Ambassador Dobrynin does not forget to congratulate Kissinger on his birthday, offering to sing "Happy Birthday" for him. Kissinger prefers to ask a favor: to keep his "KGB guys from running loose" in his neighborhood because the evening before he had run into five agents just as he "brought a girl home." [7]

A protégé of the granite-visaged foreign minister Andrei Gromyko, but a very different personality, Dobrynin arrived in Washington (where he had served previously under Gromyko as ambassador) in January 1962—just in time to be thrown into the Cuban Missile Crisis. He would stay there, *en poste*, for an unprecedented twenty-four years. A tall Ukrainian with receding, slightly graying hair, Dobrynin was the first Soviet envoy to the United States born after the Russian Revolution; in the youthful climate of 1962 Washington, he fitted in well as a *liudi novykh granits*—or Soviet-style New Frontiersman. He came of fairly humble birth, son of a plumber and an "essentially unlettered" mother (as he would refer to her), and was the first member of his family to get to university. Trained as an engineer, he entered the aircraft industry in 1944, and was less than delighted when informed he had been chosen for the foreign service. Like Gromyko, who was originally an agronomist and had been drawn into diplomacy six years earlier, Dobrynin had no prior knowledge of foreign affairs or indeed foreign languages. Obsessive Soviet secrecy being what it was, diplomatic trainees were not cleared to read foreign "bourgeois" newspapers. Instead, he had to polish his English skills with such masters of prose as the Communist *Daily Worker*.

Nevertheless, in Washington he picked up the idiom with commendable speed, where he became a lion of the Georgetown social circuit, moving around with ease. There were those who were suspicious of him, fearing that he exploited his close and confidential links with the American leadership, not to say his Slavic charm, to bamboozle them about Soviet intentions. "His winning ways," observed Sir Nicholas Henderson, who knew him well from the 1980s when he was British ambassador in Washington, "were undeniable." *⁸ The somewhat gauche Alexander Haig noted, with perhaps a touch of envy, how "admired by Washington hostesses" he was; but there was no evidence that in Georgetown (where, as noted earlier, no such thing as a secret exists), he risked more than chat about sex—as he would with his good friend Henry.⁹ Because of the prevailing anti-Semitic tone of the Brezhnev era (which he did little to challenge), Dobrynin was never quite welcome among the *Washington Post* set of Katherine Graham, its publisher. He played chess, however, with Brzezinski, who found him "an amiable bear," yet one "who could all of a sudden turn quite nasty";¹⁰ and this glint of steel was noted by others.

As Kissinger remarked once, Dobrynin certainly "knew how to talk to Americans in a way brilliantly attuned to their preconceptions. He was especially skilled at evoking the inexhaustible American sense of guilt, by persistently but pleasantly hammering home the impression that every deadlock was our fault. . . . I never forgot that Dobrynin was a member of the Central Committee of the Soviet Communist Party; I never indulged in the conceit that his easy manner reflected any predisposition toward me or toward the West. I had no doubt that if the interests of his country required it he could be as ruthless or duplicitous as any other Communist leader. But I considered his unquestioning support of the Soviet line an asset, not a liability: it enabled us to measure the policies of his masters with precision. Occasionally he would give me his personal analysis of American politics; without exception it was acute and even wise. . . . This gave us some confidence that the Kremlin would have at its disposal a sophisticated assessment of conditions here. An accurate understanding could not guarantee that Moscow would choose our preferred response, but it reduced the prospects of gross miscalculation. . . . Dobrynin was free of the tendency toward petty chiseling by which the

---

* A decade later, Ronald Reagan seems to have been equally charmed by Dobrynin. "Dobrynin was doubtless a Communist," said Reagan, according to Sir Nicholas Henderson, "but I couldn't help liking him as a human being." On his side, Dobrynin conceded that he had been more intrigued by Reagan than by any of the five other presidents he knew.

run-of-the-mill Soviet diplomat demonstrates his vigilance to his supe-riors: he understood that a reputation for reliability is an important asset in foreign policy."[11]

In Dobrynin's own words, he "accepted the Soviet system with its flaws and successes."[12]

It was to be a remarkable relationship, unlike anything similar known under other U.S. and Soviet administrations during the Cold War. It seems fair to judge, on the results that will be seen at the time of the DEFCON 3 crisis in October, that it did help "reduce the prospects of gross miscalculation," as Kissinger asserted. Equally, by and large, Kissinger and Dobrynin were astonishingly open with each other, with Kissinger giving the Russian classified material that another U.S. statesman would have jibbed at; and, as Kissinger noted, undoubt-edly Dobrynin's analysis of Washington politics—which he would, of course, be passing on to his masters in the Kremlin—was "acute and even wise." Without doubt, he was—as the popular saying went—superbly in the loop in the American capital; but how much was he kept equally in the loop with candor on what was going on in the councils of the Politburo? Moscow was never Washington. In fact, how far was Kissinger really able "to measure the policies of his mas-ters with precision" via the back channel of Ambassador Dobrynin? Crucial episodes like the Yom Kippur War may give one cause to doubt. In his own memoirs Dobrynin reveals that, during that first test of the Cuban Missile Crisis, he felt he had been shockingly deceived by his own government, by Khrushchev. He regarded it as a "fatal miscal-culation" to assume that installation of the deadly sites could have been completed without the United States discovering them.[13]

Other subsequent "gross miscalculations" on the part of Moscow, which were castigated by Dobrynin, included the invasion of Afghanistan and the planned deployment of the SS-2 missiles threat-ening Europe in the 1980s. It was a miscalculation which would end in shifting the nuclear balance decisively in favor of the United States. (Then, as miscalculations go, few—in Dobrynin's judgment—were crasser than the mildness of the Western response, under the presi-dency of Lyndon Johnson, to the invasion of Czechoslovakia in 1968. It encouraged Moscow, a decade later, to move into Afghanistan: a par-allel with Munich thirty years earlier, when British and French pusillanimity over the threat to Czechoslovakia emboldened Hitler to make war on Poland in 1939. Equally, Dobrynin claims to have been kept uninformed by Moscow over the 1968 invasion of Czechoslovakia.)

There was always the conundrum as to whether Dobrynin really did have as much influence in Moscow as he pretended, and as Kissinger believed, and, domiciled for so long in Washington, how well informed he was on realities in Moscow. He was, for instance in his memoirs (written in 1995), unable to provide a convincing explanation as to why the formidable empire proved to have feet of clay, crumbling so suddenly, and so completely. James Billington, librarian of Congress and a Russia expert, reckoned that Dobrynin "took D.C., fooled it, manipulated everybody."[14] Here Billington was largely supported by another Russia expert, Ambassador Arthur Hartman, assistant secretary of state for European affairs under Nixon (and Reagan's ambassador to the USSR for over five years): "Everybody in D.C. opened their hearts to Dobrynin, but it was hogwash what he wrote about Russian policy; he was continually being proved wrong."[15]

In total contrast, however, on the issue of the reliability of the Soviet ambassador was one of Kissinger's close associates on the missile negotiations, Jan Lodal: "Dobrynin never lied, never exaggerated. If he didn't want to say anything, he would just keep quiet. That was why Henry venerated him."[16]

Mao's warning in 1973, "Take care, the Polar Bear is going to punish you,"[17] would not have fallen on deaf ears with Kissinger. It was essential to expedite dealings with Moscow—certainly before the KGB could pick up just how indiscreet Kissinger had been in Beijing, in passing to his Chinese hosts classified material on Soviet military capabilities, such as rocketry—of which even U.S. intelligence was unaware (and he would continue to do so). Nevertheless, rising to the bait, within a week of his visit to Beijing, Kissinger notes "the Kremlin reversed itself and invited Nixon to Moscow."[18] That was for May 1972. The 1973 summit between Nixon and Brezhnev, in return for the eventful Nixon visit to Moscow the previous year, was to take place in June. That May, Kissinger set off to Russia to lay the groundwork.

Once again, Secretary of State Rogers was kept out of the loop rather gracelessly. In preparation for the 1972 summit, the State Department had prepared a voluminous report. By this time, as per

Kissinger's own admission, "relations had so deteriorated" that there was no joint input. Well might one ask, where was the adversary: in Moscow—or Washington? Kissinger saw to it "that the President's report always gave some credit to Secretary Rogers," but he adds with frankness, "though of course stressing the central role of the President and by implication my own." [19] In March, Rogers sent a memo to the president saying that he planned to "take personal charge" of summit planning. Three days later Nixon "dropped in" on a meeting between Kissinger and Dobrynin, to give the order that Kissinger was to be in charge. It could hardly have been more humiliating for Rogers. Once again, one is left wondering why he didn't chuck his resignation in the president's face—with some force. So Kissinger and his team would slip in and out of Moscow, without even the American ambassador knowing they were there. It was perhaps not surprising that even Kissinger's admirers, and staff, took to calling him "the Lone Ranger." [20]

Arriving in Moscow on May 4, 1973, Kissinger was whirled by car, at a hundred miles per hour (reflecting his host's passion for powerful cars), from the airport to Zavidovo, the Politburo's hunting preserve, some ninety miles away. It was the Soviet equivalent of Camp David, and considered a great honor for Kissinger to be invited there. He was, they told him, the only foreigner, apart from Tito and President Urho Kekkonen of Finland, to be so privileged. (At the summit the previous year, Nixon had only been taken as far as Brezhnev's dacha on the Moscow River just outside the city; the KGB had teased the president's Secret Servicemen by making it as difficult as possible to keep up with the mad speed of the Russian cavalcade.) Kissinger's own account of the stay is more than faintly hilarious. There is always an element of farce, and of the ridiculous, about high-level summits, which often seem more designed to gratify the media than for the serious matters under discussion. Perhaps Churchill started the ball rolling, forcing grandees like Tito to watch endless movies in the evenings. Macmillan used to dread visits to Ike at Camp David, where evening hours would be whiled away watching "more thundering hooves," as the president treated his guests to yet another Western; on one particularly crucial meeting, at the time of the Suez Crisis, little was discussed save Ike's prowess at being able to hit a golf ball clean out of the White House grounds. A baffled Khrushchev was distracted by being taken to a

Hollywood shooting of a can-can performance. We have already seen Richard Nixon reduced to an anodyne babble by tourist fatigue in China; at home he would drive his entourage, and guests, to despair with endless replays of George C. Scott's *Patton* at critical times—the beleaguered president clearly saw himself in the central role. One is reminded sometimes of the famous historic "summit" between the three almighty triumvirs on Pompey's galley, as depicted by Shakespeare in *Antony and Cleopatra* where Lepidus, "a third of the world," is carried off drunk. The apparent vapidity of summitry was carried on into the Bush and "Yo, Blair" era: the twin microphones, Blair fiddling endlessly with the jacket button he could never do up, Bush's backslapping small-town Texan camaraderie, the simian look-alike stances—all done mainly for the public image.

So it was with Brezhnev. His particular obsession lay with powerful, elitist cars; in advance of summits, his ambassadors would let it be known what model he currently coveted. At Nixon's visit the previous year he had wheedled out of the Americans a $10,000 Cadillac limousine (one is reminded of native chieftains being bought off with gifts of beads). In the Cadillac, with the host himself at the wheel, Kissinger was driven at hair-raising speed down narrow country lanes to Zavidovo. Brezhnev's favorite form of entertainment at Zavidovo was a wild boar shoot. There at an "over-sized Swiss chalet," built by the East Germans, Kissinger was clad in military-style hunting attire, complete with high Russian boots. Disliking all forms of blood sports, he told his host that he would come along purely in "my capacity as an adviser." After a lot of "heavy joshing" (at the expense of his underlings, and often—in the Russian way—larded with unpleasantly anti-Semitic undertones*), from the blind Brezhnev dispatched a gigantic (and handpicked) boar that had come to eat the carefully prepared lure.[21]

While waiting for another in the gloaming (he missed the next two shots), Brezhnev expatiated to Kissinger on the evils of the Chinese: they were treacherous and arrogant—in fact, "cannibals." Now they

---

* Typical of Brezhnev's stock of jokes produced at Zavidovo, which Kissinger relayed to Nixon: "Two Jews meet: one asks, 'Abraham, did you hear that Izak's dacha burned down?' Abraham says, 'So what, it is none of my business.' 'It is really none of my business either,' the first one says, 'but it is pleasant nonetheless.'" (Memorandum to President, 5/11/75, Kissinger archives).

were building up a nuclear arsenal; the Soviets could not accept this—
"something would have to be done." Kissinger thought he was "clearly
fishing for some hint of American acquiescence in a Soviet preemptive
attack. I gave no encouragement," and dismissed it as macho hunting
talk. But the next day Ambassador Dobrynin said Brezhnev had
"meant every word of it." Kissinger warned that the United States
would "not be indifferent to an attack on China. Then, abruptly,
Brezhnev switched from menace to sentimentality. Recalling the early
story of his life, in World War II, he suddenly became an old, tired and
bumbling man, saying that 'his theme now was peace.' "

Kissinger was to leave Zavidovo wondering which of these two
very Russian personalities was the real Brezhnev, jointly with Nixon
the most powerful person on earth. Regardless of the slaughter of the
boars, he came away regarding the episode as "a single, brief glimpse
of humanity that was not repeated while I was in office." [22]

Given the Russian's penchant for the Dostoyevskian *Doppel-
gänger*, perhaps the two faces of Brezhnev were but two aspects of the
same old bear: the shaggy eyebrows, the coarse features that matched
his rough conversation, but the very Russian sentimentality that lurked
below. In return, according to Ambassador Hartman, Brezhnev quite
liked Kissinger: "Henry had a real gift for the theater; and Brezhnev
loved it." [23]

Don Kendall, a close personal friend of Nixon's, who—as chairman
of Pepsi-Cola—had been one of the first U.S. businessmen to "open
up" Russia commercially, under Khrushchev in the 1950s, had rather a
different view of the Bear. He would tell Kendall outrageous anti-
Semitic jokes; then—nudge, nudge—"Don't tell Henry!" Kendall's
overall view of Brezhnev was that "if he had been born in the U.S., he
would have been head of the Barnum & Bailey Circus!" [24] Kissinger,
naturally given to pessimism, and awed with alarm at the Soviets' nuclear capability, tended to view the scene through darker-tinted glasses.
Traveling to Russia with Nixon the previous year, Pete Peterson, then
secretary of commerce, saw it through rather different lenses. Visiting
Brezhnev's famous dacha just outside Moscow (admittedly, some
thirty-plus years later) Peterson contrasted unfavorably "the multimil-
lion-dollar swimming pool with every kind of automation—and yet
just outside abandoned rusting farm equipment which they couldn't

repair — hence their contemporary need to buy grain from us." To him it signified "the total failure of the Soviet collective farm system, whereby dealers in tractors and spare parts were not integrated." He found that "the only category in which the Soviets were *reasonably* competitive was in heavy power equipment. But it was a retarded economy, desperately needing help. . . . I saw the Soviet economy, much weaker than we thought, so I said to Henry, 'We have an irrational policy, why should we be selling to the Soviets to help them? They need us far more than we need them. . . . We should resolve the existing political and defense problems before creating new ones.' "

Peterson, who was chairman of the Council on Foreign Relations when I interviewed him, claimed, "Yes, I did see what Reagan saw: the weakness of the Soviet economy — though I do think that Reagan's claims of his defense policy bringing down the Soviets were overrated." Nevertheless, he was "more and more astonished, looking backward, only that we were so frightened. . . . I cannot stress how sick their economy was." Of the 1972 talks, he was surprised that "Henry couldn't believe that Brezhnev would want to spend a whole day talking about sales of natural gas — I told Henry that it was very important for your whole position of détente." [25]

Talking to the author about the same time, Kissinger explained how he, too, had "differed with my conservative friends — I didn't think the Russians were as strong as they did . . . in my view, the USSR was weaker than it looked, and not likely to engage us in a sustained confrontation — but they might have made a *mistake*. The neocons believed the USSR was designing WMDs to destroy us . . . every time I went to the USSR the machinery struck me as so cumbersome that they couldn't possibly launch this kind of surprise attack, first strike that would succeed. The CIA believed as I did; the military intelligence was, as always, pessimistic." [26]

But could Kissinger do business with Brezhnev, when it came down to the nitty-gritty? At the first summit in 1972, he had found himself comparing the Soviet general secretary unfavorably with the supple and sophisticated Zhou, in whose company he had so recently been. On arrival at Zavidovo in 1973, like some nouveau riche Texan, Brezhnev had instantly asked Kissinger how much such an establishment would cost in the United States. Kissinger came up with a guesstimate of $400,000; "Brezhnev's face fell." Diplomatically, Kissinger's assistant Hal Sonnenfeldt suggested $2 million. Brezhnev, "vastly reassured, beamed." In Beijing, the sophisticated Chinese leaders had left their Western guests in no doubt about their cultural superiority. Kissinger observed, not without sympathy, how "China had absorbed conquerors and had proved its inward strength by imposing its social and intellectual style on them. Its leaders were aloof, self-assured, composed. Brezhnev represented a nation that had survived not by civilizing its conquerors but by outlasting them . . . with a culture that had destroyed its traditions without yet entirely replacing them. . . . He [Brezhnev] sought to obscure his lack of assurance by boisterousness, and his sense of latent insecurity by occasional bullying." Symptomatic, he thought (in 1972), was the fact that "One eats Chinese food gracefully with chopsticks; one could eat most Russian food with one's hands . . . one could barely face the prospect of the next round."[27]

Already in 1972, he had found the Bear on the verge of waning physical power. He wasted precious time at the complex 1972 arms talks fiddling with a toy cannon, traditionally deployed at meetings of the Politburo—doubtless to awaken his elderly subordinates. But the cannon refused to fire, distracting the Soviet leader from the "profundities" of his guest. Finally, it went off with a roar, and Brezhnev "strutted round the room like a prizefighter who has knocked out his opponent." In Brezhnev, Kissinger saw then a quintessential Russian "mixture of crudeness and warmth; at the same time brutal and engaging, cunning and disarming. While he boasted of Soviet strength, one had the sense that he was not really all that sure of it." He noted real concern about the significance of the Nixon trip to China, Brezhnev feeling that the president's remarks there had "downgraded the Soviet Union." To the author, Kissinger reflected that, in retrospect, "I saw him as something of a forerunner of Gorbachev. . . . He had I think a dim view that Russia needed peace. This came out in his 1973 visit to Washington—he was so anxious to be treated as an equal."[28] In contrast, Nixon—perhaps not surprisingly—quite warmed to the unattractive side of Brezhnev: the elements of the coarse talking, the excellent raconteur, as well as the brutal politician. The anti-Semitism of his humor (at Kissinger's expense) was unlikely to put Nixon off—

on the contrary! Compared to his predecessor, Khrushchev, in Brezhnev, Nixon found no inferiority complex, no need to play the part of the uncouth peasant.[29]

There was no doubting, however, that these fragile Soviet sensibilities had been rudely, and profoundly, shaken by the Nixon démarche to China. The distinguished journalist Joseph Kraft recorded attending Soviet Armed Forces Day in 1972, and noted: "A sadder party there never was."

Kissinger, however, was constantly having to pander to the things that worried Brezhnev. Would he, for instance, be courteously received in America in June 1973? Even the apparent technical lead of the Soviets could not quite bridge that gap. It made for difficult negotiations. At Zavidovo, there was one other problem too: the ever-present lurking menace of the KGB, so much an endemic manifestation of Russia's perennial inferiority complex. The Americans had brought with them an anti-bugging device, a "babbler," but Kissinger couldn't stand the noise of cocktail party chat it made, and instead finally identified "one absolutely secure" place for their secret conversations. It was the balcony outside Brezhnev's own study![30]

One needs go back, briefly, to the exchanges at the 1972 summit in Moscow. It made history in being the first time that a U.S. president visited Russia—and it was Nixon the renowned anti-Communist. His welcome was modest; yet, on the whole, it seems to have proved more of a success for Nixon—then at the peak of his powers, and authority—than for Kissinger. It was all notably about SALT, the Strategic Arms Limitation Talks, an immensely complex, and high-tech issue, currently being negotiated between the two sides in Helsinki—where seven rounds, since Nixon had taken over in 1969, had already lasted thirty months. In charge of the U.S. team was a gentlemanly and well-briefed Georgetown lawyer, Gerard Smith. The main issues were (1) the positioning of ABM sites,* (2) the number of SLBMs† allow-

---

* Still a hot issue in 2007.

† Submarine-launched ballistic missiles, such as Polaris and Trident.

able, and (3) what increases in the size of ICBMs* and their silos should be permitted. The limitation of these ghastly weapons of mass destruction was fundamental to the philosophy of both Nixon and Kissinger, and Kissinger had put in much hard work in Washington through the Dobrynin back channel. (Even the Kremlin's top U.S. expert at the time. Georgi Arbatov, praised this back channel, in that it "made it easier for Kissinger to manipulate events by excluding the pressures of Congress and public opinion."†[31]) But, in playing the Lone Ranger in the Moscow negotiations, on technical matters in which even his encyclopedic knowledge was not intrinsic, he seems to have become unseated on item number three.

It all rotated around a diabolical doomsday weapon called a MIRV, the acronym for a multiple independently targetable reentry vehicle — what Gerard Smith rated as "the most significant development since the ballistic missile."[32] (In 1969 he had urged Nixon to call a halt to testing before it was "too late," and Kissinger subsequently came to agree.[33]) In layman's language the MIRV meant a rocket which contained three or more nuclear missiles, each of which could hit a separate target — say, Washington, Philadelphia, and New York, or, concentrated, plaster American ICBMs in their subterranean concrete silos. It was, simply, a force-multiplier. In the words of John Newhouse, a considerable and respected expert on the subject, "almost no one in Congress knew what a MIRV was."[34] But the Pentagon did, and were developing their own, but deeply feared it in Soviet hands. To begin with it was very hard to target the separate warheads of a MIRV, which could wipe out the advantage of the U.S. anti-missile defenses, still on the "Star Wars" list. Because of superior technology, the Americans could devise MIRVs small enough to fit into their existing vehicles. So far, despite monumental strides made since the Cuban Missile Crisis, the Soviets could not. But they were developing a monster rocket, the SS-9, with a huge throw weight (a favorite term in the technicians' jargon), which might

---

* Intercontinental ballistic missiles.

† Even Kissinger's not uncritical biographer, Walter Isaacson, tended to agree: "For all of its drawbacks, the back-channel method was producing some notable successes. The Berlin and SALT agreements were not perfect, but they were accomplishments that the State Department had not been able to achieve" (*Kissinger,* p. 327).

be able to carry even more MIRV warheads than the Americans'. So one of the deadly SS-9s could automatically put the United States at an estimated disadvantage of six to ten. To attempt to match it would necessitate a huge ratcheting up in the arms race—and U.S. defense budgets; all of which Kissinger and Nixon were pledged to combat.

What both men wanted from SALT was a stop to the SS-9 program—and its even bigger successors, then being projected. Brezhnev, on the other hand, had the abolition of the American ABM project as his top priority, arguing that such a successful defensive weapon would present the United States with a first-strike capacity. To the man in the street it all sounds like science fiction, but to the negotiators it was deadly—in every sense—earnest, and the way "was strewn with pitfalls," in the words of Nixon[35]. But he and Kissinger had gone to Moscow in 1972 at least as ardent to succeed as Brezhnev, and willing to compromise. It seems that this ardor to succeed, coupled with the Lone Ranger instinct, may have led Kissinger into committing a serious technological error. He was no ballistics expert, nor even particularly distinguished in mathematics, but was determined to lead the talks himself, not entrusting them to expert underlings. On the Soviet side, however, there was already Ambassador Dobrynin, who was a qualified aeronautical engineer; and then, without warning, Brezhnev wheeled in a formidable expert called L. V. Smirnov, a deputy premier in charge of all Soviet defense industries.

Not, presumably, one of the vodka clan, Smirnov sounds like a creation of Ian Fleming. Kissinger describes him as "bullet-headed, heavyset, and brilliant; he made it clear that only superior orders could have landed him now in a position that so severely taxed his limited resources of self-control." Kissinger's "lighthearted banter" drove Smirnov—literally—ballistic. He did not think it at all appropriate to the solemnity of the matters under discussion. When Kissinger began revealing U.S. knowledge of Soviet missile details, "Smirnov's irritation turned to frenzy," and the ice-cool Gromyko had to take him out of the room and calm him down. Finally, Kissinger claims, he won over L.V., and they "got along famously. He turned out to be one of the ablest and most intelligent Soviet leaders with whom I dealt." He "knew everything about weapons"—and came to exhibit "a wicked sense of humor."[36] We have only Kissinger's word for this latter. But it may have been under Smirnov's harassment, over meetings that went on to a numbing 4:00 A.M., that the Lone Ranger became unseated. Concerning the vital statistics of the Soviet behemoth rockets, according to Raymond Garthoff, an expert on Gerard Smith's SALT team, Kissinger fell into the trap of confusing diameter with volume. Thus, if the limitations proposed permitted the Soviets to increase the diameter of the new generation of ICBMs, and the concrete silos housing them, by only 15 percent, through simply increasing the length they could enlarge its *volume* by a massive 30 percent; large enough to contain any number of even the Soviets' primitive but deadly MIRVs.[37] Garthoff's dismay was reinforced by John Newhouse: "Nixon and Kissinger had . . . all but ignored the opportunity to kill MIRV."[38] Even Jan Lodal, who was the number-cruncher among Kissinger's assistants, and remained a friend and admirer, thought that he had made a fundamental "gaffe." The Pentagon was instantly appalled when signaled the news. It would take much rejigging and finessing before the Lone Ranger's gaffe was corrected, and it threatened seriously to impede the vital process of SALT, while leaving a legacy that would run on into the Reagan years.

Kissinger, explaining himself, says, "With respect to silo dimensions, I was determined to transform our delegation's non-binding unilateral statement into a binding mutual definition."[39]

Kissinger took the news of a draft agreement to Nixon, plus the Pentagon's "wobbling" reaction, and angry noises from the right in Washington. He found the president stretched out, prone, having a massage. Lying there naked, in the adversary's capital, Nixon had taken what Kissinger rated as "a heroic position from a decidedly unheroic posture."[40] He ordered Kissinger to accept what the Soviets were offering: "He would not be swayed by politics at home; and he would not be pushed by the Soviets beyond what I had suggested." "The hell with the political consequences," Nixon quotes himself as saying."[41] Kissinger deemed it "one of the more courageous decisions of his Presidency."[42] After several more all-night wrangles, on May 26, 1972, the ABM Treaty was signed in Moscow. The news was announced by Kissinger at a press conference held in as bizarre circumstances as had surrounded much of the 1972 summit. It was at 1:00 A.M., in Moscow's Starry Sky nightclub. Kissinger spoke from the grandstand. Marvin

Kalb described the scene as looking "like the Roseland Ballroom, vintage 1935, Kissinger stood on the dance floor, the Frank Sinatra of diplomacy, occasionally clutching his only prop, a standing microphone."[43] It was his forty-ninth birthday. Nixon and Kissinger returned heroes; the liberal press, such as the *New York Times* and *Washington Post*, led the applause. The *Chicago Sun-Times* declared "Henry Alfred Kissinger has ceased to be a phenomenon. He has become a legend, and the word is not lightly used."[44] What could have been a nicer birthday present! (And it would give a great boost to an unpopular president, to help achieve that landslide in the November elections.) However, infuriated by Kissinger's Lone Ranger technique were powerful figures on the right such as Paul Nitze, Admirals Elmo Zumwalt and Thomas Moorer (then chairman of the Joint Chiefs of Staff), and Senators Henry "Scoop" Jackson and Barry Goldwater—as well as the much tried leader of the SALT team, Gerard Smith (who had been quite shabbily treated, and sidelined, on flying to Moscow to join the conference just as it was ending, late in the day).

Nevertheless, the overall results were rated subsequently by John Newhouse (far from being a Kissinger fan) as "the backbone of today's arms control."[45] Kissinger's equally critical biographer, Walter Isaacson, thought that, despite the MIRV setback, "the development of a working relationship with Moscow was an achievement of enormous historic magnitude, made even more so by the coup of accomplishing it at the same moment as a new tie was forged with Beijing."[46] Nixon's biographer, Stephen Ambrose, assessed that "with the ABM Treaty specifically, and détente generally, Nixon had done what none of his predecessors had been able to do. The Moscow summit was a great achievement."[47] Could it have all happened without the Lone Ranger?

At the same time, the news from Vietnam could hardly have looked more promising. Then, it was three weeks after Nixon's and Kissinger's triumphal return from Moscow in 1972, a little noted event took place in Washington: unknown burglars broke into the Democrat offices in the Watergate building.

Between the Moscow summit of 1972 and Zavidovo in May 1973, implementation of the SALT I agreements lagged. In Washington, the

Pentagon and the Senate got at them; in Moscow, it was the nationalist, hawkish marshals, reinforced by the KGB.[48] Perhaps most critical
of all, the dynamo that had pushed them through, Richard Nixon, had
begun to lose his drive. Under the domestic pressures that were crowd-
ing in on him, he was—so Kissinger frequently noted—more and more
distracted from foreign affairs. Thus, in Zavidovo in May 1973,
Kissinger would find himself with a bargaining hand that had become
significantly weakened. As we now know from material recently
emerging from the former Soviet Union, Brezhnev was determined not
to take advantage of Watergate; but it was the weakness from within
that was so disabling to Kissinger. The talks at Zavidovo were mainly
a continuation of the Moscow talks of the previous year (which is why
these were so relevant to events in 1973), and—more immediately—a
preparation for the Washington Summit in June. Perhaps the salient
feature was the reaffirmation of the principle of détente, a most elusive
concept, but which would always remain top of Kissinger's agenda. We
risk jumping ahead, but on October 8, 1973, shortly after he had been
confirmed as secretary of state, in a speech in Washington* Kissinger
expounded precisely what détente meant to him:

- We will oppose the attempt by any country to achieve a
  position of predominance either globally or regionally.
- We will resist any attempt to exploit a policy of détente to
  weaken our alliances.
- We will react if relaxation of tensions is used as a cover to
  exacerbate conflicts in international trouble spots.[49]

There are other key passages to be found in Kissinger's memoir
Years of Upheaval. Détente, he believed—explaining in part the apparent contradiction in U.S. Middle East policy—"did not prevent resistance to Soviet expansion; on the contrary, it fostered the only possible psychological framework for such resistance."[50] His overriding
philosophical belief was that "America must commit itself to a moral
opposition to Communism, not just geopolitical opposition to Soviet

---

* To the Pacem in Terris Conference.

encroachment, or its policy will be based on quicksand. But while I sympathize with this point of view, a statesman must relate general theorems to concrete circumstances."[51] At the same time, he felt that, dictated to by military planners, "Leaders committed the cardinal sin of statecraft. They lost control over events."[52] And, in a significant prediction (the writing was dated a decade before the fall of the Berlin Wall): "The major, *long term question is whether the Soviets can hold their own bloc together while waiting for the West to succumb to a long period of relaxation* [Kissinger's italics] and to the temptations of economic competition. . . . If the West saw to containment, I was convinced that it would win its historical bet. The Soviet Union's economic system was glaringly weak."[53] In 1973, Kissinger noted, the Soviets had a growth rate of only 1.5 percent, "about equal to population growth" (though it may seem that, as of that date, the Soviet predicament was seen more clearly by other members of the Nixon administration, such as Pete Peterson and James Schlesinger).

Kissinger was a strong believer in the device of linkage, and leverage, in détente with the Soviets. Thereby U.S. compromise on one front—on missiles for instance—should be linked to concessions on other fronts; say, over Vietnam, or the Middle East, or trade. Both Nixon and Kissinger placed great hope in using their opening to China, as well as détente with Moscow, to put pressure on North Vietnam to honor its commitments to the peace agreement. It was the carrot accompanying the stick. Though the nuance may be overstrong, in the opinion of John Newhouse, the aim was "less at promoting an arms control agreement than in securing an exit from the war."[54] As far as Vietnam was concerned, however, the success with either of the Communist behemoths was sorely limited—the line being from Moscow and Beijing: "We won't interfere with Vietnam's affairs"; though the flow of Soviet arms was reduced. As far as trade was concerned, in 1969, following the Soviet invasion of Czechoslovakia, Nixon had punished the USSR by imposing restrictions on commerce. The liberal press had revolted, and Nixon relented. Then, in 1972, "before anyone knew what was happening," admitted Kissinger[55], the Soviets—their incompetent agronomy resulting in a nation desperately short of grain—had bought up nearly *one billion dollars'* worth of grain, almost the whole of the U.S. surplus, on bargain-basement terms. Dubbed in the United States "the Great Grain Robbery," it was a shrewd Soviet coup. Early in 1973, Washington learned of another potential shortfall in the Soviet harvest. To help them out—the carrot to SALT—Nixon submitted to Congress an agreement to extend the Most Favored Nation (MFN) agreement.

It provoked an unexpected row, from an unexpected quarter, which—claimed Kissinger—"blighted U.S.-Soviet relations ever since."

Senator Henry "Scoop"* Jackson, representing Washington state since 1941 until his death in 1983, belonged to the right wing of the Democratic Party. A dedicated Cold Warrior, anti-Communist hardliner, and a contender for the presidential election of 1972, he had formerly been an ally of Kissinger's. But he had fallen out over the ABM Treaty. He strongly believed in the principle of meeting evil with force; he once declared memorably "I'm not a hawk or a dove. I just don't want my country to be a pigeon." Boeing, manufacturer of the B-52 bomber, was the main industry in his state, and he fought hard to have the ABM manufactured there too. All these factors had brought him into collision with Kissinger in 1972. According to John Newhouse, Scoop's aversion to his works was becoming phobic.

Then, urged on by his vociferous and ambitious thirty-two-year-old assistant, Richard Perle, Jackson had also become the leading element in the human rights cause of obtaining exit permits for the thousands of oppressed Jews penned in by the Soviet Union. Possibly as a response to the Kissinger carrot, the anti-Semitic Brezhnev[56] permitted 35,000 Jews to emigrate in 1973, compared with only four hundred in 1968. But Jackson and his allies wanted more. In August 1972, however, the Presidium of the Supreme Soviet cruelly imposed a substantial exit tax on emigrants. By the end of the next year, it had begun to slow the exodus to a trickle again; Kissinger found the ruling "nearly inexplicable" in light of what détente had seemed to achieve—except possibly as "a panicky reaction to Sadat's expulsion of Soviet troops from Egypt."[57] But that was how the Polar Bear could behave.

Said Kissinger, the "genie was out of the bottle." Two months later

---

* The nickname, apparently, was given him by his sister after a popular comic strip character.

Jackson sponsored a bill in Congress that would preclude granting MFN concessions to any Communist country that restricted emigration. It was, Kissinger considered, quite counterproductive insofar as it actually resulted in substantially reducing Jewish emigration. By September 1973, the liberal press was in on the act, with the *New York Times* leading the pack, professing to see—in Kissinger's words—"no difference between Watergate and the Soviet police-state repression of dissidents." He quoted: "The world now sees a de facto Nixon-Brezhnev alliance against dissent in each other's country."[58] The analogy was absurd, but Watergate, of course, was at the nub of the matter, as Kissinger saw it—and as will be examined in the next chapter. The furor nearly caused Brezhnev to cancel his June trip to the United States; pointedly he did not bring his wife. Eventually he removed the offensive emigration tax. But the damage to détente, at least its spirit, had been done. For "the growing enfeeblement of the President had changed all previous assumptions . . . By then [April 18, 1973], Nixon was badly wounded."[59] But Jackson and his allies now wanted more: Soviet easing of emigration laws on *all* nationalities—not just for Jews. This was an interference in their internal affairs the Soviets could never possibly accept. At his speech of October 8, 1973, Kissinger questioned, "almost despairingly," but farsightedly: "How hard can we press without provoking the Soviet leadership into returning to practices in its foreign policy that increase international tensions?"[60]

The redoubtable Scoop was not the only source of trouble Kissinger encountered in Washington. The Pentagon thought he was giving too much away on the missile accords (though at the same time they persisted in reducing the United States' conventional forces). The snubbed State Department went to the other extreme and called for a moratorium on all MIRV testing. The SALT negotiations in Geneva had now stalled, in effect stalemated as Kissinger had reached Zavidovo in May 1973. And, against the spirit—if not the actual provisions—of the 1972 accords, the Soviets had already carried out testing on the new, potent SS-17. As if all this wasn't enough, Kissinger was now presented with heavy, if not menacing, pressure from Brezhnev to sign up on his Agreement on the Prevention of Nuclear War, a surprise proposition with which the Bear had suddenly confronted him in Moscow the previous year, sugarcoating it as "a peaceful bomb." It was highly intricate, and subtle, but within it Kissinger at once spotted "a dangerous, Soviet maneuver to lure us into renouncing the use of nuclear weapons, on which the free world's defense after all depended." Kissinger saw through it as a "colossal piece of effrontery," for "Given the Soviet superiority in conventional weapons, such a move would demoralize our allies and deeply disquiet China, which would see it as a sign of the much dreaded U.S.-Soviet collusion. . . . It was strong stuff. We were being asked to dismantle the military strategy of NATO and at the same time to proclaim a virtual U.S.-Soviet military alliance designed to isolate or impose our will on China or any other country with nuclear aspirations."[61]

Moreover, "In a Middle East war, nuclear weapons could not be used by either side." The agreement was full of insidious dangers for the West. On the other hand, Kissinger did not want to reject it out of hand, because so much else was at stake—not least Brezhnev's pending American visit. Gromyko was warning that the visit could be conditional on progress with Brezhnev's treaty. So Kissinger indulged in evasion, and stalling—at least until peace in Vietnam seemed to have been assured.

To help the United States out, Kissinger had sought the assistance of an imposing, adroit, and experienced British ally—Sir Thomas Brimelow*. Cherubic, and unflappable, but with a piercing intelligence, "Tom" was *the* Foreign Office expert on the Soviets, and on Russian behavior. He was also one of the world's top experts on drafting convoluted documents, and a consummate master in the art of stalling—which course he had proposed to Kissinger in the run-up to Zavidovo, knowing full well that the aging Brezhnev was not strong on patience.† He and Brimelow agreed that the objective should be "to give them enough of the form without any substance."[62] Brimelow produced a document for Zavidovo which, Kissinger generously admitted, "owed, in fact, more to British than to American expertise." Brimelow's role, was, he stressed, "an example of the Anglo-American

---

* Later Lord Brimelow, permanent undersecretary at the Foreign and Commonwealth Office.

† The author had gained some insight into Tom Brimelow, and his technique, in the course of writing *Macmillan*.

'special relationship' at its best, even at a time when the incumbent Prime Minister [Heath] was not among its advocates. There was no other government which we would have dealt with so openly, exchanged ideas with so freely, or in effect permitted to participate in our own deliberations."[63]

It was a handsome tribute to an ally.

What emerged from Kissinger's briefcase at Zavidovo, then, was a counterproposal about "180 degrees removed from his [Brezhnev's] original design." When they turned to it, in the best tradition of summitry, there was a "pettifogging debate" as to "whether someone should read out the entire text or only the disputed portions and if so who." Hal Sonnenfeldt deployed his talents to endeavoring to read Brezhnev's briefing paper upside down ("methods by which he kept abreast of my activities in Washington," teased Kissinger); and there was much popping out onto the Bear's discreet and secure balcony for consultations by the American team. Finally, after considerable haggling, agreement was reached, "In short, in over a year of negotiation we had transformed the original Soviet proposal of an unconditional renunciation of the use of nuclear weapons against each other into a somewhat banal statement that our objective was peace, applying as well to allies and third countries and premised on restrained international conduct, especially the avoidance of the use or the threat of force." Theoretically, at least, it would make "it impossible for the Soviets to turn on either NATO or the Middle East without violating the agreement. And it even gave us a kind of legal framework for resisting a Soviet attack on China."

In retrospect, though Kissinger doubted, with a touch of cynicism, whether the agreement was "worth the effort,"[64] it satisfied the Bear—as well as saying something for Kissinger's ever-developing skill as a patient, persistent negotiator—which would be required more than ever in five months' time, October 1973. And the summit in Washington could now go ahead, in June.

On June 16, Brezhnev's Barnum & Bailey circus hit town. With him he brought the elements of comic theater Kissinger had witnessed in Zavidovo. In his most boisterous form, he immediately expressed a desire to drive a Lincoln Continental around Washington; a wish promptly thwarted by the White House Secret Service, appalled by the danger to all concerned.* Flown in to Camp David (he must have noted how rustic and thoroughly un-capitalist its cabins were compared with "million-dollar" Zavidovo—and there was no boar shoot laid on for him), he greeted Kissinger with a fulsome kiss on the lips ("the only time in our acquaintance," Kissinger rejoiced).[65] A heavy smoker (despite attempts at reform by Mrs. Brezhnev), he at once showed off "his new toy: a cigarette case that released its contents one at a time, at pre-set intervals." Kissinger noted how the Bear had all sorts of ingenious schemes for beating the system; one was simply "to carry two of these pocket safes around at the same time." Another eccentricity, which was to dog his kindly and thoughtful hosts with confusion throughout the trip, lay in the two watches he carried, one set on Moscow time, the other for Eastern Daylight Saving. Time became an obsession with him; yet he kept forgetting whether Moscow was ahead of or behind Washington, thereby causing repeated upheavals to his hosts' planning, as well as meal regimes. When flown out to San Clemente, California, where there was a three-hour difference from Washington, and twelve hours behind Moscow, he became hopelessly confused, grumbling all the time, and producing regular pandemonium among the American staffers.

There were further moments of threatened chaos at the highly formal (and no country can be more formal than the United States on such occasion) state arrival of the two leaders at the White House. After the Nixons' arrival, and solemn playing of "Hail to the Chief" by the Marine Band, Brezhnev arrived, to be greeted by a portentous fanfare. But, instead of returning the salutes of the official guard, he suddenly set off into the crowd, "and began to shake hands like an American politician on the campaign trail."[66] Nixon's chief of protocol was nearly beside himself, and again when Brezhnev—rescued from the

---

* In Zavidovo in May, when Brezhnev had expressed a desire to drive himself while in the United States, Kissinger had swiftly disillusioned him, with the warning that it was:
"One thing our Secret Service won't allow you to do."
Brezhnev: "I will take the flag off the car, put on dark glasses, so they can't see my eyebrows and drive like any American would."
Kissinger: "I have driven with you and I don't think you drive like an American!" (Memcon to Nixon, 5/11/73).

crowd—digressed lengthily with old comrades he recognized on the receiving line.* So the elaborately prepared schedule started off with a long delay. It was to be the same all through the trip. Then the rest of the Soviet delegation failed to turn up; and when they did Brezhnev launched into a forty-five-minute-long peroration on the history of Soviet-U.S. relations; among the homely platitudes trotted out: "We Russians have an adage—life is always the best teacher." [67]

Were these harassing tactics? Probably not. On the other hand, the Americans had plenty on their own side to worry them. For Kissinger, and Nixon, the visit could hardly have come at a less propitious moment domestically. Senator Ervin's Watergate Committee hearings, televised all day to every corner of the United States, were gathering steam; the very week of Brezhnev's visit, the key witness, John Dean, the former White House counsel—the man with the "smoking gun"—was due to testify. To add to Nixon's public humiliation, in front of the Ruler of All the Russias, only one week's suspension was allowed of the hearings—not a day more, so that they were actually resumed on the day of Brezhnev's departure: "giving the Soviet leaders," wrote Kissinger, "an unprecedented personal opportunity to watch the public indictment of the President with whom they had just been negotiating." [68]

The Soviet guests, so Kissinger noted, remained "baffled" by Watergate; at first they interpreted it as a right-wing plot aimed at détente. When he was in Zavidovo, they had said "they hoped it would soon be over; they were not eager to have the General Secretary of the Communist Party buffeted by the treacherous currents of American domestic controversy on a visit to Washington." We now know, however, from Russian sources published post-glasnost, that Brezhnev was determined not to take advantage of Nixon's humiliation; it was not just gentlemanly behavior on the part of the Bear—more like hardheaded pragmatism, though it was an opportunity his wilder predecessor,

---

* According to Victor Israelyan, a senior member of the Soviet Ministry of Foreign Affairs whom we shall meet again later, and who was in Brezhnev's entourage in Washington, there was a retinue of about four hundred Soviet diplomats and their families to greet Brezhnev that day; he was "astonished by the number of these 'advisers' and 'experts,' most of whom were absolutely useless during the trip." (*Inside the Kremlin During the Yom Kippur War*, p. 99).

Khrushchev, would almost certainly not have passed up. Kissinger himself noted that "It took them nearly two years before they moved aggressively to exploit our domestic upheavals by supporting proxy forces in Africa."

For the present talks, Kissinger saw that there was "no choice except to pretend that our authority was unimpaired. For that, we had to do business as usual. We could afford no appearance of hesitation." But "Nixon's mind was troubled and distracted." Kissinger found that Nixon lacked all the "sense of direction and self assurance of the previous year." It was, he reckoned, "the only time in my association with him that his usual sure touch deserted him in talking to a Communist leader."[69] Fortunately there were essentially no crucial negotiations that remained unfinished. Again the world should perhaps be grateful that it was the Bear and not the unpredictable Nikita Khrushchev who was then at the helm.

How much did the atmosphere in the United States infect Brezhnev? Possibly it manifested itself in the endless fussing with his two watches. The precision-minded Americans were driven to distraction by Brezhnev's private time zone. One meeting in the Oval Office dragged on till 3:30 P.M., with Brezhnev then demanding dinner and the "famished American delegation sprinting for the White House mess."[70] On another occasion, at Camp David, two hours after a session was due to begin, the Americans could spot the Russians chatting away on their veranda, in full sight of the president's quarters. Nixon, confessed Kissinger, "was more patient than I felt." On June 21, Brezhnev and entourage were flown off to California to the San Clemente White House in Air Force One. Kissinger couldn't help noting how much less lavishly appointed it was than Brezhnev's opposite number in the Communist USSR. With an engagingly American gesture, a stetson with a Western belt and toy revolver was placed in Brezhnev's cabin on the plane; "he eschewed the hat but found the belt irresistible," giving an imitation of his favorite film star, John Wayne, drawing the revolver over the Grand Canyon. On arrival, the West Coast time zone threw him, and his twin-watch system, into a major crisis, prompting him to go to bed the moment the party arrived—at 6 P.M.

Meanwhile, the two most powerful men in the world were settling the future of mankind between them.

The most meaningful talks took place on the very last day of the visit, June 23. At an unscheduled noon meeting, Brezhnev vented his passionate hatred of the Chinese: "His ire was not free of racial overtones. The Chinese were perfidious and they were sly in concealing their real aims." He condemned the Chinese Cultural Revolution as a sign of "moral degeneration, asking what kind of leaders would oppress their people while making propaganda all around the world." Remarked Kissinger snidely, it was "as if the Gulag Archipelago of concentration camps and extermination had never been heard of in his fatherland of socialism." Then Brezhnev came out with a statement full of menace: "that any military agreement between China and the United States would lead to war."[71]

At the very end, the talks turned to the Middle East. At Zavidovo the previous month, Brezhnev had already hinted at the threat of a new war there, remarking how difficult it was to hold back his Arab allies. Gromyko's final warning had been "the Middle East is a most urgent place." As noted in the previous chapter, Kissinger had dismissed the threat of war as bluff—on the received wisdom from U.S. intelligence that it was unlikely, because war would lead to an Arab defeat, "from which the Soviets would be unable to extricate their clients." That evening, Nixon gave a cocktail party around the San Clemente swimming pool, for Hollywood celebs prepared to make the two-hour journey; a family dinner was to follow. But, at 6 P.M., once again the two-time Bear pleaded fatigue and requested dinner forthwith. To hell with the celebs! At 7:15, after the appropriate toasts, Brezhnev embraced the president and excused himself. A grateful Nixon retired— to catch up on sleep before flying off to Paris in two days' time.

Suddenly, at ten o'clock, Brezhnev rang Kissinger, demanding "an immediate meeting with the President, who was asleep. It was a gross breach of protocol. For a foreign guest late at night to ask for an unscheduled meeting with the President on an unspecified subject on the last evening of a State visit was then, and remains, unparalleled." It transpired that Brezhnev had been seized with an overwhelming desire to discuss the Middle East. So, at 10:45, Kissinger and a somewhat ruffled president, dragged from slumbers, were called upon while the Bear "made his most important proposition of the entire trip." It was that "the United States and the Soviet Union agree then and there on a Middle East settlement, based on total Israeli withdrawal to the 1967 borders in return for not peace but an end to the state of belligerency." It would be a peace imposed jointly by the United States and the USSR, and it should be kept strictly secret; he didn't vouchsafe how this could be done. Kissinger saw Brezhnev as threatening a new Middle East war—unless his terms were accepted. Kissinger repeated the ritualistic objection that there would be no chance of launching a serious peace process before the Israeli elections at the end of October. In private he dismissed the proposals on the grounds that "for Nixon to force the issue at the height of Watergate hearings would have added the allegation of engaging in a diversionary maneuver to the charge of betraying an ally."

Nevertheless, the Soviet warning was clear and—for whatever reason—it was not heeded; though David Frost was to pick up on it in the Nixon interviews of five years later. It was what the CIA had failed to spot, or Kissinger was too preoccupied, and Nixon too distracted, to take on. Shamefacedly, Kissinger had to admit in his memoirs: "we would not forget the conversation in Nixon's study when the Middle East exploded a little more than three months afterward."[72]

For all the wrangling over rocketry high-tech, going to Moscow and the Zavidovo boar shoot, Brezhnev's coming to the United States, getting to know the Russians, and vice versa, merely talking together at different levels helped draw the ever-mistrustful Soviet leaders into an atmosphere of trust. At least everything was done to persuade them that the United States had no intention—in fact, in real terms, no capability—to launch an attack on the USSR's struggling society. Who can precisely tell, but the indications from post-glasnost Moscow writings are that Kissinger's 1972 and 1973 gambits were to pay off when the next major challenge hit the two superpowers, that October. "My fear," Kissinger stressed to the author in August 2004, "was always of sliding into war by miscalculation."

"As per 1914?"*

"Yes, exactly. It's hard to believe, knowing what we do now, that World War I could *ever* have happened." In retrospect, he saw Brezhnev "as something of a forerunner of Gorbachev. . . . he had I think a

---

* It was the ninetieth anniversary.

dim view that Russia needed peace. This came out in his 1973 visit to Washington—he was so anxious to be treated as an *equal*. I always thought that Russia would sooner or later have to disgorge the East European states . . . almost all the Soviet gains that were made in 1973 were due to our weaknesses rather than to their strengths."[73] Critics could, perhaps, accuse him here of being somewhat wise after the event. Nevertheless . . .

According to the accompanying Ambassador Dobrynin, Brezhnev's reception on the White House lawn had been "the moment of his greatest triumph. What could be greater than his being placed on a footing equal to the American president."[74] Though one thing which had been difficult to eradicate in Brezhnev that summer in the United States was the very Russian suspicion that Watergate had, somehow, "been a plot by American opponents of détente";[75] which may have been one good reason why Brezhnev was to prove so steadfast to the Nixon-Kissinger line during the most testing stresses of the Yom Kippur War. The veneer of trust was still of questionable depth.

Said Nixon, in 1973 and 1975, "Without détente, we might have had a major conflict in the Middle East. With détente, we avoided it."[76] To critics like John Newhouse, however, "The visit was of little or no lasting importance. It did produce an accord, called the Prevention of Nuclear War Agreement [the original Soviet proposition, much watered-down by the adroit Tom Brimelow], the exact import of which was never clear."[77] It was, however, what Kissinger had wanted all along: "We gained a marginally useful text," he claimed. "But the result was too subtle; the effort too protracted; the necessary explanations to allies and China too complex to have the desired impact."[78]

Nevertheless, says Newhouse, shortly after the visit the Soviet rocketeers began testing four new ICBMs; by that August, three had already been successfully tested with MIRVs. Perhaps in response, Kissinger in July wrote to the Pentagon urging the development of the long-range cruise missile—a "cheapy" which, with conventional warheads only, was to prove the most deadly weapon in the U.S. Air Force armory in both wars against Saddam Hussein.

Was détente then dead? Some of the high-tech targets, maybe; the spirit survived. SALT limped on, eventually to become START, the Strategic Arms Reduction Treaty.

· In Kissinger's summing up, the SALT discussion had "laid bare the ambiguities of East-West relations in the nuclear age. Both sides were painfully aware of the risks of war."[79]

He continued to believe "that Brezhnev was sincerely prepared for a prolonged period of stability." Yet, almost immediately, in the short term "the perception of Watergate slowed the pace of diplomacy. Brezhnev took himself out of the direct line of fire in the U.S.-Soviet negotiations. There was no sense involving the prestige of the General Secretary with the possible collapse of the Nixon Presidency. As in negotiations on the Year of Europe, diplomacy became more bureaucratic, less bold . . . Watergate did not permit us the luxury of a confrontational foreign policy." But he was convinced of the absolute necessity of "a long-range policy that avoids either confrontation for its own sake or acquiescence in Soviet expansion."[80]

CHAPTER 8

A LONG HOT SUMMER

"One of the most vindictive, cheap actions that I have seen the Congress take. And it's not just Cambodia, it's going to hurt us murderously with the Chinese, because if they think that the Congress can do these things to us in Cambodia, what are they going to do to us elsewhere?"

— Henry Kissinger, on Congress axing of
support funds for Vietnam, June 28, 1973[1]

"It was like living on a volcano. . . . Unless I made a recommendation, Nixon would have done nothing."[2]

"So it fell in part to me, in part to Haig, to both our staffs, to bolster our wounded President whose fortitude compelled respect and whose suffering evoked a curious warmth. For the worst punishment that befell Nixon was the knowledge that in the final analysis he had done it all to himself."[3]

— Henry Kissinger

WHEN I STARTED to study Kissinger's copious memoirs covering the period of 1973, I was at first awakened, if not shocked, to read how — at every critical moment in his stewardship of U.S. foreign affairs — Watergate was seen to be playing a baneful role. There it was, again and again, from that fateful moment when Len Garment had first come into his office to open Pandora's box, always lurking to impede, if not destroy, Kissinger's endeavors. In the intervening years, the sordid, tragic story of Watergate had receded into the far reaches of my memory; then, there it was, like some evil genie constantly breathing over Henry Kissinger's right shoulder. On a further reading, I had a second take: a faint suspicion that maybe the author "doth protest too much," using Watergate as a cover for his own sins of omission and foreign policy setbacks. In our first conversations, he himself somewhat reinforced this revisionist view, saying, "Well, yes, maybe I did exaggerate the importance of Watergate in my memoirs."[4] It was an honorable confession. But, finally, on a much closer study, rereading *Years of Upheaval* against other documentation of the times, I reached my own conclusion that, no, he had not exaggerated one bit.

Between the murder of President Kennedy in November 1963 and the terrorist attacks of September 11, 2001, Watergate was quite simply the single most destructive blow to the body corporate of America. Its echoes linger on, and an outsider is left with the question: "If even the bitterest foes of Nixon could have seen where the pursuit of Nixon would lead, would they still have pressed the attack home so relentlessly?" Many responsible foreign politicians, and even those close to the administrations of JFK or to the honorable Dwight Eisenhower, regarded Watergate as a minor, pardonable peccadillo. Symbolizing the French view, the distinguished ambassador currently in London, Gérard Errera, a man of probity who was serving in Washington in 1973, remarked, "Why all the fuss? Why is wiretapping so important? We do it all the time!"[5] In Washington I was frequently to hear the refrain, inter alia, from those most intimately involved in the Kennedy era: "Well, we all did it. (But we got away with it!) Why all the fuss over Nixon?" Was it the lying about the crime, rather than the crime itself? At least part of the answer has to be because it *was* Richard Nixon, whose persona inspired more hatred than any other president in human memory (including George W. Bush).

For Richard Nixon, as that terrible, long, hot summer of 1973 began, it all seemed "as if a convulsion had hit Washington."[6] Events followed swiftly on the resignation, or sacking, of Ehrlichman and

Haldeman. Immediately after their departure at the end of April, so Kissinger noted to the author, "The chase got worse. The press said 'Well, here's proof that they're all bad.' "[7] The following week (May 2), on the Hill the Senate Democratic Caucus adopted a resolution halting all funds for military activity in Cambodia. The following day, the House of Representatives Appropriation Committee rejected the Addabbo Amendment, sponsored by New York representative Joseph Addabbo, which would, in effect, have prohibited the use of funds for all military activities in Southeast Asia, including Vietnam as well as Cambodia. But a week later, on May 10, the House voted for it, 219–188. Under the pressure of Watergate, Vietnam was beginning to unravel; and—to Kissinger's utter dismay—the unraveling would swiftly pick up momentum. As June arrived, a short while before the Brezhnev state visit, Nixon admitted he was feeling "discouraged, drained, and pressured." It showed during the visit. He asked Haig whether he shouldn't resign, but Haig's answer (according to Nixon) was a "robust no," urging him to listen to the records of the Dean meetings and "construct an unassailable defense based on them."[8]

On May 8, 1973, the Senate Watergate Committee began its nationally televised hearings.

On May 15, the powerful Senate Foreign Relations Committee, by a vote of 13–3, approved a ban on any present or past government funds to finance U.S. combat or bombing activities in Indochina.

On May 17, the same committee voted 15–0 for war powers legislation restricting the president's ability to wage undeclared war for more than thirty days without congressional approval.

On May 18, Archibald Cox was appointed special prosecutor.

On May 31, the Senate itself voted 63–19 in favor of the Eagleton Amendment, sponsored by Missouri's Thomas Eagleton,* to cut off all funding for bombing in Cambodia and Laos. At the same time, it re-

---

* And, briefly, George McGovern's pick as vice presidential running mate in 1971.

jected (17–63) Robert Taft Jr.'s amendment to permit partial bombing to continue against North Vietnamese troops in Cambodia.

By early June, a torrid month in Washington anyway, the pace was heating up, on all fronts.

On June 3, John Dean told Watergate investigators that he had discussed the cover-up with Nixon at least thirty-five times. (That evening, according to Woodward and Bernstein, Nixon began listening to the famous tapes.[9])

On June 7, the House adopted an amendment "barring the use of any funds for reconstruction aid to North Vietnam."* The vote was 44–18.

On June 13, Watergate prosecutors found a memo addressed to John Ehrlichman, describing in detail the plans to burgle the office of Daniel Ellsberg's psychiatrist.

On June 16, Brezhnev arrived. The Dean testimony was postponed one week.

On June 24, Brezhnev departed.

On June 25, the Dean testimony resumed. Before the Ervin Committee, Dean outlined a political espionage program conducted by the White House, and said Nixon was participating in the Watergate cover-up within days of the burglary.

That same day, the full House voted for an amendment prohibiting use of funds for combat activities in Cambodia and Laos by 240–172. An amendment deferring the cutoff date to September 1 was defeated.

On June 27, the president used his prerogative to veto the Cambodia rider. That day the House mustered its largest antiwar vote to date—241–173. It fell just thirty-five votes of the two-thirds constitutionally required to override the executive. The Senate promptly reacted by voting 67–29 to attach a new bombing ban amendment to a bill on the national debt. According to Kissinger, Nixon then surrendered to Congress in a "compromise." When he protested to the president, he was told it was too late. "He had yielded to *force majeure*—a

---

* This had been a key part of the Kissinger peace package.

surrender that would have been inconceivable had not the John Dean testimony drained all his inner resources."[10]

On June 28, the day after the snub from the Senate, the House Appropriations Committee set an effective cutoff date of August 15—just over six weeks' time.

Kissinger was furious, and bitter. It was, he declared to Defense Secretary Melvin Laird, "one of the most vindictive, cheap actions that I have seen the Congress take. And it's not just Cambodia, it's going to hurt us murderously with the Chinese, because if they think that the Congress can do these things to us in Cambodia, what are they going to do to us elsewhere?"[11] With the Chinese, it was all so much a case of not losing face—as it had been over many centuries. In the view of Stephen Ambrose, the decision of Congress signaled the end of American involvement in Indochina. The war dragged on; but in effect Congress had already lost it, accepting defeat and a terrible fate for millions of their onetime South Vietnam allies. There was no way Nixon, or Kissinger, could stem the tide of defeat now.

In Washington that fetid summer of the febrile year of 1973, there was a mounting rabidity in the media as it now began to report every unverified accusation. It was the time that TV really hit its stride in the United States; its impact especially strong in the universities.[12] Suddenly something unprecedented since the McCarthy era—live daytime TV coverage of the hearings—had transformed Watergate into a huge nationwide media event, in everybody's house. The country had become consumed by Watergate, to an extent few can still remember. "Not since Pearl Harbor," recalled Stephen Ambrose, had the capital "been so completely concentrated on one event—not even the Army-McCarthy hearings of 1954." Democratic politicians, he noted, "talked darkly about the coming of fascism to America and denounced the Imperial Presidency they had done so much to create."[13] There was even Republican senator Chuck Percy of Illinois rating it "the darkest scandal in American political history."[14]

And the pounding went on, with reporters now beginning to investigate Nixon's tax status. Never before, remarks Ambrose, "had the

American people learned so much, so soon, about the inner workings of an Administration."[15]

From Nixon's overwhelming victory of only eight months previously, his government was now definitively on the run. It was not only Kissinger who was disturbed by it, but Haldeman, for one, noted with dismay the progressive disintegration in those summer months of Nixon himself, and his government; no one now "could avoid the impression he was no longer in control of events . . . like a figure in a Greek tragedy he was fulfilling his own nature and thus destroying himself. . . . I am convinced that he genuinely believed his version of events, which was essentially that he had been let down by faithless retainers."[16]

As the summer heat mounted, there was hardly a single issue of U.S. foreign policy, at which Kissinger had labored so hard, which was not affected. "It was like living on a volcano," he recorded, and, "Unless I made a recommendation, Nixon would have done nothing."[17] But, as mere adviser on national security, he lacked authority— while William Rogers continued to preside flaccidly at Foggy Bottom, with no influence in the White House. It was an intolerable, and dangerous, situation. Meanwhile, Kissinger himself found it hard to ward off the gloom, and general malaise, afflicting both the White House and the country at large, as witness this telephone exchange of June 29, when he let his hair down to a sympathizing William F. Buckley Jr.:

> B: . . . I imagine you're suffering a little bit. I'm sorry for you.
> K: Well, it's not one of the more glorious moments in American
>   history. . . . You know, to dismantle the country . . . because
>   of what was a collection of petty crimes, unworthy, and
>   everything else, but still this is a dramatic dismantling of our
>   foreign policy, of our Indochina policy . . . they know damn
>   well we are in the process of negotiating the end in
>   Cambodia. . . . And if this thing comes apart now we're
>   going to have the Chinese move far left to steal the
>   Communist parties. We'll have a bellicose Soviet policy and
>   no public opinion to deal with it.
> B: Yeah, yeah, yeah. I wish certain things which aren't easy to

say over the phone. . . . I wish the guy in charge had a better means of communicating this kind of thing to the American people.[18]

June became July. On July 13, Nixon's former appointments secretary, Alexander Butterfield, revealed that all conversations and telephone calls in Nixon's office had been taped since 1971.

This reflected a piling on of the pressure by that industrious couple on the *Washington Post*, Bob Woodward and Carl Bernstein, and their mysterious source, Deep Throat. One of the most important pieces of information which the hard-worked Deep Throat, Mark Felt, supplied was that Nixon had been taping all his conversations in the White House. In turn Woodward leaked the information to a member of the Ervin Committee; in consequence Butterfield was questioned about the tapes. Curiously enough, at almost the same time the Supreme Court, acting on Nixon's instructions, was drawing up tough new laws on pornography. The target was the original *Deep Throat*, starring Linda Lovelace, which had become world-famous overnight; but behind the pornographic moviemakers, Nixon, to his credit, was trying to strike at the Mafia, which had moved in on distribution profits of the movie. The courts missed both main targets, but settled for sentencing the unfortunate actor Harry Reems, who had merely supplied the male part (only earning $250 for all that expense of energy), to five years imprisonment.* American press comment at the time was: "Throat cut, world mourns." To students of history, it may seem somehow bizarre that, while the *Washington Post*'s Deep Throat was persecuting Nixon for his "immorality" over Watergate, the president in his turn was attacking the original *Deep Throat* on not dissimilar grounds.

On July 18, Nixon was alleged to have ordered White House taping systems to be disconnected.

---

* By strange coincidence, *Deep Throat* was first released in June 1972 — the same month as the Watergate break-in. The stars were never reemployed; Linda Lovelace died penniless in a 2002 car crash; Harry Reems, later pardoned, after serious drinking problems retired to become a born-again Christian. The Mafia got off scot-free. Some would see similarities when Ford pardoned Nixon, while his underlings remained in prison.

On July 23, prosecutor Archibald Cox subpoenaed the recordings of nine presidential conversations and meetings.

On July 25, Nixon refused to turn over the presidential tape recordings to the Senate Watergate Committee or to the special prosecutor.

On July 26, following Nixon's refusal to hand over nine tapes, the Senate Watergate Committee subpoenaed several of them. Supporting the earlier Senate vote, the House also voted barring use of funds for reconstruction aid to North Vietnam unless specifically authorized by Congress.

Congress then adjourned for the summer recess until after Labor Day, doubtless well pleased with its work. On July 29, the *New York Times*, reaching back into history, wrote with enthusiasm: "Viewing the proceedings one thinks more of 1789 than of 1973."[19] By the beginning of August, Gallup reported the president's popularity rating down to 31 percent, the lowest since Truman's last month in office, lower even than Lyndon Johnson's worst in 1968—and this less than a year since Nixon's all-time success of the November elections. How the mighty were falling! Even a loyal supporter like Republican senator Barry Goldwater was becoming critical. And was it surprising that, as the hammering of an already unpopular president continued, so his grasp—particularly on foreign affairs—slackened? All through August, as the struggle over the tapes surged forward, "the President's situation" (in his biographer Ambrose's words) "seemed desperate, only to get worse. Every time he counter-attacked, he lost ground."[20]

If that wasn't enough, on August 7, *The Wall Street Journal* reported that Spiro Agnew, the vice president whom the party apparatus had imposed on an unwilling Nixon the previous year, was under suspicion of extortion, bribery, tax evasion, and graft while governor of Maryland in the 1960s—and also under scrutiny by a Baltimore grand jury. On October 11, 1973, Agnew was to become the first American vice president to resign from office on account of criminal charges. For Nixon, what was almost worst about the threat to the despised Agnew was that—as Haldeman had put it in the spring—Agnew was his "insurance policy," because "not even Nixon's worst enemy would want to get rid of him if it meant that Agnew would become President

. . . an Agnew resignation would hurt Nixon far more than it would help him." [21] Next, Nixon's closest pal, Bebe Rebozo, was to be investigated by the Ervin Committee for accepting $100,000 in cash from Howard Hughes, the eccentric billionaire, as a campaign contribution. By September, it was the combination of Watergate, and then Agnew, that made it all but impossible for the president to concentrate on foreign affairs, once his great interest—and forte.

On August 15, Nixon appeared on national television, "looking drawn and a little sad," recorded Stephen Ambrose, "he repeated what he had been saying all along, that he was innocent of any wrongdoing, and asserted that 'the time has come to turn Watergate over to the courts.' " As he had done back in May, Nixon accepted "full responsibility" for any abuses and expressed "regret that these events took place," without specifying what the abuses and events were. Once again he insisted that he had "no prior knowledge" of Watergate; he had never "authorized nor encouraged subordinates to engage in illegal or improper campaign tactics." [22]

In his memoirs, Nixon claimed that his speech had "hit a responsive chord." Supportive telegrams and phone calls poured into the White House: "People were tired of Watergate," he claimed.[23] What wishful thinking!

On August 22, Nixon announced on TV the appointment of Henry Kissinger as his secretary of state, in place of William Rogers, though his official confirmation by Congress would not come through for another month.

But Watergate pounded on, no longer grinding or creeping but galloping ahead, and out of all control.

On August 29, Judge Sirica ordered Nixon to surrender nine tapes for the judge's private review. The White House announced it would appeal. This was the first major legal defeat in Nixon's battle to maintain control of the tapes.

On September 5, the *Washington Post* alleged that Nixon had been tapping his own brother's telephone.[24]

At this point it may be worthwhile to draw aside to review Kissinger's perceptions of just how Watergate was affecting his workings, his handling of foreign initiatives. It was a skein that would run consistently all the way through his memoirs of that period; as he saw it, nothing, but nothing, was left untouched by the ever-accelerating drama of that one brief moment of folly. In his memoirs, he recalled writing to a friend back in May in general terms: "The country seems in a suicidal mood,"[26] and, elsewhere, how, "With every passing day Watergate was circumscribing our freedom of action. . . . Nixon no longer had the margin of maneuver or the personnel for the intricate minuets with which he had managed the affairs in the first term. Both he and I had been reduced to fundamentals. . . . So it fell in part to me, in part to Haig, to both our staffs, to bolster our wounded President whose fortitude compelled respect and whose suffering evoked a curious warmth. For the worst punishment that befell Nixon was the knowledge that in the final analysis he had done it all to himself."[25]

Kissinger particularly noted the effects that Watergate had upon foreign friends and allies during the Year of Europe negotiations. Michel Jobert of France, and only the obnoxious Jobert, tried to take advantage of America's calvary. Already in June he was recorded as having insinuated that the purpose of the Year of Europe had been "to ease our domestic situation." The Germans were left wondering, like everyone else, how President Nixon's domestic disaster would affect his foreign policy. In Britain his very good friend, Burke Trend, Heath's cabinet secretary, was "compassionate"; but, wrote Kissinger, "the policy of a great power is sustained by respect, not compassion."[26] As far as that major commitment of Kissinger's was concerned, "Watergate muffled the thrusts of our initiative" and "made us more persistent than prudent."[27] Summing up, Kissinger was left with absolutely no doubts that "the single most corrosive factor was Watergate. The Year of Europe might well have succeeded but for the way the scandal seeped into every nook and cranny of the project. A strong President at the height of his prestige, with an American consensus behind him, could have made a compelling case for the moral unity of the free nations. . . . Had not Nixon become a political liability to the European leaders, it is highly improbable that they would have been so insistently aloof." Nevertheless, "in the perspective of nearly a decade," he was left regretting "the callousness with which some of our allies reacted to Nixon's loss of authority. Here was a man whose entire public life had been devoted to strengthening the Atlantic Alliance."[28] These were hard words, and they were directed mainly toward the French.

As far as dealing with the Bear, and the vital issues of détente were concerned, back at the time of his Zavidovo visit in May, Kissinger had felt that America, through Nixon's enfeeblement caused by Watergate, had lost both "the stick and the carrot,"[29] for "the corrosion of Watergate . . . stripped away both the incentives and penalties needed to conduct an effective policy towards Moscow." The domestic crisis had "changed all previous assumptions." Nixon was already showing signs of being "badly wounded."[30] As noted in the previous chapter, during Zavidovo, his "nightmare was that under the conditions of Watergate it was wildly risky to provoke a confrontation with Moscow . . . our leverage was weak."[31] It certainly did not add toward the ideal conditions for negotiation such as his heroes Metternich and Castlereagh would have required. Always, Kissinger's residual fear remained: that of the Soviets being "tempted into a confrontational stance . . . sliding into war by miscalculation."[32]

Finally, as the Soviet delegation returned from the U.S. summit, they understood full well how it had been "overshadowed by Watergate."[33] Though James Schlesinger, the incoming secretary of defense, insists that "We certainly thought that Brezhnev was taking advantage of the weakness showed up by Watergate,"[34] it was equally not then given for Kissinger to perceive that Brezhnev had committed himself against such a path, of rocking the boat, regarding America's domestic problem as but a "little local difficulty." In fact, he would remain reasonably steadfast, despite contrary pressures from his entourage—and especially over the next major crisis that was so soon to break—war in the Middle East.

After meetings in Paris in early June with Mao's emissary, Acting Foreign Minister Ji Pengfei, discussing a Cambodian settlement, Kissinger noted how at that point neither he himself nor Zhou Enlai had yet "appreciated quite how far Presidential authority had been eroded by Watergate . . . so we proceeded buoyantly enough."[35] But the atmosphere would slowly change. A month later, on July 6, as Sam Ervin ratcheted up the pressure, in key negotiations over the future of Cambodia, Kissinger was informed that Zhou was "getting nervous."

"The tension in Peking caused by the new and unexpected turn of events in Washington was revealed in an encounter that same day between the Chinese Premier and a visiting Congressional delegation headed by Senator Warren Magnuson. . . ." Watergate had heretofore appeared as an incomprehensible domestic squabble in America, its impact on our foreign policy obscure. "But now it seemed, possible, even likely, that China would have to deal with a President whose authority was so weakened that his commitments had become so unreliable that—to use a favorite Chinese phrase—his word no longer counted." The impassive Zhou revealed himself to be "visibly irritated." It was just after the House Appropriations Committee had set its cutoff date of August 15, which an angry Kissinger had damned as "one of the most vindictive, cheap actions that I have seen the Congress take." Kissinger felt that, with the Chinese, he was "staking too much on a losing hand." [*][36] As always, the vital issue of face was involved.

But nowhere were the consequences seen to be more injurious than in Vietnam. If Brezhnev—and, by and large, Mao too—were not prepared to exploit Watergate to the American disadvantage, the same could not be said of Le Duc Tho and his comrades in Hanoi. On the contrary: they would use it to twist the dagger at every opportunity. They were, after all, fighting a total war with every weapon available, with ultimate—and total—victory the only acceptable option. Within a few weeks of Kissinger shaking hands with Le Duc Tho on the definitive peace treaty, the North Vietnamese were already beginning to cheat. In contrast to the Soviet and Chinese puppet-masters, Hanoi wasted not a second in taking advantage of American disarray over Watergate, seizing every opportunity to reopen the war. By March 1973, they were already moving men and offensive weapons across the Demilitarized Zone into the South, under cover of the newly signed peace agreement—"before the ink was dry." [37] Within the next three months some thirty thousand troops and thirty thousand tons of mil-

---

* There is a curious aside here. According to Jussi Hanhimaki in *The Flawed Architect*, Kissinger privately told both the Chinese and Russians that all he wanted was a "decent interval" before the North swallowed South Vietnam. I was unable to verify this allegation.

itary equipment had been passed into the South. By March 29, the last U.S. ground forces were removed from South Vietnam—the battlefield where so much American blood had been expended. In March and April there were halfhearted U.S. air strikes on the North—and that was about all the increasingly distracted Nixon was prepared to do. They were, as Kissinger saw it, very much conditional on Watergate. There was a one-day strike on the Ho Chi Minh Trail, which "combined every disadvantage," thought Kissinger: it was "too short to be effective, too blatant to be ignored, and too hesitant to have the desired psychological impact on Hanoi."[38] Already in March, in this context, Kissinger was noting a "different Nixon in March 1973. He approached the problem of the violations in a curiously desultory fashion. He drifted. He did not home in on the decision in the single-minded, almost possessed manner that was his hallmark."[39]

Even staunch supporters of the war like Kissinger's good friend Stewart Alsop were questioning whether the South Vietnamese had by now "learned to defend their own turf," and if they hadn't, would they ever?[40] Very soon Kissinger was watching the whole of his Sisyphean achievements in Paris the previous year begin to fall apart. "Watergate," he wrote in glum disgust, "destroyed the last vestiges of hope for a reasonable outcome. For the first time in the post-war period, America abandoned to eventual Communist rule a friendly people who had relied on us."[41] The same would apply to Cambodia too.

In April, Thieu paid a visit to the United States. So far, though America's "ally," he had been shabbily received, allowed to meet American presidents only in outposts like Guam, Hawaii, or Midway— never the continental United States. Now in Washington none but the vice president, Spiro Agnew, already under a darkening shadow, was detailed off to host him. At the arrival ceremony only one other cabinet member, the secretary of labor, was there to greet him. According to Kissinger, at the official dinner the guests were "appallingly few. Most senior members of the Administration had found some excuse for being out of town. It was a shaming experience."[42] One asks oneself, could they not have been honest with the poor man, and told him—bluntly—that he and his country were shortly going to be thrown to the wolves?

James Schlesinger, then still director of the CIA, had told a meeting of the National Security Council's WSAG committee on April 16 that although Hanoi was not gaining popular support in the South, a more important criterion was how it judged Washington's reactions. By that date the total increase of fresh North Vietnamese regular troops funneling into the South, or sanctuaries in Laos or Cambodia, was greatly in excess of those prior to the 1972 Easter offensive. Observed Kissinger, "The normal Nixon would have been enraged beyond containment at being strung along like this; but Watergate Nixon continued to dither."[43] The dithering was infectious, and fatal. By April 23, the week after the Garment eye-opener, Kissinger perceived that "the President was not prepared to order any kind of retaliation."[44] A questioning mind might ask here: if already by March the president was in such bad shape, why didn't Kissinger, with his super-sensitive fingertips, not guess that something was wrong, before Garment's revelations in mid-April? One suspects that the answer might perhaps be that Kissinger didn't *want* to know more, and Nixon certainly did not want to tell him.

In May and June, Kissinger flew to Paris, three times. The trips were adroitly juxtaposed between his talks with Brezhnev in Zavidovo and the United States—but they must also have been highly fatiguing.* In Paris, he held further anxious confrontations with Le Duc Tho (much to the apprehension of Thieu and Saigon, understandably). En route he received a valuable intelligence intercept of how Viet Cong commanders were being briefed in the field. It was horrendously accurate: the Watergate investigations, this claimed, revealed that Nixon must "resign because he no longer has enough prestige to lead the United States. . . . Even if President Nixon remains in office . . . he will not dare to apply such strong measures as air strikes or bombing attacks in either North or South Vietnam, because the US Congress and the American people will violently object."[45] One can well imagine what a boost to morale this would have afforded battle-weary troops in the field.

Kissinger dubbed his dealings with the elusive Ducky a "charade,"

---

* Could anyone but a man of Kissinger's superhuman endurance have juggled quite so many balls in the air? The Yom Kippur War would prove that, well, yes, he could.

which—he thought in retrospect—could only have added to "further demoralization" in Saigon. Le Duc Tho had "gloated" to him over the congressional pressures besetting the White House. On June 13, Kissinger held a major press conference in the Majestic Hotel, Paris. Compared with what he was saying in private, his comments were restrained. Knowing that he was addressing a largely hostile and disbelieving audience, he outlined six points where the U.S. Government was "quite concerned" about the manner in which the treaty obligations were being handled by the North Vietnamese:

> One, the inadequate implementation of the cease-fire.
>
> Secondly, the continued infiltration into South Vietnam and the continued utilization of Laos and Cambodia as corridors for that infiltration.
>
> Three, we were concerned about the inadequate accounting for the [U.S.] missing in action.
>
> Fourth . . . the violations of the demilitarized zone.
>
> Fifth . . . the inadequate cooperation with the International Control Commission and the slow staffing of the two-party Military Commission.
>
> Sixth . . . the violations of Article 20 requiring the withdrawal of foreign troops from Laos and Cambodia.

Kissinger's last questioner, representing Hearst Newspapers, asked: "If this agreement doesn't work out, do you envisage negotiating a third agreement?

"Dr. Kissinger: It is a prospect I cannot face today. (*Laughter*)." *[46]

In the plain language that the Pentagon and CIA would probably have used in preparing Kissinger's briefing for these mild revelations: the North Vietnamese were building up their forces, both outside and inside South Vietnam, for the "final push." The date would be entirely

---

* To recap on the fundamental points of the January peace accords, these included: Release of POWs within eighty days; cease-fire to be monitored by International Control Commission (ICC); free and democratic elections to be held in South Vietnam; U.S. aid to South Vietnam to continue; North Vietnamese troops could remain in South Vietnam. (The last was a particularly deadly provision—tantamount to permitting buildup of a residual fifth column inside the body of South Vietnam.)

of their choosing. The previous year their spring offensive had been seriously blunted by U.S. mining of the harbors, as well as—perhaps—by the new reluctance of China, post-Nixon visit, to give its full-bodied support. But now they were simply waiting for the word from a wilting Congress in Washington—waiting for a definitive ruling that America would no longer support its ally militarily. It was a matter of time.

The story in neighboring, bomb-battered Cambodia was just as bad—and would get infinitely worse in a manner that no one, not even Henry Kissinger, could have foreseen. No country, wrote Kissinger, had endured such a succession of miseries: invaded and partially occupied by the Viet Minh in 1965, bombed by the U.S. Air Force from 1969 onward—then wracked by civil war culminating in the ruthless genocide of Pol Pot, which killed possibly one-third of its people, notably the leading and educated cadres. Consequential on the U.S. bombing campaign, for the catastrophe which overtook Cambodia, Kissinger himself was held responsible by liberal America—some going so far as wishing (to this day) for him to be charged with war crimes. Kissinger, however, was quite clear where the ultimate blame lay: "It was Hanoi," if it was anyone, that brought the war to Cambodia and made possible the genocide by the Khmer Rouge. But, beyond Hanoi, Kissinger pointed an accusing finger at Nixon's foes in Congress, who had sought, "and[47] succeeded, in imposing on Cambodia the restrictions they had failed to inflict on South Vietnam. Their failure over South Vietnam meant that we were strong enough there to prevent collapse;* but their success over Cambodia doomed the country and therefore South Vietnam as well." Kissinger had attempted to bring about a cease-fire in Cambodia as well as Vietnam, but the Khmer Rouge had rigorously objected, launching a new offensive. They wanted the civil war to continue—on their own deranged terms.

In maintaining Kissinger's delicate balancing act with the neutralist Prince Sihanouk, who—since 1954—had proved to be the most realist leader in Cambodia, neither China nor the USSR was helpful, in being at odds with each other over the Cambodian leadership.

---

* For rather less than two years, one should perhaps interject.

Kissinger quotes a French priest, Father François Ponchaud, who had worked in Cambodia right to the end. He wrote—with the most admirably Gallic resort to Cartesian *reason*—what Kissinger considered to be perhaps the best account of the Cambodian holocaust: it was, Father Ponchaud thought, "a perfect example of the application of an ideology pushed to the furthest limit of its internal logic." [48] Robespierre would have understood. Typical of the growing isolationism of Capitol Hill, there was the much respected veteran congressman, and former speaker, currently Democratic majority leader, Thomas P. "Tip" O'Neill paraphrasing Bismarck to declare that Cambodia was "not worth the life of one American flier." [49] As Congress voted, in June, for cutting off all funds for military operations in Indochina—across the board—Kissinger "was desperate." A bombing cutoff in Cambodia would, he insisted, "destroy our only bargaining chip—and the sole stimulus for Chinese involvement. Zhou Enlai needed to be able to argue to the Khmer Rouge that he had brought them the end of our bombing, in exchange for a compromise involving Sihanouk." The current negotiations "were our last throw of the dice." [50]

Then, on June 25, had come the Eagleton Amendment, slashing funds immediately. By August, Kissinger was reckoning that Congress "had doomed Sihanouk." [51] China was beginning to react badly; Kissinger was told by his friend Zhou Enlai, coldly, that a visit scheduled for August 6 was no longer "convenient." In Cambodia, as in Vietnam, he reckoned that, behind the actions of Congress, the deadly hand of Watergate had "destroyed the last vestiges of hope for a reasonable outcome." He added, prophetically, that the pattern once established would not end soon. "We will have to pay for a long time for the precedent into which we stumbled that summer." [52]

Increasingly Nixon, like other unpopular presidents, was paying the bill for having alienated Congress. His hubristic treatment of his political foes after the stunning electoral victory of November 1972 had asked for trouble. As Kissinger remarked to the author, "He was so eager to get a vast majority himself, he didn't campaign for Republican congressmen. He feared getting involved in local disputes. But if he had made significant gains in Congress, this would have scared the Democrats into making them supportive over continuing logistic support for Vietnam." [53]

As it was, Nixon's further alienation of Congress—already so un-
remittingly hostile to him in person—made it almost certain that its
first acts from the inauguration onward would be to cut off all funds
for prosecution of the war. To carry out his policies Nixon had to have
the support of Congress; to obtain that, he had to have more Republicans than Democrats on the floor. Nixon's biographer, Stephen Ambrose, was of the opinion that, had Watergate never happened, "there
would still have been a war between Nixon and Congress."[54] Possibly,
but it was surely Watergate that made it all so intractably difficult. In
response to Congress, Nixon reacted by rolling himself into a ball, like
a very prickly hedgehog, interpreting congressional opposition as "the
culmination of a personal attack on him by the ideological enemies of
a lifetime."[55] It was one of the many chinks in the armor of a very
flawed personality. For its part, flexing its muscles to resist every measure emanating from the White House, Congress set to cutting all support for the forces of General Thieu at every turn. Every single request,
overture, or threat that the beleaguered and distracted president would
make to Congress would be countermanded, thrown out with contempt, or turned against him.

Summing up in his book *Diplomacy* on the blighting consequences
of Watergate, Kissinger declared that without it "Nixon might have
been able to rally the country to his style of diplomacy."[56] Later in the
same book, Kissinger wrote, "But for Watergate, Nixon might have
been able to translate the very tangible foreign policy success of his first
term into permanent operating principles. . . . But Nixon's capacity to
lead collapsed as a result of Watergate."[57] Vis-à-vis the Soviets and détente, he reckoned that, in those harrowing months, the American
leadership found itself in the position of a swimmer "who, having just
barely escaped drowning, is being urged to cross the English Channel
and is then accused of pessimism when he displays a lack of enthusiasm at the prospect."[58]

It was perhaps interesting that General Al Haig, Nixon's powerful
chief of staff in replacement of Haldeman, thought that Kissinger
"never quite realized fully how much damage Watergate was developing."[59] This view certainly does not mesh with the views of others, not
least Kissinger himself. Winston Lord, who was with Kissinger on
most of the Chinese, Russian, and Vietnamese negotiations, remained

convinced that "Watergate was a significant influence on our policy, certainly by the end of 1973, and notably with China and Russia, where the momentum slowed down." It also "very much weakened our position with Hanoi. . . . It contributed fundamentally to the unraveling of Vietnam as Hanoi perceived presidential weakness and Congressional assertiveness . . . It was quite outrageous of Congress to cut off aid—absolutely immoral—shocking." Lord still felt, emphatically, that, without Watergate, "South Vietnam might possibly have been saved."[60]

Occasionally, very occasionally, Kissinger could joke wanly about Watergate. In July, welcoming the Pakistan ambassador, Sultan Khan, to his office, he cracked: "Good morning, Mr. Ambassador. This is Miss Ryan. She is here to take notes. Nothing that is said here will go out of this office. My staff may be incompetent, but they are loyal. (*Laughter*)" But, as that grisly summer ended, he was predicting no comedy. "Indochina will be the first great Watergate tragedy."[61] All he could continue to strive for was to insulate himself totally from the "inner circle" deliberations on Watergate.[62] It was the wisest, and most statesmanlike, thing that he could do.

On August 22, Henry Kissinger was nominated U.S. secretary of state. He had waited a long time, his loyalty to Nixon prodigiously tested.

CHAPTER 9

TO SECRETARY OF STATE

"Absence of power corrupts. And absolute absence of power corrupts absolutely."

—Henry Kissinger[1]

"I was the glue that held it all together in 1973 — and I'm not being boastful."

—Henry Kissinger[2]

I T WAS AT A televised news conference that Nixon finally announced appointment of a new secretary of state. Baldly he commented: "Dr. Kissinger's qualifications for this post, I think, are well known." ("He did not elaborate," remarked Kissinger with economy of words.[3]) The long anticipated deed of dispatching William Rogers, and replacing him by his pressing NSC adviser, had been performed in true Nixonian style. Six days previously, without even running it past Kissinger, the president had summoned Rogers, intending to ask for his resignation. Since by now America's two top statesmen had little or no commerce between them, Rogers came well prepared for the summons. To the great relief of the man who dreaded personal confrontation, before Nixon could open his mouth, Rogers — once his old friend — submitted his letter of resignation. Says

Kissinger, "It was a classy performance." [4] Rogers departed with grace and dignity.

Kissinger had still heard nothing; then, at San Clemente on the 21st, only the day before the formal announcement, while floating on his back in the swimming pool, Nixon casually apprised Kissinger of his appointment. It was done "without warmth or any expression of anticipation of close cooperation," but then, as Kissinger, ever the realist, construed the unusual circumstances of his promotion, "We both realized that for Nixon my appointment was less an act of choice than a step taken against his will in hope it would mitigate catastrophe." [5] Nixon, in his jealousy, "didn't want me in such a visible position," Kissinger once told me. [6] On the other hand, the realist knew that he both wanted, and needed, Kissinger more than ever before; though still, to the end, Nixon desired to run his own foreign policy. Now, at the nadir of Watergate, he—and the nation—had to have Kissinger. It was neither a graceful validation nor an elegant promotion.

The job had certainly been a long time coming, with no shortage of frustrated nudging from the candidate himself; even though he had (as Missouri Democrat Stuart Symington observed) been "Secretary of State in everything but name." [7] But, as he himself once remarked whimsically, but meaningfully, to Arthur Schlesinger, "Absence of power corrupts. And absolute absence of power corrupts absolutely." As recorded earlier, back in the beginning of the previous winter he claimed to have decided that if the job that he felt should be his continued to be denied him he would retire and seek the tranquil embrace of an Oxford college to write his memoirs. Then, in April, came Garment's revelation of the "full horror" of Watergate. To the author, he reminisced in Paris, "If I had acted wisely, I suppose I should have accepted David Bruce's suggestion back at Christmastime to retire . . . but after the Watergate revelation, I was the glue that held it together in 1973—and I'm not being boastful." [8]

Now the progressive collapse of presidential power made it quite impossible for him to abandon ship. (Also, so many challenging ploys were underway—such as détente, China, Vietnam, and Europe, not to mention the growing rumbles in the Middle East.) He had undoubtedly, observes Stephen Ambrose, made himself "difficult." [9] To this author he remarked that, from July 1973, "It was certain Rogers would have to go; and one never trusts those who follow. Who knows. . . . It was clear to me that I couldn't do the job with Rogers there; so it became impelling that I should take over. . . . Nixon from June onward knew that I was holding the government together. But for Watergate, I would certainly have left; it was *definitely* my intention."[10] Of Rogers, he had remarked critically to me the previous year, "Rogers could never develop a sense of being subordinate to Nixon—he was too vain and and too indolent. So I was often accused of achieving domination in foreign affairs. Fearful of the *New York Times*, Rogers would never touch Vietnam. He wouldn't challenge Nixon, nor would he carry out exactly what Nixon wanted; that's why I slid into power."[11]

For Kissinger, the news brought not just the natural elation of a highly ambitious man at having reached the ultimate peak; he was also "oddly relieved," recalling how Winston Churchill, summoned by Destiny in 1940, felt "liberated." There were many congratulatory calls; not least, and most generously, from William Rogers. He told Kissinger that he "would find it's a great department." Dobrynin was swift to offer his, and Brezhnev's, warm congratulations (to which Kissinger replied, referring to Dobrynin as "not just a colleague, but a personal friend," and speculating as to whether he had also been promoted to be a member of the Politburo![12]). Whatever Kissinger's mood of exaltation, he found it "passed rapidly" as he had to undergo the grueling process of confirmation hearings in Washington—while the nation, and the world, stood on the brink of crisis. They lasted until September 21. Inevitably, there was opposition. The wiretapping episode was thrown up against him; as was the bombing of Cambodia. In the end only one senator out of sixteen in the Foreign Relations Committee, George McGovern, the recently defeated presidential candidate, voted against him—on rather feeble grounds. In Washington the general attitude among patriots on the Hill was, as Ambrose noted, "Thank God we have Henry. Let's confirm him so he can run foreign policy while we get after Nixon for Watergate."[13] It also turned out to be Nixon's only action that summer that got general approval from the reporters.

On the 22nd, Kissinger was duly sworn in as the fifty-sixth U.S. secretary of state, following in the daunting footsteps of great incum-

bents from Thomas Jefferson through George Marshall. He was accompanied by his parents and children, in the East Room of the White
House—under the "genial but ambivalent auspices" of President
Nixon. The president's remarks at this solemn ceremony, lacking any
trace of warmth, "ranged from the perfunctory to the bizarre," recalled
Kissinger. Having referred to the intense congressional opposition he
had encountered, Nixon sought to explain that the appointment, in
Kissinger's recounting, "represented yet another historic first, for three
reasons: I was the first naturalized citizen to become Secretary of State;
the first Secretary of State who had visited Peking and Moscow before
his appointment; and the first Secretary of State since World War II
who did not part his hair. He did not amplify the first two points but
he pursued the last topic relentlessly, speculating as to what category
Dean Rusk,* who had no hair, belonged." [14]

To Nixon, Kissinger responded with gravitas and some emotion,
referring to his early life in Nazi Germany, where he had "seen what
can happen to a society that is based on hatred and strength and distrust, and that I experienced then what America means to other people, its hope and its idealism." [15] For some unaccountable reason, after
the swearing in the first lady declined to join the receiving line.
Nixon himself seemed "to be driven by his own demons," thought
Kissinger. Nevertheless, it was an elating day for him, as well as
being as memorable in its incidental bizarreness as Brezhnev's visit in
America. [16]

In what also might have been construed a first (additional to not
parting his hair), Kissinger, uniquely, continued to run the National Security Council while taking over the State Department. As he would
later admit, "it did not work." [17] But, while Nixon floundered ever
deeper in the morass of Watergate, this made Kissinger—in effect—the
most powerful man in America, and, ipso facto, the world; it was also
a decision that would widely arouse apprehension and criticism. Having wrestled with it from the outside, as an antagonist, he now found
the great apparatus in Foggy Bottom, in the intricacies of its bureaucracy, a body "wondrous to behold"; but one that, left to its own de-

---

* Secretary of State for John F. Kennedy and Lyndon Johnson.

vices, tended "toward inertia rather than creativity." Like other secretaries before and after him, he would do his best to shake it up. He found himself now established "in a spacious and elegant suite of offices," which contrasted sharply with his former NSC quarters down in the basement. They were "on a regally high floor with a magnificent view of the city of Washington and its monuments."

The downside was that his deputy seemed to be "almost a mile down the corridor," so that by the time Kissinger had returned to his office he would have forgotten the purpose of his visit; there being, of course, no such device as e-mail in those days. In keeping with the physical grandeur of his office, he found himself in charge of "a colossal enterprise," in which the incumbent had to "grapple with many mundane or highly technical subjects. He is forced to champion unpopular causes, such as the annual appropriations for foreign aid."[18]

The new secretary of state was shocked to discover how his new department had come to resemble "an enormous cable machine,"[19] where too often policy filtered upward in response to minor events originating abroad. "Cooky-pushing" was an in-house term for it. Though it was too late in Nixon's presidential term to undertake any fundamental reorganization of State, Kissinger determined that he would not allow himself to become engulfed in a flood of paper. He insisted on "thoughtful memoranda." Jan Lodal, one of his "note-takers," commented on how "as a university professor, Kissinger insisted that these accounts would be absolutely accurate. He probably expected that they would never be released. So I would lock myself up immediately after the meeting. After I had taken notes, I'd lock the door and let no one in, and write the report absolutely verbatim. . . . It then went straight to the President and was never doctored."[20] Thus the memcons were totally reliable. As he had done in the NSC, he drove his staff "mercilessly." Impatient with finding twenty thousand people in the State Department, he was quoted as quipping that, while at Harvard "it took me ten years to develop the relationship of total hostility to my environment, I want you to know that here I have done it in eighteen months."[21] Many could not stand the pace, and resigned. He brought in his own men: Helmut Sonnenfeldt was placed in charge of East-West relations; William Highland, trained in the CIA, was charged with Intelligence and Research; young Winston Lord (who had come close to resigning from the NSC over the Cambodian operation) was put in charge of the Policy Planning Staff. Lord, an expert on China with a Chinese wife, Kissinger came to regard as one of his "best collaborators," [22] and the even younger Peter Rodman was brought in to help with speechwriting. Another former colleague, and personal friend, Lawrence Eagleburger came in as executive assistant, charged with translating "concept into policy." Meanwhile, Kissinger also spent the month's interval between his nomination and confirmation to conduct a systematic talent search within the foreign service to bring forward the best and brightest.

On September 12, he held his first conference with the Washington press corps, where—already—he was assailed over the secrecy of his foreign travels, with the hope that this would now change. It was a key meeting. His good friend, and later biographer, Marvin Kalb of NBC, led the pack with a rap on the knuckles: "I want to say as strongly as possible: State Department reporters have an absolute right to cover the Secretary wherever he goes, even if he is on a delicate mission. . . . Second point is that because you are a newsworthy individual in your own right, and in your activities as an adviser to the President, there ought to be an arrangement whereby through some pool system or otherwise we are always informed of what you are about as you do it."

Kissinger replied, "Well I would point out that I have taken no secret trips since my trip to Moscow last year."

Kalb: "Yes, but, for example, last summer we didn't know until the next day that you were actually in Paris. Even until the time you were negotiating with Le Duc Tho."

Murray Marder (of the *Washington Post*): "We really have two problems before us." He stressed the first as "a profound crisis of public confidence in both government and in the press."

Another journalist (Barry Shield) followed up by calling for far more of Kissinger's dealings to be "on the record," while Alvin Rosenfeld riled Kissinger by suggesting "a much more moralistic tone from your press corps at State than you found recently in the Senate Foreign Relations Committee."

Kissinger responded with an imposing declaration of fundamentals: "I am interested that you say the press corps is more moralistic than the Senate Foreign Relations Committee. I think we must understand that in policy-making you cannot always think in moral black-and-white terms. You must approach your overall objectives in stages. The difference between a policy-maker and a prophet often has a tragic quality to it. That is not to say that the long-run objective should not have a moral quality to it, but on a day-to-day basis we cannot use abstract moralism as an excuse for a universal cynicism in criticizing our efforts." He continued: "Let me make a few final points. . . . First, the Department is totally demoralized. It is merely a big cable-clearing factory, not a policy-making machine. There is a tendency to maneuver to avoid disaster, not create policy. And I admit that much of this is my fault. I must give the Department a sense of confidence, a sense of the future. We need to think of where we want to be five years from now. . . . The second problem I have is to resolve the two jobs, the two hats I wear (as adviser to the President), so that other departments will not cry foul as I reinvigorate the Department of State and begin to play a major role in the policy-making process." With a small staff on the NSC, he observed how, although there had been "some bitching," nevertheless morale was very high, "because I made them feel that we were doing something very important." [23]

The next day he had a visit from the financier, former secretary of the treasury, and ambassador to France, Douglas Dillon. Dillon remarked: "This is a nice office." Kissinger replied that he had "told the curator I wanted to use some modern paintings in my new office. He was horrified. He said no Secretary of State ever used modern paintings." Not the last time that his choice in art would draw criticism, he then consulted Dillon on how to get the best staff, remarking acidly, "One thing I notice with the foreign service officers is a problem; they worry a lot more about their career than what service they can provide." [24]

Within forty-eight hours of his confirmation, Kissinger delivered a major address at the United Nations. There was a hitch when an overheated piece of equipment ate a page of his draft; nevertheless, he was able to appeal eloquently for the nations of the world "to move with us from détente to cooperation, from coexistence to community."

He went on to mention every key region, but (possibly on account of the drama of the overheated machine) omitted to mention Europe, later admitting how, in this, the Year of Europe, he "paid the price; the omission being added to the catalogue of my neglects."[25]

He spoke again in New York, on October 4, to the U.N. General Assembly delegations congregated at the Metropolitan Museum of Art, this time pledging in visionary terms that "the United States is ready to begin the journey toward a world community. Our sights will be raised even when our tread must be measured."[26] As the shakeup within Foggy Bottom proceeded, so Kissinger made it his external priority, speaking with a strong voice, "to remind Americans and our friends around the world that our government was functioning and purposeful and the master of events."[27]

Two days after his speech to the U.N. delegations, however, his visionary thoughts were interrupted by major war breaking out in the Middle East.

So it was that during this dangerous period from August to October 1973, Kissinger had his hands full with entrenching himself in the State Department, and reorganizing it to his liking. For once his mind may well have been distracted from the foreign scene, his eyes off it.

Then, on October 10, another crisis that had been rumbling for some time struck the battered administration. Spiro Agnew, the man whom the Constitution dictated would succeed Nixon in case of his impeachment, resigned. He had pleaded guilty to having accepted $29,500 worth of bribes while governor of Maryland. Agnew narrowly avoided going to prison through a plea bargain, which the former attorney general of Maryland sarcastically rated the "greatest deal since the Lord spared Isaac on the mountaintop." Nixon, upon whom Agnew had been imposed as a most unwilling choice, never spoke to him again. The scandal, and the resignation, could not possibly have come at a worse time. Because of the threat of impeachment that seemed to be approaching ever nearer, the replacement of the vice president, who—though constitutionally "only a heartbeat away" from the White House—was normally a sinecure appointment, now became a major issue. As Stephen Ambrose described it, "Washington was all in a tizzy, not with events in the Middle East,* nor with developments in the State Department and in the Department of Defense,† which were not noticed at all, but with the selection of Agnew's replacement."[28] Names most often bandied about were Nelson Rockefeller (a liberal Republican, and Kissinger's onetime mentor), Texas Democrat turned Republican John Connally, George Bush Sr. and the not widely known conservative from California, former B-movie actor Ronald Reagan.‡

There were, however, objections to all these front-runners. Finally the choice fell to Gerald Ford, a homely, wholesome and unnewsworthy congressman, whose main claim to fame had been as an unshakable football linesman at the University of Michigan. The only person to occupy the office who had been elected neither to the presidency nor the vice presidency, the noble and incorruptible Ford was to prove the best possible choice in a time of catastrophe.

Next came an event which should have been source of pure joy to Kissinger, the ultimate accolade coming on the heels of his appointment as secretary of state. On October 16, an officer interrupted a WSAG crisis meeting on the Middle East war to bring in a news bulletin from Oslo, announcing that he and Le Duc Tho had been awarded jointly the Nobel Peace Prize—for their efforts to end the Vietnam War. Kissinger claims he had not even known he was a candidate: "I threw the dispatch on the table. My colleagues read it with astonishment rather than jubilation; they congratulated me but without real passion. For we were all ill at ease." There was, he commented, "no comparable honor."[29] On the other hand, there was no peace in Vietnam; with breach after breach by Le Duc Tho's compatriots, the news from that ravaged country had never been worse. In view of the con-

---

* War had broken out, without all but minimum warning, four days previously.

† Where James Schlesinger, a "new broom," had recently been appointed at the early age of forty-four, to succeed the briefly tenured Elliot Richardson.

‡ In the view of Conrad Black, in his recent biography, *Richard Milhous Nixon: The Invincible Quest* (2007), had Nixon chosen Rockefeller or Reagan, "Nixon would have had nothing to hide from anyone, his word would have prevailed over anyone else's"; and had Reagan been chosen, thinks Black (a staunch conservative), it "would probably have spared the country the dreary Carter interlude" (pp. 894, 930). Black muses that Reagan might also have "won the Cold War" a decade earlier.

tinuing aggression by the North it did seem a grotesque irony that Le Duc Tho had been honored with a peace prize. To Dobrynin, very privately, he mocked: "I figure it like Groucho Marx said, 'any club that took him in, he does not want to join.' I would say anything that Le Duc Tho is eligible for, there must be something wrong with it."

In this latest triumph, however vicarious, Kissinger nevertheless had time for a thought of empathy with Nixon, on how painful the moment must have been for him. He had yearned more than anything for recognition as a peacemaker: "In fact," he remarked generously in his memoirs, "the major decisions that had ended the Vietnam war had been his." [30] At the same time, he penned an amicable note of congratulation to his partner in the prize. But back came one more slap in the face for America—and Kissinger; Ducky refused to accept the Nobel Peace Prize.* Such "bourgeois sentimentalities" were not for him; moreover, the Paris agreement, he claimed, was not being implemented by the United States. Meanwhile, in the United States the award was receiving slings and arrows from a thoroughly grumpy press. The *New York Times* uncharitably dubbed it "the Nobel War Prize," while in the *Washington Post* that same day George Ball (undersecretary under both Kennedy and Johnson, and by this time an articulate opponent of the Vietnam War) was quoted as suggesting that on the evidence, "The Norwegians must have a sense of humor." The *Hartford Times* queried "Honor Without Peace?", and the *Richmond Times-Dispatch* damned it as an "Ignoble Nobel." [31] In Oslo two members of the Nobel Committee resigned in protest.

The honor rapidly turned to ashes in the mouth of the new secretary of state. In November he requested the Nobel Committee to donate the entire proceeds ($1.3 million) to a scholarship fund for children of American servicemen killed or missing in Indochina. Warned that the award ceremonies in Oslo might provoke massive demonstrations by antiwar groups, he found an excuse to be represented by proxy by the U.S. ambassador. Eighteen months later (April 30, 1975), as the North overwhelmed South Vietnam, Kissinger felt constrained to return the gold medal too.

---

* He was only the second person to turn it down, after Jean-Paul Sartre in 1964, who refused on the rather infantile grounds that it might impair his writing.

It was an unpleasing story. History might possibly come to judge it a pity that the Nobel Committee could not have held off their award for a yet more distinguished contribution in the cause of peace, following the war that—far from Vietnam—had just broken out in the Middle East.

CHAPTER 10

A Dagger Pointing at the Heart of Antarctica

"I don't see why we need to stand by and watch a country go Communist because of the irresponsibility of its own people."

—Henry Kissinger[1]

"Chile was 'destabilized' not by our actions but by Chile's constitutional President."

—Henry Kissinger[2]

WHILE KISSINGER'S CONFIRMATION as secretary of state was still pending, an event took place in far-off South America which would not normally have received major space in the world press. There was a coup in Chile, in the course of which the president, Salvador Allende Gossens, was killed. An unknown army general, Augusto Pinochet, took power. The elimination of a Marxist leader (the only one ever to have been freely elected) who, for the past three years, had proved a thorn in the side of Washington might have caused a small holiday in the heart of Nixon. In relation to other events at the time, however, it did not seem to rate much more than the famous spoof headline: "Small Earthquake in Chile; Not

Many Killed." * Of his hearing news of the coup in Santiago, Kissinger recalled in *Years of Upheaval* how it was only of "peripheral concern" in Washington, "eclipsed by the Year of Europe, the Soviet summit, the Middle East." [3] He might have added Watergate, Vietnam, his own appointment to the State Department: a distraction even confirmed by one of his harshest critics, Christopher Hitchens. [4] Three pages later, Kissinger observed how, occurring in the middle of the disputatious hearings for his own confirmation to State, it "slowed down American reactions" to the coup.

Not for the last time Kissinger found himself puzzling on the U.S. dilemma: how "to reconcile its geopolitical interests and its concern for human rights?" Poor Chile, "caught up in a domestic debate transcending it; it had to carry the burdens of Watergate as well as of Vietnam." [5] Yet this seemingly small episode in a small, remote country of little importance in Kissinger's world order would, with its ramifications, come back to haunt him in the later years of his life like no other single issue.

In presidential elections of September 1970, Allende and his left-wing coalition, Unidad Popular, had won by a tiny, precarious majority of only 1.4 percent of the vote. The vast majority of Chileans, 62.7 percent had actually voted against him, but the vote had been split in a three-cornered contest. In a straightforward election, the present incumbent, the liberal Christian Democrat leader, Eduardo Frei, would have been an almost certain winner, but the Chilean constitution disbarred him from succeeding himself. His successor as leader of the Christian Democrats, Radomiro Tomic, lacked Frei's appeal—but nevertheless polled a respectable 27.8 percent. A sixty-two-year-old doctor, Salvador Allende possessed many attributes of the Latin American bourgeoisie, including a multiplicity of mistresses, but what shocked leaders of the Western world about him was that he was a dedicated Marxist, and a disciple of Cuba's Fidel Castro. Thus, in September, he became the world's first freely elected Marxist leader of a Western country. It was only two years after Brezh-

---

* Composed in the 1930s by Claud Cockburn, to win title of the world's dullest headline; I used it as the title for my 1972 book *Small Earthquake in Chile*.

nev's tanks had crushed the elected government of Czechoslovakia's reformist Alexander Dubček. What was further shocking about this "Small Earthquake" of September 1970 was that it happened, not in unstable Bolivia (whose political setup was once described as "the long-playing record—33 revolutions per minute"), but in the country designated for its stability—in terms then regarded as praise—as "the England of South America." Chile's influence in the Latin American world, and beyond, was immense; and—far from being an isolated island in the Caribbean like Cuba—it bordered on three unstable nations.

Occurring in the years of the Cold War, the potential danger of a Marxist Chile as an importing center for Communism seemed incalculable. The reformist zeal of Eduardo Frei had been regarded, from Kennedy onward, as the great hope of Latin America. Chile had received the largest handouts of aid of any country on the continent, but domestically Frei had not been seen as going fast enough; unemployment and housing in the *poblaciones*—shantytowns—remained acute. Washington had been warned well in advance of the possibilities, and consequences, of a 1970 Allende victory by the U.S. ambassador in Santiago, former journalist Edward Korry, who had covered Soviet incursions in Eastern Europe in the 1940s and 1950s. Well in advance, Korry had pronounced that an Allende victory would be tantamount to "a Communist takeover." But little seems to have been done about it. According to Kissinger, State sat on it—assuring the White House that Jorge Alessandri, the Conservative candidate, would win. Kissinger claims that, for vital months prior to the crucial election, he had been unaware of joint proposals from Korry and the CIA for measures to "head off Allende"[6]—presumably by selective bribery and corruption (though CIA director Richard Helms, in his autobiography,[7] disputes the latter charge). It did not achieve priority status. But when Nixon received the news of Allende's election, he became, in the words of Kissinger, "beside himself."[8] For the past decade, Nixon had "lambasted" previous administrations for permitting Communist power to take root in Cuba; and now it looked as if another Cuba was coming into being under his own administration—and most strategically placed on the mainland of South America.

As Kissinger recalled, for the administration it came in "an autumn of crises, which in one month, saw the arrival of 20,000 Soviet military personnel in Egypt; the hijacking of four airplanes in Jordan by the Palestinians; a Syrian invasion of Jordan; and the discovery of a Soviet submarine base in Cienfuegos, Cuba. What President would not have been deeply concerned at the appearance of a Communist base in the Western Hemisphere in these circumstances?"[9] On TV, on October 7, Nixon declared (in the context of Vietnam), "We had more than enough on our plate without planning assassinations or kidnappings." To David Frost, he put it glumly in one of his 1977 TV interviews: "If Allende should win the election in Chile . . . then you have Castro in Cuba, and what you will have in Latin America is a red sandwich, and eventually it will all be red."[10] Added to this, Nixon had his own personal reasons for being antipathetic to Latin Americans in general; he could never forget his reception in Caracas in 1958, when—as vice president—he, and his wife, Pat, had been spat upon by demonstrators, narrowly escaping injury or possibly even death.

Had all this happened in the time of an Ottoman sultan, bearers of such bad news as Korry and Helms would have both summarily lost their heads; as it was, both, most unfairly, were to be disgraced subsequently as fall guys.* At a meeting on September 15, 1970, summoned by Nixon, and attended by Helms, Kissinger, and John Mitchell (the attorney general, who was subsequently to be convicted and sent to prison for involvement in Watergate), Nixon displayed himself almost rabid with fury at Allende's election, taking it out on the CIA, and Helms personally. Educated at Le Rosey, the smartest school in Switzerland, speaking French and German, and living in Georgetown with an English wife, Helms (whom I got to know well in Washington in the 1980s) typified the kind of civil servant Nixon most distrusted. Helms recalled him ranting: "Truman had lost China. Kennedy had lost Cuba. Nixon was not about to lose Chile."[11] A short time later,

---

* The sacking of Helms, one of the most honorable of CIA chieftains, in February 1973, just weeks before he had reached pensionable age, was condemned by Kissinger as "surpassing pettiness." There was, he added, "No public servant I trusted more" (Helms, *A Look Over My Shoulder*, p. x).

Korry on a visit to the White House received a similar blast, with Nixon pounding his fist in the palm of his hand: "That sonofabitch, that sonofabitch. . . . Not you, Mr. Ambassador. . . . It's that bastard Allende." [12]

It was, nevertheless, an epithet which the president would doubtless come to use about Korry in the weeks ahead. Nixon appears to have been triggered by a meeting at the Connecticut house of his friend the ubiquitous Don Kendall of Pepsi-Cola, who had with him Augustin "Doonie" Edwards, publisher of Chile's respected and principal opposition journal, *El Mercurio*. Edwards had just taken precipitate flight from Santiago, and would find refuge with Kendall for the next three years.[13] Kissinger himself considered that Nixon was "hysterical in 1970 about Chile," regarding himself as "the tool, not the innovator." [14]

At the September meeting, a shaken Helms recalled (to the Church Committee in 1975), "the President came down very hard . . . he wanted something done, and he didn't much care how." Trying to head Nixon off, he deemed, would be like "Standing mid-track and shouting at an oncoming locomotive." That might indeed have been more effective. Helms scribbled hastily on a pad, words that later zinged across Washington:

> One 10 chance perhaps, but save Chile
> worth spending
> not concerned risks involved
> no involvement of Embassy
> $10,000,000 available, more if necessary
> full-time job—best men we have
> game plan
> make the economy scream
> 48 hours for plan of action[15]

Nixon ordered that all knowledge of the conversation be kept (as usual) from the secretary of state, but also from Ambassador Korry and even the CIA chief in Chile. Helms considered it "the most restrictive security hold-down that I can remember." [16] Up to this point, for Kissinger Chile (or even South America as a whole) had barely been on his screen at all; he described Chile, once, unflatteringly, as no more than "a dagger pointing at the heart of Antarctica." Now its significance in the all-important Great Game of the Cold War became apparent, and impelled by Nixon's intense pressure, "unfocused and born of frustration" to "do something," he and Helms became galvanized into action.

It was impossibly late in the day for the CIA to evolve a reasoned "plan of action" out of the hat. Its first ploy was to produce what Kissinger would describe as the "Rube Goldberg* scheme." Thereby the Chilean Congress would be pressed to stage a new election (which it could do, in perfect accord with the constitution, on grounds that the vote for Allende had been too close to call); Alessandri, in second place, would be confirmed, but would promptly resign; which would leave Frei legitimately free to run again in an immediate special election. Track I, as it was called, "was not invented by Nixon," Kissinger claimed, "but by the now overwrought ambassador in Santiago [Korry] and backed by the State Department. It had my full support."[17] However, the constitutionally minded Chilean politician would have none of it.

Under maximum pressure from the White House, and with minimum time for thoughtful research, the CIA choice now fell upon the engineering of a military coup. Hunting around for a progenitor, local operatives fell upon a dubious figure, a disaffected general, Roberto Viaux. Having already been involved in one failed coup against the Frei government, he produced a scheme which involved kidnapping the Chilean chief of staff, René Schneider, who was considered to be pro-Allende. In Washington, within inner circles of the 40 Committee it was dubbed Track II. While the plot was gestating, between September 26 and October 5, Kissinger was out of town, among other things holding fresh meetings with representatives of both North and South Vietnam in Paris. In the meantime, the CIA had reported to Haig that

---

* Reuben Garret Lucius Goldberg (1883–1970) was a popular American cartoonist who won a 1948 Pulitzer Prize for his political cartooning. He was renowned for his cartoons depicting machines designed to perform simple tasks in the most complex, convoluted manner. There were high school Rube Goldberg contests around the United States, challenging students to make the most complex machine to perform a simple task. The nearest British equivalent was William Heath Robinson (1872–1944).

prospects for a coup looked "even dimmer than before." On October 15, Kissinger received a briefing from Thomas Karamessines (the CIA director of plans, who had been involved in the tracking down and killing of Che Guevara in Bolivia three years previously). Not encouraged, Kissinger instructed Karamessines to "turn off" the Track II scheme. That same day he confirmed to Nixon: "That looks hopeless. I turned it off. Nothing would be worse than an abortive coup."[18] Nevertheless, Kissinger records, Karamessines did receive from him that day a "general mandate to 'preserve our assets' in Chile on the (clearly remote) chance that some other opportunity might develop." Whether or not Nixon might have persisted with the Viaux project had it not been for Kissinger is not clear; Kissinger however was positive that with his "turning off" instruction of October 15 it was "the end of both Track I and Track II." Nixon now became "resigned to an Allende presidency." (In his biography of Helms, Thomas Powers, however, adds the rider that "it is easier to get the CIA moving than to halt it. A kind of local inertia gets under way, and things grind steadily forward after the policymakers have shifted their attention elsewhere."[19] Anyone with experience of intelligence work would confirm this.)

Despite the instructions to the CIA in Washington, on October 22, the Viaux group went ahead on its own, "in defiance of CIA instructions" and without Kissinger's knowledge. It resulted in a botched operation, suggestive of the worst of CIA-inspired projects. Schneider resisted his kidnappers; was shot, four times, and died in the hospital. Viaux was apprehended, and sent to prison. The law-abiding Chileans were profoundly shocked, and Allende received a considerable (but temporary) boost as a result. He took up office on November 3, after signing the Statute of Constitutional Guarantees to reassure the Christian Democrat opposition and gain their support. On the 5th, Kissinger addressed a memorandum to Nixon, judging that *the dangers of doing nothing are greater than the risks we run in trying to do something.* He went on to recommend that we "oppose Allende as strongly as we can and do all we can to keep him from consolidating power, taking care to package those efforts in a style that gives us the appearance of reacting to his moves."[20] This, in sum, would remain the guidelines of U.S. policy for the remainder of the Allende era.

Nixon now resorted to economic measures against Chile; as far as Kissinger was concerned, Allende went on the back burner—a "cool and correct" stance was adopted.[21] Kissinger came to regard Track I and Track II as "an insane plan; I don't think I ever knew exactly what it was.* And we didn't trust Korry's judgment, because he had been so wrong about Tomic and the Christian Democrats—so we cut him out. Even Rogers called him 'a loose cannon.' " As he repeated to me several times in the Chilean context: "I had other things on my mind."[22]

Almost immediately after Allende's confirmation in office, Nixon's worst fears were realized. Allende proceeded with his Marxist transformation of Chile at breakneck speed, regardless of his tiny mandate, and of promises made to the Christian Democrat opposition to respect the constitution. Proclaiming *La Vía Chilena al Socialismo* (the Chilean Path to Socialism), he surprised observers by the fact that his Socialists would be more radical, would go even faster, and more ruthlessly, down the road to Marxification than even his more cautious colleagues of the Communist Party inside his Unidad Popular coalition. Within his first month in office, he announced plans to nationalize the immensely rich U.S.-owned copper mines with derisory compensation; private property and farmland would be expropriated in extenso, while his intentions toward Cuba were made plain a few days after his inauguration with the ceremonious unveiling of a statue to Che Guevara in Santiago. The secretary general of Castro's Cuban Workers Federation was in attendance. Even more challenging was Allende's recruitment of the extremist left-wing MIR (Movimiento de Izquierda Revolucionaria), outside the existing police and *carabinero* structure, for his own private security force—described as the "Group of Personal Friends," with its own undisclosed budget. To Che's friend (who had been with him in Bolivia), France's "loose cannon" revolutionary, Régis Debray, who moved in, Allende confided openly that he regarded his constitutional "deal" with the Christian Democrats as purely tactical, and that he would impose on Chile an "irreversible" revolution. Elsewhere, in his book published already in 1971, Debray

---

* Indeed, in their complexity some confusion about them does emerge from his memoirs.

(who was ever anything but discreet about what his friends told him) quotes Allende as saying: "As for the bourgeois State at the present moment, we are seeking to overcome it. To overthrow it!" [23] In fact, all this followed quite rationally from minutes of Chile's Socialist Party back in 1967 which declared: "Revolutionary violence is inevitable and legitimate . . . only by destroying the bureaucratic and military apparatus of the bourgeois state can the socialist revolution be consolidated." [24]

Those autumn months of 1970, I became personally engrossed in Chile's travails over the course of prolonged conversations with Chilean graduate students at Oxford, who were deeply concerned about their country's fate—many years before I had met Kissinger, or knew anything about his involvement over Allende. I had just written two books on the revolutionary Commune of Paris, of 1871,* and when an opportunity presented itself to visit Chile in company of an American journalist friend (William F. Buckley Jr.), I leapt at this opportunity to get experience of a real revolution in process. I planned to stay in Chile a week or two, and file one or two articles; instead I ended staying several months, writing *Small Earthquake in Chile* (which would appear a year before the Pinochet *golpe*—coup)—and becoming enduringly taken with the subject. What I found in January 1971 proved to be—I consider—a useful supplement to the current story. Together with the Yom Kippur War, events in Chile in the 1970s comprised one area of Kissinger's stewardship in which I had the advantage of some direct experience.

My introduction to Chile was to meet Pablo Neruda, the Marxist poet, at his Pacific hideout of Isla Negra; wonderful poet, but a fairly horrible human being—as anyone who has seen the movie *Il Postino* will recognize. Like Allende (who was about to send him as ambassador to Paris), Neruda struck me as the epitome of the "Champagne Socialist"—full of sentiment about the poor of the earth, but relishing a high bourgeois life. Moving to Santiago one was forcefully aware of

---

* *The Fall of Paris: The Siege and the Commune, 1870–71* and *The Terrible Year.*

the poverty, deprivation, massive unemployment, and resentments of the urban poor in their slum *poblaciones*, hotbeds for social revolutionaries like Allende; but nothing as bad as Lima, or Brazil. I found Ambassador Korry, intelligent and cultured with firsthand experience of what Sovietization meant in Eastern Europe, to be a deeply unhappy man. Already he was beginning to realize that he was being cut out in Washington; he had warned about what was likely to happen in Chile, but was now impotent to do anything about it. U.S.-Chilean relations were at rock-bottom, as Allende's socialization of the country galloped ahead at ever increasing speed, his famous "90 Days" already rocking the Andes. Under a policy of agrarian reform about as radical as anything seen in Eastern Europe, Chilean *latifundos* were being taken over—down to farming areas of less than two hundred acres—often through illegal *tomas* (takeovers) by semiguerrilla groups of Guevarist extremists of the MIR. On flimsy excuses of fiscal irregularity, smaller as well as larger private enterprises were also being expropriated by the insertion of government *interventors*. There had already been soaring wage increases, some as high as 40 percent, even 65 percent. To pay for all this, the powerful U.S. copper companies, which—representing an investment of almost one billion dollars—formed the backbone of the Chilean economy, were being grabbed. Washington retaliated by blocking Chilean credits.

Politically, the way ahead was mapped out with abundant clarity by Allende in his conversations with Régis Debray: "to begin with," declared the *compañero presidente*, his Unidad Popular regime would contain opposition "with their own laws. Then, we shall meet reactionary violence with revolutionary violence, because we know they are going to break the rules." [25] And Castro—Allende's new best friend—was coming to town shortly, just to rack up the pressure on *los yanquis* a bit more; while more and more radical leftists were moving into positions of power. Meanwhile, as well, heavy financial pressure was applied to the opposition parties; the principal opponents of Allende's Marxist experiment in the media were being effectively silenced by a combination of officially orchestrated strikes, financial pressures on their advertising revenues, and rank intimidation. *El Mercurio*, the oldest newspaper in all the Hispanic world, an honest and most honorable journal, which would lead the vanguard of opposition to Allende over the next years, was a particular target.

At the university, I met an enraged professor, Claudio Véliz, director of its Institute of International Affairs. Originally well left of center, Véliz backed Allende at the 1970 elections, but was rapidly changing his mind. His black beard was bristling with rage. His beloved university was being politicized, wrecked before his very eyes. It was the student supporters of the MIR: "These mad kids want to turn us into an institute of anti-imperialist studies." Pressure was on to extend a voice in the running of the Governing Body to even the lowest-grade nonacademic employee—so that the porters (who were Marxists) could have a vote. A few weeks after our conversation, Véliz arrived at the university one day to discover he had been locked out, his door screwed shut. *Mirista* students had simply moved in and taken over the building. Véliz left for Australia—and a distinguished international career—like thousands of refugees from Allende's Chile, never to return.

Almost while one watched, Santiago was becoming polarized, into exultation and euphoria on the one hand, something akin to the mood of Russia in 1917 that John Reed described in his classic account, *Ten Days That Shook the World*; on the other side, deepest dark gloom. The confrontation was hotting up daily; ten-thousand-plus "visa-less foreigners" were reported to be entering the country. To my simple, British, conservative mind, what Allende and his zealots were doing to this relatively prosperous, and stable, little country was alarming. Yet it was a fascinating time for a historian of war and revolution; it was all happening here. As it became swiftly clear to me, however, it was not in Santiago that the main revolutionary action was taking place, but down in the countryside far to the south. There the *reforma agraria* was really biting. Hundreds of thousands of hectares of farm and forestry properties were being expropriated, either legally or illegally. Of course, the Chilean *campesinos* had a case. Although real poverty was nowhere as desperate in Chile as elsewhere in South America, land hunger had long been a gnawing evil. When Allende's predecessor the Liberal Eduardo Frei came to power, between 2 percent and 5 percent of landowners possessed an estimated 75 percent of the land, and there was only an average of a hectare per person to go around. Much of the land was inefficiently farmed. Under Frei's reform laws, properties of over two hundred acres could be expropriated. These were fiercely disputed, but with the advent of Allende, his new minister of agriculture, a Cuban-trained apparatchik called Jacques Chonchol—whose love for the *latifundistas* was about as warm as Stalin's for the kulaks—made it clear at once that he intended to accelerate Frei's program out of all recognition.

For the young firebrands of the MIR, down in the southern province of Cautín, things were still not moving nearly fast enough. They were reportedly creating Guevara-style guerrilla *focos*—comparable to the Viet Cong safe areas in South Vietnam. Meanwhile Allende turned a blind eye, pretending they didn't exist. In fact, as I came to discover, he was using the MIR much like the SA storm troopers in the early days of Hitler, doing the dirty work out of sight. A young Chilean journalist, of liberal inclinations, Pablo Hunneus, filled me in with details of at least eighty-six *fundos*, embracing an area of 400,000 acres (in fact, there turned out to be several times that amount), which had already been taken by the MIR down in the two southern provinces of Cautín and Valdivia alone—the breadbasket of Chile. Groups of them were being led by a mysterious figure called Comandante Pepe* who—a little like the freebooter Strelnikov in *Doctor Zhivago*—roamed the countryside at will, carrying out expropriations and setting up armed revolutionary committees wherever he went. Hunneus had himself tracked down Pepe up in the wild Andean foothills close to the Argentine frontier. He reckoned the aim of Pepe's *miristas* was to establish bases to counter a coup by the Chilean right wing. In defense, property owners were beginning to import machine guns from over the border. The situation looked menacing. The Allende government had been enraged by Hunneus's articles, formally declaring that Pepe was a figment of his imagination. Deplorably, but rather typical of the foreign press corps as I remembered from my days as a foreign correspondent in Germany in the 1950s, apart from Hunneus, not one of the vast corps of national and international press, who

---

* The self-appointed rank has a Castroist derivation.

were tumbling over themselves in the bars of Santiago, had taken the trouble to go down south and investigate.

I decided that I would. Accompanied by a courageous Chilean journalist as my interpreter, we set off on the two-day car journey. My pass was that I was a British historian of the Paris Commune (I was fortified with the jacket of my recent book), not unfavorable toward Marxism. Looking back on it, it was a foolish risk to have taken, and possibly dangerous—especially for my interpreter. But this was all before the days of the hostages of Beirut, let alone Iraq; and we were dealing with Chileans, who (at least until the advent of Pinochet and his thuggish acolytes) were a humane people. Up in the Andes, where Hunneus had mapped out, after passing more and more MIR revolutionary slogans, eventually we entered dense forest and jungle country close to the Argentine frontier. The whole neighborhood exuded a miasma of neglect, of slow death. We came to a roughly painted sign:

TERRITORIO LIBERADO

At the head of a posse of armed *miristas* we encountered the legendary, fictitious Comandante Pepe himself: a smallish man dressed predominantly in black: black trilby, black leather jacket with a ruff collar, black knee boots, black hair, black mustache, lively black eyes and freckles, over-tight jeans held together with a string, a large automatic and Bowie knife slung from a rawhide belt. He looked every English boy's image of a Latin American outlaw, a Zorro figure. His real name was José Gregorio Liendo, age twenty-six and of petite bourgeois origin, his father a dairy-worker. He was a student at Valdivia University—the great hothouse center for the MIR—and had now spent four years *conscientizando*, or working on, the local *campesinos*. His number two, twenty-three-year-old Valentina, a tough number also of bourgeois origins, had been sent to school in Maryland, then returned to join the MIR out of impatience with President Frei's reforms. They and their group of out-of-work *campesinos* had moved into the house of the owner of the logging complex, Señor Kunstmann, and expelled him. Altogether Pepe and his *compañeros* had "liberated" nearly a million acres in the area. According to Valentina, "There are 25,000 of us *miristas* now—next year there will be 50,000—the year after, 100,000, all out among the *campesinos*, spreading the revolutionary word."

We sat down and discussed the *reforma agraria* at length. Some of the *miristas* were suspicious of us, and hostile; but not Pepe—who was very forthright. "Remember," he declared, "for centuries a minority has abused the majority in this country, and now it is the turn of the majority to abuse the minority, and there is bound to be injustice in the process." Pepe came across as a romantic of considerable charm, such as Latin America specializes in. He manifested a deep human involvement with the *campesinos*. In a war, I would like to have had him with me. We turned to discussing bourgeois versus Marxist truth. Pepe insisted that the Paris Commune had been provoked by economic injustice. He brought in some of the *campesinos* for a good old-fashioned all-American bull session. I studied their faces. Some looked just like schoolboys, one or two had disagreeably vindictive sneers, and one could without difficulty imagine them operating as dispassionate killers. After a lengthy dialogue Pepe confronted me: "Do I have the impression that you are not a Marxist?"

"You could be right!"

Then, almost in a whisper: "But if you were a Chilean of my age, you would be with *us*, wouldn't you?"

"Quite possibly."

Later that night I reflected how we were all regarding South America with Cold War eyes, neglecting that the revolutionaries of the MIR had their own agenda, and the agenda of youth.

Things developed on a moderately free and easy basis. Pepe did not seem to be worried by my dialectical shortcomings. But some of his team began to look menacing. We departed before things could get rough. But before we did, I asked Pepe about the future, to which he replied meaningfully: "Historically there is bound to be a counterreaction against the Allende government, a right-wing coup. As a *mirista*, as a Marxist, my historical view is that the longer time passes, the more difficult it will be to reverse the popular processes—therefore the left wing will have to react sooner than later. If you see a man about to hit you in the face, you don't just stand there waiting for the blow, do you? Of course, we'll defend ourselves, *hasta la muerte*; but we must organize, and we feel there is not much time." Several times he repeated with chilling emphasis "Civil war in Chile is inevitable."

At the gate, Pepe bid us *adíos*, with a greeting for "my good friend

Jacques Chonchol" (Allende's Cuban-trained minister of agriculture, in charge of the *reforma agraria*): "He was here two weeks ago." A few days later I was interviewing Chonchol down in Temuco. Trained in Cuba, like many a theoretical ideologue, he had never worked the land himself. I questioned him about his strategy of land reform. He said he had a simple formula: "If a proprietor tells me he employs thirteen people, I tell him that's far too few, you must multiply by ten." Not surprisingly, the unhappy landlord now employing 130 bodies cannot afford the wage bill and has to sell up, or simply move out. When we arrived at the delicate issue of the MIR and the illegal land seizures, I inquired "And what about this Comandante Pepe?"

Looking me straight in the eye, he replied: "All an invention of the press . . . I doubt if this Pepe exists. Even if he does he has little significance."

I could not help remembering Pepe's parting remark: "He was here two weeks ago." It seemed to confirm what a dirty, double game Allende and his regime were already playing with their myrmidons of the MIR. They were using the MIR as the left hand of official policy, with the aim of provoking a half-cocked uprising through creating an atmosphere of panic among the landowners—which they could then crush. Pepe's chilling words continued to ring in my ears. "Civil war in Chile is inevitable." He had insisted "it is likely that there will be a right-wing coup within the year." In fact, it would be two years and eight months before the coup would take place, mounted by the army with the object of averting just the kind of civil war that Pepe considered inevitable.

The notion of "arming the workers" proved to be a fantasy which acted against Allende, insofar as it terrified the middle classes of Chile, so that centrists like the Christian Democrats ended in supporting the Pinochet coup. In September 1973, the MIR fought back against it; they were the only ones who did. A few days later, on September 21, 1973, it was reported that Pepe had been captured together with seventeen of his men; two weeks later the London *Times* announced his execution. I learned that the day after the coup he and a group of his *mirista* followers had attacked the nearby *carabinero* post we had visited on the Argentine frontier. They had been repulsed and fled, but were apparently given away by *campesinos* who had previously been his *compañeros*. Pepe was sentenced, and shot summarily. Reportedly he had comported himself with courage. I was not surprised, but felt saddened by the news. Pepe, as I remembered him, for all his considerable charisma was an amateur—like his hero, Che. I could not entirely make up my mind whether these *miristas* were serious guerrillas—or just overgrown students playing the part. But then, what was Che? The execution of Pepe and his men was a final testament to just how bitter divisions had become in this gentle country; in part explaining why a thoroughly alarmed military regime would react with the shocking brutality displayed by Pinochet after September 1973. Fear breeds terror.

I left Chile with gloom in 1971. If ever there was a man bent on shooting himself in the foot, ruining his country in the process, it was President Salvador Allende. When Kissinger wrote years later in his memoirs that he had been "brought down by his own incompetence and inflexibility," or "by forces in Chile that he had himself unleashed, and by his inability to control them"[26] I was not in disagreement. He was indeed "marching inexorably toward a fate which he both dreaded and invited."[27] In 1971, I returned to England convinced that, sooner or later, he would be deposed; the only thing that surprised one was how much later. In the two years between my visit and the publication of *Small Earthquake*, the scene I watched from England grew worse by the day. Inflation would rise from 163 percent in 1972 eventually to 350 percent. Between 1971 and 1973, the Chilean GDP declined by an average of 5.6 percent "negative growth." A once reasonably successful agricultural country would be forced to purchase chickens from France, as food imports rose by 149 percent. (This despite, or perhaps because of, the fact that by September 1973 the government could lay claim to being "in legal possession" of 61 percent of all irrigated farmlands—i.e., the best—in the country.) The plight of the Chilean middle classes became critical; food shortages grew, and more and more private companies fell into the hands of the *interventor*. Breaches of the constitution were being heedlessly perpetrated by the Allende regime. Fear spread as reports multiplied of Cuban and Czech arms entering the country, together with the growing influence of Castro.

What was Washington doing about it? In fact, since the initial reactions of 1970, far less than has been suggested in the aftermath. After November 1970, no evidence has arisen of any further coup plotting by the CIA. With some reluctance, Nixon accepted the "cool and correct" policy toward Chile. To meet Allende's seizure of the U.S. copper companies, America, with perfect propriety, invoked the Hickenlooper Amendment from 1962, which cut off aid to any country expropriating U.S. property. When, a year later, Allende was forced by the economic crises he had fathered to repudiate Chilean debt payments, the international banking community hesitantly followed up with a freeze on credits. Meanwhile, the Chilean opposition, rallying slowly after its defeat, tried—with modest success—constitutionally to stem the tide of takeovers in the private sector, as well as to put a halt on the shipment of arms from Cuba. Recognizing that the biggest internal threat in Chile was Allende's intent to "starve out" the opposition parties, and their media, Kissinger's 40 Committee responded by earmarking some $1.5 million in financial support. (On resistance from the new ambassador, Nathaniel Davis, Ed Korry's successor, some of it however was withheld.) Newspapers under threat, like *El Mercurio*, received covert subsidies purely to keep them in business (according to Davis, just under a million dollars between November 1971 and December 1973). Without this, *El Mercurio* would almost certainly have folded. Recalling how, for many years, the CIA kept Britain's valiant, liberal, and outspoken magazine *Encounter* financially afloat, was this a misdirection of covert funds? I think not; Kissinger for one claimed that "democratic institutions in Chile would have been destroyed without our assistance"[28]; it was probably an accurate prediction. Ambassador Davis, though no pawn of Kissinger's, substantially agreed. (Ironically enough, these CIA funds seem also to have preserved the independent entity of *El Mercurio* even on into the repressive days of Pinochet.)

As was later revealed, however, the sum of $1.5 million was small beer compared with what the Soviets, including the KGB, were spending for their purposes in Chile. (For 1972 alone, a figure of between $600 and $950 million has been put forward.)[29] Interestingly enough, no cuts in U.S. arms sales to Chile were made during these years of standoff; in fact, they would be increased threefold to Allende, who would in effect receive more U.S. military equipment than Pinochet.

Between 1971 and 1973, credits for military purchases rose from $5 million to $12.4 million; a curious paradox when at the same time other forms of aid were cut off. There was a twin reasoning behind this paradox, which clearly showed the hand of Kissinger: suspension of arms sales risked alienating the Chilean military, whom Washington thought might one day become their allies against Allende. Secondly, it would have given Allende an excuse to purchase Soviet equipment—with all that that signified in terms of becoming a client of the Kremlin, as the Egyptians had discovered. The Soviets were dangling offers, reportedly up to $3 million, in arms purchases—which, to the United States, would have represented an unacceptable encroachment into the Western Hemisphere.

Toward the end of 1972, things began to heat up in Chile; there was a prolonged national strike of truck drivers, which received wide support across the country (and, indeed, subsistence funds from the treasury of the 40 Committee). The previous winter, during Castro's prolonged visit, there had already been massed demonstrations by angry housewives in Santiago, beating empty pots and pans in protest against food shortages. In the south, Pepe continued to be increasingly in the news, as at least eight other guerrilla *focos* were reported to have been established—along with accounts of Cuban arms depots building up in the urban *poblaciones*. By May of 1973 the *New York Times* published an editorial warning of the dangers of civil war in Chile, and laying blame firmly at the feet of Allende.

The following month, there was another hamfisted attempt at a coup by an armored regiment in Santiago; Ambassador Davis noted how its legal-minded leaders even "obeyed all traffic lights and at least one tank stopped to fill up at a commercial gas-station."[30] The CIA was in no way involved in this failed coup—nor, it appears, did they even have advance knowledge.[31] It gave rise, on a "relatively quiet" Independence Day, to the following conversation between Nixon and Kissinger, which was—if nothing else—revealing in its jocular innocence about another supposed partner in the Chilean conspiracy, ITT:

P: . . . You know I think that Chilean guy may have some
    problems.

K: Oh, he has massive problems. He has definitively massive problems.

P: If only the Army could get a few people behind them.

K: And that coup last week—we had nothing to do with it but still it came off apparently prematurely. . . .

P: Well, we won't have to send the ITT down to help, will we?

K: [*Laughs*] That's another one of these absurdities. Because whenever the ITT came to us we turned them off. I mean we never did anything for them.

P: I never even knew they came.

K: . . . You didn't know it. I didn't tell you because it required no action and I listened to them and said "Thank you very much" and that was that.

P: Frankly you know we left it to Helms and he and the Ambassador and so forth, they screwed it up. . . .

K: Oh yes, you remember, if we had in '64 they put in $2 million behind Fray [*sic*]. . . . We might as well given nothing.

P: Right. Did you enjoy your visit to LA last night?

K: . . . I saw the opening of *Gigi*. The music was very nice but the play isn't nearly as good as the movie was.

The *tancazo* coup, as it was called, collapsed, but it marked the beginning of the end of the road for Allende. He was now forced to bring generals from the armed services into his cabinet, giving them key roles. On September 6, Allende warned that there was enough flour for only three or four days. Two days later the air force fell upon a large weapons cache hidden in a textile plant; many of the caches being discovered were of recent Cuban or Czech origin. There were increasing indications of Cuban agents, and Cuban arms, deployed in the country, and a kind of panic, not manifest heretofore in Chile, began to seize the "silent majority" of anti-Marxists. Were Castro and Brezhnev poised to pull off a Czechoslovak-style takeover in Chile?

Records of memcons and telcons, released in recent years, show an exceptional paucity of communication between Kissinger, the White House, and security organs concerning Chile in the run-up to September 1973. Between the crucial months of June and September there were no conversations at all between Kissinger and Nixon on the subject. Both had "other things" on their minds; Chile was distinctly off even the back burner. Despite the legions of left-wing devotees beavering away at the legend, no compelling evidence has yet been adduced connecting Kissinger or the White House with the September 11 coup. Christopher Hitchens speaks of a "thesaurus of hard information" in *The Case Against Henry Kissinger*,[32] but is unconvincing. There were even stories, of rivaling fantasy, that the ubiquitous Vernon Walters (then deputy director of CIA) had been spotted directing the coup from the adjacent Hotel Carrera.

In reality, how the attitude of the CIA in Washington, acting under the direction of Kissinger and the NSC, had altered since October 1970 is revealed in an exchange between the Santiago chief of station and his superior in Langley, chief of the Western Hemisphere division, in November–December of 1971. The chief of station had sent a memorandum suggesting that his mission should be to "work consciously and deliberately in the direction of a coup" through fresh contacts within the Chilean military.[33] Back came a sharp rap on the knuckles, stating: "We cannot accept your conclusion . . . nor can we authorize you to 'talk frankly about the mechanics of a coup' with key commanders, because the implications of that amount to the same . . . in sum, stay with history as it unfolds, don't make it."[34] One could almost visualize the final phrase being uttered in a Harvard tutorial by Dr. Henry Kissinger!

Possibly the last communication to Kissinger from William Colby, director of the CIA in succession to Helms, comes in a memcon dated August 25, assuring him that the Santiago station "would not be working directly with the armed forces in an attempt to bring about a coup nor would its support to the overall opposition forces have this as its objective."[35] This seems to offer the conclusion that, right up to the last minutes of Allende's regime, the CIA was not involved in any projected coup plotting. In sum, in the three years since Allende's confirmation in power, could it be found that Washington had executed actions against Chile that lay any distance beyond the norms of international banking or trade law? The ruthlessly inquisitorial Church Committee would come up with the conclusion that it "found no evidence" that the CIA was "directly" involved in the 1973 coup. In his book *Modern Chile*, Mark Falcoff queries: "if a military coup (as op-posed to contingency planning and intelligence gathering) was what Washington wished, why did the 40 Committee so persistently with-hold what it could so easily have given: the necessary authorization?"[36]

Along almost every avenue, one meets the reality that, since the turn-offs of Track I and II in October 1970, Kissinger himself had largely lost interest in Allende and Chile. Never over-enthusiastic in the first place, he had, after all, many "other things" on his mind. But conspiracy theories die slowly. Remarked Kissinger, "In the theology of the left, Allende's collapse *had* to be the malign work of others."[37]

Had Allende himself been conversant with the works of Byron, with what accuracy he might have quoted the following:

> *I have been cunning in mine overthrow*
> *The careful pilot of my proper woe.**

The Pinochet coup on September 11, 1973, was carried out with swift and brutal efficiency. That morning, the Chilean armed forces began by securing the main centers in Chile. Before noon, Allende's government headquarters at La Moneda Palace was surrounded by tanks; then came Hunter fighter-bombers to strafe the building with rockets. By 2 P.M., Allende, who had courageously come into La Mon-eda as soon as he received warning of the attack, was dead, defended to the last by a loyal group of *miristas*. Immediate reports said that, as Pinochet's men worked their way into La Moneda, he had committed suicide with a submachine gun given him by Castro. But alternative legends soon began—with Castro claiming (on the basis of what infor-mation has never been revealed) that he had been murdered by the in-surgents. Whatever, there was no doubting that the *companero presidente*—like Comandante Pepe—had died bravely, one good rea-son why the myth about Allende continued with such force. Ambas-sador Nathaniel Davis thought that Allende's last address, without a single note, and his explicit appeal to the people not to "sacrifice them-selves," would "go down in Chilean history as a moving statement of the aspiration of the Chilean left."[38]

---

* "Epistle to Augusta."

I have tried to indicate how little input Washington had in events leading up to the coup; but how much, or how little, did Kissinger know in advance? Circumstantial evidence looked suspicious — certainly to the American press at the time. Three days before the coup, Kissinger had Ambassador Nathaniel Davis to his office in Washington. It was their first encounter, but Kissinger wrote that it had "entered the mythology of American culpability as a conspiratorial meeting to fine-tune the plot against Allende."[39] Kissinger hotly denied this; nominated secretary of state just two weeks previously, he had asked for a list of the ablest senior State Department officers. Davis was invited to Washington and was subsequently — hence the reason for being interviewed by Kissinger — appointed director general of the foreign service. All Davis knew of the coup was the developing crisis in Santiago that everyone was talking about; Kissinger ordered him to keep the American embassy out of it. To the very last hours, it seems that Pinochet himself was ambivalent about launching the coup and the CIA remained uninformed on its details. It was a failure of intelligence, not for the first or last time in 1973.

Though obviously not displeased by the news of Allende's fall, Nixon's comment on the telephone to Kissinger on the 16th was: "Well, we didn't — as you know — our hand doesn't show on this one though."

Kissinger replied, "We didn't do it.[40] I mean we helped them. [*garbled*] created the conditions as great as possible." Kissinger's critics assiduously endeavored to find some sinister connotation in this tormented sentence, but none of it quite seems to add up to a smoking gun of complicity in the Pinochet coup.

As news began to reach North America about the excesses being carried out in Pinochet's post-coup purges, on September 26, Senator Edward Kennedy deplored the Nixon administration's "policy of silence" on the spate of executions. On October 11, Kissinger warned Admiral Ismael Huerta, Pinochet's foreign minister, who was visiting the United Nations, that Chile would pay "a heavy price" if it resorted to brutal repression. Huerta replied that the government's first priority was to control the "internal situation."[41] Though providing little excuse for the regime's brutality, something of the fear felt by the Chilean armed forces may be gleaned from remarks made by Castro to the East Germans three months after the coup: "In our embassy in Santiago we had a large group of combat troops. We had to hand weapons sufficient for a battalion. Our troops were instructed to defend and protect President Allende once the order was given. Unfortunately Allende neglected to take such precautions."[42]

Having observed Allende's Chile in operation at first hand, it never ceases to amaze me that the *compañero presidente* continues to this day to be such a folk hero across the world, and not only among the way-out left. How did he ever achieve such a heroic legend? Was it in part because he died violently, like Che—or Princess Diana? Macaulay's famous dictum, "We know no spectacle so ridiculous as the British public in one of its periodical fits of morality," seems to apply here equally. Proportionate to "morality" about the martyrdom of Allende comes a condemnation, much of it unreasoned, about the responsibility of Henry Kissinger. In the United States alone a vast industry engaging scholars, like Peter Kornbluh of the Chile Documentation Project, at the National Security Archive in Washington, have been laboring away, turning out pages of incriminating documentation by the thousands. Pressure by the human rights coterie became so acute, as noted earlier, there was a time two decades later when Kissinger hesitated to travel anywhere near cities like Judge Juan Guzmán's Madrid, just in case some overzealous moralist might wish to arraign him as Pinochet had been in Jack Straw's London. But is there some Macaulayan hypocrisy at work here? Professor Niall Ferguson has drawn shrewd parallels between attitudes to the "disappeared" (2,279) in Pinochet's Chile and the dead (around 200,000) in the CIA-led coup in 1954 Guatemala, commenting: "you will search the bookshops in vain for *The Trial of John Foster Dulles* or *The Trial of Dean Rusk*." He goes on to query pointedly why there was no outrage when Nixon and Kissinger had trooped off to the court of Chairman Mao in China, who was "guilty of many more violations of human rights than all the right-wing dictators put together."[43]

In 1987, nearly seventeen years after my first visit, I returned to Chile, for an interview with President Pinochet. It was supposedly the first he had permitted to a foreign writer. We spoke for nearly an hour, in the course of which he observed that his government had never "practiced" torture. On the other hand, he also assured me that, were he to lose the election, the following year, he would get out. Unlike Allende's Jacques Chonchol back in 1973, in this context at least he spoke the truth; Pinochet lost the election, the first in nineteen years, and promptly handed over the presidency. In economic terms, the Chile I found in 1987 was a very different country to that under Allende; under Pinochet, whatever might be said about his human rights record, it had acquired a new, and firmly based, economic prosperity—which remains the envy of Latin America to this day.

Though *Small Earthquake in Chile* was published back in 1972, a year before Pinochet seized power, since then I have found little in my views about Allende that I would modify now. If anything, recent releases of documents from the former Soviet Union have hardened them. Most notably, the Mitrokhin Archive (Volume II)* reveals with extraordinary clarity the closeness of KGB links to Allende, hitherto suspected, but nevertheless not proven. According to Nikolai Leonov, the KGB's leading expert on Latin America (dispatched there in the guise of being a journalist), under Yuri Andropov, all KGB efforts were "aimed at causing the greatest possible harm to North American dominance in this part of the world. So we supported politically, sometimes by sending weaponry or other aid, anyone who was against United States dominance." 44 Andropov's priorities were "to strengthen—discreetly—the Soviet footholds in Chile and Peru"; but nothing was to be done "that would cause complaints about our activity." Mitrokhin considered that, back in 1970, the KGB "may indeed have played a significant part in preventing Allende being narrowly beaten into second place." In contrast to the CIA, KGB money was "precisely targeted." Most damningly, the KGB files reveal how "In a cautious way Allende was made to understand the necessity of reorganizing Chile's army and intelligence services, and of setting up a relationship between Chile's and the USSR's intelligence services. Allende reacted to this positively."

---

* *The Sword and the Shield: The Mitrokhin Archive and The Secret History of the KGB,* by Christopher Andrew and Vasili Mitrokhin (2005). Mitrokhin, a former KGB archivist, is regarded to have been possibly the most valuable intelligence asset ever to have come over to the West.

If Allende was not actually a paid-up agent on the KGB books, he now seems to have been extraordinarily close to it, with KGB contacts regularly passing him sums of money for his personal use. In February 1973, for instance, $400 was paid to Allende for unspecified "valuable information" he had provided, and (so Andropov reported to the Politburo): "Allende set this channel apart from the usual unofficial government contact and used it for handling the most confidential and delicate matters (establishing contact between Chile's and the USSR's armed forces, consulting on the use of Chilean atomic raw materials, organizing co-operation between the Chilean and Soviet security services)." Andropov, Mitrokhin continued, went on to note that the KGB had "succeeded in exerting a definite influence on Allende," who was, in turn, "systematically informing us on the situation in the country and in Popular Unity, on his own personal plans, and so forth." Could anything have been much more double-faced? The KGB (of all people) was also recording information about Chilean torture chambers under Allende—a matter on which apologists in the West are reticent. On February 17, 1973, at a secret meeting with a KGB operative in a villa in the suburbs of Santiago, Allende passed on his fears of a coup: "Allende is very much counting on Soviet assistance in this matter," the Lubyanka was informed.

By the spring of 1973, however, even the KGB was beginning to write Chile off. There was talk about a $30 million cash loan, but this was considered by Nikolai Leonov, the director of KGB ops in South America, to be "like putting a patch on a worn-out tire." Leonov recorded that the KGB no longer believed in Allende's success.

On his death, for the KGB, says Mitrokhin, "Pinochet represented an almost perfect villain, an ideal counter-point for the martyred Allende. Pinochet himself played into the hands of hostile propagandists." As did the activities of his notorious DINA secret service: Operation Toucan, approved by Andropov on August 10, 1976, was marked up as being "particularly successful in publicizing and exaggerating DINA's foreign operations against left wing Chilean exiles." It specialized in publication of forged letters from its director, the much feared Miguel Contreras, to Pinochet—which were accepted by even major newspapers in the West as genuine. The *bien-pensants* Allende fans were avid customers. Mitrokhin records how, in 1976, the

New York Times published sixty-six articles on the abuse of human rights in Chile, as compared with only four on Cambodia. One final note of relevance from this KGB file: following the Nixon visit to Moscow in 1972, and Brezhnev's return to Washington the next year, which represented the high point of Soviet-American détente, the KGB sent orders to its outstations to "be cautious" in Latin America.

So, in interfering in the affairs of a sovereign state, did Nixon and Kissinger behave improperly? Times and standards change. Nineteen seventy was a time of perceived maximum peril in the Cold War. Only a decade from the Cuban Missile Crisis, Castro and his influence on the continent of South America was regarded in Washington as a grave threat; and not only in the context of the Western Hemisphere. Acting like a Foreign Legion for the Soviets, Cuban mercenaries were already popping up in hot spots like Angola in Southwest Africa. Perhaps the atmosphere of the times was well expressed by Kissinger with his remark of 1970: "I don't see why we need to stand by and watch a country go Communist because of the irresponsibility of its own people."[45] If a historian can find any excuse, or explanation, for the excesses and abuses committed under Pinochet, it may be that history tends not to circle gently, but moves in strong swings of the pendulum; a violent swing producing a violent reaction. Allende's experiment in Marxism was no "small earthquake," and the shockwave in fear and hatred that it produced was, inevitably, of comparable force.

In the United States the full impact of the Pinochet coup was perhaps not apparent until the fall of Nixon in 1974, and the report of the Church Committee (or, more properly, the United States Senate Select Committee to Study Governmental Operations with Respect to Intelligence) of 1975–77. Out of the whole Allende episode, the U.S. intelligence community would emerge one of the principal losers—in a defeat from which it may well not have recovered at the time of writing. The hearings came against a backdrop of the ending of the Vietnam War, and the Watergate revelations. Americans were fed up with war, and with "spooks," and intelligence activities as a whole—which they no longer considered to be a front line of defense of the nation. The dam broke on December 22, 1974, with the *New York Times* publication of a lengthy article by Seymour Hersh, which detailed CIA operations over the years, dubbed "the family jewels." Covert action programs involving assassination attempts against foreign leaders, and subversion of foreign governments, were reported for the first time. Among matters investigated were the assassinations of foreign leaders, such as Patrice Lumumba of the Congo, Rafael Trujillo of the Dominican Republic, the Diem brothers, Ngo Dinh Diem and Ngo Dinh Nhu, of Vietnam, Kennedy's plan to use the Mafia to kill Fidel Castro—and, notably, General Schneider of Chile. Under recommendations and pressure from the Church Committee, President Ford issued Executive Order 11905 (ultimately replaced in 1981 by President Reagan's Executive Order 12333) to ban U.S.-sanctioned assassinations of foreign leaders. But the hearings, the most extensive review of intelligence activities ever to be made available to the public, were to become almost a McCarthy-style witch-hunt against all forms of "secret intelligence"—and an exercise in self-hatred, and self-harm.

It was, in effect, putative CIA activities against Allende which constituted the straw that broke the camel's back, or the bucket of water that submerged the dam, whichever metaphor one cares to choose. Although, as has been seen, the CIA was trumped all along the line by the KGB, and actually had only the most modest input in Chile after 1970, yet it was Chile, preeminently, which brought lasting punishment down on the head of the American intelligence community. Through the Church Committee, it was to become "a treasured exhibit in the chamber of horrors of American foreign policy."[46] Emblematic was the fate of Director Richard Helms, who was fined and disgraced—for not telling what he construed to be against the honor of the service (though he continued to be revered within the profession). Both he, and Ed Korry too, deserved better of the American establishment.

Unfairly, when it came to the future effectiveness of the CIA as an organization, what would count in the book with the Church Committee of 1975 over Chile would not be the CIA's restraint from 1971 on, but the rash options imposed on it by Nixon in 1970. In fact, one might almost conclude by agreeing with Kissinger—that it would have been better if the CIA had done nothing (save perhaps its rescue of the opposition media). The Pinochet coup would have happened of its own, Chilean accord, anyway, with or without any input from Washington—if not in September 1973, then at latest a few months down the road. For America, as Ambassador Davis construed it, the contest lay "between covert action and abstention in a skewed political struggle."[47]

At issue too, and not only within a coterie of American opinion, was the reputation of Henry Kissinger, as head of the NSC throughout the Allende years.

On May 31, 2001, while Kissinger was enjoying a stay at the Ritz Hotel in Paris, a French judge served a summons on him relating to crimes committed under the Pinochet regime back in the 1970s. It was, Kissinger said, "unprecedented—a secretary of state pursued in a foreign court on twenty-four-hour notice about alleged human rights abuses without being told the subject matter of the inquiry. I contacted the deputy chief of mission of the American embassy in Paris—an ambassador not being in residence."[48] He consulted the State Department, the White House and the French Foreign Ministry. The problem was that to resist the summons on principle would have turned the issue into a cause célèbre, leaving open its substantive content.

Without changing his schedule, Kissinger left Paris the following afternoon, and the judge's inquiries were directed to the U.S. State Department. A questionnaire was then submitted and answered by the State Department, with the assistance of Kissinger's legal advisers. These questionnaires were returned to the French foreign minister. Kissinger goes on to note that "No response was ever received from the judge or other French authorities. (The inquiry turned out to be a red herring. It concerned a Frenchman engaged in anti-Pinochet activities who disappeared from Buenos Aires, about whom no American records seem to have existed. No American agency was involved in his fate. The first time I learned his name was from the court proceedings.)" Three years previously Pinochet himself had been arrested in London, on orders of the Labour home secretary, Jack Straw, and held for nearly two years—on an application by a Spanish judge. His unprecedented detention, in a foreign country for crimes against humanity committed in his own country, without any request for extradition from his own country, marked a watershed in international law.

Later in 2001 again, an Argentine judge applied to the U.S. State Department for a deposition by Kissinger to aid the investigation of

Operation Condor, an organization set up jointly by right-wing military governments in Latin America, namely Argentina, Chile, Uruguay, Paraguay, Bolivia, and Brazil, during the mid-1970s, with the object of combating left-wing subversion. Its activities led to a number of covert killings—including that, allegedly, of Orlando Letelier, a former minister of Allende's, in the middle of Washington, D.C. in September 1976. Allegations were made of official U.S. support, but these have never been documented. In any case, so far as Kissinger is concerned, their date puts them outside the remit of this book. The following month, a civil suit was filed in a Washington, D.C., court by the family of the late General René Schneider, former commander in chief of the Chilean army, alleging Kissinger's involvement in his killing in October 1970. They were attempting to sue Kissinger and Helms (then director of the CIA) for $3 million. The very next day, on the twenty-eighth anniversary of the Pinochet coup, Chilean human rights lawyers filed a criminal case against Kissinger, along with Pinochet and other Latin American leaders, for alleged involvement in Operation Condor—on behalf of ten alleged Chilean victims. These questions were dealt with in 2002 by the same procedure outlined above. "No response was ever received," says Kissinger.[49] The Argentine queries were never pursued. Also in 2001, journalist Christopher Hitchens wrote a scathing critique, *The Trial of Henry Kissinger* (later adapted into a film), which accused Kissinger of war crimes, particularly in the context of Cambodia and Chile. In sum, nothing has ever come of these various charges.

Nevertheless, one may recall the imputations made against ex–prime minister Harold Macmillan by Nikolai Tolstoy in *The Minister and the Massacres*, which—though proved to be unfounded—made a misery of a distinguished elder statesman's old age.[50] Similarly, the Chile allegations were a source of constant, nagging anxieties in Kissinger's later years. He has to be prudent in which countries he flies to. The controversy rumbles on, as late as 2003 spreading to the august pages of *Foreign Affairs*, which in turn led to the angry resignation of an eminent member of the Council on Foreign Relations, Kenneth Maxwell. At least one point made by Maxwell in his article would probably not be disputed by Henry Kissinger—and certainly not by this author: "Allende might have fallen by his own weight, victim of his own incompetence, and not become a tragic martyr to a lost cause." The Chileans finally dealt with Pinochet themselves; he died a short while later, in December 2006, aged ninety-one, disgraced as much in Chile for his secret account with the Riggs Bank as anything else. In the outside world, however, there is little sign of the barrage against Kissinger falling away.

CHAPTER 11

THE WAR OF ATONEMENT

"A generation that has taken a thrashing is always followed by one that deals out the thrashing."

—Bismarck

"The overwhelming victory of the 1967 Six-Day War proved to be an albatross that almost doomed Israel in 1973."

—Walter J. Boyne[1]

W E NOW REACH the dramatic high point of this story of 1973 and Henry Kissinger: the crunch, the crisis, an episode presenting material not just for one but numerous books in itself. The Yom Kippur War may seem to loom large in these pages; but it did then. Not only did it threaten world peace, change all conceptions about the Middle East, and impose upon Western economies the worst energy crisis since World War II, but—in its unprecedented documentation, massive accumulations of those telcons and memcons—it also shows the workings of Henry Kissinger in power as nothing else does. Set against a backdrop of domestic meltdown in Washington, the events of October 1973 should certainly not have been unforeseen, and would not have been—under normal circumstances. Yet they were to have unforeseeable consequences, imposing upon the foreign-born Harvard professor an unanticipated role of Olympian significance, and bringing him to a pinnacle of lasting, but unexpected, fame. What led up to the October War as it would be known in Egypt, or the Yom Kippur War as it would be labeled in Israel (and the West), was a lethal distillation, over the past months, of Israeli hubris, Arab zealotry, and Egyptian cunning, a failure of both U.S. and Soviet intelligence—and of Watergate.

At six on the morning of Saturday, October 6, Kissinger was sleeping peacefully in his thirty-fifth-floor suite of New York's Waldorf-Astoria. Two days previously he had been speaking at the Metropolitan Museum of Art to delegates to the new session at the United Nations, in the course of which he deplored, philosophically, the self-destructive instincts of man. He was preparing a further speech for that day. Suddenly, at 6:15 A.M., Joseph Sisco*—the excitable assistant secretary for Near Eastern affairs whom Kissinger had inherited from the State Department—"barged" into his bedroom. Sisco told him that Israel and Egypt and Syria were about to go to war. He had been warned by the U.S. ambassador to Israel, Kenneth Keating, who had been summoned urgently to Prime Minister Golda Meir's office two hours previously. "We may be in trouble," she had warned Keating. Sisco, relates Kissinger, was "confident, however, that it was all a mistake; each side was really misreading the intentions of the other." He thought that if Kissinger "set them right immediately," he could get matters under control before the shooting began. Kissinger viewed this as "a flattering estimate of my capacities. Unfortunately, it turned out to be exaggerated."[2] In fact, contrary to every expectation and intelligence analysis, the shooting had already begun—and a new major war in the Middle East was underway. The date had been appointed with supreme adroitness by the attacking Arab nations; it was Yom Kippur, the Day of Atonement, the holiest day of the year for Jews. As Kissinger reminds us, it was "a day spent in fasting, prayer, and reflection; it is supposed to remind man of his insignificance in relation to God . . . in which, according to tradition, God decides the destiny of all mortals for the coming year."[3] For the Arabs in 1973 it was also the

---

* A native of Chicago, Dr. Sisco was the son of Italian immigrants. His mother died when he was nine, and his father, a tailor, raised the five Sisco children in modest circumstances.

first day of Ramadan; thus all round the most unlikely day to start a war. For the Arabs it would also be a day of destiny, changing all ideas in the Middle East.

Little suited Kissinger's temperament better, however, than a crisis and he immediately went into action with a barrage of telephone calls and signals from the Waldorf: to Haig (Nixon was hiding out from the current D.C. storm, over Agnew's resignation, in Key Biscayne), to the Israeli and Arab representatives, to the British ambassador (Lord Cromer), to the U.N. secretary-general (Kurt Waldheim). Of particular significance was the fact that his very first call that morning, already at 6:40, was to the Soviet ambassador, and his good friend, Anatoly Dobrynin. Despite the developing cataclysm, throughout the day Kissinger's sense of humor was never entirely to desert him. The exception was when (by 7:51 A.M.) the U.S. Navy commander had failed to expedite messages to the Soviet embassy, and received the full force of Kissinger's well-known impatience with nonperforming subordinates.* Clearly woken up by Kissinger's early morning call, Dobrynin seemed completely, and convincingly, bemused, by the news Kissinger gave him. He was looking forward to taking off for a relaxed weekend, and "quite a nice dinner" at his house in Maryland. Kissinger dissuaded him. The Soviet ambassador repeated each statement of Kissinger's, to the point of the caller exploding with irritation. It was the kind of irritability only acceptable between old-established friends.

K: We are urgently communicating to the Israelis.
D: You?

---

* K: When I ask you to do something, it must be done that second . . .
  H: [Commander Jonathan Howe] I will look into it.
  K: Get these people off their behinds. What conceivable reason not to have them sent there yet? (Kissinger, *Crisis*, p. 23).

Later Kissinger made a heavy joke of this to Dobrynin, suggesting that his KGB operatives might help dispose of a few "bodies" out of Washington, referring presumably to the chastised navy officer in charge of communications in the Situation Room (Commander Howe survived, to become a full admiral, commander of the U.S. Fleet in the Mediterranean).

K: If I kill some people and get the bodies to you can you get them out of the city?
D: Ha ha ha. (*Crisis*, p. 22).

K: Yes.

D: Communicate to the Israelis?

K: If this keeps up . . . —there is going to be a war before you
   understand my message.[4]

Kissinger's motives in making communication with Dobrynin his
first priority was twofold: one, to ascertain whether the Soviets were
"in the plot," backing their Arab client states to attack Israel for whatever purpose; and, two, to judge how war in the Middle East might affect the U.S.-Soviet Great Game of détente, the top priority, on which
so much diplomatic and political capital had already been expended.
All through the ensuing weeks and months of crisis in the Middle East,
this second concern would remain Kissinger's overriding consideration; more than the carnage to the respective client states of the region,
or their mutual security—more too than the subsequent oil threat to
Western economies. At the back of Kissinger's reasoning was also the
opportunistic ambition that the Yom Kippur War could provide a lever
to get the Soviets out of the area; even though this ambition might perhaps seem to sit oddly with all the professions of amity and détente.
But was this opportunism something Metternich and Castlereagh
would have let pass them by?

Kissinger had another four or five conversations that morning with
Dobrynin. It was plain that Dobrynin had not been put in the picture
by Moscow. He complained about his level of communications;
Kissinger generously offered Moscow access to the U.S. end of the hot
line. But—more important—by the end of the day Kissinger felt reasonably reassured that the Soviets were not behind the Arab attack. (It
subsequently emerged that Brezhnev had been warned the previous
day. The source still remains a mystery; it was not, apparently, the
KGB or the Soviet embassy in Cairo or Damascus.) As the day progressed, it became equally clear that Israel was not the aggressor; which
is what ran totally across the preconceptions of the befuddled minds of
the Western intelligence agencies, committed to the rationalist view
that an Arab-initiated attack would be tantamount to a quest for suicide. No one, however, seemed to question whether Sadat shared the
same rationale. For the Soviets—rational people—to be behind it

would, equally, have amounted to assisted suicide. Khrushchev, maybe; but surely not Brezhnev.

After his first call to Dobrynin, Kissinger then rang the Israeli embassy in Washington. The ambassador, Simcha Dinitz, also a friend of Kissinger's, was away in Israel, observing Yom Kippur. In his absence, Kissinger spoke to Dinitz's deputy chief of mission, Mordechai Shalev, and chided him for not having gotten to him a message of the previous day—which, in the mounting tension, was to reassure Egypt and Syria that Israel "had no intentions to attack." Shalev told him that, as of fifteen minutes ago, Israel was taking "precautionary measures," including "mobilization of some troops." Kissinger replied with emphasis that "We are in touch with the Soviets and the Egyptians*, urging the utmost restraint. Dobrynin has said they will cooperate with us. We are setting up special communications.† We would like to urge you not to take any preemptive action because the situation will get very serious if you move."[5]

Next, at 7 A.M., he telephoned the Egyptian foreign minister, Mohamed el-Zayyat, who was attending the U.N. meeting in New York. Previously Kissinger had used the back channel to Cairo via Zayyat. Kissinger read him the Israeli message verbatim, repeating his warning given to the Israelis not to attack, and got the same fuzzy response as he had gotten from Dobrynin—having to reread the message to him. It made him "reasonably sure" that Zayyat was also not dissembling; Sadat had not kept Zayyat in the loop. He got no response from the Syrian U.N. mission. At 8:15, Zayyat came back with Cairo's reply; it claimed that there had been an Israeli "provocation" with naval units attacking Egyptian positions in the Gulf of Suez. Kissinger then telephoned Abba Eban, Israel's much respected foreign minister, a veteran diplomatist of South African origin since the early days of Israel's existence. Eban considered that such a move was inconceivable, especially on Israel's holiest day. Kissinger agreed. Five minutes later, at 8:29 (3:29 P.M., Middle East time) an agitated Shalev was on the line

---

* He did not reveal when, or by what means; his own back channel to Sadat?

† At that point, since the Six Day War of 1967, the United States had had (officially) no relations with Syria or Egypt.

again: Egyptian and Syrian planes had been attacking all along the front for the past half hour; he knew nothing about the alleged Israeli naval attack. A second conversation with Eban passed on a firm insistence from Prime Minister Golda Meir that the story of the Israeli naval attack was "false."

"Her Hebrew vocabulary," relayed Eban, "is very rich and she poured it on," emphasizing that "our action so far has been defensive."[6] Kissinger immediately proceeded to send "flash messages" to the kings of Jordan and Saudi Arabia urging them to use their influence to avert hostilities. Later that night Jordan's King Hussein, America's constant lone friend among the Arabs, came back expressing concern; Faisal of Saudi Arabia emphasized Arab solidarity. Both would remain on the sidelines of the conflict.

At 8:35, Kissinger was on the telephone to Haig, who was with Nixon in Key Biscayne. Haig seemed as surprised as the others.

> K: We may have a Middle East war going on today.
> H: Really?

Kissinger then filled him in on what he had gleaned.

> K: First I thought it was an Israeli trick for them to be able to launch an attack although this is the holiest day.

He repeated the gist of his earlier conversations, adding, "All I want you to know is that we are on top of it here."

This might be considered as something of an exaggeration.

He continued: "I think what happened is the Russians told the Egyptians . . . that there will not be any progress unless there is stirring in the Middle East and those maniacs* have stirred a little too much."[7] Kissinger then gave the former military man his strategic interpretation (to which he would cling for the next few days)—that the Israelis would hit back hard, and win. A call to Secretary-General Waldheim at the U.N., who was in a position to delay or speed up Se-

---

* Note the same noun used by Kissinger when dealing earlier with both North and South Vietnamese.

curity Council meetings, had the aim of allaying any fears of an Israeli preemption. By mid-morning, Kissinger had the president himself on the line. Nixon's first observation was, echoing Kissinger, that "the Russians claim to be surprised." Kissinger reported that a meeting of the Security Council was likely to take place already that day, to which Nixon remarked, "We ought to take the initiative. Can't we get the Russians to?" With some wisdom he then urged Kissinger: "Don't take sides. Nobody ever knows who starts wars out there." Kissinger responded by outlining "two problems . . . the long term, I think it is impossible now to keep maintaining the *status quo ante*. On the immediate thing, we have to avoid getting the Soviets drawn in on the side of the Arab group. If they join us in a neutral approach . . . that would be best."[8]

In another call to Dobrynin, Kissinger then warned that if the Soviets took a position where "you will have to defend the Arabs," it would force the United States into defending Israel. "We are then in a hell of a mess. It will affect a lot of friendships."[9]

Dobrynin: "I understand."

At 10:55 A.M., Kissinger was telling Shalev: "I want to inform you on a personal basis only for the Prime Minister that we have proposed to the Soviets that we jointly call—the U.S. and the Soviets—a Security Council meeting and [for a] return to the cease-fire line. [This is] an attempt to smoke them out to see if they were behind it and give us a basis for leaning towards your position in the actual debate. This only for the Prime Minister."[10] Toward the end of the morning, Kissinger had Shalev again on the line, who told him—in a note of unsustainable optimism:

S: The information that I have on the military situation is that in the Syrian front the attempt by the Syrians to advance have (*sic*) been halted. On the Egyptian front I know about 16 Egyptian planes down, some of the Egyptian troops crossed the Canal and our people are dealing with that now. I wouldn't like to be in the shoes of those that are being dealt with.

K: (laughs) Well, that is what we are counting on.

S: You shouldn't worry.

K: We are operating on the assumption that you will win.

S: There isn't the slightest doubt.

K: But it would be helpful to us if you kept me informed.

At 2:30 P.M., Kissinger took off to Washington, having summoned an emergency meeting of WSAG, the crisis tabernacle within the National Security Council, now in the hands of Kissinger's able and reliable deputy General Brent Scowcroft. He also instructed Scowcroft to set up a plan to move the U.S. Sixth Fleet toward the Eastern Mediterranean danger area. It was clear that the NSC's inside information lagged behind what Kissinger had already determined. Combined intelligence reports had failed to find any "hard evidence" of a coordinated Egyptian-Syrian offensive. Director of the CIA William Colby still thought that Israel had initiated the attack. Defense Secretary James Schlesinger * (like Kissinger, also Jewish) supported this thesis, remarking that it would be the first time in twenty years when a Mideast war had *not* been started by Israel. Only Roy Atherton, Sisco's deputy, did not concur, observing that it would be "the last day in the year when they would have started something."

By mid-morning, in his sixth conversation with the Soviet embassy, Kissinger was yet more emphatic in his warnings to Dobrynin, quoting the president's "very grave concern" that the war should not be "used to destroy everything that it has taken us three years to build up." He warned that "If you take the position of support all out for the Arabs, that would be in effect encouraging what seems clearly to us an Arab attack." In the Security Council, the United States would be prepared "to take a neutral position if you do, and we are prepared to

---

* Nominated by Nixon on May 10, 1973, from being director of CIA for only five months, Schlesinger became secretary of defense on July 2, at the youthful age of forty-four. But, as a university professor, researcher at RAND, and government official in three agencies, he had acquired an impressive background in national security affairs. Outlining the basic objectives that would guide him, in particular, Schlesinger saw a need in the post-Vietnam era to restore the morale and prestige of the military services; modernize strategic doctrine and programs; and shore up a Defense Department budget that had been declining since 1968. He maintained that the theory and practice of the 1950s and 1960s had been overtaken by events, particularly the rise of the Soviet Union to virtual nuclear parity with the United States, and the effect this development had on the concept of deterrence. Schlesinger believed that "deterrence is not a substitute for defense"; over détente he would collide with Kissinger.

make a joint resolution just calling for [a return to the] cease-fire line."
He stressed his personal assessment that Arab incursion into "Israeli
territory" would not last seventy-two hours before the Israelis turned
the tide. Although Washington, he revealed, had already received "an
urgent Israeli request for additional military supplies," it had not responded. But, "If it gets out of hand, we will be forced to that." Then
the Soviet Union and the United States would find themselves on opposing sides. Privately, it was worrying to him to learn that—two days
previously—Soviet civilians had been withdrawn from Egypt and
Syria. To Dobrynin, he concluded, plaintively but forcefully: "Your
Arab friends were terribly deceitful. . . . We are taking this matter extremely seriously." Later that Saturday afternoon he stressed to Dobrynin his conviction already that the war would end in military
victory for Israel. "Then everyone will come to us. . . . No one should
think they can diddle us along."[11]

At the end of a hectic day, the most hectic since he had taken over
as secretary of state (while still remaining head of the National Security Council), Henry Kissinger was not a happy man. As far as impelling the Security Council to move, the British (with whom as we
have seen relations were already at best cool), were "getting cold
feet."[12] Backing Egyptian representations, they would only support a
resolution for a simple cease-fire—but not for a "cease-fire ante"
(meaning, back to the lines held by Israel on pre 1967 Egyptian and
Syrian territory). "This faces us with a problem." To Lord Cromer, the
British ambassador, Kissinger generously confessed that "Our worst
mistake was to throw you out of the Canal Zone," referring to the Suez
debacle of 1956. However, he then pulled no punches; referring to the
impasse of the Year of Europe in Copenhagen, he declared that it
"doesn't apply with regard to the Eastern Mediterranean." He added,
"It is in the interest of everybody, including Western Europe, not to
run across us in this particular instance." (This was a thinly veiled menace that would become more pointed as the oil crisis developed.) The
Soviet position was equivocal. With Haig's concurrence, Kissinger
pressed. "We have to be prepared to take them on . . . we cannot be the
soft guys in this crisis."[13] In his longest call to Dobrynin, that evening
Kissinger repeated to him that in the Security Council he would be
calling for "a de facto return to the status quo ante" lines.[14] He hoped

the meeting would not turn into a "propaganda battle," warning if it did "our only protection is to be extremely tough and to teach the facts of life to people who like to make great speeches and we will see what is more important—a speech or reality. I will be very brutal. That will be our strategy."[15] That was surely plain speaking; once again, undoubtedly facilitated by those chummy relations he had fostered with the Russian. Shelved now were the earlier jokey conversations. He also let Dobrynin know meaningfully that he was pursuing his own communications with what was still a Soviet ally—Egypt.

At home, however, the president was increasingly embattled by Watergate where the issue of his surrendering the tapes was moving inexorably through the courts, and now by the pending resignation* of Vice President Agnew. "His authority," noted Kissinger, "was deteriorating daily"; the president looked like providing little command in the crisis.

Kissinger's long day ended with his chairing a WSAG meeting in Washington. One good piece of news was that Soviet naval units pulling out of Egyptian ports were heading *west*; i.e., away from the battle zone, suggesting a desire for noninvolvement. On the other hand, although Kissinger persisted in his conviction that "By Tuesday, or Wednesday at the latest, the Arabs will be defeated," already that day Washington was receiving urgent pleas for help from Golda Meir. Her generals were informing her that things were going worse than could possibly have been anticipated. Kissinger was told that there was "a real bridgehead across the Canal," and that Israel had suffered sixty dead and 110 wounded. "You have to multiply that by a hundred to get the equivalent American casualties," he informed Haig—the general who had been through Vietnam, and who would have understood that equation. "If we suffered six thousand dead and fifteen thousand wounded in one day. No joke." The Egyptians, however—so Zayyat told him—had already suffered five thousand killed†; and after such a loss, how could they go back to where they had started from? In a further conversation with Cromer (at 9:38), he declared "we are quite determined that if the Israelis go beyond the present cease-fire lines that

---

* On October 10.

† This soon turned out to be a gross exaggeration; the actual number of Egyptian troops killed in crossing the Suez Canal had run only into the low hundreds.

we will push them back," commenting acidly: "I think cleverness is the national form of stupidity of the Israelis."[16]

During the course of that busy day, Kissinger had also managed to find time, in Washington, to give an important briefing to the Chinese ambassador, Huang Zhen. It was revealing not only in its remarkable openness, couched in terms almost as if Kissinger had been addressing his own inner councils of the NSC, but also in the clarity of his assessments at that very early point in the developing crisis. He explained to Huang that "our strategic objective is to prevent the Soviet Union from getting a dominant position in the Middle East. That is our basic objective. Israel is a secondary, emotional problem having to do with domestic politics here." He went on to predict: "By Tuesday and Wednesday if the war isn't ended, the Arabs will be pleading with us to get this [a cease-fire] for them since within 72–96 hours the Arabs will be completely defeated. We have to think of that situation, not of today's situation when they have gained a little territory."[17] Events may have been about to prove the timing to be somewhat faulty, but not Kissinger's underlying conclusion.

What was actually happening in the Middle East? At 2 P.M. (Middle East time) that afternoon of October 6, a concerted onslaught by the Syrian and Egyptian armies struck the Israeli positions. Syria attacked on the bleak Golan Heights in the north (which Israel had seized from Syria only after hard fighting in 1967).* In the south, Egypt crossed the Suez Canal into Sinai in five separate places, with a force roughly equivalent to the whole of NATO—a combined total of over three thousand main battle tanks (mostly modern Soviet models), or about six times the total number in the British army today, to Israel's armor numbering two thousand.

The timing was immaculate; being the first day of Yom Kippur, a national holiday when most of Israel's population could be expected to be at the synagogue, or at home (though this might also have worked

---

* In 1967, Israel had seized from Syria half of the strategic Golan Heights, from Jordan the West Bank territories, and, in the south, from Egypt the whole of the Sinai Peninsula.

to Israel's favor, with empty roads assisting the mobilization of reserves). Secrecy on the part of the attackers was all but perfect. The
CIA's spies-in-the-sky had failed to spot the huge Arab buildup. Even
the much vaunted Israeli Mossad had been unable to provide more
than twelve hours' warning. As a result, by the beginning of the third
day the IDF, the Israeli Defense Forces, would be sent reeling out of
its bunkers along the Suez Canal, while the Syrians had penetrated to
within an alarming ten-minute drive of the Sea of Galilee in the north.
Israeli losses had indeed been grim.

What had gone wrong? One needs to look back to the Six Day War
of 1967. Here, by wiping out their air forces in a brilliant preemptive
strike, Israel was able to shatter the combined Arab coalition forces in
a lightning campaign of Old Testament quality, where a mighty foe had
been smitten "hip-and-thigh" with a great slaughter by Samson, "with
the jawbone of an ass." The tiny nation was as astonished by its own
success as the Arabs were dismayed. A huge amount of real estate had
been acquired, but no peace settlement achieved, while the Arabs (notably Egypt and Syria, with their total populations of well over forty
million to Israel's three million) were left humiliated, and bent on revenge. By contrast Israel had lapsed into a dangerous state of hubristic
complacency. In Tel Aviv shortly after the 1967 victory, I recall that
disturbing encounter with General Ezer Weizman, the larger-than-life
architect of the air force triumph, and later to be president of Israel.*
A massive, swaggering figure who with his close-cropped blond hair
and blue eyes could almost have doubled for a 1940s Luftwaffe ace, he
commented on the great military triumph Israel had just won; then
asked, rhetorically, what should they do now? Sticking my neck out,
rashly, I replied I thought Israel had about a year in which to make a
"good peace." He cut me off at the knees, lambasting me as a "Limey
armchair historian," and he then proceeded to boast, in disquieting,
and unashamedly racist, terms, that Israel "can lick any combination of
Arabs that come against us." [18]

It was a boast that exemplified how, six years later, Israel's guard
was down. Defense spending was cut; infantry tactics and antitank fire-

---

* See chapter 6, p. 122.

power neglected; intelligence gathering lapsed. Meanwhile, on the other side a vast armory of the latest Soviet weapons was pouring in. Above all, they included numerous batteries of SAMs, surface-to-air missiles which had recently proved lethal to the U.S. Air Force in Vietnam. United Nations negotiations had failed, as had the Israeli doctrine of deterrence. Worst of all, the Israeli high command deluded itself, by applying its own standards, that their enemy would not risk war to obtain a limited military objective. Which was precisely what Egypt's President Sadat planned to do—aiming not for a decisive victory but to impose losses on Israel that would force political and territorial concessions.

Thus was the stage set for a Bismarckian reversal; but here the time gap was not a generation, but only six years. As military commentator Walter Boyne observed, victory in the Six Day War proved to be "an albatross that almost doomed Israel in 1973."[19] Or, to borrow the subtitle of a book about another part of the Middle East, *A Catastrophic Success.*[20]

Sadat achieved surprise partly through his own, apparent, pretended indecision, where a false alarm in May 1973 persuaded the Israeli chief of staff, Dado Elazar, to mobilize prematurely—costing the nation an estimated $35 million. Determined not to get caught out again, his director of intelligence, Eli Zeira, misinterpreted the signs as October approached, taking the immense Egyptian military activity and the construction of huge sand ramparts along the west side of the Suez Canal to signify only maneuvers—yet again. As Sadat remarked scathingly after the war: "The Israelis mocked at our building activity saying that the Egyptians always like to build pyramids!"

In retrospect, it seems extraordinary that so many great brains should have been so blinded to this enormous army moving up, so visibly, through the open desert.

Confusion on the part of the Arabs' backer, the Soviet Union, also played a role in misleading Israeli—and U.S.—intelligence. The Kremlin was not itself clear how far it would go in the event of another Middle East war. Taking advantage of the prevailing U.S. weakness, still reeling from Vietnam, it had sought to increase its influence in the Arab world. But it was not courting responsibility for either another crushing Arab defeat, or a decisive military victory over Israel.

Thus Israel was caught on the wrong foot. Although it could mobilize nearly 10 percent of the population, there were no reserves immediately available in either the north or south to face a powerful onslaught. And, as always, the tiny nation was caught in the grim bind of having no space in which to mount a fighting withdrawal while its limited manpower and ammunition meant it could not face a war of more than ten days. On the other hand, the Egyptians were prepared to take as many as 25,000 casualties in crossing the canal (in fact they lost only two hundred in the first assault stage).

On October 6, behind pulverizing artillery barrages, the Arab allies attacked with far greater élan, indeed fury, than they had shown in 1967. Though the standard of tank crews was low, and the Soviet tanks were no match for Israel's British Centurions, with their unbeatable 105mm gun, the Syrian soldier was very brave; while the Egyptians were much better officered on a tactical level than ever before. What was missing—a defect inculcated by the Soviet overlords—was any flexibility by the higher commands. This would tell in the latter stages of the war.

Both Syrian and Egyptian attacks went in under a dense umbrella of SAM batteries, some of them the most modern the Soviets could supply. The Egyptians alone had 150 batteries. The SAMs went far to neutralize the superiority of the Israeli Air Force, inflicting most of its unacceptably heavy losses that first day. Meanwhile, the attacking infantry carried with them powerful Sagger missiles, which—handled with great courage—proved capable of neutralizing the other key Israeli advantage—its strong armor. Between 1967 and 1973, in their underestimation of Arab military potential, both the IDF and IAF had failed to take either weapon seriously enough. By the end of October 8, the IAF had lost nearly fifty aircraft, most of them to SAMs; by the following day, the Israelis had lost somewhere near five hundred tanks. In Sinai, using powerful fire hoses to level the twenty-meter-high Israeli ramparts of sand, General Saad el-Shazly, the able Egyptian commander, had gotten his tanks across the canal at a number of points. The Bar-Lev Line, named after the IDF chief of staff, a system of defensive works constructed by the Israelis in Sinai following its capture in the 1967 war to protect against an Egyptian attack across the Suez Canal, was seriously breached. Momentarily it looked as if Israel might have to withdraw from Sinai altogether. In the north, throwing in mass attacks on the narrow front of the Golan Heights, the Syrians had all but broken through, with their tank commanders able to look down on the amazing—and highly vulnerable—panorama of the Sea of Galilee. Orders were prepared for the defenders to blow the vital bridges across the Jordan. On both fronts, because of the lack of organized reserves, the Israelis were only able to throw in piecemeal—and very costly—counterattacks; a style of warfare totally at odds with their doctrine.

Kissinger's early optimism had clearly been tinged by Israeli hubris. If the intelligence service had failed the administration, Kissinger—as the major figure in U.S. policy-making—could not avoid his share of remorse at his own myopia when the first rumbles of trouble had reached him from the Middle East earlier in the year. As late as the week before Yom Kippur, he had been warned by Gromyko (in a message for Nixon): "Your assessment and ours do not fully coincide, even if at first sight it seems that we do since both sides feel the situation is complicated and dangerous. But we have a different assessment of the danger because we feel the possibility could not be excluded that we could all wake up one day and find there is a real conflagration in that area. That has to be kept in mind. Is it worth the risk? A serious effort has to be made for a solution because a solution will not just fall down from the sky." Gromyko continued, reminding the Americans "I recall the conversations you had with General Secretary Brezhnev here and then in San Clemente on this and your words that you considered the problem of the Middle East most important, and that you would take it up. I certainly would be most interested in what you might say."[21] The message seems to have fallen on stony ground. In his mea culpa Kissinger could offer the mitigating circumstances—as he had put to this biographer over the Chilean debacle—"I had other things on my mind." Indeed he had: to recap, there had been China and Russia, the troublesome Europeans, ending the Vietnam War, not to mention the nagging cancer of Watergate. But now he would expiate this dereliction with a superhuman deployment of energy over, not weeks, but months in the ongoing crisis. Remarkably, he even managed to devote considerable time to his speech to the U.N.

•   •   •

In his memoirs, Kissinger referred to the second day of the war as "A Sunday of Stalling." Nevertheless, it was in fact a day of powerful and threatening advances by the Arab armies at the battlefront; and of intense maneuvering and manipulation behind the scenes at the U.N. Kissinger described the United Nations as being "paralyzed by obstruction from all sides." "The Soviets were stalling; Egypt, depending on which ambassador one believed, was either stalling or preparing for a cease-fire in place; Israel wanted time to complete its mobilization; Syria had not been heard from. Only the United States was prepared to go to the Security Council, but our preferred resolution amounted only to a sophisticated delaying tactic because no other Council member was likely to support us." [22] Calling for a Security Council meeting that evening, Kissinger was aiming for a vote by Tuesday or Wednesday (the 9th or the 10th, the third and fourth days of the war). Kissinger continued to assume that by then the Israelis would be winning.

This was certainly not how it seemed in the "Pit," IDF headquarters outside Tel Aviv. In the office of Israel's unyielding prime minister, Golda Meir, there was consternation. Moshe Dayan, the war hero who was now minister of defense, was in a state of nervous collapse, talking melodramatically of the "ruin of the Third Temple." There were bitter mutual recriminations. Already supplies of ammunition were running down; air force losses were getting close to the perilous "red line" of danger. The use, in extremis, of Israel's nuclear weapon, "Jericho," was even discussed.* Washington, where Kissinger was essentially in charge, was appealed to for an all-out airlift.

In his first conversation with Haig that morning, Haig asked Kissinger, "Are the Israelis panicking?"

> K: They are almost. They are anxious to get some equipment
>   which has been approved and which some SOB in Defense
>   held up, which I didn't know about. I think, myself, we
>   should release some of it.

---

* Kissinger always hotly denied, and several times to the author, that Israel had ever mentioned this possibility to the United States, and certainly not as any form of blackmail for assistance.

H: I think so too.

K: I think if the Arabs win, they will be impossible and there
will be no negotiations. A change would be ascribed to our
domestic crisis.

H: . . . The Israelis are shocked by the confidence of the Arabs
. . . this might make easy negotiations.

K: . . . depends on how we conduct ourselves. We must be on
their side [the Israelis] now so that they have something to
lose afterwards. Therefore I think we have to give the
equipment.

H: What are we talking about, ammunition and spares?

K: Let me see, I have it here. [Reads from list.] What we can do
is send those which have already been approved.

H: Do we airlift them?

K: We don't have to do anything. They are sending a plane over
and we could do it on the ground—that they were picking
up things they have already ordered. My profound
conviction is that if we play this the hard way, it is the last
time they [the Israelis] are going to listen. If we kick them in
the teeth they have nothing to lose. Later if we support
them they will be willing to help with Jewish emigration or
MFN [Most Favored Nation] or other stuff.*23

This was an exchange that showed clearly how, despite the all-
embroiling crisis, Kissinger was still able to think laterally—with the
Great Game with Moscow foremost in his mind.

Next Kissinger received a call from Eban, warning him that the
night had been "not particularly good." A key Israeli garrison on
Mount Hermon had fallen to the Syrians: "We're not at full capability
because of the special circumstances of yesterday." The "special circumstances" referred to Kissinger's messages recommending restraint
to Israel; these were adumbrated in a bitter personal message from
Golda Meir—which, according to Kissinger, "raised our blood pres-

---

* MFN status for Soviet trade was being blocked by the amendment put forward by
Senator Scoop Jackson, making it conditional on Jewish emigration from the Soviet
Union.

sure." In a manner that would become familiar, she was passing on to
the United States the blame for Israel's current difficulties: "You know
the reasons why we took no preemptive action. Our failure to take
such action is the reason for our situation now. If I had given the chief
of staff authority to preempt, as he had recommended, some hours before the attacks, there is no doubt that our situation would now be different." So America, i.e., Kissinger, was to blame. It could hardly have
been more pointed. But, in fact, given the state of Israel's defenses,
would things really have been different?[24] However, requesting that the
United States postpone a vote until the 10th or 11th, Meir still reckoned that by then Israel would have regained the offensive on all
fronts. Meanwhile an Israeli 747 (just one), with markings painted out,
was speeding to an out-of-the-way naval base in Virginia with instructions to pick up urgently needed special equipment. Notably this comprised the latest Sidewinder air-to-air heat-seeking antiaircraft missile.*
Considering the losses Israel had already suffered, it may have seemed
like a mere token of assistance.

Shortly thereafter Nixon was on the line, putting with the lucid
perceptiveness of which he was, however spasmodically, still capable,
this nagging apprehension: "One thing we have to have in the back of
our minds is, we don't want to be so pro-Israel that the oil states—the
Arabs that are not involved in the fighting—will break ranks."[25] There
followed a conversation with Secretary of Defense Schlesinger, to
whom Kissinger passed on the Israeli "shopping list," which included
"forty Phantoms, which of course is out of the question, but the President's inclination is that if the Israelis will be able to pick it up, to give
them some other stuff, laying claim for diplomatic—[sentence unfin-
ished]. . . . Do you think you could handle it at Defense so that it
doesn't leak?"[26]

It was a tall order, typifying Kissinger's predisposition for covert
action. Schlesinger thought he could "manage it," but was to be embarrassed as news promptly leaked out. He stressed the importance the

---

* Named after the sidewinder snake, which detects its prey via body heat and also because of the peculiar snakelike path of flight the early versions had when launched. The
Sidewinder was the first truly effective air-to-air missile, widely imitated and copied
subsequently.

Israelis were attaching to the Sidewinders: "In fact, they are sort of quietly desperate about that," adding, "Their air losses have been substantial because of the SAMs. There is something very peculiar about the
Egyptian front," Schlesinger said. "They [the Israelis] seem to want
Egypt to come in—[the] Egyptians didn't move their forces heavily
across the Canal last night. The Israelis seem to be lying back."[27] While
it was IDF strategy to hold back its main defenses from the canal, it
may also have been that Pentagon intelligence was taken in to the extent of not grasping the seriousness of the threat to Israel in Sinai.

By late morning Dobrynin was on the telephone, complaining:
"I'm really nailed down. I'm still waiting for a message."

Kissinger replied, derogating the role at the U.N. being played by
America's difficult traditional ally, Ted Heath's Britain.

> K: We are waiting for your message. We are holding off the
>   British until we hear from you. We don't want to talk with
>   them till we hear from you.
> D: Okay, I will call you even before the translation.
> K: Good.[28]

To Haig that afternoon, a mistrustful Kissinger came on the line to
remark, "I am beginning to think those sons of bitches in Moscow are
schnookering us,"[29] regarding agreement over the Security Council
meeting. He had had no further word from Dobrynin. Then the ambassador telephoned to relay a rambling personal letter, "from boss to
boss,"[30] Brezhnev to Nixon. "It turned out to be essentially another
stall. Either Moscow was genuinely baffled as to what to do or it was
operating on a different estimate from ours. . . . Clearly, the Soviets
wanted to let the war run its course a little longer or else they did not
have as much influence with their Arab friends as we had thought."[31]

That afternoon Kissinger confirmed to the Russians that the president had decided to announce their call for a meeting at 5 P.M. In effect both Washington and Moscow were now stalling, waiting to see
which way the cat would jump for their respective clients, with neither
side eager for a cease-fire that might reverse their advantages. Kissinger
told Eban—somewhat sardonically—that, at the U.N. the United
States "in this case wouldn't mind if you sacrificed eloquence to

length," and went on to remark that "My impression, quite honestly, is that they [the Russians] were taken aback by what the Arabs did this time. . . . So, there are no Russians involved."[32]

So far Washington had not been taking Israel's cries of pain too seriously. Then, late on the evening of the second day of fighting (the 7th), Nixon was admitting to Kissinger, "The doggoned Syrians surprised me. They're doing better than I ever thought," though the Israelis were "doing damned well." Urging the need to speed a cease-fire, the president was met by Kissinger's reply that "It's a little premature."[33]

Meanwhile in the Middle East, Asad and Sadat were paralleling Israel in their pleas by begging Moscow for more supplies. Both requests were granted top priority by the patron nations. Now, to the consternation of Europe, Saudi Arabia deployed the oil weapon, raising prices and cutting production, first by 5 percent, then by 10 percent. The hurt was immediate and there were more urgent calls for a cease-fire.

From Egypt, via Kissinger's intelligence back channels, there came suddenly a surprise communication from Egypt, from Sadat personally, inviting the United States "to take charge of the peace process." Kissinger judged this as extraordinary, given that "at the United Nations we were advocating he give up territory that his armies had just captured." Up till that point, somewhat dismissively—perhaps—Kissinger admitted that he "had not taken Sadat seriously. Because of the many threats to go to war that had not been implemented I had dismissed him as more actor than statesman."[34] Kissinger would soon revise his opinion; now already a process was sparked in that swift-moving mind.[35] At the end of the day in a WSAG meeting Colby of the CIA came up with the thought that perhaps Sadat "intended to make only a limited move across the Canal." It was the best intelligence guess yet. Kissinger agreed: "My judgment is that he *will* cross the Suez and just *sit* there. I don't think he will penetrate further."[36]

On the 8th, there were few developments—except for a pressing call from Ambassador Simcha Dinitz, returned from Israel, speaking in anguish of Israel's "very heavy casualties both in human and equipment. . . . Hundreds." He stressed the effectiveness of the Soviet SAM batteries against the Israeli Air Force. That evening Nixon, speaking to Kissinger, was at his best, focused on events in the Middle East.

N: . . . The one thing we have to be concerned about, which you and I know looking down the road, is that [the] Israelis, when they finish clobbering the Egyptians and the Syrians, which they will do, will be even more impossible to deal with than before and you and I have got to determine in our own minds, we must have a diplomatic settlement there.

K: I agree with you.

N: . . . We must not get away with just having this thing hang over another four years and have us at odds with the Arab world. We're not going to do it anymore.

K: I agree with you completely, Mr. President.

Kissinger then went on to explain his tactics so far that week with the U.N., while Nixon continued to his Jewish secretary of state:

N: I'm not tough on the Israelis. Fortunately, the Israelis will beat these guys so badly I hope we can make sort of a reasonable [proposal]—You and I both know they can't go back to the other [1967] borders. But we must not, on the other hand, say that because the Israelis win this war, as they won the '67 war, that we can just go on with status quo. It can't be done.

K: I couldn't agree more.

Kissinger continued on a somewhat rash note of premature optimism, that—as far as threats to U.S. oil—"no one has made a peep against us yet." Nixon concluded his analysis of the battle on the Canal.

N: They'll cut the Egyptians off. Poor dumb Egyptians, getting across the Canal and all the bridges will be blown up. They'll cut them all off—thirty or forty thousand of them. Go over and destroy the SAM sites.

It was a remarkable prediction of what would happen, once General Ariel Sharon appeared on the scene—but meanwhile immediate events of the next few days would make it seem an improbable scenario.[37]

"The gods are offended by hubris," observes Kissinger[38] and the 9th was the day Israeli hubris was well and truly pricked by the gods. The day began with an urgent call from Ambassador Dinitz to Kissinger at 1:45 A.M.:

> D: I hope I didn't wake you . . .
> K: It's all right.

Israel was in serious trouble. In the first eighteen hours of fighting, the Egyptians had gotten 90,000 troops, 850 tanks, and 11,000 vehicles across the Suez Canal—for a loss of 280 soldiers. The IDF had previously estimated it would take them at least forty-eight hours to shift heavy equipment. Most of the Bar-Lev defensive line had been occupied.[39] The kind of preemptive aerial strike, which had gained Israel swift superiority in 1967, was now ruled out by the presence of the Russian SAMs—on top of the heavy warnings emanating from Washington. With this glum knowledge, at 8:20, Dinitz was at the White House, accompanied by his defense attaché, Mordechai Gur. Kissinger was accompanied by General Scowcroft. The Israelis now revealed that their losses had been "staggering and totally unexpected." They had lost forty-nine aircraft, including fourteen of the high-performance U.S. Phantoms—almost entirely victims to the SAM missile batteries. But what came as even more of a shock was the admission that they had lost five hundred tanks, four hundred of them on the Suez front alone; many from new RPG-7 infantry rockets and guided antitank missiles provided by the Soviet Union. A number of the Israeli tanks had been lost on their way to the battlefield through improvident maintenance. Israel was urgently calling for resupply. But as far as Phantoms were concerned, this would present a major problem for the United States, insofar as the sophisticated aircraft were only coming off the production line at a rate of about two a month, and there was hardly any surplus available.

Kissinger was shocked by the news from the Israelis. Dinitz asked to stay behind, privately, for five minutes; things were so bad, he said, that Prime Minister Meir wanted to fly secretly to Washington to plead with Nixon for urgent arms aid. Kissinger "rejected the visit out of hand and without checking with Nixon."[40] That would be a display of panic that might bring in all the uncommitted Arab states. As it was, the Israeli reverses threatened to throw out all Kissinger's previous calculations, on which he was basing his hopes of achieving a cease-fire. Reporting to a special meeting of WSAG (but holding back on the full extent of Israeli tank losses), Kissinger was met by skepticism. From the hopelessly ill-informed CIA, Colby reported that Israel was doing well on the Syrian front, and "holding its own" on the canal.[41] Schlesinger was concerned that meeting Israeli demands for more arms might seriously blight U.S.-Arab relations. Meanwhile Dinitz had been diligent stirring up congressmen to the Israeli cause; Kissinger was being deluged with calls from Capitol Hill pressing for arms to be rushed to Israel.

Events now moved quickly; by the afternoon Dinitz was reporting to Kissinger that the IDF had destroyed a hundred Syrian tanks up on the Golan that day alone. But the overall situation remained shaky. A conversation with the British ambassador, Lord Cromer, that afternoon showed Kissinger sharing with his principal ally only the bare minimum of what he knew; Heath was not being helpful at the U.N. By that night Kissinger was thoroughly alarmed that, in the new situation of extreme danger for Israel, the Soviets might see a window of opportunity to enhance their hand with the ascendant Arabs. As he put it in *Crisis*, "We saw an opportunity to start a peace process by convincing the Arab states that the Soviets could provoke a war but not achieve diplomatic progress; hence American diplomacy was indispensable. Diplomatic progress required an Israeli military success but not in a manner that united the Arab world against America"[42] (i.e., an eighteenth-century victory, such as a biographer of Metternich might have understood, rather than a twentieth-century one).

It was the most impossible circle to square. And a stalemate could only lead to triumph for the Soviets—leading also to the strong probability of another war. That was what, for Kissinger, the Great Game was all about, limiting, if not removing altogether, Soviet influence in the Middle East.

On the 10th, Nixon once again lapsed into distraction. It was the day that Agnew resigned. Kissinger was forced to admit to Dobrynin (as if he didn't already know, but as "a sign of my great confidence in you"): "We are having a major domestic problem . . . coming to a head early this afternoon."[43] It was, also, an excuse now for Kissinger to continue stalling on the cease-fire until Israel had had more time to regain her strength on the battlefield. Moscow's aggressive representative at the U.N., Yakov Malik, should be temporarily put on a leash—Kissinger beseeched Dobrynin. Meanwhile Soviet replacement arms were flooding toward Egypt, planes flying in breach of Turkish airspace into Syria. Kissinger was angered with the slow response of the Pentagon to Israel's pleas. To his deputy, Scowcroft, that evening he urged that "the Defense people are just going to have to stop dragging their feet. First, the Israelis are going wild. They think we are stabbing them in the back." He asked Scowcroft, a man he trusted implicitly, for his personal judgment. Scowcroft replied that he feared "If we settle into a stalemate, we will have big trouble. . . . We either have to go for a cease-fire or a massive reequipment." Kissinger asked, "If there is no resolution in forty-eight hours, can we get through the weekend?"

"I don't think we can," Scowcroft replied.[44]

It was clear that the transport planes sent by El Al could not pick up all the equipment required so urgently by Israel. Meanwhile some twenty Soviet transports were flying into Syria from Hungary. Kissinger appreciated that an airlift of this magnitude could not have been improvised—"it must have been organized for several days." What were the Soviets up to? He remained suspicious of the Bear. "Were they helping their most hard-pressed associate to keep it from collapsing, or were they encouraging a new onslaught?" Even years later, such was the obfuscation of Kremlin policy it has never become entirely clear. "What the Soviets hoped to achieve is hard to fathom. Their ambivalence gave us a chance to play for time and recoup."[45]

In the meantime, it gave the United States a bona fide excuse to step up resupplies to Israel. Kissinger began by resorting to the highly unreliable device of employing charter firms; but few were willing to risk their planes in a war zone. Then Israeli pressure persuaded Kissinger to take the gloves off, and use U.S. military planes—thereby draining all available sources of tanks, shells, and planes currently protecting NATO. Here would be provided one more source of annoyance for America's European partners.

That night Kissinger reviewed the situation: "We would maintain contact with the parties. Our aim was to slow down diplomacy without appearing obstructionist, to urge a speedup of military operations [by Israel] without seeming to intervene, and then to force a cease-fire before . . . unforeseeable events could rip the whole finely spun fabric to smithereens."[46]

But the next day, the swiftly moving kaleidoscope of the Middle East suddenly shifted. As the Egyptians consolidated their gains in Sinai, Israel hit back with full force against the Syrians in the north. The next day, the 12/13th, the U.S. airlift to Israel began in earnest. That evening in Washington an exchange laden with meaning in another crucial context, which concerned even more vitally Kissinger's role at the center, took place between him and General Brent Scowcroft.

> S: . . . The switchboard just got a call from 10 Downing Street to inquire whether the President would be available within 30 minutes for the Prime Minister. The subject would be the Middle East.
>
> K: Can we tell them no? When I talked to the President he was loaded.
>
> S: We could tell him the President is not available and perhaps he can call you.
>
> K: I will be at Mr. Braden's* and the President will be available tomorrow morning our time.[47]

It was the day after the resignation of Agnew had placed heavy new pressures on Nixon. Unmistakably, though Kissinger was always reluctant (through a sense of loyalty to Nixon) to admit it, the inference was that the president was drowning his sorrows in alcohol—an added debility at this time of crisis! On the evening of the 12th, Kissinger had

---

* Thomas Braden, Washington TV journalist.

to hurry to the White House to attend Nixon's announcement of the choice of Gerald Ford to replace Spiro Agnew as vice president; it would prove to be a historic choice, but with no bearing on the war raging in the Middle East. Nixon was briefly elated; but in his memoirs, Kissinger noted, Nixon, in his despair, had "failed to realize that it was a tribute above all to Ford."[48]

Suddenly the tide of battle turned, definitively. After suffering huge tank losses, both the Syrian and Egyptian onslaught ran out of steam. The IDF recovered its balance, and—with its usual panache and brilliance on the offensive—struck back. What told were the following factors: superior (British) tanks; superior training and organization, versus the ponderous Soviet-style command system; Maverick anti-tank missiles flown in on the U.S. airlift; Israel's interior lines connecting the fronts—but, above all, the traditional Israeli soldier's sense of having his back to the wall. After an appalling carnage of Syrian tanks, comparable to a World War II battle, Israeli tanks broke out of the Golan Heights, reaching to within twenty miles of Damascus. Much more dramatic, however, was what took place on the Suez Canal. Aided by her interior lines of communication, such as had given the Germans an enormous advantage in both world wars, the IDF was able to rush its armored forces south to Sinai after countering the Syrian threat in the north. Here the distance was only a matter of some 250 miles, or one night's travel; but considerably less for what still remained of Israel's redoubtable fighter-bomber force.

On the Suez front Sadat now committed a fatal blunder. Acting to forestall the predicted Israeli counterblow, and out of sync with the Syrian high command, he ordered his commanders to break out of the twenty-five-mile perimeter they had won on the east bank of the Suez Canal. Abandoning his intention to fight only a limited engagement, they were to strike for the vital Gidi and Mitla passes in central Sinai, which had proved so decisive in the Israel campaigns of both 1956 and 1967. Hold them, some of his advisers felt, and Egypt would be protected against any offensive Israel could muster. But they disregarded the vital factor of the SAM sites located to the west of the Canal—their trump card. Their Soviet suppliers had refused to give them mobile— i.e., *offensive*—missile weaponry, so as not to antagonize the United States excessively. These could not readily be relocated on the east side of the canal; now, once out of their protective belt of ten miles, Egypt's Soviet tanks would be sitting ducks for the Israeli Air Force, equipped with the latest antitank missiles.

At 9:04 on Sunday morning, October 14, Kissinger reported to Nixon: "The Egyptians have launched a big offensive and it is hard to know exactly what is going on in an early stage of an offensive . . . the last information we have that is not absolutely firm is that they may have reached close to the Mitla Pass. . . . There are two possibilities, one that the Israelis were trying to draw them beyond the SAM belt in order to knock out a lot of their forces."[49]

In fact, this is precisely what was happening. Sending in their elite 21st Armored Division, carefully husbanded heretofore, the Egyptians had blundered into a Balaclava-like trap and were annihilated; in one engagement eighty-six out of ninety-six of the latest Russian T-62 tanks were destroyed, while overall by the end of the 14th, they had lost some 250 of the 330 tanks in their regained territory on the eastern shore of the Suez Canal—at a cost of four Israeli tanks. The remainder of the Egyptian tank force never regained the west bank.

Once again, one cannot help but be struck by Kissinger's prowess as a military analyst; constantly, so the documents reveal, he seemed to be at least one leap ahead of what intelligence the various U.S. agencies were providing. Yet, as a Harvard professor, he had been essentially untrained in the science of military affairs. The suspicion arises, was he receiving special information? Intelligence from decrypts?* Or from what source? When I taxed him on the subject once more, on my return from Egypt in 2008, he responded, "Yes, I had been receiving day-by-day intelligence from the Soviets—but they weren't really in touch; and from the Israelis. But fundamentally," he insisted, "it was my own analytical deduction."[50] From the onset of the Arab attack on October 6, under combined pressure from Dinitz and the supporters of Israel in Washington, the main bulwark of Kissinger's underlying conviction that Israeli arms would ultimately triumph never shook, though the parapets may have crumbled a bit.

Nixon's response to Kissinger on the morning of the 14th was to

---

* A notion suggested by British intelligence experts; viz Professor Christopher Andrew of Cambridge (interview, 2/28/08).

reveal him in focus, thinking—as was his wont—well beyond the immediate battle raging in the Middle East. Kissinger outlined to the president the cease-fire situation: "As of yesterday we started out with the idea of a ceasefire and a return to the pre-hostilities lines. Incidentally, should the Israelis clobber the Egyptians that will turn out to be a pretty good position. Then we move to a simple ceasefire . . . the Egyptians are demanding a return to '67 borders; now that is absolutely out of the question, short of a huge [Israeli] defeat," to which Nixon replied: "I think we have got to get some way. Look we have got to face this—that as far as the Russians are concerned, they have a pretty good beef insofar as everything we offered on the Middle East, you know what I mean, that meeting in San Clemente . . . we were stringing them along and they know it. We have got to come off with something on the diplomatic front." And later in the conversation, Nixon told his secretary of state: "We have got to squeeze the Israelis when this is over and the Russians have got to know it. We have got to squeeze them goddamn hard. And that's the way it's going to be done. But I don't know how we can get across now; we told them before we'd squeeze them and we didn't." Kissinger went on to propose a peace conference which would invoke Security Council Resolution 242, which spoke of withdrawals, but which "doesn't flatly say the '67 borders." He then complained angrily about the disappointing performance of number one ally Britain over formulation of a cease-fire resolution at the U.N.: "On the immediate specific issue, where the British are behaving badly, they are just passively sitting there picking up the pieces: they are not shaping anything."[51]

In the short, twenty-mile stretch between Ismailia and the Great Bitter Lake on the Suez Canal (which I remember well from my last days with the British army in 1947), the Egyptian tank debacle of the 14th had left a vacuum, a hole between the Second Army to the North, and the Third to the south. Very much like the ill-fated French Second and Ninth Armies in May 1940, each thought the other was guarding its flank; through that gap had rushed Hitler's panzers, to bring about the total collapse of France a few weeks later. Possibly aided by U.S. Air Force intelligence reconnaissance, a spy plane, the SR-71 Blackbird, which, flying over the battle zone had spotted the "open seam" in the Egyptian order of battle and passed it on to Israel, an aggressive

fair-haired divisional commander called Arik (Ariel) Sharon saw an opportunity. He had been a front-line commander in both the 1956 and
1967 campaigns in Sinai.* The two Egyptian armies each had the bulk
of their forces on the east side of the Canal, and Sharon urged the high
command to be allowed to attack and, in a bold thrust, envelop the
enemy from the rear—as indeed General Erich von Manstein had done
on the Meuse in 1940. Whereas in 1940, the bold stroke had presented
the Wehrmacht the glittering options that would paralyze the opposing team—of either heading straight for Paris, or swinging north to
trap the British Expeditionary Force up against the coast (as they did),
in 1973, Sharon gave Israel the option of threatening Cairo, or of
swinging north to trap the Egyptian Second Army against the canal, or
south to trap their Third Army. The last was the option they chose.

After the drubbing the IDF had received, General Elazar and the
commander in Sinai, Chaim Bar-Lev, hesitated and two useful days
were lost. Sharon came within an inch of being sacked for insubordi-
nation (which would have put paid to any future political career). But
eventually the daring scheme was accepted. Operation Abiray-Lev (in
English, Valiant or Stouthearted Men) was put into action. At first
Sharon got little more than a squadron of tanks across the Suez Canal.
For a while, after bitter fighting around the Chinese Farm south of Ismailia and Deversoir on the Bitter Lakes,† it looked as if the thrust
might be contained, Sharon repulsed. Still by the 17th, U.S. intelligence
was not attaching too much importance to the development, with even
Kissinger not yet appreciating the extent of it.

Reporting to Nixon at 8:44 on the morning of the 17th, Kissinger
told him:

K: On the military front, it looks still like a stalemate. . . .
N: . . . this Israeli raid [Sharon, across the Suez Canal] was not
    that big, huh?

---

* In a headstrong attempt to capture the Mitla Pass in 1956, thirty-eight of Sharon's men
were killed, a mishap that was to set back his military promotion. He was actually in retirement in August 1973, but called back for the war and put in command initially of a
reserve armored brigade.

† Once a British army base near where the author served in 1947.

K: Apparently not.

N: I gathered that.

K: There is a tank battle going on now in Sinai and we don't have any report of its outcome yet.

In fact this was the beginning of Israel's decisive breakthrough, not just a raid. At 1:40 P.M., Nixon was claiming to Kissinger:

N: A most successful morning. . . . They [the Arab foreign ministers] were happy. . . .

K: . . . seems to be a tank battle going on.

N: I think it's a stalemate, I really do.

K: I do too.[52]

Given the context, it is hard to see why Nixon found the Arab ministers "happy" but they would not remain so for long. Sharon's tanks were now swarming across the canal on a huge roller-bridge, fanning out behind the Egyptian lines on the far side, and knocking out the deadly SAM batteries so that the IAF could dominate the battlefield.

It was in fact the epitome of the "expanding torrent," as advocated by Liddell Hart in the 1930s, carefully studied by his keen disciples among the young Israeli general staff—and exploited to help win the campaigns of 1956 and 1967. Since its early days the IDF had a unique policy of publishing, in Hebrew, books it considers of particular relevance. We historians can sometimes claim too much influence for our books, whereas it is always rewarding to learn that leaders occasionally benefit from one's work. When I visited Israel shortly after the Six Day War, to speak about my book *The Price of Glory: Verdum 1916*, apart from my disturbing encounter with General Ezer Weizman as described earlier, I was also received by General Chaim Bar-Lev, then Israeli army chief of staff. Greeting me affably, he made some obliging remarks about *The Price of Glory*. Having thanked him, I then expressed my puzzlement; why on earth had they bought it? What had the static Western Front, 1916, to do with their remarkable, modern style of highly mobile, blitzkrieg warfare? He replied: "When you go down to our lines on the Suez Canal, you will see why. The Egyptians are shelling us night and day, and we are losing two to three men each week—which Israel with its tiny population just can't afford. The sanctity of life is very fundamental to us. So we want to explore which side got it right at Verdun—the Germans or the French. So which side did?"

I replied that, in my view, it was the kaiser's Germans; they dug deep and held lightly. In effect, that was precisely what Bar-Lev did in the line which was to bear his name. The fate of the Bar-Lev defenders on October 6 was grievous; but had they emulated the French, and placed a large number of defending troops up in the front line, in shallow fortifications, when Sadat attacked the consequences would have been horrendous, if not catastrophic. My second book published by the IDF, *To Lose a Battle*, an account of the Nazi blitzkrieg on France in 1940, had been published just eighteen months before the Yom Kippur War. That October I was actually in Algiers, waiting for an interview with President Houari Boumédienne. Meanwhile, I tried anxiously to follow the course of the battle on the Suez Canal. Suddenly the penny dropped: in Sharon's westward thrust the Israelis were pulling off a very close replay of Wehrmacht General von Manstein's crossing of the Meuse, which decisively broke through between the French defenses in May 1940, and which I had analyzed in great detail. My hunch was confirmed a few months later by a distinguished Israeli expert on the war, Chaim Herzog—who later became president. "Arik," he said, "was very grateful to you. You should get a medal!" It was never to come; but it seemed to me ironic at the time that a Jewish army should have resorted to a Nazi strategy to win a battle—but it did, and it worked.

In his memoirs Sharon may have claimed rather more than his share of a truly remarkable victory; nevertheless, by the third week in October when a cease-fire was imposed, Israeli columns had reached the port of Suez, severing the Egyptian Third Army from its supplies of food and water—a timely triumph which would lead to him becoming the unrelentingly tough boss of Israel a decade later. Only a cease-fire could now avert a terrible calamity for the Egyptians.[53]

Meanwhile the resupplying of both sides went on, threatening to make the conflict more dangerous, more capable of escalation and of

spreading outside the area. Pari passu was the quest for a cease-fire resolution at the United Nations. Underlying the latter there seemed
(were it not for the huge issues involved) instincts that were somewhat
primeval, if not schoolboyish with each of the backers (United States
and USSR) striving to get the best deal for their respective combatant
clients. When, in the first days, Israel had seemed to be getting the
worst of it, Kissinger sought a cease-fire based on the status quo ante
lines of October 6—so at least the menacing Golan Heights could be
regained; then, as Israel's counterattack surged forward, he sought a
cease-fire in place—i.e., on the prevailing battlefront lines. On their
side, initially the Soviets would only support Sadat's insistence that any
cease-fire would have to be based on Resolution 242, which would
return Israel to her pre-1967 borders. Then, as the tide of war turned
dramatically against the Arabs, with both Damascus and Cairo threatened, they and their Soviet backers argued with increasing anxiety
for the cease-fire in place. There was little give-and-take on either
side. Kissinger was progressively infuriated by the unhelpfulness of
America's European allies, notably Britain, which tended toward the
Arab resolution. This would be totally unacceptable to Israel, and consequently vetoed by the U.S. delegation to the U.N. He recorded in
his memoirs that, as of October 10: "The Soviet initiative for a cease-
fire in place was now on the table in the worst possible circumstances
for our strategy: If the Soviets pushed their proposal at that juncture,
it would have had nearly unanimous backing, including by our European allies. On the other hand, Israel, with the pre-war situation not
yet restored, would have refused. Had we gone along with the Soviet
plan and pressured Israel to agree, the war would have ended in a clear-
cut victory for the Soviet-supplied Arab forces. The United States's
position in the post-war diplomacy would have been severely
impaired."[54]

As noted earlier, in his conversation with Nixon on the 14th,
Kissinger had expressed his frustrations about the disappointing performance of number one ally Britain over formulation of the vital
cease-fire resolution at the U.N. Despite the standoff with Moscow,
Kissinger's telcons with Dobrynin continue generally to reflect their
earlier friendly and jokey relationship, while those with the Heath gov-

ernment in London and the British ambassador in Washington, Lord Cromer, remained frosty. The exception was the foreign secretary, Alec Douglas-Home, to whom in his memoirs Kissinger regularly, and reverentially, referred as "that rarest of statesmen, one whose integrity disarms even his critics . . . inspired confidence in full measure . . . he stood for the common values of freedom. There was literally no one whom we trusted more," and "one of the wisest and most decent men I have had the privilege to meet. We never questioned that for him, Atlantic partnership was a moral necessity; unlike his Prime Minister, he did not see Britain's European vocation as requiring the loosening of transatlantic ties built up over three decades."[55] Basically, the *froideur* all harked back to the unhappy course of the ill-chosen Year of Europe negotiations earlier in the year, in which—for Dr. Kissinger—Ted Heath and Michel Jobert of France had vied for role of number one villain.

As pointed out earlier, with de Gaulle's defection (in Israeli eyes), when he had halted deliveries of Mystère aircraft during the Six Day War of 1967, the United States had replaced France as Israel's principal source of military hardware. Following Golda Meir's anguished calls for an urgent airlift of arms, on October 10, Kissinger records having been woken to the "ominous news of the Soviet airlift to Syria."[56] As far as Israel's pleading was concerned, with the weight of Pentagon expertise behind him, James Schlesinger for one was skeptical that an army "could run out of ammunition without warning. . . . It is impossible that they didn't know what their supply was—and suddenly they've run out of it." Kissinger replied, parenthetically, and with some acidity: "I have no doubt whatever that they are blaming us for their own failures," and later, with growing impatience: "Look, they fucked it up. . . . I bet you they didn't expend as much in the whole Six Day War as they did in one day of this offensive . . . they are living in 1967. All day long yesterday they were telling me they were heading for Damascus and they were going to stop on the outskirts. This morning they tell me they will use public transportation if they can. Now obviously they can't make it."[57]

Fearful of aggravating the Arabs into using the "oil weapon," Kissinger was equally inclined to caution—initially. At first small quantities of equipment—notably of the new, state-of-the-art Maverick antitank missiles—were collected from U.S. bases by camouflaged El Al commercial planes. Then Kissinger introduced the ruse of utilizing private air charter companies; but this soon turned out to be a fiasco as the proprietors "ran scared" of their aircraft being intercepted and shot down. In any case, the quantity of arms shippable by such means was minimal—and disappointing to the Israelis.

In Washington, Kissinger was coming under unwelcome domestic pressure, orchestrated by his friend, the tireless Israeli ambassador, Simcha Dinitz. Senator Hubert Humphrey, the former Democratic vice president and Nixon's opponent in the 1968 election, was performing as the typical Washington politician under pressure from the Israeli lobby. On the 12th, he was remonstrating with Kissinger, "I just don't think we can let that little country that we have so much interest in get clobbered." Kissinger was robust, telling Humphrey: "You understand, keep in mind that whatever we do give them, they come back the next day asking for five times as much." When Schlesinger informed Kissinger that Scoop Jackson had been badgering him for "fifty Phantoms within twenty-four hours," Kissinger retorted brusquely: "Tell him to go screw himself!" Schlesinger then reported back: "We will go ahead with the package, which consists of 30 Sky Hawk A4s, 16 Phantoms, 125 tanks, including 65 M60s [Pattons], and a whole range of other things." That evening Kissinger was sharply reproving Dinitz: "I was very upset by the harassment from the pro-Jewish senators this afternoon. As if we had not done enough." And, again the following day, telling him how he had been threatened again by Jackson with a congressional investigation: "I must say this—if I get one more threatening call by anybody I am going out of the supply business. With all my friendship I am not going to stand for it." Dinitz protested his innocence, but Kissinger continued menacingly: "If it turns out that we are going to be under attack for mismanagement in a crisis, we will have to turn on you. I don't care who does it, if that happens, we will defend ourselves."[58] These abrasive exchanges seem hardly to reinforce suggestions that Kissinger was excessively favoring Israel in the war. Certainly Golda Meir did not think so.

That Sunday, the 12th, Haig had been advising Kissinger that the Soviets had alerted three airborne divisions. With the news of the Russian airlift and troop moves, Kissinger now warned Dobrynin that it would "force us to do at least the same."[59] He and Nixon now shifted into top gear. "I wanted a demonstrative counter to the Soviet airlift," recorded Kissinger.[60]

That day the heavy U.S. airlift began in earnest, flown in its entirety by U.S. planes, including giant C-5As which could carry a quantity of tanks or compact Skyhawk A-4 fighter-bombers in their vast hulls. Some 25,000 tons of equipment was earmarked for shipment. The selection of a new vice president was resolved on the 14th by the appointment of Gerald Ford. Yet now the crisis over the release of the Watergate tapes and the start of impeachment proceedings was but a few days away. Still Nixon, that day, was able to take a coherent and strong line over the airlift, observing to Kissinger, "We are going to get blamed just as much for three planes as for three hundred—not going to let the Russians come in there for—with a free hand. On the other hand, this is a deadly course, I know, but what I mean is, Henry, I have no patience with the view that we send in a couple of planes even though they carry some 60 [sentence unfinished] . . ."

Nixon continued: "The purpose of supplies is not simply to fuel the war; the purpose [is] to maintain the balance . . . and then—because only with the balance of that area, can there be an equitable settlement that doesn't do in one side or the other. That is really what we are talking about. . . . We ought to tell Dobrynin—we ought to say that the Russians—that Brezhnev and Nixon will settle this damn thing. That ought to be done. You know that."

"K: Exactly. Exactly right."[61]

In his desire to shut the Soviets out, this was however not what Kissinger really thought—as would be seen during his trip to Moscow the following week.

When Schlesinger reported that there were problems of diplomacy within the State Department, Kissinger erupted with fury. To Haig late on the night of the 12th, he complained about "having a massive problem with the Israelis, because the sons of bitches in Defense have been stalling for four days and not one airplane has moved . . . not one God damn shipload—not one has moved. And they are now out of ammunition. They are stopping their Syrian offensive."*

"Oh boy," was Haig's response. Kissinger then called on him to "throw the fear of God into Schlesinger" over refueling snarl-ups. Haig promised to do so. The next morning Kissinger was demanding—via Scowcroft at NSC—the names of any official "who is inventing obstacles and have him removed." He was also savage with the Portuguese when initially they hesitated over use of U.S. bases in the Azores for the airlift. He told Schlesinger that "I just told them we wouldn't bargain. If they reject, we remember. When the crisis against which they want to protect themselves occurs . . ."†62 Schlesinger was however able to reassure him that eighteen giant transports packed with munitions would shortly be flying in, direct to Tel Aviv, refueling in the Azores.

To Alec Douglas-Home on the morning of the 13th, Kissinger voiced his suspicions that continued to nag him about the Soviet role in the conflict: "My impression is that if they tricked us on this, they will pay the price of our entire relationship. They have all to lose." Home replied expressing concern that "our credibility will be completely lost if we were to make the public initiative and he [Brezhnev] would not have it. He himself has given us the conditions to which he would agree to a ceasefire."63 In his quest for a cease-fire Kissinger was still finding little support from the Austrian U.N. secretary-general, Kurt Waldheim, an ineffectual figure already enfeebled by rumors of a war crimes past in World War II. He reported that the Egyptians, still advancing, would accept a cease-fire only if the Israelis agreed to withdraw to the pre-1967 lines. Kissinger replied: "Yeah, well, that's out of the question."64

Later that afternoon, in a series of conversations with Dobrynin, Kissinger voiced his suspicions that "you tricked us," and then warned

---

* As seen earlier, this was not strictly true. The Israelis, having defeated the Syrians, were shifting their forces down toward Sinai. Whether from panic, or design, they had exaggerated their ammunition problems for U.S. consumption (telcon 12/10/73, 11:54 P.M.).

† The Portuguese government under Marcelo Caetano was currently in deep crisis, in fact on the brink of revolution.

him that, because of the Egyptian attitude and the Soviet arms shipments, the president "can no longer observe any restrictions that I gave
you yesterday on flying American planes." That "we are prepared to
stop when you are." [65] The ante was rising, so were tempers. Kissinger,
in his memoirs, dismissed one note from Moscow as "pure inso-
lence." [66] Resorting to hard talk, Kissinger in an unusually long conversation warned Dobrynin on the evening of the 13th: "You sent in
140 airplanes. Maybe why the Arabs are so tough now." And another
emphatic warning designed for the Bear's consumption, "We will not
under any circumstances let détente be used for unilateral advantage."
He went on to express fears that the United States and Soviets were
"obviously on collision course . . . [but] I had absolute confidence—
you have never lied to us before," and then, more challengingly: "Why
do we have to deal with you [on matters] that depend on Sadat, why
not deal with Sadat directly?" He ended declaring that "The President
is extremely agitated."

The Russian's response to this tirade was somewhat incomprehensible: "In my telegram [presumably to Brezhnev?], I will quote,
unquote you. I can assure you—otherwise [situation] is dangerous." Kissinger concluded, reminding Dobrynin that "We had an
understanding to work on the basic issue in January. This has been
completely disregarded now. We will not let ourselves be pressured
into it." [67]

On the 14th, Kissinger was maintaining the pressure on his Russian
friend: "You know, Anatoly, we all know now what is at stake, because
if this goes on much longer—"[68]

In his second conversation with the president on the morning of
the 14th, although his initiative for a cease-fire had been thwarted, he
was able to assure Nixon that "a massive airlift" was underway, with
planes landing in Israel every fifteen minutes, the massive transport
planes capable of flying in five or six of the compact Skyhawk A-4s in
their capacious bellies, along with the 25,000 tons of equipment. It was
a remarkable display of American technological ability. Nixon, now—
briefly—back in command of the situation, instructed Kissinger to tell
Brezhnev that "the peace of not only this area but the whole future relationship is at stake here and we are prepared to stop if you are." [69]

Later that day, Schlesinger was reporting to Kissinger that twenty

Phantoms had been sent, plus "the TOWs. As you know, they have never appeared out there before so there will be a certain dramatic effect." *[70] The following day Schlesinger was revealing to Kissinger that the Israelis were also pressing for special bridging equipment, clearly indicative of Sharon's intentions on the Suez Canal, and how things were moving there. (Hitherto the U.S. government had banned export of such matériel, in case the Israelis might be contemplating any such offensive move into the heart of Egypt.) Kissinger suggested to the WSAG[71] that the United States should maintain its resupply "at least 25 percent ahead of the Soviets," following up with an increased sea lift, given that in the Black Sea the Soviets were loading ships with enormous quantities of matériel, including their most modern weaponry. The situation was beginning to look increasingly dangerous each day that went by.

Reporting on the scale of the airlift to Senator Jacob Javits of New York (one of the leading Jewish congressmen), Kissinger urged him to "say something kind" in this context about the beleaguered president. By the 17th, he was able to tell Nixon that "we are pouring in arms at a rate about 30 percent greater than they do." That same day an elated Dinitz, after passing on congratulations to Kissinger on his award of the Nobel Prize, told him that "Golda talked to me on the telephone. She said people are crying in Israel. She went to the airport and saw American guys coming with the planes and said it was one of the most exciting sights of her life."[72]

It must have been an exhilarating moment for Kissinger. Yet the doubt has to remain whether in fact Israel would have won the Yom Kippur War without the massive U.S. airlift, which was to cause such an impact both on détente and the West's oil supplies. To what extent had Golda been genuinely panicked by the shock of that first week of bad news, or deliberately exaggerated Israel's dangerous expenditure of munitions to gain maximum U.S. commitment? Certainly by the 18th, Sharon's bridgehead across the canal, with some three hundred tanks

---

* These were the latest U.S. wire-guided antitank missiles. Some eighty-one TOW launchers and 2,010 missiles were rushed to Israel. Israeli commandos flew to Fort Benning, Georgia, that same month to train on the systems. They returned home in time for decisive action both on the Golan Heights and in crossing the Suez Canal.

pouring into it and up to eight miles in depth, was already secure, while the fearsome Israeli air weapon was unleashed as Sharon's armor swiftly mopped up two-thirds of the SAM sites west of the canal. Through the skill of Israeli mechanical crews more than half of its damaged tanks were repaired on the battlefield; while between them the Egyptians and Syrians proved able only to return 5 percent of theirs.

Israel was saved.

CHAPTER 12

THE CRISIS: DEFCON 3

"We are all Semites together."
—Saudi Foreign Minister Omar al-Saqqaf, October 17, 1973[1]

Two invitations now arrived on Kissinger's desk (on the 16th); one, from Brezhnev, to come urgently to Moscow; the other, from Sadat,[2] even more unexpected. Both would profoundly affect the progress of the war, and the peace negotiations beyond it. Already on the second day of the war Kissinger had received, via the Cairo CIA station (since the United States had no direct relations with Egypt), a secret message from Hafez Ismail, Sadat's security adviser, with whom Kissinger had held those two abortive meetings earlier in the year. The content was not significant; it simply repeated the familiar formula, unacceptable to the United States, calling on Israel to withdraw from all the occupied territories. Kissinger regarded this as only an opening gambit; but what he read into it—as constituting "extraordinary" significance—was the intimation that Sadat might be prepared to deal with the United States as a key player in the peace process, at least on a level with Sadat's Soviet ally. It displayed statesmanlike moderation, in that Sadat was not going to use America "as a whipping boy—as Nasser had done in 1967."*[3] Kissinger found it particularly promising in that here was a country "that had attacked our ally and whose aims were being thwarted by American arms." Up till that point, he admits, he had "not taken Sadat seriously." Now here, "amazingly," at the crisis point in the war, and before Egypt faced any immediate threat of losing, was a further, more direct approach, couched in language that could scarcely be warmer or more friendly: "Egypt will welcome Dr. Kissinger in appreciation for his efforts. The Egyptian side will be prepared to discuss any subject, proposal or project. . . .

"With warmest regards. Hafiz Ismail."[4]

Early on the 16th, Kissinger replied in the same vein: "Dr. Kissinger greatly appreciates the thoughtful invitation of the Egyptian side to visit Egypt. Once a ceasefire has been achieved, he would be glad to give that invitation the most serious and sympathetic consideration."[5] Kissinger interpreted that Sadat, though he could readily have used the airlift as an alibi for the Egyptian setback in Sinai, was "tired of spilling blood for futile causes." Unlike his predecessor, Nasser, he was "willing to forego posturing for attainable progress." Moreover, he had "taken the measure of Soviet support: always enough to keep tensions high, never enough to bring about a settlement."[6]

Armed with this exchange, the next morning Kissinger met the delegation of Arab ministers† in Washington in a more self-confident frame of mind—although the strategic significance of the Sharon incursion across the Suez Canal was still not fully apparent to Kissinger, and possibly not even to Sadat. The previous day, ominously, the Saudi deputy foreign minister had warned the European ambassadors that, unless they pressed the United States to change its policy, Saudi Arabia would reduce its oil production. The exchange of Wednesday the 17th in Kissinger's office in the State Department was a forthright one, with Omar al-Saqqaf, the Saudi minister of state for foreign affairs (described by Kissinger in his memoirs as "gentle and wise") leading off

---

* Egypt's Gamal Abdel Nasser (1918–1970), a powerful demagogue and preeminent Arab nationalist, turned virulently on America following the Arab defeat by Israel in 1967.

† From Saudi Arabia, Kuwait, Morocco, and Algeria (memcon, 10/17/73).

with an expression of fears of a "major power confrontation in the Middle East, which would hurt the U.S.: The Russians would be seen as doing something for the Arabs, while the U.S. is helping the other side. This is something we do not want." Kissinger responded: "This is exactly what is bound to happen if there is an inconclusive outcome and if there is Great Power confrontation in the area." More aggressively, Abdelaziz Bouteflika* from Algeria, weaned in the war against France, recalled how in that eight-year-long struggle, the Algerians "did not ask for a ceasefire before determining the specific conditions of peace." (This throughout the Algerian war of liberation had constituted a fundamental, and successful cornerstone of Algerian policy.) Bouteflika went on: "You can't tell people to stop a war and expect that they automatically will do so. . . . You can guarantee the honor and dignity of Israel, but do not sacrifice the honor and dignity of the Arab countries on that altar." Kissinger pointed out, gently, to the Algerian that it had taken four years of war for them to obtain a solution, and that in Vietnam "my colleague, Le Duc Tho, tried to follow the Algerian example, but did not succeed. . . . There are different precedents for different situations." Thinking ahead to his possible future role as a mediator, still substantively undefined—and toward his shuttle diplomacy of the even more distant future—he foresaw: "The most dangerous thing now would be for me to travel in capitals before the framework of what we want to achieve is set out."

Studied today, this reads like an utterance of almost visionary caliber. In the same vein, Kissinger went on to declare that "The problem which worries me most is the Palestinian people." He urged his Arab interlocutors to "use your influence with the Arabs and the Palestinians to find a *realistic* solution which incorporates the territorial integrity and existence of all the states in the area. Such negotiations should not be used as a new form of political warfare" (author's italics). He continued, taking the ministers into his confidence about the state of the war: "My assessment of the immediate situation is that the Arab armies have done better than expected, but that they do not have the ca-

---

* Later to become president of Algeria and a staunch ally of the United States in the war against terror. It is worth recalling the role in orchestrating the October War which had been played by Houari Boumédienne, Bouteflika's then boss.

pability to push Israel back to the 1967 borders." Foreign Minister Bouteflika: "I can assure you that they can do it." Letting this challenge pass, Kissinger warned: "If we make a diplomatic move and fail and war breaks out again our influence to lead events will be diminished."

An hour later, the discussion with the Arab foreign ministers continued with Nixon in the Oval Office. At that very moment, Nixon was confronting the face-off with the special prosecutor, Archibald Cox, which would lead to the opening of impeachment proceedings against him. He no longer, recalled Kissinger, "had the time or nervous energy to give consistent leadership";[8] nevertheless, he handled the meeting "masterfully and without a sense of strain." Says Kissinger, "Nixon with his mastery of intangibles knew exactly how to strike the right note: to promise a major diplomatic effort without committing himself to a particular outcome."[9] Remarkably, Nixon seems to have been at his best—and his worst—that day. Exuberantly, he promised Kissinger as a negotiator, then, to Kissinger's "horror," implied that this "ensured success. He returned to a familiar theme from his first term, assuring his guests that despite my Jewish origin I was not subject to domestic, that is to say Jewish, pressures." Saqqaf, the polished diplomat, turned this oafish, typically Nixon, slight aside, remarking mildly, "We are all Semites together." As he left the Oval Office, Saqqaf threw a bouquet, but a provocative one, to Kissinger: "The man who can solve the Vietnam War, the man who could have settled the peace all over the world, can easily play a good role in settling and having peace in our area of the Middle East."[10]

There appears to have been little or no mention of the oil weapon; yet only the day before the Saudis had threatened to cut production. Was Kissinger to be criticized for a deficit of attention when it came to the economic facts of life?

At the end of the talks on the 17th, Kissinger telephoned the president to designate it "a most successful morning." The Arab foreign ministers had gone away "happy." Meanwhile, Soviet premier Alexei Kosygin had flown to Cairo, and had not returned "happy," enlightened, or encouraged by what he had heard. On the Sinai front, Sharon's raid had expanded into a torrent of three Israeli armored divisions, supplied by an ingenious, homemade roller-bridge. Across it rolled Avraham "Bren" Adan's 162nd Division, which then raced south, with

the intent of cutting off the Egyptian Third Army before it could retreat west back into mainland Egypt. At the same time, raiding forces
fanned out to destroy the Egyptian SAM batteries east of the canal. By
October 19, the Israelis had managed to construct four separate bridges
just north of the Great Bitter Lake under heavy Egyptian bombard-
ment, pushing some three hundred tanks west across the canal—
roughly equal to the number of Egyptian tanks they had destroyed in
the brutal, decisive battle of the 14th on the east bank. Taking this on
board, and having been briefed by a triumphant Dinitz, to his deputy
at the NSC, General Scowcroft, Kissinger remarked on the night of the
18th: "They are going across with more tanks. I am afraid it will turn
into a turkey shoot. . . ."

> S: The real danger is, the Egyptian army is going to panic.
> K: Once they get across the division strength, that means the
>   SAM belt is gone. When they [the Egyptians] see the army
>   from top and bottom, they are going to disintegrate. They
>   are not that good. They won't be able to get supplies.
>   They'll die of starvation. What I can't understand is how
>   they [the Israelis] broke through the Canal.

This proved, once again, to be a perceptive analysis of military realities. The conversation ended with Kissinger concluding: "When all
is said and done it is a Soviet defeat . . . that should make them [the
Arab states] realize they had better get on our side."[11]

As Kosygin returned to Moscow, the pressure for a cease-fire to
rescue Egypt—and the Kremlin—was growing irresistibly.

Kissinger had just ended the daily WSAG meeting on the morning
of the 19th, when Dobrynin telephoned (at 11:04) "with an urgent
message from Brezhnev to Nixon." It suggested "that the U.S. Secretary of State and your closest associate, Dr. Kissinger, comes in an urgent manner to Moscow to conduct appropriate negotiations with him
[Brezhnev] as with your authorized personal representative. It would
be good if he could come tomorrow, October 20. I will appreciate your
speedy reply.

"Sincerely, L. Brezhnev, October 19, 1973."

Kissinger received this breathless summons with some glee. At last the logjam was breaking up, with dramatic speed. Returning to the lighthearted banter of earlier days, Kissinger's instant riposte after Dobrynin had read out the signal was: "You are friendly, aren't you?"[12]

As was his wont, pressure galvanized Kissinger. Half an hour later he was back on the line to Dobrynin, with Nixon's agreement. At first, testing the water, he asked, however: "Why should Gromyko not come over here?" Dobrynin's response was that the triumvirate, the collective leadership in the Kremlin of Brezhnev, Kosygin, and Gromyko, all wanted to be present—another indication of the urgency which they were attaching to the "summons." Would Dobrynin accompany him?

> D: Yes, if you don't mind I would like to go both ways.
> K: Well as long as you sit in the front compartment.

(The suggestion being that Kissinger did not relish Anatoly backseat driving to Moscow and back.) Then, more seriously: "Anatoly, when the Soviet government makes such a proposal on the basis of urgency it is not a matter we take lightly." In a later call, Kissinger cautioned (without actually spelling out the word *Watergate*) that the trip would "present us with enormous domestic difficulties." He went on to stress the U.S. assumption "that no unilateral actions will be taken while I am in transit."

> D: What do you mean?
> K: No military threats. And I am assuming both of us will keep
>   the situation calm—I don't believe while I am there I will be
>   able to negotiate a final settlement. I will be able to
>   negotiate a cease-fire. . . .
> D: Okay.[13]

Kissinger packed his bags for the following day. That evening there was a brief meeting, eleven minutes long, in his State Department office. Present were Schlesinger, from Defense; Colby, director of CIA; Admiral Moorer, chairman of the Joint Chiefs of Staff; and Scowcroft, Kissinger's deputy at the NSC. Illustrative of how many balls he had aloft in the air at once, he instructed Scowcroft to make sure it was known that the Chinese had been properly warned in advance of his Moscow trip re the dinner they were holding for him at the Mayflower Hotel that night. He explained the strategic advantage of the trip, coupled with his mandatory appearance at the Chinese dinner, in that it would delay the cease-fire a few days, giving the Soviets "a face-saver"—and the Israelis more time to consolidate their gains. "I will work for a simple ceasefire, with maybe a call for negotiations. The trouble is Israel doesn't want anything, but I may have to include a reference to 242*," he explained. "Everyone knows in the Middle East that if they want a peace they have to go through us. Three times they tried through the Soviet Union, and three times they failed." However politely delivered, this would in effect be Kissinger's message in the next few days. In staccato orders, bearing the imprint of presidential authority, he instructed: "Keep the aircraft going to Israel so Israel will be grateful and can't say we screwed them in their hour of triumph." Once again, the tone of his underlying sentiments about the Israelis came through loud and clear. His final thought was "We can't humiliate the Soviet Union too much"; and then he was observing that he could not afford to postpone his long-scheduled trip to China any longer. Colby interjected: "It's only two weeks. Then put it off again if necessary." [14]

It was, as Kissinger explains in *Crisis* [15] the worst possible time to leave Washington, from the domestic point of view. Nixon was negotiating the release of the Watergate tapes (which would lead to the Saturday Night Massacre†, while two days later the House of Representatives would start impeachment proceedings). Meanwhile, during these October days, Nixon, still as brilliant as ever in his long-range conceptions, became increasingly erratic as Watergate moved relentlessly in on him. Daily Kissinger found himself having to take charge; and, earning little support from America's European allies, as well as slender comfort in the world at large, it was the tiller of the West super-

---

* U.N. Resolution 242, calling for a withdrawal of Israeli forces from the areas occupied during the 1967 war.

† Attorney General Elliot Richardson and Deputy Attorney General William Ruckelshaus resigned rather than fire special prosecutor Archibald Cox as ordered by President Nixon. Solicitor General Robert Bork carried out Nixon's order.

ship he held in his hand. Before leaving the following day, there was a drama with Haig when he expressed Nixon's desire to "go out tonight and announce your trip."

Kissinger: "Impossible. . . . My honest opinion is that is a cheap stunt. It looks as if he is using foreign policy to cover a domestic thing. . . . I would not link foreign policy with Watergate. You will regret it for the rest of your life . . . if he gets that mixed up with foreign policy, Al, then he has to do this with the Jewish community. It will forever after be said he did this to cover Watergate. I really would plead with you." Eventually, after Kissinger in a subsequent call declared that it was going to be "no joy to be in Moscow under these conditions," Haig persuaded Nixon to back down, and make two separate announcements.[16]

Before he left Washington, one of Kissinger's last communications came from an elated Dinitz, reporting "We have taken a town 35 miles from Cairo, which is halfway between the Canal and Cairo." At the front, things were moving rapidly indeed. In *Crisis* Kissinger summed up: "we had achieved our fundamental objectives: we had created conditions for a diplomatic breakthrough. We had vindicated the security of our friends. We had prevented a victory of Soviet arms. We had maintained a relationship with key Arab countries and laid the basis for a dominant role in postwar diplomacy. And we had done all this in the midst of the gravest Constitutional domestic crisis of the century." In conversation with one of his Democratic critics on the Hill, longtime Arkansas senator J. William Fulbright, Kissinger explained meaningfully—and with patience: "The thing we all have to remember is with all this détente talk, without the détente Kosygin would not be in Cairo. The Soviet press would not be accepting our airlift and all hell would be breaking loose."[17]

So, during all this time of intense, and dangerous, crisis in Washington, and fierce battle in the Middle East, what was the view from the windows of the Kremlin? If we lucky historians have enjoyed one rare benefit through living in the murderous and turbulent twentieth century it is surely that, as almost never before, through the collapse of hitherto opaque, totalitarian regimes—and their subsequent exposure—we are privileged with unique views of "the other side of the hill." After 1945 we were treated to a comprehensive insight into the workings of Nazi Germany and Imperial Japan, in all their vileness. Thus too, with the fall of the Berlin Wall, the coming of perestroika and glasnost, we were able to glimpse inside the stony exteriors of the rulers of the Soviet Union two decades previously. One who recorded the scene there, with what seems like remarkable fidelity and lack of prejudice, was Soviet apparatchik Victor Israelyan. Born in 1919, for more than forty years Israelyan served in the Soviet Ministry of Foreign Affairs, rising through the ranks to become one of the Soviet Union's leading diplomats, specializing in disarmament negotiations. Having worked with all the postwar Soviet foreign ministers, from Vyacheslav Molotov, Andrei Vyshinsky, and Andrei Gromyko on through Eduard Shevardnadze, and having established diplomatic ties particularly to the United States, Israelyan was privy to the inner meetings of the Foreign Ministry. As a senior ranking expert (appointed as one of a four-man task force set up during the Yom Kippur War), though not actually within the Politburo itself, he was brought into many of its deliberations, as well as being well informed on the mindset of its chieftains and all the hushed gossip in darkened corridors.

From these dangerous days Israelyan comes across as a kind of Boswell to the Politburo, his account buttressed by the recollections of Dobrynin. Describing himself as "a typical product of the Soviet system and its obedient servant," Israelyan was forced to retire in 1987, a casualty of a system that was about to collapse under the weight of its own contradictions. In disillusion he moved to Pennsylvania State University. He could not then imagine that the regime in whose service he had spent his life was about to collapse. Though damning of the whole structure, and not sparing those involved in its decline and demise, Israelyan makes no attempt to excuse his own role; he explains how "the irresistible desire to understand the Soviet Union's foreign policy fiasco" led him to write his book *Inside the Kremlin*.[18] In a foreword to Israelyan's book, Soviet expert Alvin Z. Rubinstein writes: "Not since Trotsky's writing in the 1930s has a witness to the foreign-policy-making decision process of the Communist Party's top leadership provided us with so substantive a work."[19]

At variance with perceived truths, Israelyan gives a picture of a torpid collectivity in steep decline, ruled over by a somnolent, but by no means yet senescent, Brezhnev—not the brutal ravisher of the Prague Spring, but a sagacious if not benign paternal figure. The Politburo comes across as a time-serving body where nobody would raise his head until Brezhnev had committed himself, fearing a swipe of Father Bear's paw: "a team of political chameleons, adaptable, guided primarily by the desire to keep their positions."[20] The poker-faced Gromyko was always particularly circumspect; which, thought Israelyan, was what had allowed him to remain foreign minister for twenty-eight years. Yuri Andropov, the KGB chief who had assured Khrushchev in the early 1960s that the Soviet Union could conquer Western Europe in seven days, sat silent, "unwilling to argue." Only the military men, notably Marshal Andrei Grechko, tended to thump the table as the crisis developed. What comes across loud and clear was that the Kissinger-Nixon initiatives striving for détente, all those meetings at Zavidovo, Washington, and San Clemente, had stored up valuable capital of goodwill—which would pay handsome dividends over the next highly dangerous week. If, with his instinctive Russian anti-Semitism, the Bear did not entirely trust Kissinger, he seems to have come to think that Nixon would never pull a fast one on him, would never launch a surprise U.S. attack on the Soviet Union—which for so many years had haunted Stalin and Khrushchev.

Israelyan opens his account by recalling how Thursday, October 4, 1973, had been "an ordinary weekday full of the usual bureaucratic fuss." Summoned suddenly at 7 P.M. to the Foreign Ministry high-rise building on Smolenskaya Square, in "one of the most remarkable" of the meetings he had ever attended, he found a stunned Gromyko repeating, several times, that a Middle East war was going to begin at 2 P.M. in two days time.* Present were Vasili Kuznetsov, his first deputy, and Georgi Kornienko, head of the U.S. department. Gromyko insisted that the Politburo had done everything it could to talk Asad and Sadat out of attacking. He thought that the negotiations between Brezhnev

---

* To this day there remains a mystery, which Israelyan was unable to resolve, as to who actually tipped off the Soviets. It seems (see Israelyan, p. 15, and Richard Lebow, *Between Peace and War*, p. 220) that it was neither the Soviet embassy, nor the KGB, from Cairo. No tapes appear to have been kept of Politburo discussions—unlike Nixon's—hence much reliance has to be placed on Israelyan's account.

and Nixon that summer had created a good foundation for a political solution to the Middle East problem, and that a military conflict would ruin things.* Parallel to U.S. Middle East policy as of the beginning of October 1973, a "no war, no peace" policy was equally the most acceptable to the Kremlin. The usually impassive Gromyko was "clearly annoyed."[21] It was thought that Sadat should have been obliged by the Soviet treaty of 1971 to consult or at least inform the Soviet government of the decision to attack well in advance; yet he had given the ambassador in Cairo, Vladimir Vinogradov, not the least hint.

On the 6th, *Pravda* was set to claim that Israel was whipping up tension for an attack. Israelyan commented laconically on how the Soviet leadership was just deceiving itself with its own propaganda. (As an interesting aside, Israelyan explains the silence of the Soviet media throughout September came from the fact that it had been so preoccupied with the coup in Chile as to preempt "reports on other international problems." In contrast, Kissinger would claim he was distracted from Chile by events in Moscow.) The Politburo recognized that Vinogradov was being bypassed by Sadat, and fed with obvious untruths. Many years later Vinogradov would express his bitterness at the way in which Sadat had deceived him. The Soviets were clearly being shabbily treated by their Arab client states; Israelyan claims that Sadat and Asad had "strictly prohibited informing the Russians about the date before the day of the attack"—but he also blames a policy that was "rather two faced, ambiguous and contradictory, as was the foreign policy of the Soviet Union in general."[22] He adds: "I have the impression that he [Sadat] sincerely believed he could be a champion of Soviet-American détente and at the same time a supporter of anti-imperialist, anti-American forces and movements all over the world."[23]

---

* This is also reinforced by the signal sent from Gromyko to Nixon on September 28 (Kissinger archives, memcon 9/28/73) with an articulate warning on the Middle East: "Your assessment and ours do not fully coincide, even if at first sight it seems that we do since both sides feel the situation is complicated and dangerous. But we have a different assessment of the danger because we feel the possibility could not be excluded that we could all wake up one day and find there is a real conflagration in that area. That has to be kept in mind. Is it worth the risk? A serious effort has to be made for a solution because a solution will not just fall down from the sky." Gromyko went on to recall the conversation Brezhnev and Nixon had held in San Clemente that June. The question arises—and always will—because of Watergate, was Nixon paying attention that day?

Though Nixon found it hard to believe that the Egyptians and Syrians could move without the knowledge of the Soviets, Israelyan stresses how "disappointed" Brezhnev was by the behavior of their Arab clients: they would be "sorry they have not followed the advice of the Soviet leadership," he said, while the militant Andrei Grechko, minister of defense and (at 70) a veteran of World War II, wanted the Arabs to "be punished for their disobedience." He doubted they could win the war "the way they are waging it."[25] Expressing residual contempt for the Arabs, Marshal Victor Kulikov, chief of the general staff, complained: "They do not listen to us. They pretend to be their own military strategists."[26] In the past mistrust of the "Arab brothers" and their military competence had led to Kremlin rejection of their requests for the most modern Soviet weaponry. Early on in October, Brezhnev too was foreseeing another Arab defeat, fearing that this time, armed with Soviet weapons, it would be regarded as a challenge to Soviet military might. There was harsh criticism at the shortsightedness of the Egyptian "operational pause" of October 14, in not pushing on to capture the vital Sinai passes.[27]

Therefore an early cease-fire was seen as the best solution, and Brezhnev hoped for U.S. collaboration here. He had welcomed Nixon's early appeal. Israelyan speculates on what would have happened if the Kremlin had agreed with Washington's "genuine or tactical suggestion" aimed at a joint cease-fire resolution in the first days of the war; instead the Soviets had blundered by deciding to "act in accordance with the position of Egypt"—even though Sadat had brusquely expelled the advisers in the run-up to war. The Politburo felt itself committed to supporting "the legitimate demands of the Arab territories occupied by Israel since 1967," but was depressed by the news that Sadat would not meet the Soviet proposal halfway. In fact the Politburo was furious at his "stubbornness." Says Israelyan, it was "torn apart" by this dilemma, accepting "that a cease-fire resolution, which included provisions that Israel immediately withdraw to the 1967 borders would inevitably cause a confrontation with the U.S. and its veto." At the heart of Kremlin policy, there lay a fundamental contradiction in its "desire to please its 'Arab friends' while at the same time maintaining friendly cooperation with its superpower partner."[28] Meanwhile, at the U.N., the cease-fire status quo ante, as proposed informally by Kissinger, had no chance of passing the Security Council. There Moscow's aggressive representative, Yakov Malik, was like "a lion growling in a cage," pursuing a hard line on his own.[29]

On October 12, Israelyan notes, the Politburo held a meeting that was "perhaps the gloomiest throughout the Yom Kippur War."[30] The United States was beginning to resupply Israel (Andropov believed, wrongly, that they had been doing so since the very beginning of the war). There were rumors of 150 American pilots going to Israel disguised as tourists. The Kremlin was still caught up in its "futile attempt to combine two incompatible courses of action."[31] Kissinger's proposal that Britain introduce at the U.N. a cease-fire in place resolution was seen to have failed. Israelyan, however, challenges Kissinger's suggestion that "the Soviet Union had been stringing us all along never intending to have a cease-fire."[32] How, asks Israelyan, "could the grand master of diplomacy have failed to see that the Soviet Union's quest for a speedy cease-fire was guided by the desire to assist its clients in a deteriorating military situation, the same way the American policy aimed at delaying the cease-fire was in the interests of its client, whose military situation was improving very quickly. The motivations of the two superpowers were the same."[33] Gromyko is recorded as suggesting, sagely, that perhaps both the Soviets and the Americans should stop military supplies entirely?

The Politburo attempted to analyze the impact of Watergate on U.S. policy. According to Israelyan in a particularly significant passage, "the consequences of the Watergate scandal were grossly underestimated in the Soviet Union." It had not been widely discussed in the Soviet press, and Brezhnev had made it clear at a press conference that summer "that he had never given any thought to whether the Watergate scandal might have weakened President Nixon's foreign policy position and he did not intend to exploit the issue." That was a purely "domestic American affair," and it would be "quite indecent and quite unsuitable" for a Soviet leader to intervene in any way.[34]

Prior to Kosygin's flying visit to Cairo, on the 16th, at a Politburo meeting the previous day (described by Israelyan as held amid an atmosphere where his task force was "almost in a panic," with only Brezhnev remaining in a "cheerful mood"), Brezhnev instructed Kosygin to warn Sadat of "the growing American reluctance to take concrete measures to stop the war." Moscow had accepted that the tide of war now seemed to be turning. Kosygin in his turn warned an unreceptive Sadat of the danger presented by Sharon's penetration across the canal; he was astonished to see Cairo streets full of young people who seemed not to care. It was not how he remembered Moscow during the Great Patriotic War. Sadat had dismissed the Israeli thrust as "a small episode, nonsense." Kosygin went on to warn Sadat that if the Arabs were going to lose as many as a thousand tanks in a week, the Soviet Union could not replace them. He also voiced the very real Soviet fear that the moment the Arabs started to use oil as a political weapon a NATO military force would "descend on the Middle East." It was a fear that would prove to be quite unfounded; nevertheless, says Israelyan, a serious concern that "the Arab oil embargo would complicate and broaden the Middle East conflict prevailed in the Kremlin." Equally there was apprehension that China might exploit any Soviet embarrassment to move in to the region; this "sometimes overshadowed other concerns of Soviet leaders."[35] Kosygin's visit had clearly not been regarded as a success by the Politburo. It was abundantly clear that Sadat did not like Kosygin, or the Russians in general; equally Israelyan was critical of the Soviet failure to understand Sadat. As a professional diplomatist, he blamed the "orthodox, doctrinaire Soviet approach to world developments."[36]

It was clearly this mood of apprehension which persuaded the Kremlin to send for Kissinger. Meanwhile, the Soviet media kept stoking up the propaganda war against Israel—and U.S. arms deliveries. Not until the 18th did they mention that *seven* Israeli tanks had crossed the canal; by now the actual number was around three hundred. But, says Israelyan, the lies were for the Soviet public, "the Soviet leaders knew the bitter truth."[37] Hence the urgency of the Kremlin's invitation to Kissinger.

Kissinger departed Washington on Saturday, October 20, in a mood of qualified optimism, but on the way three things occurred to ruffle his equanimity. First came the announcement that the Saudis were cutting oil production—a warning shot of what lay ahead. Next, without consulting him, Nixon was suddenly aroused into "an unusual flurry of diplomatic activity." A personal letter dispatched to Brezhnev while Kissinger was in midair granted him "full authority" to conduct the forthcoming discussions. Another emissary might have regarded this as a flattering demonstration of presidential confidence. But to Kissinger it was deeply compromising in that it immediately deprived him of his fallback ploy of pleading that he needed to consult the White House before making any commitment. Further, the message went on to suggest that Kissinger was empowered to discuss a global cease-fire cum political settlement; something which contravened the whole of Kissinger's strategy of dealing with the two separate issues. Kissinger, angered, flashed back a message to Scowcroft objecting: "I must be in a position to insist to the Russians that I must pass the proposals back to the President for his consideration. Any reference to full authority would undercut this ability." Then, third, there would come (the next morning, Moscow time) news of the Saturday Night Massacre. Kissinger recorded leaving as "a firestorm was sweeping through Washington."[38] What had happened was that Special Prosecutor Cox had refused to accept Nixon's summaries of the White House tapes; he insisted on having the tapes themselves. Nixon responded by firing Cox, which led to the resignation of both the recently appointed attorney general, Elliot Richardson, and his deputy, William Ruckelshaus. The inexorable path to impeachment lay imminently ahead. In consequence, as far as Moscow was concerned, more not less authority was devolving on Kissinger's shoulders.

Kissinger reacted with unusual irritation to Nixon's démarche, signaling Scowcroft: "My position here is almost insoluble. If I carry out the letter of the President's instructions it will totally wreck what little bargaining leverage I still have. Our first objective must be a cease-fire. That will be tough enough to get the Israelis to accept."[39] Meanwhile, with Haig another testy exchange took place, on an open line, with Haig begging: "Will you get off my back? I have troubles of my own."

Kissinger: "What troubles can you possibly have in Washington on a Saturday night?" Haig then told him of the Saturday Night Massacre, adding: "and all hell has broken loose." Kissinger later excused himself on the grounds of "two weeks of too great tension and too little sleep."[40]

Nevertheless, the Moscow negotiations proceeded with unprecedented speed. Matters were undoubtedly accelerated by Kissinger's stalling because of his date with the Chinese in Washington, which had provided another forty-eight-hour delay—time for Israel to further its gains against the Egyptians. Meeting him at the airport, Gromyko then escorted the American team "at the customary racing-speed" to the guest villa on the Lenin Hills overlooking the Moscow River. "No sooner had we been installed than we were served the obligatory heavy meal that immediately cut down our mobility."

It was dinnertime in Moscow, but only midday in the United States. There then followed a "private" dinner with Brezhnev in the Politburo office—regardless of the fact that the Americans had just eaten. The Bear was up to his old double-watch act from San Clemente. Kissinger found "the atmosphere was not without its bizarre aspects. . . . The convivial second meal was taking place at the very moment that both sides were introducing thousands of tons of war matériel daily to opposite sides in a desperate war, each seeking to reduce if not eliminate the influence of the other."[41] Such are the paradoxes of history. But, as Kissinger noted, "no evening with the Soviet leadership could be complete without some bluster."[42]

In view of the news from Washington, Kissinger deemed it all the more important to obtain a cease-fire before the Kremlin was tempted "to take advantage of our domestic debacle." But many in the Kremlin were deeply suspicious of Kissinger. The fact of his being in Moscow without Nixon caused some of the age-old, atavistic anti-Semitism of the Russian to rise close to the surface. Israelyan gave voice to this mistrust: "The Kremlin leaders and the Soviet diplomats viewed Kissinger differently . . . a well-known American bourgeois historian."[43] Regarding him as "a self-promoter," Kuznetsov (for twenty years the Soviets' first deputy foreign minister) even suspected Kissinger of having invited himself to Moscow—in his own personal interest. Himself critical of Kissinger, Israelyan in his book accused him of exerting "much effort into depicting himself as a creator and originator of American foreign policy, thereby downgrading Nixon's role and prestige in that area." While in Moscow, he claimed, Kissinger "did his best to keep the U.S. Embassy in Moscow unaware of his stay."[44]

Israelyan goes on to record how Gromyko warned "Don't give him a finger—he will bite off your hand." Though himself Jewish-

Armenian, Israelyan spoke of both "the covert and the outspoken anti-Semites" speculating, and joking, about Kissinger's Jewish identity: "How can a Jew be an anti-communist if he was born in Germany and became a political scientist when he settled abroad, following the pattern of Karl Marx?" And: "Why should the Soviet Jews emigrate to Israel and not to the United States, where Zionists are dominant in business, the media; where now a Jew has become the foreign minister; and most probably the next American President is going to a Jew as well." * And so on.[45]

Brezhnev too was surprised that Nixon trusted Kissinger to the extent of giving him full authority to act on his own. For almost thirty-six hours negotiations proceeded, ending in Brezhnev and Gromyko accepting Kissinger's text with only minor editorial changes.[46] It reflected Sadat's swift change of heart, realizing at last just how badly the battle had turned against him, and applying maximum pressure on the Soviets in a "desperate appeal." To the Soviet ambassador in Cairo, Vinogradov, Sadat pleaded: "I can fight the Israelis but not the United States. I cannot cope with the huge flow of American tanks and aircraft. We destroy them, but the flow goes on."[47] Several times he repeated that Egypt could not match the military might of the United States.

This was a highly significant statement, putting maximum pressure on the Soviet Union. If the war went on with Soviet weaponry being destroyed wholesale, displaying its inferiority, other client states would become increasingly reluctant to purchase Soviet equipment—or to commit themselves any further to Moscow. Brezhnev may privately have enjoyed some *Schadenfreude* at the expense of an unruly client, who had disobeyed Kremlin warnings not to launch the disastrous war in the first place ("he got what was coming to him," quotes Israelyan[48]), but it also placed him in a quandary. The war had to be stopped, at all costs; a cease-fire had to be reached, within hours: "If Kissinger learns of Sadat's appeal to me, his position will be much tougher," Brezhnev admitted to the Politburo on the 21st. But Kissinger, tucked away in the guest villa in the Lenin Hills, was receiving all the latest from Wash-

---

* An observation which demonstrated either total ignorance of the U.S. Constitution, or was a hopelessly loose prophecy.

ington. Hafez Ismail, for the first time, was admitting a serious threat to Cairo from the Israelis. Their tanks had thrust out to a point less than thirty-five miles from the Egyptian capital. Egypt would now be prepared "to separate a cease-fire from an overall settlement."[49]

Meanwhile, the hard-liner, Syria's Asad, was still holding out against a cease-fire; he thought he could recapture the Golan Heights. Brezhnev was placed in a major quandary; if the flow of Soviet hardware could not redress the balance, and if a cease-fire were to fail—what other options remained open to his embarrassed regime? A physical intervention by Soviet forces? Unthinkable—too dangerous; but a threat, maybe? Kissinger takes up the story: on the afternoon of the 21st, "to our amazement, Brezhnev and Gromyko accepted our text, with only the most minor editorial changes. . . . After only four hours of negotiation, the text of the cease-fire resolution was agreed."*[50] It was, commented Kissinger, "extraordinary speed for any negotiation but particularly for one with Soviet leaders, considering the need for translating everything, checking the texts, and frequent interruptions as each side huddled together for consultation." No one in the Politburo opposed the text: altogether an achievement which showed the Bear—and Kissinger—at their respective best. Instructions were sent out to American and Soviet representatives John Scali and Yakov Malik at the U.N. "I do not remember," remarks Israelyan, "such harmony in words and deeds of the two superpowers at the United Nations throughout the entire period of the Cold War."[51] There was some mutual backslapping; even Gromyko cracked a joke, telling Joe Sisco, "I am ready to hire you in the Soviet Ministry of Foreign Affairs,"[52] and referring to his ally, Sadat, as "a paper camel"; while Brezhnev cracked that "what Kosygin could not achieve in three days of negotiations in Cairo with our friend Sadat I could achieve in three hours with our adversary Kissinger."[53]

There were also two hitches: in the American camp, somehow Lawrence Eagleburger had failed to send off the vital signals; as he recalled later (in a special memo for Kissinger), amidst a noisy hubbub the secretary of state walked in to the room occupied by his staff with

---

* The text agreed was to become U.N. Security Council Resolution 338 (Kissinger, *Crisis*, 304–5).

a roar: " 'What, the cables aren't out yet?!' I looked up, to find you standing in the middle of the room with smoke issuing from nose, eyes, and ears, and *no one* else. . . . All twenty or thirty people—no doubt led by Sisco—had exited with a speed and facility that would have put Houdini to shame." The only one present, apart from Eagleburger, was the valiant Winston Lord. Electric storms—in the stratosphere—were blamed. Furious, at the time Kissinger saw the situation as "far from funny. Altogether, at least four hours were lost and much Israeli confidence in us."[54] Potentially much more serious, however, was a glitch on the Soviet side. From Egyptian-occupied north Sinai, Russian-made Scud missiles were fired at the small port of El-Arish, where U.S. matériel was currently being unloaded for the Israeli army. Although Sadat had expelled the Soviet advisers before the war began, the Scuds were nominally under Soviet control. But when—in the late afternoon of October 22—Ambassador Vinogradov passed on an Egyptian request to the pugnacious minister of defense, Grechko, the latter yelled back: "Go the hell ahead and fire it!"[55]

When he heard the news, Gromyko was "outraged" and promptly had Grechko's order rescinded. But the missiles had been fired. Fortunately they missed the target; nevertheless, the order could have led to a most dangerous escalation. The brushwood had become inflammably dry.

Kissinger was pleased—and intensely relieved—as, after copious toasts of brandy all around, he terminated his emergency visit to Moscow. He wrote in *Crisis*, "The United States had achieved its strategic objectives: (1) it had fulfilled its obligations to Israel; (2) it had reduced the Soviet role in the Middle East and was in a position to do so at an accelerated pace once the peace process evolved; and (3) it had maintained friendly relations with the Arab world—indeed, based on messages with Ismail, there was every prospect of a fundamental shift in Egypt's heretofore sole reliance on the Soviet alliance."[56]

But, was this over-egging the pudding? And what had been the cost? In getting a cease-fire, on his terms, had he not expended a goodly chunk of the capital which had been so laboriously stored up by détente? Yet, to avert danger of a major confrontation in a disputed area, wasn't that what it was all about? When I put it to Kissinger he tended to agree with both propositions.[57] Victor Israelyan, advancing a Russian point of view, thought that Kissinger had exploited the Soviets through gaining "the impression that Brezhnev was so eager to preserve at least the spirit of détente that he would make a major concession." Brezhnev himself had fallen victim to the "incompatible principles of Soviet foreign policy—the desire, as the Russian proverb says, to kill two hares with one shot."[58]

From Washington, Nixon was able to reassure Golda Meir that the Moscow deal meant that it would "leave your forces right where they are."[59] Once Eagleburger and Lord had gotten communications working again, Kissinger received a message from Meir suggesting that he visit Israel "on the way back from Moscow." Kissinger thought it "a nice way of putting it":[60] Tel Aviv was hardly on the direct route, but— as this was where any trouble over the cease-fire was likely to come from, at four hours' notice he taxed Brezhnev's cumbersome traffic control by flying south instead of west, on the afternoon of Monday, October 22.

That afternoon in New York the United Nations Security Council adopted Resolution 338, for a cease-fire.

In his last conversation with Dinitz before leaving Washington for Moscow, such a visit to Israel had been implied. Golda Meir told her ambassador that Kissinger would be received "with open arms."

K: Women shouldn't say that to me.
D: There is a certain age when they are safe even from you, Mr.
    Secretary.[61]

In *Years of Upheaval* Kissinger subheads his October visit to Israel as "tense," but then goes on to describe it as one of the most moving moments of his entire government service. The tone of the underlying communications, telcons and memcons, suggests however that, in his talks at government level, there was a great deal of tenseness. Kissinger describes vividly his reception at Lod Airport: "Soldiers and civilians greeted the approaching peace as the highest blessing. Israel was heroic but its endurance was reaching the breaking point. Those who had come to welcome us seemed to feel viscerally how close to the abyss they had come and how two weeks of war had drained them. Small groups of servicemen and civilians were applauding with tears in their

eyes. Their expression showed a weariness that almost tangibly conveyed the limits of human endurance. Israel was exhausted no matter what the military maps showed. Its people were yearning for peace as can only those who have never known it. . . . She had had enough casualties—its 2,000 killed being the equivalent of 200,000 Americans.*
. . . Deep down, the Israelis knew that while they had won the last battle, they had lost the aura of invincibility."[62]

Within the government, the mood was very different from the atmosphere of hubris he had encountered shortly after the triumph of the Six Day War. Particularly shaken was the vauntful Moshe Dayan, who, as minister of defense having gotten it badly wrong, was most under fire. It was "his tragedy," wrote Kissinger, that "like Moses, he was permitted a glimpse of the Promised Land but the journey to that mountain top had deprived him of the ability to implement his own vision. Like most talented and artistic men, he knew his own worth; he was not free of vanity."[63] For Golda Meir, "Miss Israel" as Kissinger had unkindly once nicknamed her, "the battle was already a thing of the past"; she was getting ready for the next one. Already Kissinger suspected that the Israeli army was breaking the embryonic cease-fire agreement (news of Egyptian agreement actually came through while he was conferring with Golda Meir), at least in spirit, in their determination to destroy Egypt's encircled Third Army. They had cut all its supply routes—except for one secondary road near Suez at the far south of the front. It was soon clear that Israeli forces were continuing to advance beyond the agreed cease-fire lines. In her turn, Mrs. Meir was suspicious that in Moscow Kissinger had been engineering a "secret" deal to impose the 1967 borders; she "explored all the possibilities of American duplicity."

Speaking to her, Kissinger found that her nation's insecurity "was so pervasive that even words were daggers."[64] Kissinger, in his memoirs, records "an emotion-laden visit,"[65] but there seems to have been little warmth in their exchanges. In sharply marked contrast was the remarkable degree of warmth that would emerge in his forth-

---

* Or four times the number of Americans killed over ten years of Vietnam—equalling twice the Israeli losses in 1967—and over a space of three weeks.

coming dealings with the ruler of Egypt, Anwar Sadat—as is revealed most tellingly from the tone of the communications, the telcons and memcons, exchanged. The relationship between Israelis and American Jews has often been a prickly one; although Israel would not have been created but for U.S. support post-1945, its gratitude for deliverance (in the long term) and deliveries of life-saving military hardware (in the short term) has seldom been extravagant. Emigrés from Eastern Europe were not unknown sometimes to dub American Jews, odiously, as "Yids." There was feeling, never far below the surface, that America owed Israel a living; already gratitude for the arms deliveries of the previous ten days was perhaps starting to look a bit perfunctory by the third week of October 1973. As Dayan in his heyday was wont to remark: "Our American friends offer us money, arms and advice. We take the money, we take the arms and we decline the advice."[66]

Israel did not necessarily feel safer with a Jewish secretary of state; Golda Meir herself was prone to snide remarks at Kissinger's expense—such as: "Now we both have Jewish Foreign Secretaries—the only difference being that our Foreign Secretary [Abba Eban, the suave former South African] talks better English!"[67] On Kissinger's side, apart from a select few close friends and colleagues like the later assassinated Yitzhak Rabin, he never felt particularly at ease in—or with—Israel. At the time of its creation back in 1948, as a Harvard freshman Kissinger had opposed it, taking the view that a separate state in the Middle East would be "a potentially historic disaster." He thought the Zionists would have been "better off forming a federal state with Jordan."[68] As he observed on several occasions to the author, he regarded the Israelis as a "hard, unforgiving, and ungenerous" and "maddening people."[69] His sentiments about Israel were residually complex, but strongly tinged with pessimism. He remarked to the author that he could not conceive of being secretary of state in circumstances which might see the demise of Israel; yet he thought its chances of survival beyond the mid-twenty-first century were slim. When I once put to him a proposal of a Nuclear Free Zone to embrace the whole Middle East, inclusive of Iran *and* Israel, he responded (with courage, I thought), "Intellectually, I would support that; but emotionally I can't."[70] For him, personally, he always found relations with the Israelis "very difficult—especially for a Jew. Yes, I was very suspect. They had no understanding for anything that was less than 100 percent support. They expected me, as a Jew, to be totally on their side; I couldn't be."[71] On a more social plane he had been heard to complain, with feeling, sybaritically, "How one million Jewish mothers collectively can cook such awful food is an historical wonder worthy of a good Ph.D. study!"[72] Golda Meir he admired, as belonging to "the pioneer generation, to whom every square inch of Israeli territory had been gained with Jewish blood. She was a heroic warrior; the idea of giving up territory for diplomacy caused her great pain . . . she was tough with the Arabs, and would never have negotiated territory away." He contrasted her with Moshe Dayan and his "rather ambivalent, patriarchal treatment of the Arabs," finding it "too condescending."[73] His irritation with her and her team could be profound. In October 1973, it can hardly have been agreeable to come from the ever-lurking anti-Semitism of the Soviet Union to a people not exaggeratedly philo-Semitic toward American Jews. With Israel and the Israelis it was always a most difficult tightrope he had to walk—especially for a *Jewish* secretary of state.

While in Tel Aviv on October 22, Kissinger held three separate conferences with Mrs. Meir (which received only the briefest reference in *Crisis*). In the first,[74] a foursome attended only by Kissinger and Golda Meir, the director of her office, Mordechai Gazit, and Peter Rodman from the NSC staff—very much tête à tête—a dark suspicion reigned over the U.S.-Soviet talks just finished. Had there been a deal at Israel's expense? Hardly had they sat down in the guesthouse near Tel Aviv with Golda alone for fifteen minutes before notes were taken, Kissinger at once did his best to reassure the Israeli prime minister about reference to Resolution 242. He explained that it really meant "nothing"—that the reference had been inserted because Nixon had come "under tremendous pressure from the Arabs and from the oil people for a return to the 1967 borders"; while, in Moscow, "Brezhnev screamed for more than 242; he wanted 'full implementation of all UN resolutions.'" Meir, in contention, argued vigorously over the text: "But the resolution doesn't say 'direct negotiations' . . . 'negotiations . . . between the concerned under appropriate auspices aimed at establishing a just and durable peace.' That's what bothers us. What does this mean?"

Dr. Kissinger: Nothing. Until there are negotiations.

Then, defensively:

Dr. Kissinger: I drafted it.
The Prime Minister: I thought so.

Prime Minister Meir was clearly unhappy. Kissinger weaved around, then came down to the burning issue of the return of Israeli POWs.

The Prime Minister: This means a great deal to us. And no one
    has greater experience with prisoners of war than you.
Dr. Kissinger: If I were you—I'm not advising you—I would
    not begin negotiations until it happens. You'd be entitled to
    do nothing.
The Prime Minister: I can't live with it.

Then speaking very much as the "Mother of Israel," always deeply concerned for "her boys:"

The Prime Minister: How can I face the mothers and wives of
    these men? . . . The Arabs, they couldn't care less. . . . They
    just don't care about human lives. Sadat doesn't have to
    meet the wives; I do.
Dr. Kissinger: My strategy in this crisis, as I explained to Dinitz
    several times, was to keep the Arabs down and the Russians
    down.

It was a sentiment he would hardly have repeated to Brezhnev— or to Sadat the following month.

The Prime Minister: I know what you did. Without you, I don't
    know where we would have been.

Then, directly regarding the cease-fire, which had still to be declared*:

> The Prime Minister: The Egyptians haven't said anything. They
>   have said that the fighting continues.
> Dr. Kissinger: You won't get violent protests from Washington
>   if something happens during the night, while I'm flying.
>   Nothing can happen in Washington until noon tomorrow.
> The Prime Minister: If they don't stop, we won't.

This was a declaration, designed reflexively to sweeten the ever-suspicious Israeli leader, which Kissinger would swiftly regret. For the triumphant Israelis, winning all along the line, it was an encouragement they hardly needed. Was Kissinger being deliberately duplicitous here? Too clever by half? Was it part of his deliberate policy, of putting each side in debt, prior to the actual peace negotiations beginning? Or did it simply reflect excessive battle fatigue—seventeen days of nonstop crises, culminating in these two high-pressure trips to Moscow and Tel Aviv? (His biographer, Walter Isaacson, thought it was a "bad mistake.")[75] Later that day, while talks in Tel Aviv were still continuing, news came through that Egypt had accepted the cease-fire. But Israel had been given its opening to complete the definitive encirclement of the Egyptian Third Army. In years to come Kissinger's slip would be used by the Arabs to accuse him of duplicity and unfair bias toward Israel. Around the table in the Israeli guesthouse, there was "a mixture of relief, exultation, and resignation—veering between hope and suspicion."[76] It was suspicion that probably prevailed. In his foursome with Golda Meir, Kissinger ended by assuring her that the supply of arms would continue. She was, evidently, not entirely persuaded, still on her guard.

> The Prime Minister: But there is a phrase in there about "if the
>   war ceases, the funds won't be expended."

---

* The cease-fire went into effect at 7:12 A.M. Middle East time, 1:17 P.M. Eastern Daylight Time.

Dr. Kissinger: But you have a commitment from the President
 to replace all your losses. That you have.

Kissinger continued, telling her of his conversation with the Arab
foreign ministers in Washington the previous week:

I said the Soviets can give them equipment, but not a settlement.
I will get involved but not until objective reality makes it possible. So, whether they hate us or not, they will have to talk
to us.

It was a meaningful forecast. He then went on to question whether
Sadat could survive. Golda Meir riposted, yes, "Because he is the hero;
he dared. . . . So in Egypt they think they won."

The conversations continued over lunch, with the full teams on
both sides participating. The hard-liner minister of defense, Dayan, observed, "I'd like not to stop"; to which Kissinger replied, now being a
little more specific: "I'll be on the airplane. Just say you'll stop at 1800,
provided they do. What we're communicating to the Russians is that
we've been informed you'll stop at 1800 provided they stop."

Turning to Peter Rodman: "Make sure I notify the Soviets from the
plane that the Israelis have agreed to this." Kissinger expressed doubt
about "the Arabs starting war so quickly again . . . [although] they
fought better than in 1967." Dayan agreed: "I'm sorry to say they did.
They kept fighting." The Syrians had fought "a sort of jihad. They
fought not professionally well, but emotionally well." Jihad: here was
a new word for the Americans. Kissinger closed that round of the talks
by predicting the beginning of the forthcoming peace negotiations:
"We're not going to float an American plan. That's not my plan or my
method. I've been telling this to every Arab minister. They ask me,
'Will you use your influence with Israel?' And I say, 'There is nothing
to use our influence about.' " It would be, he forecast dramatically, "an
historic event, even if it totally stalemates—which I expect, frankly."[77]

The meetings in Tel Aviv closed with a briefing from the Israeli mil-
itary, who revealed just how hard the fighting had been. The Israeli Air
Force had lost a total of 102 planes, to over five hundred Syrian and
Egyptian planes; the Syrians had lost about 1,000 of the 1,700 tanks

they had on October 6, but were receiving many Soviet tanks by ship; "in a few days they'll be completely ready for another strike," General Zeira, the director of military intelligence, said. On the other hand, the Egyptian army was "more or less destroyed in its offensive capacity." In Cairo there were only two tank brigades. General Elazar, the chief of staff, regretted—meaningfully—that "Unfortunately, we didn't manage to finish the Third Army. We think it is possible to do it in two, maybe three days." Elazar spelled out clearly that the Israeli objective was to "destroy and capture its forces." Not picking up on this, Kissinger, having expressed Nixon's admiration for Israel's winning "a great military victory and a great political victory—Arab acceptance for the first time of direct negotiations," was sent off by Golda Meir with an emotional evocation, recalling how the past days had been "our worst ever . . . we had many bitter hours."[78] Kissinger records emplaning from Israel that night "elated and yet somber. We had achieved our strategic objective, but it had only opened the way to an unknown terrain that would require discipline, unity, and purpose to traverse."[79]

As William Quandt, who served as number two in Kissinger's Middle East office for two years from August 1972, wrote in his excellent book, *Peace Process*, whatever Kissinger may have told Dinitz in advance, he had gone primarily to Moscow "not to gain time for Israel's battlefield success but to obtain Soviet and Arab agreement to a cease-fire resolution that could serve as the basis for a subsequent diplomatic effort. If Brezhnev and Sadat were prepared for a simple cease-fire, then Kissinger would press for a quick end to hostilities. He had no interest in seeing Sadat humiliated, especially in view of the encouraging tone of U.S.-Egyptian exchanges over the past two weeks . . ." Quandt continues that Kissinger "later claimed that he was very tough with the Israelis,"[80] on insisting that they adopt defensive positions and do not violate the cease-fire. Yet there would remain, at the end of the stressful visit to Israel, that ambiguity.

During his overnight flight home, Kissinger received cables from Scowcroft and Haig warning him that he would be "returning to an environment of major national crisis" as had resulted from the Saturday Night Massacre. At a brief stopover in Heathrow, the British foreign secretary, Alec Douglas-Home, briefed him on the details. Impeachment proceedings against Nixon were beginning. The British press was reveling in the news. Wrote Kissinger, "I was heading back toward the capital of a nation that, even while contributing to peace in the Middle East, was consuming its authority at home."[81] On reaching Washington, the crisis would intensify at the same time as Nixon's input became more erratic. The hostile media was rejoicing in each fresh item of Nixon's discomfiture, relegating news of peace in the Middle East to a lower priority. A president under sentence, Nixon was drinking—which, for a man with a very low tolerance for alcohol, did not help his ability to focus. Kissinger would be increasingly on his own, at the summit of the pyramid of world power.

Hardly had he reached his office than signals were pouring in, from all sides, accusing him of double-dealing. Around 9:30 A.M. on the morning he returned, the 23rd, U.N. Secretary-General Waldheim was reporting to him that Egypt had formally complained of Israeli cease-fire violations. This was shortly reinforced in a series of messages from the Soviets; one, from Brezhnev, indicated the degree of alarm in that, most unusually, it was addressed directly to Kissinger, and not to Nixon. The Israelis were still attacking—in clear contravention of the cease-fire. They had now completely surrounded the Egyptian Third Army, cutting off its last tenuous supply route. This had been confirmed by Soviet reconnaissance planes. Brezhnev labeled the Israeli action "unacceptable" and a "flagrant deceit." Kissinger was furious with the Israelis; but also blaming himself to a certain extent for having "emboldened them"* in his last exchanges with Golda Meir. He immediately got on the phone to Ambassador Dinitz, who returned with a personal assurance that no actions had been "initiated" by Israel. Kissinger seethed, commenting acidly in his memoirs: "I thought she was imposing on my credulity with her definition of 'initiate.'"[82] It seemed to him utterly implausible that the Egyptian Third Army would take the offensive when it had just been saved from destruction.

---

* He wrote, in *Years of Upheaval*: "I also had a sinking feeling that I might have emboldened them . . . to gain their support" (p. 569).

At noon, Dinitz called, declaring that Israeli forces would not withdraw from the positions they now held.

Shortly after midday, another urgent message arrived from Brezhnev, this time addressed to Nixon himself, and sent down the hotline—the first time this had been utilized during the Yom Kippur War. "Esteemed Mr. President," it began—a form that presaged trouble. It accused Israel of "treachery" and insisted the United States and Soviet Union "jointly" impose the cease-fire. The new word "jointly" began abruptly to have a menacing connotation.[83] Meanwhile, from the U.N. the U.S. representative, Ambassador John Scali, warned that the Soviets' pugilistic Malik was "acting like a goddamn idiot," proposing a separate U.N. resolution. Kissinger instructed him to "tell Malik to calm down," followed more toughly by: "You tell Malik to hold his water or I will send him to Siberia. I know Brezhnev better than he does. Ask him if he has ever been kissed on the mouth by Brezhnev, as I have."*[84] Then came further trouble from Tel Aviv—in the shape of a "blistering" communication from Meir. She declared forcefully that it was "impossible for Israel to accept that time and time again it must face Russian and Egyptian ultimatums which will subsequently be assented to by the United States."[85] Was this the language of a junior, and hugely indebted, ally? Kissinger's temperature was rising. In an angry conversation with Dinitz, he exclaimed: "Jesus Christ, don't you understand?" (To which, it was alleged, Dinitz replied suggesting that "his Government might be more persuaded if he were to invoke a different prophet!")[86]

Meanwhile that afternoon, a frantic Sadat sent an urgent message direct to Nixon through CIA channels; that this was also unprecedented indicated the true gravity of the situation. Sadat proposed that the United States (with whom Egypt had had no diplomatic relations since the Six Day War of 1967) should now "intervene effectively, even if that necessitates the use of forces" to implement the cease-fire. This was dangerous stuff: where would it put the Soviets, Sadat's putative ally? Kissinger was also, more than ever, fearful that Sadat might fall—

---

* Activity at the U.N. would finally result in a subsequent resolution, Number 339, being passed that evening. Reaffirming 338, it "urged," not "demanded," that the warring parties return to previous lines. Kissinger notes that it had been reedited to meet Israeli wishes—a gesture "not requited in Israel" (*Years of Upheaval*, p. 575).

to be replaced by a radical, pro-Soviet leader. But he found Sadat's "extraordinary proposal" as equally unrealistic as it was that America should "run diplomatic interference" while Israel strangled a trapped Egyptian army. He wrote in *Crisis* that he had been adamant that he would not grant what Israel wanted, i.e., "a free hand to destroy the Egyptian Third Army. . . . Israel seemed determined to end the war with a humiliation for Egypt. We had no intention of seeing Sadat destroyed as a consequence of an Israeli challenge to a ceasefire we had negotiated and cosponsored."[87]

That evening Kissinger had a soothing exchange with his friend Dobrynin, just returned from Moscow. "Dobrynin: The most important thing is the agreement between you and Brezhnev and the whole situation in the Middle East. If we hold firm that it doesn't matter what happens, we will survive. If we drag this anchor through the winds."

Kissinger responded: "You have known me long enough—I will not trick Brezhnev. That is the stupidest thing I could do. Even if we win this one, we could never have a trusting relationship again. We cannot control everything the Israelis do."

There followed, that night, a much less temperate exchange with Dinitz, with Kissinger calling on him to "put that Jewish mind to work so that when the pressure starts you can start withdrawing a few hundred yards. . . . You have cut the road. Some people on the East Bank will not have any water."

To which Dinitz retorted coldly: "They had no business being there anyway."[88] It was indicative of an Israeli mind-set that Sinai, taken by conquest from Egypt in 1967, no longer rightfully belonged to Egypt—a mind-set which would militate, long and strong, against any future peace deal.

Kissinger remained highly suspicious, seeing through an Israeli pretense to order its troops to stop firing—which "amounted to an insistence on starving out the Egyptian Third Army."[89] Nevertheless, he thought that, by the time he went to bed, exhausted, on the 23rd, "calm seemed to have been restored." He was quite wrong. The next morning, awaiting him in his office at eight, was a cry from Hafez Ismail that "the Israelis have resumed their attacks."[90] He telephoned Dinitz, rejecting his explanations and giving full force to his mistrust of Israeli actions. To Kissinger (writing in his memoirs), it was "clear that if we let this go on, a confrontation with the Soviets was inevitable."[91] And gone too would be his hopes of a new relationship with Egypt. At 9:45 he was calling Dobrynin, just returned from Moscow, preemptively warning. "Anatoly, the madmen in the Middle East seem to be at it again. . . . I want you to know what we have done." But should he not, by rights, once again have been blaming himself for that rash "emboldenment" of the Israelis while in Tel Aviv? Kissinger admits in his memoirs that "this new fighting was continuing far beyond the brief additional margin I had implied."[92] He repeated his angry messages to Dinitz that afternoon. Meanwhile, Sadat's desperate plea to Nixon arrived for intervention of U.S. troops. More disquietingly, Sadat informed the president that he was "formally" directing the same request to Moscow.

To Kissinger, the sending of American troops to the Middle East was unthinkable; even more so was the dispatch of Soviet forces. Such a force would prove "impossible to remove; there would be endless pretexts for it to intervene at any point against Israel, or against moderate Arab governments, for that matter." There followed, that afternoon of October 24, 1973, numerous further exchanges with Dobrynin, which culminated—at 7:25 A.M.—with a warning from the Russian that "Now they [Soviet leaders] have become so angry they want troops." He blamed Kissinger: "You allowed the Israelis to do what they wanted."[93] But, "You know we don't want a confrontation." Nevertheless, twenty minutes earlier, "suddenly" a bombshell from Brezhnev arrived in the White House. It was "in effect an ultimatum." Gone was the spirit of détente; it began with a peremptory salutation of "Mr. President," and ended with an equally peremptory conclusion that demanded "an immediate and clear reply." The message was a call to "urgently dispatch to Egypt the Soviet and American contingents," to insure implementation of the Security Council's cease-fire resolution. It closed with an equally clear-cut threat that if the United States did not comply "we should be faced with the necessity urgently to consider the question of taking appropriate steps unilaterally. We cannot allow arbitrariness on the part of Israel."[94]

Kissinger regarded it as "one of the most serious challenges to an American President by a Soviet leader."[95] It had to be confronted. That it had been sent off from Moscow at 4:00 A.M. seemed to indicate just "how frayed nerves were" in the Kremlin. The nervous tension was certainly no less in Washington. As if it was not enough to have the Egyptians, the Israelis, the neocon Zionists at home, and now the Soviets on his neck, the president seemed to be seriously cracking up. Kissinger recorded that that Wednesday evening, in the midst of a conversation with Dobrynin, Nixon was cutting in on the other line "as agitated and emotional as I had ever heard him. Talk of his possible impeachment increased daily." Melodramatically Nixon said that he might "physically die." For once the president was not to be reassured: "What they [his Watergate persecutors] care about is destruction," said Nixon. "It brings me sometimes to feel like saying the hell with it. I would like to see them run this country and see what they do. . . . The real tragedy is if I move out everything we have done will crumble. The Russians will look for other customers, the Chinese will lose confidence, the Europeans will—They just don't realize they are throwing everything out the window. I don't know what in the name of God . . ." In Kissinger's perception, "Here was the Watergate tragedy encapsulated in a brief telephone conversation."[96] And, at what a time for the kettle to boil over!

That evening, at 7:25, having warned Dobrynin that, if Malik were to introduce a new resolution at the U.N. raising the sending in of troops, the United States would vote against it, exercising the American veto. He issued orders to Ambassador Scali in New York to veto, "and make a very strong speech on that."[97] At 7:50, Kissinger was on the line to Haig, disclosing the latest developments.

> K: I wanted to bring you up to date on what is happening.
>   The Soviets are taking a nasty turn . . . we may have to
>   take them on.
> H: We knew this wouldn't be easy.
> K: I think we have to be tough as nails now.
> H: Sure we do. Absolutely.

Two hours later Kissinger was on the phone to Haig again, telling him of the Brezhnev letter.

> H: I think they are playing chicken. They are not going to put
>   in forces at the end of the war. I don't believe that.

K: I don't know—What's going to keep them from flying
    paratroopers in?
H: Just think of what it will do for them. Of course, their
    argument is that Israel is not complying.

(Could this have been a backhander, knocking Kissinger for his
"emboldening" remark in Tel Aviv?) Kissinger told Haig that he had
kept the Israelis informed of developments. Then: "Should I wake the
President?" Haig came back with a curt—and revealing—"No." In his
memoirs, Kissinger wrote, meaningfully: "I knew what that meant.
Haig thought the President was too distraught." What that meant, in
effect, was that Kissinger, as secretary of state and head of the National
Security Council, was now in charge, in charge of the destiny of the
United States—and of the world. It was, he recognized, "a daunting
responsibility to assume."[98]

He called an emergency meeting of the WSAG for 10:30 P.M. in the
State Department. But why, at only 9:50 P.M., on this crucial day, was
the president already asleep? Just before the WSAG was due to con-
vene, Kissinger made a further brief, but sternly admonitory, call to
Dobrynin:

K: We are assembling our people to consider your letter. I just
    wanted you to know if any unilateral action is taken before
    we have had a chance to reply that will be very serious.
D: Yes, all right.
K: This is a matter of great concern. Don't you pressure us. I
    want to repeat again, don't pressure us!

Immediately after came another conversation with Haig, with
Kissinger reminding him: "Don't forget . . . what the Soviets are playing on. They find a cripple facing impeachment and why shouldn't
they go in there." Haig's reply was: "If they do and start fighting, that
is the serious thing." He then inquired pointedly if the WSAG meeting was going to be at the White House, in the NSC? After Kissinger
remarked that it was to be in the State Department,* Haig replied:

---

* The two buildings being only a hundred yards apart.

H: He [Nixon] has to be part of everything you are doing.

K: Should I get him up?

Haig, once again evading the question, replied simply:

H: I wish you would hold it in the White House.[99]

Kissinger immediately altered the venue, explaining to the author subsequently that "it had to be absolutely clear that what came out was a White House decision." Nixon in his memoirs wrote, ex post facto, that after Haig had informed him about the Brezhnev letter, "I said that he and Kissinger should have a meeting at the White House to formulate plans for a firm reaction to what amounted to a scarcely veiled threat of unilateral Soviet intervention. Words were not making our point—we needed action, even the shock of a military alert."[100]

Yet, all the evidence points to the strong suggestion that, during one of the most critical meetings in U.S.—indeed, world—history since 1945, the president of the United States, the most powerful human being alive, was in fact incapacitated by the misery of Watergate closing in on him—or was crudely put, "loaded."* In the event, the WSAG meeting took place in the basement offices of the White House, beginning at 10:40 P.M. and continuing until 2 A.M. on Thursday, the 25th. In the chair was a former teacher of history, Dr. Henry Kissinger. Also present were James Schlesinger, secretary of defense; William Colby of the CIA; Chairman of the Joint Chiefs of Staff Admiral Thomas Moorer; presidential chief of staff Alexander Haig; General Brent Scowcroft, Kissinger's deputy at the NSC; and Kissinger's military assistant, Commander Jonathan Howe.† It was a tightly knit group. (Ambassador Dinitz was waiting anxiously in the deserted lobby of the West Wing, Israel now being under strongest U.S. pressure to behave itself, and cease all attacks on the

---

* According to Dr. William Burr of Georgetown University, editor of the National Security Archive, and a consistent critic of Nixon and Kissinger, Nixon did not even see the Brezhnev letter until the following day, "and played no part in the policy discussions that evening" (Document 71, p. 48, note 66).

† Of those present, Moorer and Colby are deceased; the author interviewed Schlesinger, Haig, and Scowcroft. Jonathan Howe chose to remained silent.

Egyptians. At one point, Kissinger interrupted the meeting to go over and brief him.)

It was unanimously agreed that the Soviet threat of intervention had to be contested; it was noted in the WSAG meeting that the CIA reported the Soviet airlift to the Middle East had ceased—the ominous implication being that transport planes were being assembled to ferry the airborne divisions, "whose alert status had also been noted." (Speaking to the author in May 2005, Schlesinger confirmed: "The stand-down of Soviet forces in Europe certainly affected U.S. judgment—or were they just bluffing? The stand-down in fact signified to us that they were preparing to send troops to the Middle East.")[101] During the evening, according to Kissinger, a consensus emerged that the Kremlin was "on the verge of a major decision." It had to be deflected—at any cost. In the small hours of the morning it was decided to place the U.S. forces, in their entirety, on DEFCON 3.* DEFCON 1 is war, DEFCON 2 a condition in which attack is imminent— DEFCON 3 the highest order of alert in peacetime. Most of the U.S. forces were at DEFCON 4 or 5—or normal states of readiness—in 1973—except for the Pacific area, on account of Vietnam, which was already subject to DEFCON 3. As Kissinger goes to lengths to explain, in effect DEFCON 3 meant very little in operational terms—but it was the lowest degree of alert that "the Soviets would notice." As the highest level of peacetime alerts, it would however administer a "sharp shock." At the same time, an equally sharp warning was sent to Sadat that, should Soviet forces appear there, the United States would have to "resist them on Egyptian soil"; it would also impose cancellation of Kissinger's peace process visit to Cairo.[102]

The 82nd Airborne was put on a state of readiness; the huge carrier *John F. Kennedy* and its task force ordered to steam at full speed from the Atlantic to the Eastern Mediterranean. These were conspicuous moves which Kissinger anticipated would be swiftly marked by Soviet intelligence. At the same time, Kissinger imposed on Admiral Moorer strictest secrecy: "Not a word of this is to leak." According to Walter Isaacson, Defense Secretary Schlesinger "rolled his eyes"; how could

---

* For Defense Readiness Condition.

such orders be hidden from two million servicemen? Never totally on board with Kissinger, it was, he thought, "typical of Henry to believe that you could keep it a secret from everyone except the Russians."[103] The official reply to Brezhnev was not dispatched until 5:40 A.M. (Washington time) on the 25th, so as to give the Soviets the maximum time to reflect on the U.S. military movements. In the meantime, Kissinger asked Scowcroft to leave the meeting to ring Dobrynin with the following message: "Tell him to desist from all actions until we have a reply [from Egypt]. Tell him you are not empowered to give any reply. I am in a meeting and can't be pulled out. There should be no unilateral actions and if they are taken it would have the most serious consequences. If he says anything you can say you have instructions not to comment. They may as well know that we mean business."[104]

Dobrynin played his hand well. As Kissinger phrased it, "two could play chicken." There came back no reassurances, only the "laconic comment that he would stand by for our reply." The Americans in the basement of the White House were left chewing their nails in a heightened sense of menace—waiting, and wondering. Was the world moving to the brink of another Cuban Missile Crisis type of confrontation? The response to Brezhnev, sent off finally at 5:40—significantly, "in Nixon's name"—was deliberately tough, rejecting all Moscow's demands.[105] It pointed out that any unilateral action by the Soviets in the Middle East would be "in violation" of the agreements reached in Moscow in 1972, and of the Agreement on Prevention of Nuclear War—which Brezhnev himself had pressed so hard upon the Americans: "Such action would produce incalculable consequences which would be in the interest of neither of our countries and which would end all we had striven so hard to achieve."[106] What could have been tougher, more uncompromising, among "friends"? Where was the spirit of détente?

The letter to Brezhnev was signed "in Nixon's name." That was a fact that gives rise to a great deal of speculation about who actually signed DEFCON 3. Who gave the order for this dramatic action? There remains some mystery. General Haig, ever the loyal soldier, remained adamant that Nixon was not "loaded," or incapacitated, that night: explosively, to me he declared it to be "nonsense." "We were worried about his health, under stress in 1973; but he was not, repeat, not drunk or loaded."[107] Several times that night, Haig recalled, he "went upstairs to see the President with the replies to the Brezhnev draft. Nixon finally gave his approval, he said 'OK, that's tough enough.' " But he did not sign it. In his own memoir, Haig admits that, prior to the WSAG meeting, Nixon had "expressed no enthusiasm for attending the meeting in person. . . . Besides, he was tired. . . . With a wave of the hand, he said, 'You know what I want, Al; you handle the meeting.' We all knew what he wanted: a worldwide military alert of United States military forces tied to a strong reply to Brezhnev."[108] For the simple mind, it seems like a terrifying dereliction of responsibility. To me, Haig went on to claim that "all the mischief came from Jim Schlesinger." He still felt bitter animosity for him.

In his turn, Schlesinger thought it "extraordinary" that Nixon was not at the meeting. Was he ill? Drunk? "I don't know—Haig would know. He was running backward and forward to and from the residence from the basement office of the NSC." Schlesinger reckoned that he, as secretary of defense, "gave the order . . . I presumed that I had the presidential say-so."[109] On the other hand, Scowcroft, whom I found in general a most reliable witness, was at odds with Haig, and fairly convincing that Nixon was "off the wall. . . . He had had a very bad day." Was he drunk? "I can't rule it out." He confirmed Haig's view of Nixon's low threshold of alcohol toleration: "Two martinis and he changed . . . he couldn't hold his liquor . . . how he held up over all those months of Watergate, I just don't know." Who gave the actual order? Scowcroft: "It should have been Schlesinger, but I am not sure who it was."[110]

Peter Rodman, Kissinger's close NSC associate, though not there, supported Scowcroft's opinion.[111] Nixon's biographer, Stephen Ambrose, writing in 1991, found there was "much conflicting evidence on both sides" as to Nixon's condition, relaying the view of Nixon's "lack of involvement in what he called the most serious crisis in Soviet-American relations since the Cuban missile crisis";[112] while Kissinger's biographer, Walter Isaacson, was much more positive about Nixon's role—or lack of one—that night: he was definitely "not part of the decision-making process that night, nor was he briefed. Kissinger never even spoke to him that night, nor did Haig or anyone else."[113]

In his memoirs (and *Crisis*), Kissinger himself claimed—perhaps with excessive deference: "As always in crises, Nixon was clear-headed and crisp." [114] To the author, Kissinger, remaining loyal to the dignity of the highest office in the land, was discreet as to Nixon's condition; he had not signed the order himself, but regarded it as a "collective decision," carried out with presidential authority. [115] However, according to Haig's biographer, Roger Morris, "Eagleburger and other Kissinger aides later told a frightening story of Nixon upstairs drunk . . . slurring his words and barely roused when Haig and Kissinger tried to deal with him in the first moments of the crisis. . . . Returning to his State Department office in the predawn hours, Kissinger gave Eagleburger an account of the drunken Nixon." [116] In Isaacson's interpretation, when Kissinger briefed Nixon at 8 A.M. on the 25th, "he was struck by the fact that Nixon seemed to be hearing it for the first time." [117]

By eight that morning, the crisis was in effect all but over. Kissinger was shocked to wake up after three hours' sleep and discover that the whole world knew about DEFCON 3 — despite his optimistic injunction to Schlesinger and Moorer. Egypt had withdrawn the request that had sparked off the crisis; instead it was asking the Security Council to provide an "*international* force" [118] to oversee the cease-fire. Sadat now "was staking his future on American diplomatic support rather than Soviet military pressure." [119] Later there came a mild and anodyne message from Brezhnev, tacitly dropping the suggestion of joint intervention and accepting the principle of a United Nations international peacekeeping force. He spoke of hopes for continuing U.S.-Soviet cooperation. The British and America's other European allies, whom Kissinger considered had not behaved like allies, were also now on board.

There followed some angry, cold, and reproachful exchanges between Kissinger and Dobrynin — who (apparently once again out of the loop with Moscow) claims first to have heard news of the U.S. alert from the radio. The previous evening, according to Dobrynin's memoirs, Kissinger had "sounded nervous as I read to him Brezhnev's message." Dobrynin claims that he only learned later "that Washington never had any real cause for alarm because the Politburo did not have any intention of intervening in the Middle East . . . nobody in Moscow wanted that." Having started his ambassadorial career at the time of the Cuban Missile Crisis in 1962, he "was not unduly alarmed at these reports in contrast to the Cuban crisis on 1962. But I was rather angry." [120]

Not having forewarned him, Kissinger had, he felt reproachfully, betrayed their friendship. Interestingly he noted that (in a manner historically, and disquietingly, reminiscent of the famous Ems Telegram of 1870 in which Bismarck had "hardened" the king of Prussia's message to France's Emperor Louis-Napoleon, and which sparked off the Franco-Prussian War), Brezhnev's confrontational letter contained a "stronger phrase about our possible involvement," which had been mysteriously inserted into the text before it reached Washington.* Early that afternoon Kissinger received a call from Dobrynin, telling him that a letter from Brezhnev was on its way to the president:

K: Is it going to calm me down or make me go into orbit again?
D: No, not orbit - Prefer to stay in orbit quietly.

Dobrynin then read out the text of Brezhnev's conciliatory letter. Somewhat in the nature of an explanatory apology, Kissinger responded, "at 4:00 in the morning I didn't try to be gentle. I thought you were threatening us. Don't—I take threats very badly." [121] Dobrynin claims that Kissinger excused himself by saying that the U.S. action had been "mostly determined by 'domestic considerations' " [122] —i.e., by Watergate. This was something which Kissinger would hotly deny to the American press that day.

So the crisis was over; though the cease-fire was fragile. But how had it seemed in the Kremlin? How had Brezhnev reacted to the U.S. counterchallenge? According to Israelyan, as Kissinger had left Moscow on the 22nd, "We thought the war had stopped and we would go back to business as usual." [123] Two days later was one of the Kremlin's busiest days, with preparations for the World Peace Congress. Meanwhile more bad news had come in from Egypt, stressing the impossible situation of the Egyptian Third Army under renewed Israeli attacks, and

---

* The implication was that the author might have been the aggressive Andrei Grechko, Brezhnev's defense minister.

coupled with Sadat's plea to the Soviet Union to act independently. Brezhnev accused Kissinger of double-dealing. He had "vowed fidelity to the policy of détente, and then while in Tel Aviv he made a deal with Golda." Brezhnev believed that Kissinger deliberately "deceived them" to further the Israeli cause. Then had followed the new, tough messages to Nixon of October 24. These "reflected the Kremlin's disappointment, anger and suspicion regarding the American position."[124] At the U.N., an overexcited and aggressive Malik had followed up to declare that "The honor and dignity of the United States and international trust in it and in the new United States Secretary of State, Mr. Kissinger, are now being subjected to searching scrutiny." But when Washington had "overreacted," going to DEFCON 3 late that night, nobody (recalled Israelyan), "including, I am afraid the Kremlin leaders—imagined that the world was on the verge of a nuclear confrontation because of a letter Brezhnev had just sent to President Nixon." Israelyan accused Kissinger of "a huge miscalculation"—but admitting, too, that at the same time "we had miscalculated."[125]

On the 25th, the Kremlin held one of the most important meetings of the war. There was a clear realization that the conflict was heading toward a confrontation with the United States. Kosygin sharply criticized Kissinger; he had "lied to us when he was here. He preferred to fraternize with the Israelis." "He is not playing by the rules," grumbled Andropov, of the KGB (and successor to Brezhnev).[126] Brezhnev, puzzled, wondered, "What is this to do with the letter I sent to Nixon?" and postponed his speech to the World Congress. "Something is wrong with the American logic," he complained. Marshal Grechko, who had previously ordered the Scuds to be fired on Israel, indulged in some saber-rattling, and suggested that the Politburo should meet the U.S. threats, and raise the ante. Andropov, taking the hard line, supported him—recommending that the Kremlin should "respond to mobilization by mobilizing." Israelyan remarks that, over the years since that day of crisis, "Many times I have asked myself what would have happened had the Kremlin responded to Defcon III with a Soviet nuclear alert and initiated military action in the Middle East or elsewhere."[127] Recalling the shooting down of the South Korean airliner in 1983, could Grechko, representing the military, have pressed the button on his own initiative, dispatching Soviet airborne troops to Cairo, or meeting the U.S. alert with Soviet countermeasures? It remains a dangerous thought. Already orders had gone out to a Soviet nuclear submarine commander to trail the carrier *John F. Kennedy*! "It was not difficult," observes Israelyan, "to imagine the consequences of such an order." [128]

Fortunately for the peace of the world, however, Brezhnev brought calm and good sense to that critical Politburo meeting. He would not react; he would be conciliatory. "We should not be provoked by American irresponsibility. I am not inclined to take measures to make Soviet troops ready for action." [129] The old Bear had spoken; his authority, says Israelyan, was "indisputable." Would historians of the future deem this to have been *his* finest hour? Or Kissinger's, playing a consummate poker hand? There followed Brezhnev's conciliatory letter of the 25th to Nixon. Perhaps, whatever else might be thought of Kissinger around that Moscow table, some element of the trust instilled by détente might be detected in Brezhnev's response?

CHAPTER 13

TO SADAT

"The crazy bastard really made a mess with the Russians."
   —Henry Kissinger, to Alexander Haig, October 26, 1973[1]

"I have been longing for this visit. I have a plan for you. It can be called the Kissinger plan."
   —Anwar Sadat to Henry Kissinger, November 7, 1973[2]

"I knew I was dealing with a great man. . . . Sadat bore with fortitude the loneliness inseparable from moving the world from familiar categories toward where it has never been."
   —Henry Kissinger[3]

THE STATE OF ALERT, DEFCON 3, was removed within thirty-six hours—almost before many residents of the United States were even aware that it had been imposed. After a sleepless night of highest tension, at midday on the 25th, Kissinger held a major press conference. At length, speaking without notes, he expounded the background, leading up to the reasons why the Nixon government had felt it necessary to take such extreme, and risky, measures. Significantly he began by meeting the criticisms of the Scoop Jackson camp that it had been U.S. intervention which prevented Israel from taking preemptive action on October 6. He then soft-pedaled

most gently the perceived Soviet threat which had precipitated the
alert—and repeatedly in response to questions. Though the United
States and the Soviet Union were, he said, "ideological and, to some
extent, political adversaries," they also had a "very special responsibility": the mutual capability of "annihilating humanity." He stressed the
overriding—and ongoing—importance of détente, while vigorously
denying Jackson's claim that morning that Brezhnev's letter had been
"brutal." The USSR was not, he declared, "threatened in any of its legitimate positions in the Middle East." Answering questions, Kissinger
stressed, "We do not consider ourselves in a confrontation with the Soviet Union. We do not believe it is necessary, at this moment." He expanded later on their "very unique relationship. We are at one and the
same time adversaries and partners in the preservation of peace." He
explained the suddenness of the crisis by pointing out that, "until yesterday," there had been no suggestion of any joint U.S.-Soviet intervention in the Middle East.[4]

Kissinger reacted angrily to a suggestion by Marvin Kalb,* the veteran correspondent of NBC and CBS, and a leading critic of Nixon,
that "domestic requirements" (i.e., the need to create a distraction from
Watergate) had been at the root of the U.S. alert. This was a comment
clearly in the minds of many journalists present that morning. But, to
Nixon afterward, Kissinger said he had "treated Kalb contemptibly" in
his reply—even though he had (according to Dobrynin) used it as an
excuse to the Soviets for the U.S. reaction. "It is," he declared acridly,
"a symptom of what is happening to our country that it could even be
suggested that the United States would alert its forces for domestic reasons." And, in response later to another probe along similar lines:
"One cannot have a crisis of authority in a society for a period of
months without paying a price somewhere along the line." He added
later: "It is up to you ladies and gentlemen to determine whether this
is the moment to try to create a crisis of confidence in the field of foreign policy as well." One particularly astute critic, Clark Mollenhoff,
asked pointedly whether Kissinger had recommended the DEFCON
decision, or had Nixon initiated it: did Kissinger now "feel that it is a

---

* Kalb, jointly with his brother Bernard, was one of the early biographers of Kissinger
(1974).

totally rational decision"? Kissinger replied emphasizing that it had been a "unanimous" recommendation by the NSC—though admitting "the President did not himself participate . . . he joined only after they had formed their judgment."

The press went away on the 25th not entirely satisfied that the DEFCON 3 risk had been justified, or that Watergate "domestic considerations" had not been involved. This was especially so of the *Washington Post*—but, after all, Watergate was "their story": the following day it commented, defensively, that "Our crisis at home was created by the President." An editorial in the *New York Times* observed "how tenuous" détente still was. A quip ran around Georgetown: "A crisis a day keeps Impeachment away."[5] In his Memoirs Kissinger later speculated: "I tremble at the thought of what fate would have been in store for us in such an environment for very many days."[6]

Shortly after the press conference ended, Kissinger heard from Waldheim at the U.N. that the contested Egyptian resolution had been dropped in favor of insertion of a neutral observer force. The crisis was over. Haig rang with his congratulations.

H: You did a hell of a job.
K: Was it all right?
H: Superb.
K: We have won. They have accepted the SC resolution. . . .
H: . . . it seemed like someone had taken their shoes away from
  them. You really handled the thing magnificently.
K: I think I did some good for the President.

To Nixon, half an hour later:

K: Mr. President, you have won again.
N: You think so?

Kissinger was congratulated on his performance by an "elated" Nixon, his mind clearly focused on his enemy, the media, not Brezhnev:

N: Al told me you slaughtered the bastards. Keep it up. . . . We
  will survive.
K: No question.

Nixon pondered on giving his own press conference but decided, "I am not in the mood tonight."[7]

Did Kissinger overreact that explosive night of October 24–25th, 1973, which could have proved to be one of the two most dangerous in the whole of the Cold War? Some critics thought so. His handling of DEFCON 3 would certainly evoke some of the sternest criticism of all his stewardship of foreign affairs. How close had the world, in fact, come to the long-dreaded catastrophe of Americans and Russians shooting at each other—to Kissinger the unthinkable? Or could the imposing of DEFCON 3 be regarded, retrospectively, as a superb ploy by Kissinger? In all crises there can occur the totally unexpected, subsidiary event which triggers off disaster. For instance, we are now told that, the following day, the 25th, the first day of the alert, at Kincheloe Air Force Base in Michigan, U.S. Air Force mechanics were repairing one of the klaxons and accidentally activated the whole base alarm system. B-52 crews rushed to their aircraft and started the engines. The duty officer recognized that the alarm was false, and was able to recall the crews before any took off.[8] To Joseph Kraft, the journalist, Kissinger admitted the next day, "We may have read it wrong . . . but at midnight you can't take chances." Kissinger's biographer, Walter Isaacson, reads this as signifying "a sign that Kissinger had gotten a bit too excited about Brezhnev's rather ambiguous previous message the night before."[9] Stephen Ambrose, Nixon's biographer, also felt that Kissinger had "grossly exaggerated the supposed threat."[10] Among America's allies, in London Prime Minister Heath's reaction was one of fury at not being consulted, all but accusing Nixon of diverting attention from Watergate, and adding, "We have to face the fact that the American action has done immense harm, I believe, both in this country and worldwide . . . without consultation with his allies."[*] It was, he declared, "without any justification in the military situation at the

---

[*] If there had indeed been no "consultation," part of the fault may well have resided in the British embassy in Washington, where the ambassador, Lord Cromer, excused himself saying there had been "no one to whom he could pass his notes for earlier transmission."

time." The British Joint Intelligence Committee had backed this up: "We are inclined to see the U.S. response as higher than necessary to achieve the desired effect."[11]

At the White House DEFCON 3 meeting, though few took the Soviet proposal of joint intervention too seriously, there were differences of opinion. Some thought the Soviets might well send airborne forces to Egypt; Colby had disquietingly produced CIA information that there "might" be Soviet nuclear weapons in the country; and there were equally disturbing reports of movements of airborne troops in Eastern Europe that suggested the first detachments might actually be on their way. Admiral Moorer expressed the sailor's view that, in the event of naval combat with Soviet forces in the Eastern Mediterranean, "we would lose our ass."[12] On the other hand, there were those who held that Brezhnev was bluffing. Kissinger took a clear line that that should make no difference: "If we remained passive in the face of the threat, the Soviet leadership would see no obstacle to turning it into reality. We had no choice except to call the bluff."[13]

Two of the more serious analysts of Cold War issues, Richard Lebow and Janice Stein, found "obvious incredibility" in the notion that the alert would deter the Soviets, had they been intent on intervention. For that they would have to be induced to believe that the United States was prepared to resort to nuclear weapons; but the threat was "obviously out of proportion." They sharply criticize Kissinger in that he "did not completely understand the technical details of the alert"; nor did he or Schlesinger consider its "escalatory consequences." It left the United States with "few options to escalate up the ladder if deterrence failed." Their evaluation was "sobering"; but they found the Kremlin's equally flawed; they were driven by "anger," while in Watergate Washington, Kissinger was operating "under stress." Both were undesirable circumstances for the background of handling "the most serious Soviet-American confrontation since the Cuban missile crisis in 1962."[14] The authors disputed Kissinger's claim that the Kremlin "backed down because the United States bared its teeth."[15] What Brezhnev wanted, in fact, was not confrontation, but to compel the United States to press Israel "to stop the fighting." In this he would prove successful.

Among those present at, or closest to, the WSAG deliberations of the night of the 24th, however, there seems to have been near unanimity that Kissinger was right. Scowcroft regarded the decision as having been "*not* a cliff-hanger at all, not like the Cuban Missile Crisis. But—if the Russians (e.g. the marshals) had reacted differently . . ." Schlesinger expressed fears that, because of Watergate, "the Soviets thought the government of the United States might be crippled, and therefore we could not react—so part of our decision to go to DEFCON 3 was to show the Soviets 'you are in error; we are in a position to react, to a justifiable reaction.' Therefore you could argue that we took a step that was beyond what Brezhnev's message called for. The stand-down of Soviet forces in Europe certainly affected U.S. judgment—or were they just bluffing? To us it signified that they were preparing to send troops to the Middle East." And what if they had sent troops? "I think we could have lived with it, and not necessarily responded in kind."[16] Jan Lodal, who was not at the meeting but had been intimately involved with Kissinger's détente talks, felt that he "was right in going for the 'big shock.' My guess is—yes it was dangerous, but if we had gone stage by stage it could easily have led to an escalation into all-out war; I mean *nuclear*."[17]

Peter Rodman, also not at the October 24 meeting, had been on most of Kissinger's missions to the Middle East. Rodman regarded DEFCON 3 as "a brilliant stroke—it shook the Russians into agreeing on a cease-fire."

"But wasn't it potentially dangerous?"

"No—it was only a preparatory warning, no question of nuclear preparation."

It was a distortion to dub it a "nuclear alert." It was a "shock effect" designed to prevent "matching escalations."[18] In a symposium edited by Richard Parker, *The October War*, Rodman is quoted, however, as having gone even further, declaring: "We should have been willing to go to war . . . or at least to put American forces there to interpose." Spelling out the wider strategy of Nixon and Kissinger, he says: "The first objective was to ensure that Israel turned the tide . . . it was essential that Israel not be defeated by force of arms—particularly Soviet arms. The next objective was to try to split the Arabs from the Soviets. . . . It was the political hope of the administration, not that they had any great plan to guarantee its achievement."

Always very close to the center of Kissinger's planning, Rodman stressed that it was Sadat's expulsion of the 15,000 Soviet advisers which had been "the turning point of modern Middle East history. It wasn't Camp David. It wasn't even the October War. It was Sadat's reversal of alliances." Though he admitted that, heretofore, Sadat had been "misjudged," this was the foundation upon which Kissinger's strategy was constructed. At the time of the alert, his sense was that "the Soviets themselves didn't know . . . what they were going to do next." [19] This was indeed a view confirmed by Israelyan's record of Kremlin deliberations.

Kissinger himself always remained unapologetic about the alert. The meeting had to be held inside the White House, so as to "make it absolutely clear to the Soviets that what came out was a White House decision." But perhaps most crucial was his assessment, stemming from the long hours of talks with Brezhnev in Moscow, Zavidovo, Washington, and San Clemente, that "I didn't feel I was taking a risk, because I had gotten to know so well Brezhnev that I felt sure his reaction would be to avoid confrontation."

But, I asked, "What if the Soviet marshals *had* won the day?"

"Well, they wouldn't have done—and even if Russian troops had been sent to Egypt it wouldn't necessarily have involved an eyeball-to-eyeball confrontation with the U.S." [20] So it was, in effect, détente that won the day; but would it, *could* it, emerge undamaged?

In Moscow, Brezhnev—at least for the time being—became conciliatory. So, had the shock worked? Then, as Kissinger was awaiting his latest message on the 26th, a bombshell landed in the shape of Nixon's own press conference, which he had decided to give that evening. Kissinger was ringing his good friend in the Washington media, Stewart Alsop (Joseph's brother), to invite him and his wife, Tish, to dinner:

K: Miss Maginnes is here.

A: I am looking at your Chief now and I am . . .

K: I am having heart attacks when he is talking about the
    Middle East. . . . I am having such a heart attack about his
    challenge to the Soviet Union which I do not believe.

Half an hour later he had Haig on the line. For once the habitually deferential, indeed reverential secretary of state let his hair down. He was sulfurous at Nixon's mishandling of the situation, to the world at large:

K: The crazy bastard really made a mess with the Russians.
H: What?
K: Didn't you listen to his press statement? First we had
   information of massive movement of Soviet forces. That is a
   lie. Second, this was the worst crisis since the Cuban missile
   crisis. True, but why rub their faces in it? Third, Brezhnev
   and I exchanged brutal messages. This has never been
   acknowledged before. Four, Brezhnev respects me because I
   was the man who bombed Vietnam.

Haig admitted:

H: . . . He just let fly . . .
K: Compare it with my press conference when I said there was
   no confrontation with the Russians. . . . He has turned it
   into a massive Soviet backdown. Brezhnev is known to his
   politburo as a man with a special relationship with Nixon
   and he is being publicly humiliated. . . .
H: The rest is just as bad. . . . He took on the press like I have
   never heard.

Haig then ended with a caution: "If you talk to him tonight, take it easy. He is right on the verge."[21] Kissinger left it to Haig to try to mollify Dobrynin and the Russians—explaining, in effect, that the president didn't mean what he said.

In his memoirs, Kissinger somewhat plays down the episode, on the grounds that he was "overwrought with little sleep." But at the time it must have seemed like a major diplomatic disaster, under other circumstances surely grounds for resignation. Nevertheless, the tenor of his remarks shows better than anything how all the stresses of Watergate were getting at the U.S. secretary of state, at that moment the last bastion of the nation. Apart from the damage done to détente, in his press conference Nixon did himself immense harm in bashing the media ("I have never heard or seen such outrageous, vicious, distorted reporting," he declared, his fists clenched, according to his biographer, Stephen Ambrose.[22]) Up in the family rooms of the White House, wife Pat and daughter Julie winced. Nixon was "determined to show," wrote Kissinger, "that despite a week's hue and cry over the 'Saturday night massacre' and despite the threat of impeachment, he was in control."[23] He was, in effect, destroyed. Nothing proved it more clearly than that disastrous press conference.

Obliging Kissinger, Haig rang Dobrynin that same evening, informing him that he had told the president "that his remarks tonight were I thought overdrawn and would be interpreted improperly."

Dobrynin: "Yeah."

Haig continued to apologize: "And I wanted you to know that he did not in any way have the intention of drawing the situation as sharply as he did."

Dobrynin, clearly annoyed, replied that the Politburo was "very angry because they consider that you created all these things by reasons we don't know — we don't want to discuss it — but artificial crisis, why? And when you compare it with even the Cuban crisis, it is really — excuse me — but it is going beyond any comparison." He continued, complaining somewhat incoherently, his good English abandoning him: "Then he created this [unclear] crisis that you are real and we are just weaker partners standing looking against braver United States. Really, we have our people too around Moscow." Haig ended the White House climb-down with: "Well, obviously, I wouldn't call if I was at all comfortable with what was said tonight."[24]

Kissinger then received a call from the British ambassador, Lord Cromer, who began on a transparently diplomatic note: "I thought the President was absolutely great," but then suggested he might have been stirring up "a hornet's nest." If DEFCON 3 had provoked shock in Moscow, the ripples were not much reduced in Western Europe. In London, Heath was seriously discomfited by parliamentary questions from the Labour opposition as to whether he had been aware of the mobilization of U.S. nuclear forces stationed on British soil. But when Cromer complained about lack of consultation of America's European allies, which "can cause a lot of unhappiness," he was cut short by

Kissinger's riposte, "The Europeans have to face the fact that the President is fed up." Menacingly, in terms that perhaps recalled his predecessor, the late John Foster Dulles, he warned, "We might reach a point where on both sides of the Atlantic there will be a need to reassess U.S. relations."[25]

Friday, October 26, was the day when Kissinger's patience with the Israelis was pushed to the limit. Incensed by the Israeli lobbying in Washington, Nixon remarked angrily to him: "Who is going to save Israel, and who will save it in the future?" There was the perennial question as to whether this kind of pressure was ultimately in the best interests of either the United States or of Israel herself. In *Crisis*, Kissinger notes: "We had supported Israel throughout the war for many historical, moral, and strategic reasons. And we had just run the risk of war with the Soviet Union . . . [but the Israelis], [m]addened by the fact that they had been surprised, beside themselves with grief over the high casualties, and deeply distrustful of Sadat, who had engineered their discomfort," were bent on ending the war "with his destruction. Their emotion was understandable."[26] Their response did not, however, serve in their best interests, let alone that of world peace.

Kissinger had several corrosive conversations with Dinitz that day, attempting to save the trapped, hungry, and thirsty Egyptian Third Army:

> K: Why don't you let them break out and get out of there . . . ?
>   Why can you not let them take the tanks with them? The
>   Russians will replace them anyway.
> D: We will not open up the pocket and release an army that
>   came to destroy us. It has never happened in the history of
>   war.
> K: Also it has never happened that a small country is producing
>   a world war in this manner. There is a limit beyond which
>   you cannot push the President. I have been trying to tell
>   you that for a week. . . . You play your game and you will
>   see what happens.[27]

Dinitz came back later that evening, appealing for compassion with what his country had suffered: "In this embassy we have three girls who have lost either a brother or a cousin in this fighting . . . if we open the route, we revitalize two or three divisions that would be a threat to our bridgeheads. We know what their intention is. . . . We cannot afford to have this army revitalize." Unmoved, Kissinger warned, "You will be forced if it reaches that point."[28] Just before eleven that night Kissinger was back, thrusting at Dinitz with a strong reaction from Nixon: "He wanted me to make it absolutely clear that we cannot permit the destruction of the Egyptian army." With it came a clear threat of invoking U.N. sanctions to enforce Israeli compliance: "I have to say again your course is suicidal. You will not be permitted to destroy this army. You are destroying the possibility for negotiations, which you want."[29]

Still arguing, Dinitz was presented with an ultimatum for Israeli compliance by the next day. Back came a letter from Mrs. Meir, addressed to Kissinger personally; it was "vintage Golda, passionate, self centered, shrewd." With her reelection imminent, it was written as much for its impact on the Israeli cabinet as for the United States government. Israel, she complained, was "being punished not for its deeds, but because of its size and because it is on its own." If she was compelled to make a concession, it would have to be imposed only on direct orders from the White House—"nothing could force the lioness to be graceful about it," wrote Kissinger.[30] ("Mad heroes" was how Kissinger apostrophized the Israelis to Scowcroft.[31])

Finally both sides, Israel and Egypt, agreed to send emissaries to conclude a cease-fire at Kilometer 101. Even then, at the last minute, there was a flurry of discord, with the Israelis complaining that the Egyptian representatives had not turned up; the Egyptians protesting that they had been stopped at Kilometer 85 (its distance from Cairo marking just how close the Israeli forces had come to the Egyptian capital) by Israeli sentries. It transpired that the ever-suspicious Israelis would not let Egyptian drivers proceed, claiming that they would "see all our placements and tanks."[32] A signal came through from Golda Meir to Kissinger, more or less blaming the Americans for this last hitch. In a subsequent message from Dinitz to Kissinger, there was an attempt at humor—the best the Israelis could muster by way of an apology: "The Prime Minister sends you her greetings and felicitations. She wants to meet with Sadat at 3:30 this evening on Kilometer 111½."

"K: I am glad she still has a sense of humor."[33]

His was clearly under challenge. At 1:30 A.M., local time, on October 28, 1973, the representatives from the opposing sides met, exchanged awkward salutes, then shook hands. It marked the first direct peace talks between Israeli and Arab representatives since 1948. An end to the fighting was agreed, and an end to another round in the Arab-Israeli conflict. In Kissinger's eyes, there came with it a closure to "the most urgent perils to the American position in the Middle East. We had emerged as the pivotal factor in the diplomacy. Egypt was beginning to move in our direction."[34] The date could hardly have been more auspicious; almost to the day that Sunday was the eleventh anniversary of the ending of the Cuban Missile Crisis. "We were nearly at the goal of our strategy," wrote Kissinger.[35]

While at historic Kilometer 101, Egyptians and Israelis were hammering out all the nitty-gritty of cease-fire arrangements—the repatriation of POWs, care for the wounded, and supply convoys for the trapped Egyptian forces—Kissinger and Egypt's acting foreign minister, Ismail Fahmy,* were holding cordial talks that would lead up to a visit to Cairo and Sadat in early November. He describes Fahmy as "bounding," like some exuberant Labrador, into his office, straight off the plane, and without any appointment, with the words that he had come "to prepare your visit." Fahmy evidently flattered Kissinger, endowing him with "diplomatic skills exceeding even my own not excessively low estimate"! He reflected whimsically on it being "in the Arab nature to believe that some epic event or personality will miraculously transcend the humdrum mess that is the usual human condition; a miracle working is a mechanism for avoiding hard choices."[36]

In effect what Fahmy was offering would turn out to be a remarkably innovative, if not romantic, turn in Kissinger's career. Of that initial introduction into the world of Arab diplomacy, he noted—with detached amusement—how Arab foreign ministers would speak of themselves as " 'brothers' but seemed never to find anything else good to say about each other!"[37] Via Morocco and Tunisia, he set off on his groundbreaking entry into the Arab world on November 5. But first,

---

* He was confirmed in his post on October 31.

on the 31st, came a visit to Washington by Sadat's recent enemy, Golda Meir. She was a different person to the leader who had, only so few months previously, boasted to Nixon " 'We've never had it so good.' The war had devastated her," as a leader who truly suffered with every bereaved family. The realization was beginning to sink in in Israel that the Yom Kippur War might have brought tactical victory, but—for the first time in Israel's precarious history—had been strategically inconclusive. Kissinger detected an "almost elemental fear" that, with the United States committed to a new relationship with the Arab world, Israel might lose its only friend. It was Kissinger's task to ram home the fact that, for the first time, "our support was not unconditional."[38] The line had been drawn, definitively, at the destruction of the trapped Third Army.

Still taking a hard line on permitting mercy convoys through to the trapped Egyptians, Meir continued to rail that "We didn't start the war," to which Kissinger responded "But you face a need for wise decisions to protect the survival of Israel. This is what you face." With her voice shaking, according to Kissinger's account, she went on: "You're saying we have to accept the judgment of the U.S.? . . . We have to accept your judgment? Even on our affairs? On what is best for us?" Her American interlocutors were driven, says Kissinger, "to a level of irritation that nearly matched our high regard for Golda."[39] Tempers were growing short with her obstinacy; at one point some members of the WSAG committee were urging that the trapped Third Army be resupplied by an *American* airlift. Kissinger remarked with heavy irony that his ultimate responsibility "was as Secretary of State of the United States, not as a psychiatrist to the government of Israel."[40] But the redoubtable lady had a general election ahead of her. Slowly she climbed down, in the face of the inevitable.

As Kissinger left Washington on November 5 for his first venture into Arab territory, the cease-fire for which he had striven so long and so hard was in place—and seemed to be sticking. But his prickly meeting with Golda Meir left him with absolutely no illusions as to how difficult would be the next steps—the achieving of disengagement, followed by a lasting peace formula. Also, before leaving, he had received warning from that well-placed journalist, Arnaud de Borchgrave, that Sadat was considering resumption of hostilities given that his senior commanders considered the encirclement of the Third Army an intolerable affront to Egyptian honor. Kissinger tended to discount this, rightly as it turned out, on the grounds that both the Egyptians and the Syrians were still at a military disadvantage.

He would, however, be agreeably surprised, if not stunned, by his reception in the "enemy camp." Arriving for the first time on Arab soil, preparatory to his first exposure to this new world, Kissinger was greeted by a majestic turnout laid on by King Hassan of Morocco: fierce Berbers in flowing red and white robes, members of the Royal Guard in scarlet and green uniforms with swords drawn. There was an awkward moment as Kissinger, clearly taken aback by this first experience of stately protocol, endeavored to shake hands with the sergeant major—who was also holding a sword in his hand. To the king he unveiled his disengagement plans; the king was supportive and sent a helpful message ahead to Sadat, declaring that "if he gets into a commitment, he will honour it." [41] In Tunisia, pausing at Habib Bourguiba's new fantasy Palace of Carthage, Kissinger found the long-surviving ruler of Tunisia equally supportive of his moves to exclude the Soviets from the Middle East. Arriving in Cairo on the 6th, Kissinger discovered the city still blacked out, the cease-fire having been in force for less than two weeks.

The next day, visiting the famous Egyptian Museum, he saw its priceless contents still protected with sandbags, the glass cabinets covered with strips of tape. But he encountered a mood "exuberant and, I judged, full of expectation." [42] He sensed a people "yearning for peace." Viewed as the savior of the Third Army, momentarily he was hailed as a hero. He himself had little idea of what to expect, and had no preconception of what kind of diplomatic partner Anwar Sadat would be. The next day, November 7, his dramatic first encounter with Sadat took place.

President Anwar al-Sadat was born on December 25, 1918, in a small village on the Nile, one of thirteen brothers and sisters in a poor peasant family. His father was Egyptian, and his mother Sudanese. He took a commission in the army, where he met Gamal Abdel Nasser. Along with several other junior officers they formed the secret Free

Officers Movement, committed to freeing Egypt from British domination and the corruption of the Farouk dynasty. Between 1942 and 1947 he was imprisoned by the British for his efforts to obtain help from the Axis Powers, often in solitary confinement in a particularly harsh jail. He opens his autobiography with pride in his ancient fellahin heritage, a peasant born "on the banks of the Nile—where man first witnessed the dawn of time."[43] So, with Kissinger, he shared immediately one thing: descent from very ancient, Semitic races. Along with his fellow Free Officers, Sadat participated in the military coup known as the Egyptian Revolution of 1952 which overthrew King Farouk. After the coup, he was assigned by Nasser to take over the radio networks that announced the news of the revolution to the Egyptian people. Though achieving no great prominence under Nasser (who, unflatteringly, nicknamed him *Bimbashi Sah*—or "Major Yes, Yes"), he was appointed his vice president and, on Nasser's death in 1970, succeeded him as president of Egypt, rising to the nominal rank of field marshal. Sadat then purged most of his fellow leaders under Nasser, and in 1971 endorsed the Jarring peace proposals—which foundered following lack of U.S. and Israeli support.* His unprivileged birthright, coupled with his harsh experience in jail, endowed him with a strong, philosophic sense of endurance. He was a man of simple, peasant tastes, with a strong element of the dramatic and the romantic. His otherwise loyal foreign secretary, Ismail Fahmy, complained of Sadat's habit of telling stories that sometimes "bore little resemblance to reality. What he said changed with the occasion and the audience."[44] It was a protean quality not unfamiliar to his American guest. He also shared Kissinger's propensity for gathering power around himself. Yet, because of America's neglect of Middle Eastern affairs, all too little had been known about Sadat's personality—until October 1973.

Arriving at the Tahra Presidential Palace on the morning of the 7th, Kissinger found himself led into a gallery packed with journalists and television cameras. There was no visible security presence, and Kissinger was mobbed and jostled, though in a thoroughly friendly,

---

* Dr. Gunnar Jarring, Swedish ambassador to Moscow, was charged by the U.N., in 1971, with a mission to evolve a compromise solution aimed at a reopening of the Suez Canal, and a partial withdrawal of the warring sides from the Canal Zone.

Egyptian fashion, bombarded with questions and blinded by camera lights. It was disconcerting. Then, suddenly, "I heard behind me a deep baritone: 'Welcome, welcome.' "[45] Strangely enough, no other account seems to have been kept of this historic meeting,[46] other than Kissinger's own vivid and rather moving description in *Years of Upheaval*. As I found it one of the more heartfelt personal passages in all his voluminous memoirs, I take the liberty of quoting it at length: "Dressed in a khaki military tunic . . . he was taller, swarthier, and more imposing than I had expected. He exuded vitality and confidence. That son of peasants radiated a natural dignity and aristocratic bearing as out of keeping with his revolutionary history as it was commanding and strangely calming. He affected nonchalance. I too did my best to pretend that there was nothing unusual about a meeting two weeks after a war in which we had armed Egypt's enemy and then—during the alert—had threatened to intervene militarily on Egyptian soil." Kissinger continued: "Neither of us wanted to show that we had a great deal at stake, even while we knew that we would soon begin one of the few diplomatic exchanges that can be called seminal." It must have been an extraordinary meeting, perhaps more of personalities than of minds. Almost immediately Sadat seems to have grasped the nettle, saying in greeting: "I have been longing for this visit. I have a plan for you. It can be called the Kissinger plan."[47] Kissinger followed by flattering his Egyptian host in turn. He expressed respect for the "stunning surprise" Egypt had achieved on October 6. Puffing at his pipe, Sadat astonished Kissinger by declaring that "the Soviet Union was the real enemy."[48] He explained with openness that he had ordered the Soviet advisers out of Egypt the previous year, partly because of the disrespect they showed toward Egyptians, but also because their presence might have clashed with his plans of attack. Its purpose was to vindicate Egyptian honor. Now that he thought this had been achieved he had only two objectives—to regain Sinai and make peace. Here was a very different, chastened Sadat from the one who had boasted to Soviet ambassador Vladimir Vinogradov in the early days of the October War: "My boys are riding on the Bar-Lev Line! We've crossed the Canal! . . . My sons are on the eastern bank of the Canal!"[49]

As he listened to Sadat's tale "of foresight and cunning, of honor and daring," Kissinger came to the realization "that I was in the presence of a remarkable man. Sadat seemed free of the obsession with detail by which mediocre leaders think they are mastering events. . . . I sensed that Sadat represented the best chance to transcend frozen attitudes that the Middle East had known since the creation of the State of Israel." It was perhaps an equally remarkable conclusion for Kissinger to reach, in so short a meeting. But he was an intuitive operator. Kissinger says he found himself explaining U.S. strategy to the Egyptian leader much as he might have done at a WSAG meeting. In his memoirs, he continued, recalling how "Nasser's policy of trying to extort concessions by mobilizing the Third World against us with Soviet support had not worked in the past and would not be permitted to work in the future." But with Sadat, Kissinger instinctively felt he could "discern no inevitable clash of interests between us." He urged Sadat to "think of peace with Israel as a psychological, not a diplomatic problem." Once the immediate tension was defused, Kissinger undertook that the priority of the United States would be to "do its utmost to arrange a genuine disengagement of [Israeli] forces back across the canal," although perhaps not as far as the two-thirds withdrawal across Sinai which Sadat had been proposing.

This would, however, constitute "the first Israeli withdrawal from Arab territory occupied for any length of time; it would create the confidence for further steps." Were Israel compelled to retreat too fast, she would dig her feet in, and Kissinger might be faced with the prospect of facing a renunciation; in which case, Israel, feeling itself imperiled by the defection of its sole guarantor, could seek its security in continuing with the destruction of the weakened Arab armies. Thus it had to be a gradual, stage-by-stage, drawn-out process, with the first priority the salvaging of the trapped Third Army. Sadat recognized that Kissinger knew better than he what Israel would accept, and remarked—to Kissinger's surprise[50]—that the Third Army was "not the heart of the matter between America and Egypt. He was determined to end Nasser's legacy. He would reestablish relations with the United States as quickly as possible and, once that was accomplished, he would move to friendship."* He also tacitly acknowledged that Egypt, and the

---

* Diplomatic relations were in fact restored, on February 28, 1974, following Kissinger's shuttle trips and the first Egyptian-Israeli disengagement agreement.

Arabs, could no longer look to the Soviets for comfort; for peace, they had of necessity now to look westward. On the other hand, through his action on October 6, he had effectively forced America to play a lead role in the Middle East—and had, incidentally, through destroying Israel's "aura of invincibility" (Kissinger's words[51]), cemented his rule at home. Abandoning any preconception he might have had about Sadat, Kissinger admitted that his performance "astonished me. He did not haggle or argue . . . it was, in truth, an act of considerable courage. Against what we later learned was the near unanimous sentiment of his advisers, Sadat decided to take his chances on the word of an American whom he did not know."[52]

Kissinger then drew up, with Sadat's full endorsement, a six-point plan for the complex process of disengagement, including the resupply of the Third Army, exchange of the wounded, and all POWs. With it would follow substantial U.S. funding to help rebuild Egypt's shattered economy—and which, over many future years, would make the country one of America's top beneficiaries of aid. To what was essentially Kissinger's draft (and which he had in part cleared with Mrs. Meir in Washington), Sadat made "only the most trivial changes." He "cut through trivia to the essential, to make major, even breathtaking, tactical concessions in return for an irreversible psychological momentum." Although it was herein that "the devil in the details" lay, as will be seen later, the issues which would subsequently bedevil relations, Sadat's was, indeed, a breathtaking performance, revealing immense courage. Paying tribute, Kissinger continued: "Wise statesmen know they will be measured by the historical process they set in motion, not by the debating points they score."[53]

Of all Kissinger's meetings that I have endeavored to describe in this book, that in Cairo of November 7, 1973, was the one in which I would most like to have been the fly on the wall: that first encounter between the Jewish refugee from Hitler and the peasant from the Nile, two statesmen who only days previously had seemed like committed adversaries. Kissinger sensed at once, in the words Margaret Thatcher would later use about Mikhail Gorbachev, that here was "a man I could do business with." But there was more to it than that. The unintended spark which flew between the two of them (what media folk might now call "chemistry") that day must have been quite extraordinary.

Sometimes, describing it to me, Kissinger would almost have a break in his voice; for Sadat would, eventually, pay with his life for that day's display of courage. How different, certainly in tone, it was from all his dealings with Golda Meir, however great his respect for the Israeli leader. On a personal level, with Sadat it was almost like a kind of instant love affair. The intellectual bond between them was something comparable to what he had found with China's Zhou Enlai. Sadat seemed to have a subliminal awareness of the grand sweep of history that paralleled Kissinger's own, and which he found in few foreign leaders. From that meeting on, Kissinger recognized in Sadat that "I was dealing with a great man." He summed up Sadat as being "more than the sum of his parts. By one of the miracles of creation the peasant's son, the originally underestimated politician, had the wisdom and courage of the statesman and occasionally the insight of the prophet. Yet nourishing all these qualities was a pervasive humanity."[54]

There was something about the man that evoked to Kissinger that day the great pharaonic statuary he had seen in the Cairo Museum, figures that were "larger than life," yet their faces "infinitely human" with their gaze leading "towards distant horizons." Such a man, wrote Kissinger years later, "was Anwar Sadat. Only the future will tell whether he started an irreversible movement of history or whether he was like that ancient Pharaoh Ikhnaton, who dreamed of monotheism amidst the panoply of Egyptian deities a millennium before it was accepted among mankind. . . . One way or another, the cause of peace will be his pyramid."[55] Seen from his point of view, Sadat declared that he "felt as if I was looking at the real face of the United States, the one I had always wanted to see." In agreement, Foreign Minister Fahmy felt that Kissinger's candor and sincerity had gained Sadat's trust.[56]

Kissinger promptly reported back to Nixon, via Brent Scowcroft, details of the Six-Point Agreement, expressing his admiration for Sadat's courage. Nixon, plunged ever deeper in the slough of impeachment proceedings, was elated. At the bottom of the memorandum he scrawled: "K — Congratulations — great job."[57] Two days later the Watergate defendants were sentenced to tough sentences. More than ever in need of support from the pro-Israel senators, on Kissinger's return

Nixon set up a meeting with fellow Republican Senator Javits of New York on November 12. Doing almost all the talking, with Kissinger sitting silent, Nixon brought Javits up to speed on the Middle East. He started: "The airlift saved Israel. It was done over the objections of the DOD and State bureaucracy. I did it because I think if you act, you should do it decisively. Also the alert. We sent a strong message. This gave them [the Soviets] a bad time." Javits responded: "Your standing in the Jewish Community is great. . . . You personally saved Israel. Henry Kissinger has been magnificent. The Jewish Community must be mobilized. . . . The Middle East can be a monument to you."[58]

Not everyone, however, shared Nixon's elation. In Egypt there were many misgivings. Chief among them were those voiced by the veteran journalist Mohamed Hassanein Heikal. Exactly the same age as Kissinger, an articulate nationalist, as editor-in-chief of *Al-Ahram*, Heikal had risen to become the most powerful journalist of his generation in the Arab-speaking world. Starting off life as a reporter covering the Battle of El-Alamein in 1942 (he was an admirer of General Bernard Montgomery), he became a close friend of Nasser's, and—for the first four years—an equally close associate of Sadat's. For a brief time in the early 1970s he was simultaneously acting as minister of foreign affairs, minister of information, editor of *Al-Ahram*, chairman of *Al-Ahram*, and author of a weekly column. What led to a breach with Sadat, and subsequently to Heikal's imprisonment, was the Kissinger-Sadat entente of November 1973.* Speaking to me in Cairo in February 2005, Heikal was vitriolic about Kissinger's role in November 1973. He had, said Heikal, "five loyalties: one to three, to himself; four, to Israel; five, to the United States!" Heikal recalled how, in June 1973, Sadat had asked him to go to Washington to talk to Kissinger, but when he questioned him about the parameters of a conversation, Sadat had hedged, warning that "talking to Kissinger is not a game—you need to be specific." Sadat elaborated: "I am not ready to commit myself—I just want to explore." So Heikal refused: "Then I can't go." When Kissinger came to Cairo in November, it was their first meeting; but

---

* Heikal resigned from *Al-Ahram* February 1974, following differences of opinion on policy with Sadat. Performing a remarkable comeback after the age of eighty, thirty years later Heikal attracted a huge audience across the Arab world glued to their TV sets every Thursday night with his hour-long one-man program of recollections.

Heikal was scathing about Kissinger being economical with the truth, in "pretending," he said, that the two had never met. "Hence my contempt for him."[59] On his side, Kissinger dismissed Heikal's account of a dinner conversation as having been "poetically imaginative."[60] Here was a conflict of two very strong, and positive, personalities.

Heikal said he regarded Kissinger as "a *gulli-gulli* man, a magician" and warned Sadat of the danger of seeing him alone. "I begged him, 'Don't start—Henry Kissinger will get everything from you.' " Sadat refused; he said, "No, it will be best to be"—and then he used French—"*en tête-à-tête*!" Heikal said he was furious that Sadat had, nevertheless—and despite all his admonitions—gone ahead and conferred with Kissinger alone, Heikal having hoped that Sadat would have had a team of negotiators (including, naturally, himself) in attendance. But Sadat had rejected this, pointing out that "Kissinger always had *tête-à-tête* meetings with leaders like Brezhnev and Mao."[61] Consequently, Sadat "put all his bets on him, and lost them. . . . Don't forget, he was a man from the tribe! I refused to join him for lunch. He said to me 'Kissinger is a man of strategy—and so am I'; what he wanted was Russia out of the Middle East—and that's a game we can do together. Sadat hated the Soviet Union—and he feared the Egyptian army, if things went wrong." Heikal praised Sadat for his courage; first, in going to war; and secondly, in leaving the campaign to the army; but he stressed how "disastrous" he had been in his negotiations with Kissinger. The following day Heikal had gone to Sadat's residence to tell him so. He found the president in bed, covered in white sheets, wearing a white bathrobe—his wife remarking that the swarthy president looked like "a flea in a bowl of milk." Not knowing what had been agreed, Heikal, as was his habit, wrote down notes of the Sadat-Kissinger meeting on six-by-eight cards, filling sixty-one of them. When he presented them to Sadat, his leader barked: "What are all these cards? . . . They are irrelevant—Don't act like a horse! Pawing the ground!"

After listening to Heikal for some twenty minutes, Sadat told him that all he had said was " 'quite irrelevant—I am disengaging with the Americans, not Israel—and this is your policy!' But it wasn't at all—Sadat had made himself a hostage to Kissinger, by kicking out the USSR. I reckoned that Sadat completely misconstrued Kissinger. At that meeting he betrayed his allies—*he gave everything away*. No, he was not a traitor, but just very misguided." That was, Heikal told me, "my breaking point with Sadat—over the disengagement lines." Out of favor, eight years later Heikal found himself thrown into the Tora prison for three months in appalling conditions, lying on the ground with only a blanket—"a prison filled with my friends—enough ministers to form a government!"[62]

Sadat was assassinated during that time—at a military parade commemorating the anniversary of the October War, by Egyptian dissidents. In his book, *Autumn of Fury: The Assassination of Sadat*, Sadat's former friend Mohamed Heikal wrote that by granting peace with Israel, Sadat had "achieved a world-wide constituency, but lost the constituency which was naturally his as President of Egypt—the Arab world." He described him as "the first Egyptian Pharaoh to be killed by his own people . . . a hero of the electronic revolution, but also a victim."[63]

With the passing years, Heikal's dissenting voice about the Kissinger-Sadat talks has risen to a loud clamor in the Arab world. Sadat died, a martyr to the cause of peace in the Middle East, as a direct consequence of the deal. When, in February 2008, I was invited to Cairo to give a series of three lectures to a prestigious audience, my suggestion that since 1973, Egypt—at least—had enjoyed thirty-five years of peace (or more than 50 percent longer than that granted Europe between the two world wars) was met with powerful criticism. The tenor of the response was that, no, it had only been a very flawed peace that Sadat purchased. There had been powerful internal discontent, and major acts of terrorism which had substantially damaged the Egyptian economy through the flight of tourism it had caused. Equilibrium had only been maintained through Hosni Mubarak's imposition of draconian and brutally repressive laws. It had not brought peace to Palestine, to the Arab "brothers" in Palestine (though one well-educated young Egyptian expressed total disdain for the Palestinians and their constant inability to govern themselves; another said, "Well, who won the October War, anyway? I don't know!"). Strongest of all was the sense that, in declaring peace with Israel, Egypt had abandoned the Arab cause, condemned the Palestinians to prolonged subjugation and misery—and, above all, led to Egypt's own isolation from the rest of the Arab "brethren." One distinguished former foreign minister of Egypt praised to me Sadat's "wisdom" in recognizing that no major power could allow the destruction of Israel; yet voiced the opinion that Sadat had failed in *not* allowing himself to be drawn into detail in those November talks. Kissinger had been better briefed—and "the devil had been in the details": that was Arab rights. Sadat's overriding hope had been that the October War and the Kissinger "deal" combined would lead to "a bigger success." And, concluded another Egyptian, wasn't the Middle East now a much more dangerous place than it had been in November 1973?[64]

In November of 1973, however, Kissinger could leave Cairo satisfied that the laborious machinery of the peace procedure had been primed. Next stop would be full-dress peace talks in Geneva, in December, but meanwhile there was a further spat with Israel. Undiplomatically, Kissinger sent his two subordinates, Joseph Sisco and Harold "Hal" Saunders, to Tel Aviv to tie up negotiations. The hypersensitive Israelis evidently took umbrage at an implied derogation, with Kissinger failing to come in person. There followed what Kissinger dubbed "another hallowed ritual of Israeli negotiating tactics." This would have meant going back to Sadat, on what had already been agreed—based on the terms, the "Six Points," drawn up with Meir herself in Washington the previous week. With elections imminent, "Golda spoke darkly of resigning in favor of a tougher negotiator," which was—wrote Kissinger, "a truly frightening prospect, which we happily knew was unfulfillable."[65] This time her bluff was called by the Americans.

As this new turbulence occurred, Kissinger was already on his travels again: first, on November 8, to consult King Hussein in Jordan, then on to the far more palatial surroundings of King Faisal in Riyadh, and finally to the shah in Iran: three monarchs who at various levels were valued allies of the West. Hussein, the brave "Lion of Jordan," America's most consistently reliable ally among all the Arabs, was feeling somewhat put out that, during the Yom Kippur War, he had been consulted by neither the Arabs, nor Washington—let alone Israel. It was the penalty he paid for being dependable. The Syrians and Egyptians had kept him out of the secret about the planned war. Later, when it was all over, Asad had confided to Hussein's prime minister, Zaid Rifa'i, that Sadat had "double-crossed" him in not revealing that he only intended to wage a limited war. Hussein had been caught "completely off guard"; on October 6, he had been motorbiking with his wife, Alia, on the pillion, when a security car had flashed him down and given him the news. True to his engagements he maintained a defensive stance. Only after it seemed as though Damascus was threatened had Hussein sent in his crack 40th Armored Brigade to bolster the Syrians, where fellow Arab units had considerably shelled it—by mistake. By assuring Israel that it would present no third front in the Egypt-Syrian operations, Jordan's essentially neutral stance had materially aided the IDF's ability to transfer units from Golan to Sinai. Hussein too wanted to see the Soviets excluded from the Middle East; he had thoroughly "played the game" with Kissinger, but derived little benefit from it. Kissinger told him that the United States proposed to treat the thorny problem of Yasser Arafat's newly ascendant Palestine Liberation Organization as an inter-Arab concern, not an international one, but this was not something Hussein would welcome.[66]

While Kissinger was away on his travels, at home the moving finger was moving ever closer to President Richard M. Nixon; the Watergate defendants were sentenced to long terms of imprisonment by Judge John Sirica (nicknamed "Maximum John" for his tough sentences); a crucial eighteen-and-a-half minute gap in the White House tapes was disclosed; and White House lawyers J. Fred Buzhardt and Leonard Garment flew to Key Biscayne to recommend to the president that he resign. In Riyadh, Kissinger's host, the absolute ruler of Saudi Arabia, must have been puzzled by the attacks on his fellow head of state in Washington. Reaching King Faisal's monumental palace, as Kissinger walked through a hall that seemed as large as a football field, he found himself reflecting on "What strange twists of fate had caused a refugee from Nazi persecution to wind up in Arabia as the representative of American democracy." Discussing matters of state with Faisal was very different from anything that had preceded it. Apart from his ritualistic, broad condemnation of Israel, the king's conversation, effected "in a gentle voice even when making strong points," was "elliptical" in the extreme. He could offer little comfort in the world oil crisis his court had imposed; what Kissinger saw as a "revolution in world affairs," he presented as a "reluctant decision taken with a bleeding heart," imposed on him by the greed of others. He thought Kissinger's step-by-step approach to achieving peace was "noble," but little more. Kissinger described the talks as "a stately minuet" in which both dancers failed to harmonize their movements.[67] This was not Sadat; nor was it Golda.

On to Iran. Again the tenor of talks was different. The shah had been America's consistent ally for thirty-seven years—and Israel's only ally in Islam. But he had his own problems, which—as of 1973—may not have seemed overwhelming, but were nevertheless visible like black clouds on the horizon. Writing ex post facto, Kissinger in his memoirs rendered passing tribute to Sadat, who alone would provide the shah sanctuary, when all others were to give him the cold shoulder—including President Jimmy Carter's America, which owed him so much. As of November 1973, the shah—having resolutely refused to allow airspace to the Soviet airlift to the warring Arab states—continued to regard Israel as a strategic linchpin in the area, but could offer little other material support. Kissinger regarded his brief visit to Tehran in 1973 as mainly "symbolic."[68]

From there he flew on eastward, to Pakistan—and Beijing. Swiftly, with all the adroitness of a Chinese chess-player who could conduct the game on three levels at once, he readjusted his mind to focus on China, and what would be his last conference with his other hero, Zhou Enlai.

CHAPTER 14

ON TO CHINA

"A sentimental journey."

—Henry Kissinger[1]

"Barely two years after establishing contact, the grizzled revolutionary [Mao] was giving a tutorial to the American Secretary of State on how to keep America's alliances together."

—Henry Kissinger[2]

FOLLOWING KISSINGER'S HISTORIC visit to his new friend Anwar Sadat, it seemed that his career as secretary of state—still only two months old—had reached a kind of summit. Or was it a watershed from which rivers would flow in different directions? They would not necessarily all flow toward the sea of success, or with equal velocity. His bringing an end to the fighting in the Middle East, establishing a cease-fire and then getting it to stick, was no small triumph; while the bridge he had created with Sadat would bring unforeseeable consequences. The peace conference in Geneva, the famous shuttle diplomacy which ensued, may have lacked the dramatic impact of the Yom Kippur War, but were essential follow-ups, of outstanding historical significance. In the meantime—having put the Middle East and all its problems temporarily behind him, he had to face the increasing difficulties for the United States in China.

Kissinger's last visit to the Chinese had been in February, on his way home from Vietnam—following what then seemed like the successful conclusion of his peace negotiations with Hanoi. In all of these, peace in Cambodia had played an important subsidiary role. Here, Kissinger deemed Beijing to be holding the key—as part of the overall deal which had followed the opening of the door to China. Zhou Enlai had agreed to support U.S. proposals for ending the war in Cambodia, which involved the intercession of Prince Sihanouk, the neutralist Cambodian leader. It was agreed that having moved to Beijing, Sihanouk—in essence a Chinese puppet—would meet with Kissinger there in August. But in the meantime, in Washington the House of Representatives—operating on its Watergate agenda of opposing the White House at every turn—had voted on July 18 to prohibit all American military action in Indochina, despite the threat of a presidential veto.* The bombing of Cambodia, much criticized, was ordered to cease on August 15. In Kissinger's view, however, this might effectively, and disastrously, remove any "bargaining leverage" with Cambodia's increasingly militant Khmer Rouge. They would now see no reason to negotiate a cease-fire. At the same time, it had "politically wounded"[3] Zhou—already vulnerable in the court of Mao, and (unknown then to Kissinger) suffering from terminal cancer of the bladder.

The very day of the congressional vote of July 18, Kissinger received a "brutal" note from Beijing. Such was the import of its synchronization with the move in Congress that Kissinger could not help but regard it as a deliberate slight. The next day, he convened a meeting in his White House office to discuss this unhelpful communication. The note accused the United States, despite Sihanouk's repeated request for a halt, "of obdurately continuing its bombing of Cambodia." Beijing fully supported Sihanouk here: "The key to the settlement of

---

* On September 10, the Senate Foreign Relations Committee reported, with a 10–0 vote, a McGovern (Nixon's defeated adversary in the 1972 election) amendment that would provide for an immediate cutoff of all funds, and the requirement of congressional approval of any renewal of U.S. involvement in the Vietnam War. On October 10, Congress jointly voted in this authorization. On October 24, the crisis day of the Yom Kippur War, Nixon vetoed the war powers legislation. On November 7, less than two weeks before Kissinger's trip to China, the House overrode the presidential veto with four more votes than the two-thirds majority required. Thus, as Kissinger left on his travels, Nixon's powers were essentially annulled.

the question," it claimed, "is held by the United States, and not by others. If the United States truly desire to settle the Cambodian question, the above reasonable demands ... should be acceptable to it."[4]

An unexpected coolness seemed to have set in on Sino-U.S. relations. Whereas the Chinese had previously urged that Kissinger return to open a dialogue with Sihanouk, now Sihanouk had said that the Americans should negotiate with the Khmer Rouge and not himself. Kissinger had been expecting an invitation to revisit Beijing, and see Sihanouk, in August. But now that had been inexplicably postponed. Kissinger regarded this as "a slap in the face," reflecting both the "turmoil" in Congress and the internal struggle in Beijing, where Zhou's influence was clearly on the wane. Most seriously, China—thought Kissinger—was washing its hands of Cambodia, and leaving that unhappy country to the mercy of Pol Pot. It was, Kissinger complained to his group in the White House, "a complete reversal of the Chinese position." Kissinger was puzzled as to whether it meant that "something more fundamental was happening to the relationship." He concluded with his suspicions that the Chinese were motivated by concern at "a paralyzed President unable to provide firm support in matters affecting their security." Ambassador David Bruce in Beijing was instructed to "pass a harsh response" back to the Chinese note, and call off Kissinger's trip scheduled for August.[5]

After this, there followed a period of a few weeks when both sides "sulked." Then the invitation was renewed. But the Yom Kippur War had intervened. In the meantime, Gromyko, in his cautionary note to Nixon about the Middle East on September 28, had appended a few remarks about relations with China. Nothing noteworthy had occurred since Brezhnev's visit in June. The situation remained "tense." But there had been no border clashes, Gromyko noted: "And we trust the Chinese leaders will not resort to such incidents. As regards the future ... can one continue to rely on the common sense of the Chinese leadership? It is hard to forecast the makeup of the future leadership. But this is something we have to think of in both our interests. As we see it, our assessments do not diverge that much. But I am interested in your assessment and in the bearing of that factor on the relations between us. You have advanced the idea in confidence that you gave priority to U.S.-Soviet relations and we cannot point a finger at anything that you have done that runs counter to what you said." Gromyko then summed up with an assurance that, as seen from Moscow, "our relations assume an irreversible character."[6] It was the letter of a friendly power to an ally, angling for information on the wild card in the pack. Then had come the Yom Kippur War, with all the strains that it had imposed on the Moscow-Washington entente.

On October 25, flush with the success of DEFCON 3 and his press conference which defined the end of the crisis, that morning Kissinger had spent three-quarters of an hour giving an intimate, blow-by-blow briefing of that crisis to Ambassador Huang Zhen. Still described as chief of the People's Republic of China Liaison Office, Huang had been the first diplomat to present his credentials on Kissinger's becoming secretary of state (on September 29), a week before the outbreak of war in the Middle East. In one of his early conversations on October 6 Kissinger had explained with clarity that "our strategic objective is to prevent the Soviet Union from getting a dominant position in the Middle East. That is our basic objective. Israel is a secondary, emotional problem having to do with domestic politics here. Our objective is always, when the Soviet Union appears, to demonstrate that whoever gets help from the Soviet Union cannot achieve his objective, whatever it is. You remember that in 1970 I once said publicly that we wanted to expel the Soviet troops from the Middle East. I was criticized, but we succeeded. . . . So we advocate now a return to the status quo ante before the fighting started." The Chinese position was that it was not possible for them to do anything, to which Kissinger responded: "I am not asking you to do anything." On their meeting in the afternoon of the 25th, Ambassador Huang had opened, sympathetically, with "You were up all night."

Displaying self-confidence, and satisfaction, good humor rather than fatigue, Kissinger replied: "Your allies [undoubtedly, with heavy emphasis] tried to throw their weight around last night. I thought I would bring you up to date on what has been happening for the benefit of the Prime Minister [Zhou Enlai]. First, let me tell you about the situation last night and today, and then I'll go back to the Moscow trip. First, Mr. Ambassador, our policy has been what I told you the first night. We have one principal objective, to keep the Soviet military presence out of the Middle East and to reduce the Soviet political influence as much as possible. I know you are going to disagree with these objectives violently."

There was laughter; Ambassador Huang interjected: "Not necessarily!" He then told Kissinger he had watched in its entirety his press conference that morning. Flattered, Kissinger commented that Zhou had once described him as "the only man who can speak a half an hour without saying anything!" He continued in the bantering and amicable tone similar to that which he had established with Huang's Soviet counterpart, Dobrynin. At length Kissinger gave the Chinese ambassador the kind of frank and open briefing he might have offered up to a meeting of the NSC. "My honest view," he said, "is that the Soviet Union has suffered a major strategic defeat, and that's why they tried to bluff us last night." The Arab leaders, he thought, had learned a lesson and that now, "if they want to make diplomatic progress, they have to deal with us."

Following this exposition, Ambassador Huang had hit back with some force, speaking of Oriental concern with face, and condemning the arrogance of the two superpowers in putting a resolution before the U.N. Security Council, "agreed upon by themselves," but not in consultation with "other countries." It was, he said, "a practice we find intolerable." Adopting a higher moral tone, coming down in support of Arab aspirations, he declared that China looked "at the perspective of which side is just and which side is not just." Weapons were important, but the people who used them more important—if it was only a matter of weapons, "George Washington would never have been victorious"—nor would the Chinese Revolution have triumphed. He refused to accept Kissinger's military assessment; he did not share his view that the Arabs had been "defeated." The Palestinians had a just cause. But he defused the situation by stressing "We are old friends. We have differences of view, but we are old friends." With a merry gibe at his assistant, Winston Lord, Kissinger had closed the session by describing his forthcoming trip to China as "a sentimental journey."[7]

On November 10, Kissinger's plane took him to Beijing via Pakistan, a "sentimental journey" in that it followed exactly the same route as on his famous, exploratory voyage of two years previously. It was his sixth visit. Zhou, though visibly drawn, with all the suave manners of the former mandarin and perhaps more diplomatic than his ambassador, congratulated Kissinger on his "whirlwind diplomacy" (the term "shuttle diplomacy" had yet to be invented), also "applauding" U.S. endeavors to reduce Soviet influence in the Arab world. Whereas the media tended to judge "progress" in terms of Taiwan, Kissinger and Zhou agreed with one another that their ties "were not cemented by formal agreements but by a common assessment of the international situation." On the Middle East, Zhou commended the shah (perhaps surprisingly in retrospect, and considering the fate that would soon overtake Iran) as "a far-sighted leader." The big danger came from "radical" Iraq* achieving local hegemony in the area. The dialogue with Zhou was of "a high order," assessed Kissinger,[8] but both he and his assistant, Winston Lord, who had been on previous trips noted that "something was missing." The old "bite and sparkle" had gone.[9] Both politically and physically the brilliant statesman whom Kissinger so admired, and liked, was on his way out. (In their massive biography, *Mao: The Unknown Story*, unrelentingly hostile to Mao, Jung Chang and Jon Halliday assert that Mao, with murderous brutality, refused to allow his loyal deputy to have access to medical help for his cancer, despite the critical worsening of his bladder tumor. Already passing blood at the time of Kissinger's visit, he was forced to die painfully, in sequestration.)[10]

It was the last time Kissinger would converse with Zhou; two months later he would disappear totally from the political scene; a year later Kissinger would visit him in the hospital, in his terminal decline. Eloquently he encapsulated their talk in his memoirs as reminiscent of "a brilliant, slightly stifling summer day whose beauty is the harbinger of a distant thunderstorm."[11] From Zhou, Kissinger went to have a long talk with Mao himself. Kissinger described him, already aged eighty, and apparently recovered from his recent pneumonia, as "that incarnation of willpower, who greeted us with his characteristic mocking, slightly demonic smile."[12] Mao looked better than he had ever seen him, making heavy jokes with sexual innuendoes—at which the female interpreters giggled obsequiously. The chairman made it plain that he, not Zhou any longer, was articulating policy. He sur-

---

* As of 1973, Saddam Hussein was still a relatively unknown, but rising, figure.

prised Kissinger by expressing concern, not at U.S. policy toward the Soviets, but at its domestic situation: Watergate. Mao could not understand what all the fuss was about; resorting to scatological terms, he "contemptuously dismissed the whole affair as a form of 'breaking wind' " (a passage that evidently presented the interpreter with some difficulty). Clearly to Mao the whole problem could be resolved by dispatching the offending journalists to some remote Chinese gulag. What principally concerned him was how it affected U.S. capacity to resist Soviet expansionism. Turning to (with Americans, the hot issue) Taiwan, Mao embraced a great Chinese sweep of millennia of history—"let it come after one hundred years": or a Cycle of Cathay. There was no urgency.

After two and a half hours, Mao concluded his tour d'horizon with warnings to "be wary of China's women"—referring unmistakingly to his machinating wife, Jiang Qing—and by applauding Kissinger's decision to take in Japan on his way home. Kissinger received Mao's condescension with detached amusement; here, "barely two years after establishing contact, the grizzled revolutionary was giving a tutorial to the American Secretary of State on how to keep America's alliances together." Sharing tutorials was not something with which a Harvard professor was unfamiliar!

The long conversation ended with Mao, returning—"like the composer of a symphony"—as Kissinger described it—"to his opening theme: would Watergate sap the authority of a President with whom he more or less agreed." [13] That concern was clearly nagging him throughout.

America's ambassador in Beijing, David Bruce, a man with unparalleled experience in most of the capitals of the world—London, Bonn, and to NATO—reckoned that Kissinger's conversation with Mao was the most extraordinary presentation from a statesman that he had ever heard; all the more so because of its spontaneity. But what did Kissinger's sixth trip, coming in such troubled times, actually add up to? Reporting to the Oval Office Kissinger claimed that his four-day visit had been "a constant success on all planes," which had resulted in a "deepening of the close identity between you and the Chinese leaders' strategic perspectives on the international situation." The two-and-three-quarter-hour session he had had with Mao had been the longest with any foreign official in recent years, and had been "very significant." Having almost gone to excess in describing that the duo of Mao and Zhou "may well be the most impressive twosome in history," the report expressed a caveat about the succession in the Middle Empire: "A worrisome aspect is the fact that on all our trips we have dealt with the restricted circle of Zhou and his lieutenants. We have had virtually no contact with other elements of the political leadership, such as the Shanghai radicals . . . we have no assurance that the PRC [People's Republic of China] will continue its policy towards us when Mao and Zhou depart. This puts premiums on solidifying our relationship while the current leadership is directing their policy."

To his embattled chief, Kissinger threw out a bouquet that may have been only partially merited; referring to "your strong handling" of the DEFCON alert. Here Zhou had "called you more courageous than President Kennedy as a leader"; and "the Chairman was vigorously supportive of you" over Watergate. Kissinger quoted Zhou as having been critical of Allende's "rashness" in Chile and Che Guevara's "adventurism"; it seemed to have been almost an aside, but Nixon, on receiving the report, was to sideline the reference.

Kissinger insisted that both Mao and Zhou "looked well and demonstrated their usual mental prowess (Mao more than ever). . . . Mentally he is extremely impressive, improving his previous performances. He led the conversation, covering all major international issues with subtlety and incisiveness and an unerring knack of striking the essential cause in a seemingly casual way. By the time he was finished he had sketched their strategic vision comprehensively and laid down the essential elements for their policies region by region. He went from issue to issue in an ostensibly random, but always purposeful, manner. And all this was done without a single note of his own, or prompting by Zhou, who once again was clearly deferential to his presence."[14]

To the author, Kissinger stressed that the November meeting had represented "the high point of our relationship,"[15] emphasizing the Chinese satisfaction at the pushing of the Soviets out of the Middle East.

This was, however, a view that would be strongly challenged later by Jung Chang and Jon Halliday in *Mao*,* from sources that were not always revealed. They saw Zhou as "a blackmailed slave, living in dread of untreated cancer and of being purged," and hidden "from outside eyes." To Mao's ambitions of world power, Kissinger in November 1973 had brought a "terminal blow." There had been no advance on the Taiwan issue, nor on full diplomatic recognition. Graver still for Mao, specifically "There were to be no U.S. nuclear weapons for China."[16] Here Kissinger consistently and adamantly denied that there had been any discussion whatsoever of any "deal" on nuclear weapons. It was "absolute nonsense," declared Kissinger to the author; the issue "was simply never discussed."[17] In the official report to Nixon, there was certainly no mention of the topic having been raised; and Kissinger's refutation was supported robustly by Winston Lord, his specialist on China who had accompanied him on almost all trips ("there was no mention whatsoever of nuclear warheads for China"), and by Ambassador Stapleton Roy, envoy to China in 1991–95 and fluent in Mandarin.[18] As regards the allegation that the opening to China had "cut loose" Taiwan, to the author Kissinger riposted "Some cutting loose. Here we are thirty-four years later . . ."[19] Winston Lord recalled that the November encounter had been a "good meeting," though not as positive as February 1973, while he agreed that by the following year "things had cooled off;"[20] with the eclipse of both Zhou and Mao, under Ford in 1975–76 the cooling off had become much more pronounced.† Yet none would agree with the assertion in *Mao* that the November meeting had closed the door to Mao's "Superpower Programme," or that "Ace schemer though he was, even he had reached the bottom of the barrel."[21]

What, however, was clear was Kissinger's disappointment that Mao's colossus would not help promote a settlement in Cambodia—which was so integral a cog in the machinery of "peace with honor" for

---

* Speaking to the author (10/28/05) Jonathan Spence, who had published a lengthy, and critical, review in *The New York Review of Books*, thought *Mao* flawed, and "strange—with absolutely no historical depth or understanding." Another reviewer, Andrew Nathan (*London Review of Books*, 11/17/05), feared that the authors' "white-hot fury" prevented them from creating an objective study of Mao. A monster, no doubt, but as demonized in the book, "How could a man like this win power!" asks Nathan.

† Both Zhou and Mao, semidisgraced, died in 1976.

Vietnam. Summing up on what in the longer term had been achieved by the opening to China, as Kissinger wrote to the author, Nixon and he had "set up a triangular relationship with Moscow, which contributed to breaking the Soviet back and winning the Cold War. China had achieved some reassurance against the forty-two Soviet divisions on its borders. I will let others decide who gained more. When an arrangement lasts thirty-five years, usually both sides gain something."[22] In his memoirs he would claim that greater things had been achieved: "We preserved the essence of a relationship crucial to world peace amidst the turmoil of the times and the stresses in both countries unrelated to our foreign policy design. Statesmen have often done much worse."[23]

Reinvigorated by his meeting with Mao, Kissinger finished his Asian trip in Japan. He was prepared to admit that, when he first came into office, "there was no major country I understood less than Japan." As with many Westerners, it did not engage his imagination. Not altogether unlike its Meiji forebears, the Japan of the 1970s was buried in self-interest, producing its cheap and reliable cars, its stunningly ingenious electronic ware, to perfect regeneration of its economy in a kind of intellectual isolation from the rest of the world. Kissinger did not in November 1973 come as a Pinkerton; instead he came by way of apologizing for not keeping the Japanese ally informed of negotiations with the traditional foe, China. U.S.-Japanese relations were not brilliant that year, suffering from much the same aches and pains as Europe—and, in addition, from the oil crisis which was about to envelop the world.

CHAPTER 15

TO GENEVA AND SHUTTLE

"Nothing so warms the heart of a professional diplomat as the imminence of a major conference."

—Henry Kissinger[1]

"I have never been in an Arab country and never had much dealings with them. I frankly thought I could get through my term of office and let someone else do it. To be honest. Now that I have started, I will finish it and with enthusiasm."

—Henry Kissinger, to Andrei Gromyko, in Geneva,
December 22, 1973

ONCE THE DUST of the Yom Kippur War had settled, the story of Kissinger and the Middle East for the rest of the year, and on into 1974, may lack the day-to-day high drama of the war. As Kissinger himself noted in *Crisis,* "Great events usually culminate not in great drama, but as a series of technical decisions."[3] The painstaking negotiations that preceded the setting up of the Geneva Peace Conference, the short-lived conference itself, Kissinger's frenetic two rounds of shuttle diplomacy, followed by a semblance of peace, are events that would hardly make the big screen; yet they were, conjointly, in terms of diplomatic breakthrough, of greater consequence for historians than the war itself. Historically speaking, was it to be a Peace of Westphalia,* which had ended the Thirty Years War in 1648?—or Versailles, which terminated the First World War in 1919 but which, after a bare generation of peace, proved only a prelude to an even more murderous conflict? For the Middle East, the jury may still be out. As the result of the Yom Kippur War, and the ensuing negotiations, the Soviet Union was excluded from the area. Through a process amounting more or less to nolo contendere, the European powers neutralized themselves. Kissinger could well regard the exclusion of the Kremlin—with all the grief, mischief, and menace that its hand in the Great Game had brought since the Suez Crisis in 1956—as one of his greatest triumphs. And it came without (at least apparently) any lasting damage to the doctrine of détente. Yet, at the same time, Kissinger was assuming for the United States the burden of responsibility for Israel, and peace in the region as a whole. Washington donned it willingly, consensually; then, as later leaders and U.S. governments replaced Nixon, progressively shirked the burden. Was it to prove a Shirt of Nessus?† Might historians one day parallel 9/11 with the poisoned shirt which had subjected the hero Hercules to such mortal torment?

Coolness in Japan on his November visit should have forewarned Kissinger, and it probably did, of what he would find among the NATO allies in Europe as he returned home. It would seem like a mixture of frostbite, and hot anger. He could blame the unpropitious initiative of the Year of Europe, and the sores which it had opened. Here he had, to an extent, also taken the blame upon himself. The Europeans—notably Britain—now had reasonable complaints that they had not been sufficiently consulted during the Yom Kippur War. The unilateral declaration of DEFCON 3 had particularly rankled. On the other hand, Kissinger could reply that the splits and divisions which

---

* Peace negotiations were held concurrently in the cities of Roman Catholic Münster and Protestant Osnabrück, about fifty kilometers apart. These two locations were necessary because the Protestant and Catholic leaders refused to meet each other. But it ended the religious wars which had ravaged Europe for many more than thirty years.

† Nessus, a centaur, attempted to rape Deianeira, the wife of Hercules, who shot him with a poisoned arrow. As he lay dying, Nessus persuaded Deianeira that his blood would ensure that Hercules would remain true to her forever. Trusting him, she spread it on a shirt and gave it to her husband. Hercules died in slow agony as the shirt burned into his skin.

Europe had revealed in a real crisis, such as war in the Middle East, proved his point about the need for a new look at NATO. Europe was not united, except possibly against the United States; which was just what the Year of Europe had been intended to counter.

There is an old Italian adage about the foolish blackbird, which at the close of January sings out: "I fear thee no more, O Lord—now that the winter is behind me." Meanwhile predators circle. Now, with memories of Prague 1968 five years behind them, could it be that to West Europeans détente had heavily reduced their fear of the Soviet Union? Would not a similar phenomenon present itself three decades later with NATO (notably France and Germany) reluctant to fight in Afghanistan?

By the end of 1973, the year, the Year of Europe, could be reckoned to have become the worst in memory for U.S.-European relations. Nixon was crippled by Watergate. Georges Pompidou of France was dying, in Germany, Willy Brandt—distracted by the urge to pursue unilaterally with the Soviets his own Ostpolitik—was sinking and would shortly be destroyed in May 1974 by a Stasi spy scandal, while in Britain Ted Heath, his blinkered gaze fixed on European union, would also disappear that year, his government weakened by labor crises. Personal relations between Heath and Nixon (and between Kissinger and Heath) had reached a nadir. For all the mutual respect between Kissinger and Sir Alec Douglas-Home, the Yom Kippur War had markedly widened the rift between the United States and Britain. As noted previously early on in the crisis Kissinger had accused Britain of "behaving badly" by not supporting U.S. cease-fire initiatives at the U.N.; "passively sitting there picking up the pieces." He warned Lord Cromer, the British ambassador, on the first day of the crisis, that it was "in the interest of everybody, including Western Europe, not to run across us"; later, on October 12, he accused the British of "dancing around," and threatening to veto any alternative British U.N. resolution. The following day, when Scowcroft had remarked, "I don't get the Brits. Why not tell them we are not going to give them any Poseidons or Polaris?" (missiles for British nuclear submarines), Kissinger had snapped back: "No, they're not going to get them anyway."[4]

He would fail to get the stubborn Brits to introduce a cease-fire in place resolution. Then, on October 26, after Cromer had expostulated that Nixon's outburst that day would "cause a lot of unhappiness" in Europe, Kissinger is on record as replying: "We have just about—the Europeans have to face the fact that the President is fed up." Menacingly in terms that recalled the words of his predecessor, John Foster Dulles, he followed up: "We might reach a point where on both sides of the Atlantic there will be a need to reassess U.S. relations."[5]* Back to Cromer: after he had refused to forward a message from Kissinger to London on the grounds that it "would cause enormous offense," on the 30th, Kissinger was charging the British of doing (according to the Egyptians) "astonishing things": such as recommending "that they didn't accept the Resolution on the Ceasefire." Cromer professed to find that "amazing."[6] At one point, such was his fury Kissinger was reported as exploding: "I don't care what happens to NATO. They can all go to hell as far as I am concerned."[7]

What had exacerbated anger in Washington in particular had been the refusal of Europe across the board, with the exception of bullied Portugal and the sturdy Netherlands (which was to suffer almost most of any from the Arab oil embargo), to permit flights with arms for Israel, or refueling, flyover rights. Turkey too had joined in refusing facilities, while Germany protested at shipments of NATO arms to Israel from Hamburg, with the ambassador in Washington complaining that its "credibility in the Arab world was at stake."[8] Britain in particular was the target of these reproaches. To his friend Lord Home, Kissinger complained, after the war was over, that the Soviet Union had been freer to use NATO's airspace than the United States, given that much of the Soviet airlift to the Middle East overflew allied airspace without challenge.[9] But even Home would add his criticism to the effect that U.S. leaders, over the years, had never paid enough attention to European views on the Middle East. To the Anglophile head of the State Department's North European affairs, William Buell, the rift "almost broke the Special Relationship."[10]

---

* In a conversation with Kissinger on November 3 (telcon), Nixon echoed the same theme: "Let's face it, we can't start having the Europeans, British, taking a . . . line on everything we try to do . . . so maybe we have to make an agonizing reappraisal of European views. We are saving their oil, after all, they need it more than we do." It was not a view European leaders would have applauded at the time.

On the British side, coupled with the *froideur* that harked back to the unhappy course of the negotiations over that ill-chosen Year of Europe earlier, there was a deep sense of resentment over the lack of consultation on the DEFCON 3 crisis. Heath himself, then chief whip to Harold Macmillan, could remember vividly how only nine years previously Kennedy had consulted Macmillan daily, if not more often, over the Cuban Missile Crisis. In the *New York Times*, he was reported as pointedly refusing to endorse the U.S. alert; while papers published from London's Public Relatives Office under the 30-year rule reprint a furious memorandum from Heath, all but accusing Nixon of diverting attention from Watergate. Then, also, because of Watergate, there was a keen sense, in Downing Street, that—given the state of vacuum at the top in Washington—little useful business could be done with an unreliable ally.[11] In his memoirs, Kissinger himself noted, in pain: "The reluctance of our allies to meet with the wounded President was palpable."[12]

Predictably, Kissinger's worst headaches came from Paris, where—with President Pompidou mortally ill—the contumelious Michel Jobert (described by Kissinger as the "impresario of elegant obfuscation") was in ascendance. During the Yom Kippur War, Jobert had castigated both Moscow and Washington for sending arms to the Middle East, adding nastily: "We see Mr. Brezhnev, the apostle of détente, and Dr. Kissinger, now a Nobel Peace Prize winner, shaking hands while sending thousands of tons of arms by air."[13] Jobert made it plain that France, though critical of the United States at every turn, would not come up with any coherent alternative solutions for peace in the Middle East; though none of this would impede France from calling for a common European policy. Kissinger noted a little wanly, thinking of Suez, how European frustration at now being a bystander where they had once been preeminent was compounded with its current dependence on the region's oil. Meanwhile, not letting the Year of Europe negotiations lie dormant, the wily Jobert proposed it should be deferred for a year: thereby Pompidou (i.e., Jobert) would assume the chair! Following the October alert Kissinger had had a "testy" conversation with France's ambassador to Washington, Jacques Kosciusko-Morizet—unsweetened by the fact that the United States had named a city after his famous Polish forebear. The ambassador criticized the "lack of consultation," either over the alert or the U.S. resolution at the Security Council. Kissinger fired back, saying "perhaps we should have told you," adding that in the crisis the Europeans "had behaved not as friends, but as hostile powers."[14]

That was tough talking. France followed up with a request that work on the long-pending NATO draft declaration be suspended as a sign of displeasure with Washington. On Kissinger's final visit to Pompidou in December,* the dying man had declared that France would play no role at the forthcoming conference in Geneva, "since it had been excluded by the Soviet Union and the United States."[15]

Kissinger remarked, with frustration, at the end of 1973 that, for whatever reason, "The unity of the industrial democracies to which we had dedicated so much effort had eluded us . . . Something deeper was involved than clashing tactical approaches."[16] Already, in mid-November Nixon had given voice to similar concerns in a special briefing to Senator Javits: "For the Europeans to go into business by themselves would be a disaster. We would be picked off one by one."[17] Toward the end of the year, Kissinger was noting—with mounting aggravation—how France and Germany, though eager to circumscribe U.S. freedom of action, were not prepared to pay "in the coin of a co-ordinated Western policy." A troubled American statesman of the twenty-first century, plunged once more into the dilemmas of the Middle East, but unable to persuade NATO troops to fight in Afghanistan, might well ask "What's new?" The "painful fact was" that, over the whole Yom Kippur War crisis, "not one of the European allies said anything in support."[18]

For America's allies, dependent as they were (unlike the United States) on Middle East oil, that was the source of anger overriding all others. In 1972, oil imports represented only 5 percent of the total energy requirements of the United States, whereas, for example, Japan had to import 90 percent of its oil from the Persian Gulf. They could accuse Nixon, and Kissinger, not unreasonably of having paid too little attention to their vital interests. Already at the end of the first week of the Yom Kippur War, on October 13 there had been a frosty con-

---

* He died the following April.

versation with Lord Cromer. After Kissinger had criticized the British lack of support over his first U.N. initiatives, and informed him that the airlift to Israel was starting, Cromer inquired: "What would be your posture vis-à-vis when the Arabs start screaming oil at you?"

In Churchillian tones, Kissinger had replied:

K: Defiance. . . .
C: Just defiance? It is going to be rough, won't it?
K: We have no choice.[19]

Already earlier in the year Arabists in the United States like Raymond Close* had been warning Washington that "under pressure from our Arab brothers"[20] King Faisal would use the oil weapon. No one had taken it seriously. Faisal however pledged Sadat (in August 1973): "We don't want to use our oil as a weapon in a battle which only goes on for two or three days and then stops. We want to see a battle which goes on for long enough time for the world public opinion to be mobilized." But (says Egyptian journalist Heikal) this fitted closely to what Sadat himself was thinking.[21]

Europe's dependence on oil had risen from 25 percent in 1950 to 60 percent—all of it imported. Twenty-five percent came from Libya. Throughout the 1960s consumers had been spoiled by a world glut of oil. But ever since Muammar al-Qaddafi took over, once Libya had broken the mold of regulated prices, things were changing. OPEC, the Organization of the Petroleum Exporting Countries, created in 1960, found it had new power. And oil and gas from the short-lived North Sea bonanza had yet to come onstream.

On October 7, the second day of the war, Nixon had begun voicing fears about oil. On the 16th, six Gulf states unilaterally raised the price of oil by 70 percent, from $3.01 to $5.12 (figures that might seem incredibly modest by 2008 standards of $130+ a barrel), without any consultation with consumers. Next day the Arab members of OPEC, meeting in Kuwait, agreed to cut production by 5 percent—and to continue reducing it by an additional 5 percent every month until Israel

---

* CIA station chief in Saudi Arabia.

withdrew from all occupied territories. Shortly thereafter, European leaders were stunned to learn that OPEC was simultaneously raising prices and cutting production. On the 18th, Saudi Arabia announced that it would exceed what had been agreed, cutting her immense production by 10 percent. On the 19th, on the eve of Kissinger's trip to Moscow, Nixon rashly and openly announced his request to Congress for the $2.2 billion package for military aid to Israel. One of Kissinger's own close advisers at the time, William Quandt, is sternly critical: "Had Nixon and Kissinger been more sensitive to these issues, they might have been more discreet in their handling of the $2.2 billion aid package to Israel, announcing it after the war was over rather than in the midst of battle."[22] In his memoirs, Kissinger too admits that the timing "could not have been more unfortunate."[23] Apparently not consulted, it would, he thought, have been much more prudent to have deferred the announcement until after the cease-fire. Promptly, the very next day, Saudi Arabia declared a total embargo on oil exports to the United States. Shortly thereafter OPEC extended the embargo to the Netherlands—the European government which had offered most support to U.S. policy, and where many of the biggest refineries were sited.

With her own vast domestic production, coupled with supplies from Western Hemisphere countries like Venezuela, the United States itself could—for the foreseeable future—shrug off the Arab measures. But to Europe, the pain was immediate, the long-term threat incalculable. Combined, the Middle East oil cuts dramatically upset the world oil market. Europe, which felt itself to be a mere bystander in the Yom Kippur War, was outraged at the apparent insouciance with which the United States had embroiled the European countries in this calamity, and there were more urgent calls for a cease-fire. Relations had seldom been more strained. On October 26, Kissinger delivered a strong, stiffening warning in person to the West German ambassador, Berndt von Staden, to the effect that "not only will European capitulation to the Arabs not result in their ensuring their oil supply, but it can have disastrous consequences vis-à-vis the Soviet Union." The Soviets could be expected "to mount even more aggressive policies elsewhere."[24]

That same afternoon Kissinger met a group of powerful oil company bosses, who warned him that the embargo could produce "a real disaster" and a "possible breakdown of the economy"; by the end of the year the supply problem could become "catastrophic" for the United States too. He told them the European performance "has been incredible to me. It is suicidal. . . . The idea that 10 million Arabs can hold up and blackmail Europe notwithstanding its military, economic and financial strength should be intolerable from the point of view of the Europeans themselves."[25]

Asking them to "tell your Arab friends that we are serious about trying to achieve a peace settlement but that they have to make an effort," he saw that "building a bridge" to King Faisal was the key.[26] Robert McCloskey, the State Department spokesman, was instructed, inelegantly, to tell journalists that "We were struck by a number of our allies going to some lengths to in effect separate publicly from us." Kissinger was irritated in the extreme by European assumptions that the United States "had the power to force Israel to do our bidding," while coming up with no efforts themselves. At the same time, they seemed unaware "that their rhetoric tended to strengthen the radical Arabs over the moderate ones . . . and enhance Soviet influence over both." He fumed, questioning what the point was of "an alliance for whose vitality partners are not prepared to curtail their freedom of action."[27] It all harked back to the futile wrestling earlier over the Year of Europe, where the allies had employed every excuse to evade action. All his fears—with which he had launched into the Year of Europe—of what might happen if the West did not revitalize its defenses, and unite to meet fresh challenges, now seemed to be coming home to roost. But it was not, as anticipated, from the Soviet bloc that that challenge came, but from the Muslim world—an unforeseen quarter—as it would so devastatingly three decades later.

Meanwhile Europe was confronted with the prospect of a cold, energyless winter—and the menace of economic disaster. Wrote Kissinger, recalling the bitterness of the moment, "Oil combined with conviction to drive Europe into ever-sharper opposition to our Middle East strategy."[28] Anxiety was shared in the Kremlin too, where Kosygin on his return from his discouraging trip to Cairo expressed fears that the moment the Arabs started to use oil as a political weapon, a NATO military force would "descend on the Middle East,"[29] though his fears proved wrong. Indeed neither NATO nor the United States alone had the intention, or the means, with which to "descend," as has been seen. Nevertheless, disquiet lingered in Moscow that the Arab oil embargo could complicate, and broaden the Middle East conflict.

After his speech to the Pilgrims, a British-American society, in December, Kissinger left London with the lonely sense of having now to pursue the Middle East peace process unilaterally. About all that was agreed was the need to hold a multilateral energy conference.

Meanwhile he was preparing the approach march for the Geneva Peace Conference. His former staffer, William Quandt, who saw him in action, analyzed his technique as being the "ability to break issues into manageable pieces that can then be imaginatively recombined into viable agreements. Mastery of details is essential to success as a sense of context and nuance." He came to believe that Kissinger's "practical skills as a negotiator and mediator were unsurpassed . . . his originality, his sense of timing, his intelligence, and even his personality served him especially well."[30] Kissinger had seen how all-embracing, all-enveloping schemes for peace in the Middle East, like those of Gunnar Jarring and William Rogers before him, always seemed doomed to failure. Instead, he would tackle it piece by piece, small bites at a time. This would require endless painstaking, patient, meticulous negotiation—all the time fighting against the mountains of Israeli insecurity, and opposed by stored-up hatreds and mistrust on the Arab side. Rushing from capital to capital at breathtaking speed suited his temperament. In fact, he positively thrived on it. He seemed to love flying (and, indeed, does to this day). On the 1974 shuttles the accompanying press corps, battle-fatigued and possibly a little awestruck, ran up a poster for him, which with pride he hangs in his study at Kent, Connecticut:

I AM HENRY, FLY ME TO DAMASCUS.

Kissinger describes from one of his subsequent shuttles how his airborne State Department–cum–National Security Council functioned aboard a special Air Force Boeing 707 (formerly used as Air Force One). By the entrance was a large electronic console manned by two sergeants, a hub of communications which could connect with any part of the world in minutes by a system of coded Teletype—state-of-the-art in those days. Through it he could send and receive all messages to and from his ground staff and the White House. An enormous volume of traffic poured in, to be processed by his hard-pressed staff. Farther back, the plane was divided into four compartments; the first, Kissinger's own personal area, consisting of two sofas which made up into beds; opposite them were a fold-out table and two easy chairs. Here the secretary worked, read, and napped (rather than slept). Next came a conference room, with a patented table that had a hydraulic technique all its own, whereby an unwary neophyte might find himself trapped between a rising chair and a descending table. Here, when the compartment was not in use, exhausted staffers would sometimes stretch out on the floor. Farther back was a working area for his senior staff, and one small table for an electric typewriter (again, state-of-the-art). Here Joseph Sisco reigned. Finally came the section which Kissinger described as "the most fun." About ten rows of first-class seats housed the traveling press corps of fourteen or fifteen handpicked journalists, representing the key U.S. media; as the shuttles progressed, Kissinger liked to think that his "journalistic companions developed a vested interest in a successful outcome." [31] On the whole, harmony reigned.

Hal Saunders,* who accompanied all the Middle East missions from the end of October, described for me some of the problems of the airborne team: "There were three to four of us on the shuttles; at Cairo there was [Joe] Sisco, [Roy] Atherton, and me (Henry, in his mind, fired Joe once a day!). It was a most powerful process—all very grueling, rigorous—disciplined—power that you could feel in your gut, in the best sense of the word . . . a hugely exciting novelty, it had never been done before." In contrast, he recalled the equipment as being "antediluvian": "On the plane there was one typewriter, one primitive Xerox. HK would then come out and tell the typist 'change that, change this'—but when the plane landed with a tilt, the old Xerox ink would run to one side and only half the page would be printed. The typists were exhausted—but I'd say 'Remember, we've never done this before!'" Kissinger himself was "indefatigable." His strategy had three simple points: "to put the U.S. in charge; get the embargo lifted; get the Europeans off our backs! All of this was powerfully articulated by Henry." (Saunders had spent eight years working with him; it was "a

---

* Saunders later became an assistant secretary in the Carter administration, participating in the Camp David negotiations.

marvelously formative experience — despite the occasionally very emotional outburst. His staff was one of the very best.")[32]

Strictly speaking, Kissinger's two famous series of shuttle trips took place, after Geneva, in early 1974. However, in effect, paving the way for Geneva required a preliminary shuttle — or at least a scamper around Middle East capitals. He would have to take in seven countries in four days — culminating with three in the same day. Each revision of text had to be laboriously transmitted, and retransmitted, to his airborne office — wherever it might be. December 16 was fixed as "G-Day." It was soon to prove an ambitious target. With some cynicism, Kissinger remarks in his memoirs, "Nothing so warms the heart of a professional diplomat as the imminence of a major conference."[33] That may be, but it little took into account hesitations and animadversions on the part of the participants. Israel, facing elections in a matter of days, was having difficulties with the amount of territory it would be willing to give up. Golda Meir was determined that the PLO should be barred from the Geneva talks. There were difficulties in getting her to agree to attend the Geneva conference at all. At the end of November an Arab summit had injected fresh tensions into the scene. Meanwhile there lurked the ever-present danger that the cease-fire, fragile as it was, might disintegrate into shooting. There were constant worries that if the Third Army ran out of supplies, Sadat would be compelled to reopen the battle. He had largely reequipped his tank forces from Soviet supplies; revisionist Egyptian historians writing after the event would claim that it was not the Egyptian Third Army on the east bank of the canal, but the encircling Israelis on the west bank who were most at danger — should Sadat resume the offensive. There were signs that he was becoming increasingly impatient. Kissinger admits that he never knew exactly what was going on at Kilometer 101, except that the delegates from the opposing armies were arguing over a matter of a few yards of desert. So he had to act swiftly, and forcefully.

On December 13, he set off again for the Middle East. The Geneva conference was due to begin in five days' time, and there was still no agreement on an agenda. Kissinger's main task, as always, was to create trust where none had existed. As agreed with Sadat, following the

Geneva conference, U.S. policy would concentrate on completion of disengagement in Sinai. His first host was that master of mistrust, the gaunt and rather sinister conqueror of de Gaulle's France, President Houari Boumédienne of Algeria, in whose court much of the preliminary impetus for the Yom Kippur War had evolved—not to mention the hotting up of the oil war subsequently. Kissinger was greeted by drizzling weather, supplemented by an "aloof" welcome. Previously his knowledge of the huge country had been limited to his admiration for Albert Camus, the great French Pied-Noir writer. As perhaps a deliberate tease, Boumédienne offered the American team (which comprised Assistant Secretary Joseph Sisco and Peter Rodman; Boumédienne was accompanied by Foreign Secretary Abdelaziz Bouteflika*) superlative Havana cigars, presented by Castro, and—of course—forbidden in America. Later Kissinger was informed that Boumédienne, a ramrod-straight figure with piercing eyes, clad in a somber black cloak, timed meetings in terms of cigars consumed; rarely were there three-cigar meetings—but this one lasted for two hours. (Rodman noted, with some awe, the large number of fat Havanas that had been laid out in anticipation.[34]) The Algerian president greeted Kissinger reassuringly, remarking (in case Kissinger had not appreciated this) that the Middle East was a "region of passion. Great problems and great passions."

Somewhat incongruously, he then launched into a discussion on Chile and Allende (in whose memory one of the main squares in Algiers was renamed). Boumédienne described his fellow revolutionary Allende as "a troubling case." Kissinger replied: "I tell you frankly that Allende faced an objectively complex situation. He wanted to make revolution, but he had no discipline, too many scruples, and too much inefficiency. We did not do anything to overthrow him." He continued, switching fronts, "I told your foreign minister that as a professor I wanted to make a study of revolution. This is why I am fascinated by Algeria. Seriously, I am fascinated by how revolutions start with inferior strength and how they convert psychological superiority into mil-

---

* On Kissinger's earlier visit to the Maghreb, Boumédienne had been absent, drumming up support for Egypt in Moscow and the other Arab capitals.

itary superiority. In your case you analyzed correctly that you were
bound to win if you did not lose. . . .

"President Boumédienne: Exactly . . .

"Secretary Kissinger: Therefore you didn't try to win in any normal sense. But for this you need great discipline. This was Allende's
difficulty.

"President Boumédienne: Perhaps we do give the Americans too
much credit!"

Kissinger repeated: "We did nothing to help him. We did not stop
his suicide."

After this rather unexpected detour to a far-off country, Boumédienne brought the focus sharply back to Soviet influence in the Middle
East, asking Kissinger: "Do you think the Soviet Union would fight
for the Arabs."

"Kissinger: No."

"Boumédienne: I don't think so." [35]

Kissinger followed up by stating that the United States wanted neither a "Soviet sphere" nor an American sphere in the Middle East, then
moved on to attack vigorously the Arab oil nations who wanted U.S.
help, but at the same time were striking at supplies.

In his report to the president Kissinger described Boumédienne as
"an impressive man, reflective and intelligent . . . he spoke very frankly
of his misgivings about whether an 'American Peace' in the Middle
East could be a just one. He thought American policy was still charac-
terized by 'the big stick.' " Kissinger, in reply, had "explained that we
were no longer trying to act as a world policeman but had to maintain
our interests and commitments even while we changed our style." [36]
He left Boumédienne feeling encouraged that Algeria, with its revolutionary stature in the Third World, would be supportive in his Geneva
strategy.

So what did Kissinger want from Boumédienne? Probably no
more than support of a man disillusioned by Soviet duplicity as witnessed during the Algerian War.

Flying back into Cairo, Kissinger noted the city was still blacked
out—a constant reminder that the front line was only 101 kilometers
distant. Underscoring this, Sadat expressed a certain impatience—
hinting that if there was no progress, he might be driven to war again,

and back into the arms of the Soviets. "You hold all the cards here," he constantly repeated to Kissinger. Meanwhile, the very day he arrived in Cairo, Nixon launched a bombshell—much as he had when Kissinger had been en route to Moscow in November. In Washington the courts were closing in ever more menacingly; there was now a furor over the missing eighteen-and-a-half minutes of tapes that had been discovered. (Kissinger still remained convinced that Nixon was in "very real ignorance"[37] of what was actually in the tapes.) As a display of reasserting his authority, Nixon suddenly summoned the Soviet ambassador for a private meeting—to talk specifically about the Middle East. Scowcroft reported to Kissinger that it had lasted half an hour, and Dobrynin had said it was one of the most satisfactory meetings with the president that he had ever had. In Cairo, Kissinger exploded; it was an extraordinary event, and "no laughing matter to have the White House announce what could only be construed as a Presidential move to strengthen our Soviet ties on the same day that Sadat had informed me that he planned to end the Soviet-Egyptian Friendship Treaty."[38] Kissinger sent back a string of angry cables; Scowcroft replied, emolliently, that it might have been worse: Haig and he had at least managed to head off a similar interview Nixon had scheduled with the Saudi ambassador.

Kissinger went on with the quest for peace, putting to Sadat the concept arrived at Kilometer 101, whereby a thinned-out Egyptian force could remain on the east side of the canal, while the Israelis would withdraw to the line of the Mitla Pass in the Sinai, a distance of some twenty miles. He left Cairo in a "buoyant" mood. Pieces for the Geneva conference were at last falling into place; and Sadat had promised to press for lifting of the Saudi oil embargo.

Moving on to Riyadh, he found the king more willing than on his November trip to modify his views on the Palestinian issue. Kissinger had been preceded by a friendly-tough personal letter from Nixon to Faisal. It started, on an almost apologetic note: "You have always given me wise counsel, and in retrospect your advice was well taken and should have been heeded. . . . Because of the far-sighted and statesman-like approach of responsible leaders in the Arab world, in particular President Sadat, we are on the verge of a peace conference which holds out greater hope for the future prosperity and stability of the Middle East than at any time in the past 25 years. This conference must not fail."

Nixon sharpened to the point, stating that Americans even understood how, "in the heat of the recent war, the need to demonstrate solidarity with your Arab compatriots led Your Majesty to institute certain measures with respect to the production and supply of oil . . . We are now in a new phase, however, and I must tell Your Majesty frankly of my concern that the American people will not understand the continuation of these measures while their Government is making a major and difficult effort over the weeks and months ahead to promote the just peace that the Arab world seeks . . . an atmosphere of growing confrontation would only work to our mutual disadvantage and to the benefit of those who wish to maintain the status quo." In other words, remove the oil embargo—or else no peace conference. Referring to implementation of Resolutions 242 and 338, in his own handwriting, Nixon had scribbled in: "You have my *total personal* commitment to work towards this goal."[39]

While Kissinger was in Riyadh, another blow descended; this time, once again, from Israel, now on the verge of elections. The draft invitation to Geneva had been rejected by the cabinet; "no reference to the Palestinians, no matter how conditional, would be accepted." It threatened "to blow up everything."[40] Kissinger had no choice but to postpone the conference by three days, to December 21.

From Riyadh, Kissinger then flew to Damascus for a first encounter with Asad—the steely dictator of Syria who had been in office for over eleven years. It would be the first visit by an American secretary of state in twenty years—since the days of John Foster Dulles.* Kissinger designated Syria as "a country with a long tradition and a short history." Both denoted unrelenting opposition to the state of Israel. He was to have a six-and-a-half-hour conversation with Asad. "Flashing dark eyes and a moustache dominated an expressive face. The rear of his head seemed to rise straight from his neck, creating the impression that the Syrian President was always leaning forward ready

---

* U.S.-Syrian relations were severed in 1967, but resumed in June 1974, following the fruition of Kissinger's Syrian-Israeli disengagement agreement.

to pounce on an unwary interlocutor." Over the course of the lengthy conversation, to his surprise Kissinger found himself developing a "high regard" for the rigid Syrian dictator; far from being "a Soviet stooge. He had a first-class mind allied to a wicked sense of humor."[41] Asad had had little or no contact with Western statesmen, and appeared to be learning English as he spoke. Kissinger risked teasing him that he might become the only Arab leader to speak English with a German accent; then opened the conversation with an extraordinarily candid exposé of America's dilemmas: "We are the only country that can bring about political progress without war. You are right in pointing out we have supported Israel. That is true. Candidly, there are strong domestic pressures in the U.S. in favor of support of Israel. We have to manage our domestic situation if we are to be helpful. Don't put us in a position where we have to take final positions, when what is required are first steps. People say if you can't get Israel to go back to the October 22 positions, you cannot do anything. If I had been stupid, I could have achieved this. That's not a problem. For me to waste capital, to waste ammunition on this would not make sense, what is a few kilometers? Pressure on Israel must be for a bigger withdrawal." As he would discover in subsequent shuttling, "a few kilometers" would prove to be in excess of what it was all about. Pressing the importance of the Geneva Peace Conference, Kissinger insisted "a peace conference provides a legal front within which negotiating activity can go on. Real solutions will occur outside the conference. We must plan it as you make military campaigns." As Kissinger paused for breath, Asad asked if it was his turn to speak, then remarked, without apparent asperity, that "as a professor you have spoken for fifty minutes. The President was an officer and officers are brief."[42] He then unrolled a map of the Golan Heights, stressing what a small area it was. Kissinger declined to draw any lines, at this stage.

In his report to Nixon that day, he reckoned the talks had given him "an insight into Syrian character and shrewdness . . . the toughest and least conciliatory Arab leader I have met. . . . I got some insight into the Syrian relationship to the Soviets. It did not give an impression that there has been much close contact between the two of them with respect to preparations for the peace conference, and he seems anxious to have direct contact with us . . . but it is clear that the Syrians will be hard to deal with." Depressingly little would change over the next three decades, yet nothing Asad said suggested he would not support the conference: as Kissinger saw it what Asad really wanted to know "was not the procedures but the outcome."[43] It was with relief that, at the end of the marathon conversation (the accompanying press corps were beginning to wonder whether the secretary of state had been kidnapped), Kissinger gleaned that Syria would not take its seat at the Geneva Conference—but on the other hand would not sabotage it.

Leaving Damascus, Kissinger flew on his shortest haul, to confer briefly with King Hussein, across the tumbling Yarmouk River in Amman, Jordan. It was a "soothing" respite to be in a friendly camp with a ruler who "did not threaten us with dire consequences,"[44] or invoke the oil weapon (Jordan had none). From there he went on to Beirut, capital of the small, prosperous and beautiful state of Lebanon where—as yet unravaged by internecine strife—the two principal religious communities coexisted happily. But the PLO, having set up its base there, was shortly to begin tearing it apart.

At last, on Sunday evening, December 16, Kissinger reached Israel, his third country that day, his seventh on his four-day canter round the Middle East. Here, as ever, lay the crunch. On the 17th, he reported to the president. "There remains one outstanding issue yet to be resolved; if it is not, the conference could be stillborn. The Israelis are determined not to sit down or negotiate with the Syrians until they receive, at minimum, a list of PoWs now held by Damascus." Golda was forthright about "disengagement." "It really means we will have come out of the war by pulling back. That's what it really is, if you call it by its right name. Just pulling back, that's what it is."[45] With what Kissinger described as "a seemingly endless capacity for self-flagellation," by 1 A.M. that night the Israeli cabinet finally gave its approval for the Geneva process to go ahead. To Kissinger it meant that now "A disengagement agreement between Israel and Egypt seemed within reach. . . . We were at last at the starting gate. It remained to be seen whether we knew how to run the race."[46]

That night his "weary staff" filed a long summary of his trip for Nixon: at Geneva, "Egypt, Jordan, and Israel will participate. Syria, historically the great spoiler of the Mid East, has decided for the time being to stay away." Kissinger regarded this as "a blessing in disguise . . . we should let Asad stew in his own juice for a while and let moderate Arab pressures and possibly some Soviet pressure build on him. . . . As I look ahead, I believe there is a real chance of an Egyptian-Israeli agreement on disengagement. . . . As for Israel, the reality of their situation is beginning to sink in. If Mrs. Meir's Labor Party wins sufficient support, at least the door is open. Israel finds itself unable to afford another attritional war, and at the same time unable to score an overwhelmingly decisive victory. They are beginning to see this very unpleasant fact." [47]

While on his short trip to Jerusalem, Kissinger found time to make a visit to Yad Vashem, Israel's poignant memorial to the Holocaust. He went alone, barring the press from accompanying him. In his memoirs he described it as "a moment of solitary reflection upon my own past, the pitilessness of history, and the human stakes in the exertions of statesmen." He would undoubtedly have been mindful not only of the members of his German family who had been swept up in the Holocaust, but also, once more, of the immense responsibility devolving upon him as America's first Jewish secretary of state—and currently its most powerful. The pilgrimage was also intended "as a reassurance to the people of Israel that I understood and would respect their fears in a process of peacemaking that was simultaneously inescapable, full of hope, and wrenchingly painful." [48] At about this time, his close associate Hal Saunders awarded him "very high marks" for the dispassionate neutrality he displayed in Israel. While Saunders had seen intelligence reports to the effect that Arabs were saying " 'Who better than a Jewish Secretary of State to move Israel?,' I *never* once saw him make a decision on Israel *because* he was Jewish." (Saunders also recalled a very emotional statement made to Israeli hawks on the breakdown of talks in 1975, which was illustrative of Kissinger's frustration with the Israeli lack of a worldview: "You make me rather fear the future of my son as a Jew in America.") [49] Not everyone in Jerusalem, however, was pleased to see the peacemaker. Extreme nationalists brandished odious, and brutally hurtful, placards of "JEW BOY GO HOME." [50] Kissinger made a point of not looking out the window of his car, but would certainly have been deeply offended.

• • •

With all the chips seemingly at last in place, Kissinger set off to Europe. En route for Geneva and the delayed conference, he stopped over briefly in Lisbon—to show appreciation for Portugal's help, almost unique in Europe, during the airlift to Israel—and then Paris. There he had one last, disagreeable, session with Ducky Le Duc Tho, just a year since North Vietnam had capitulated under the Christmas Bombing. It was an unprofitable meeting. Ducky was becoming "more unbearably insolent as America's domestic divisions gradually opened up new and decisive strategic opportunities for Hanoi." Since Congress had, that summer, effectively removed all possible avenues of aid to South Vietnam, the North was cheating with impunity right along the line. It seemed only a matter of time before a new all-out offensive would be unleashed on America's allies in the South. Kissinger had time to file a quick memcon to Nixon, which—in the light of subsequent events—reads as excessive, even unfounded, optimism: "The main significance of the meeting was that they have completely dropped their political demands against the GVN [Thieu's government in Saigon] . . . the meeting I believe was significant for this reason alone. They have unmistakably abandoned any expectation of gaining politically in South Vietnam . . . it is clear that they are even weaker than I believed . . . the NVA [North Vietnamese] got nowhere in a series of military attacks in November, and it is the GVN that has been gaining territorially in the prolonged fighting." [51]

During his stay in Paris Kissinger also called in at the Elysée to brief President Pompidou. He found him enclosed in the irritability of a very sick man, having in his illness "to strain to the utmost to maintain his customary calm and courtesy in the face of the exclusion of France from the proceedings" at Geneva, though it was, in effect, an act of self-exclusion. Kissinger continued: "I understood this proud man's attitude. On the other hand, there was not a single controversial Mideast issue—and precious few in other areas—on which France had taken our side in recent months." [52] Still pursuing the goal of a kind of Versailles-style grand settlement in the Middle East, France's attitude remained unhelpful to the strategy of limited goals which Kissinger deemed attainable. It did not diverge greatly from that of America's other European allies. While in Paris Kissinger also called on his old bête noir, Michel Jobert, at the Quai d'Orsay. With the heavy irony that passed for humor, Jobert greeted him: "Well, how do you feel after being one-and-a-half hours among your *real* friends?" Kissinger riposted suitably: "We want a strong France. Even as difficult as you are. It is better that you are strong."[53]

On that flying visit (was there ever an envoy who could cram more into his day?) Kissinger also managed to have a meeting with Bouteflika of Algeria, affirming his country's goodwill. The conversation is diverting as an example of the kind of discreet clandestinity existing *in perpetuo* between Kissinger and his foreign opposite numbers. The fact that they had met, said Kissinger, "we won't announce it, but if someone asks me we won't lie about it."

"Bouteflika: You can say we decided on it in Algiers, to meet before you went to Geneva.

"Kissinger: Perhaps we should announce it. When we want to do it secretly, we can arrange it secretly. The worst is to attempt to be secret and have it come out.

"Bouteflika: . . . We won't say where we met."[54]

The two might almost have been clandestine lovers, fixing a rendezvous at some louche hotel on the Left Bank!

Four days before Christmas 1973, the peace conference finally sat down. For all the modesty of its ambitions, Kissinger fervently hoped "with all my heart that it would mark the beginning of a process worthy of the suffering that had led to it and justifying the arduous exertion of the months just past." Certainly no human being could have put more effort into its preparation than Kissinger himself. Arriving at the Geneva airport, he addressed the world media in a buoyant mood; awaiting him was a generous message from the president, expressing his "respect and the gratitude of the American people for your crucial role in this great enterprise."[55] That night he dined with another old sparring partner, Andrei Gromyko. He confided to him (as taken down by Peter Rodman, who was present): "This is just for you: I have complained officially to the French for their behavior on the Middle East." Gromyko's response was: "Jobert never misses any forum to throw his arrows at us."*[56] Apart from this demonstration of solidar-

---

* In Rodman's notes: "The group then moved to the dining room for luncheon. The main topics of conversation over lunch were eating, drinking, and hunting."

ity at the expense of the absent French, it was difficult for Kissinger to avoid a triumphant note creeping into his voice; largely through the Kremlin's own flaccid ineptitude, it must have grieved the heart of such a seasoned diplomat to see the Soviets now so marginalized in Middle East affairs. But Gromyko had one last throw; he objected to the seating arrangements, suggesting instead that the USSR, and their former clients, Egypt and Syria, be placed on the right of the chairman, Kurt Waldheim of the United Nations, with the United States, Israel, and Jordan seated adroitly on the left. This would have displayed the Soviet Union as the champion of the Arabs, with Jordan out of the fold.

There is little diplomats love more than fussing about the shape of the table at conferences; but on this occasion Kissinger feared that all might have been lost—at the eleventh hour. Ambassador Dinitz's recollection of the episode was that it was "the only conference I know that took three months to prepare and only one day to hold—and even half of that one day was spent on the arrangement of the table. . . . We came here in the morning, each found a seat, and we sat. . . . A whole half day was spent arranging how the Israeli delegation wouldn't be seated between the Syrians and the Egyptians."[57] Waldheim proffered the simple solution of an alphabetical placement; but this too ran into difficulties. Finally a nimble-minded Israeli came up with the idea of a seven-sided table—whereby the United States sat between Egypt and Jordan, with the Soviet Union winding up between Israel and the empty Syrian seat. It was, indeed, as Kissinger dubbed it, a "Solomonic solution," played out on a chessboard.

After all that, the conference—like some rare bloom in the jungle—lasted just one day. But that was all Kissinger needed. Kissinger's first report to the White House read: "Your* strategy is working well. We are the only participant who is in close touch with all the parties, the only power that can produce progress, and the only one that each is coming to in order to make that progress." In his opener to the conference, Kissinger declared: "When the history of our era is written, we will speak not of a series of Arab/Israeli wars, but of one war broken by periods of uneasy armistices and temporary ceasefires . . . from

---

* Note the deferential "your."

two recent trips through the Middle East I have the impression that people on both sides have had enough of bloodshed . . . no military point remains to be made." He continued on an almost Churchillian note: "I cannot promise success, but I can promise dedication. I cannot guarantee a smooth journey towards our goal. I can assure you of an unswerving quest for justice."

That day was indeed, as he signaled the president, "a historic development, the first time the Arabs and the Israelis will negotiate face to face in a quarter of a century."[58] It was in its way, as Kissinger recalled in his memoirs, something of a "bizarre peace conference," in which "the public positions of the contending parties had on the whole to be seen as a counterpoint to what they were actually doing. The belligerence of the oratory was in direct relation to the conciliatoriness of the policy."[59] What was remarkable about the Geneva conference was that it happened at all. For the first time Arabs and Israelis sat around the same table. Nobody walked out, and all agreed with Kissinger's step-by-step strategy. It was the end of an American nightmare during the Yom Kippur War that Soviet arms, coupled with Soviet influence, might have triumphed in the Middle East—together with radicalism in the Arab states as panic in Israel mounted. Kissinger could well look on Geneva as a remarkable success—given particularly that it had been brought to fruition in the midst of Watergate, as White House authority was "draining away daily." He could justly regard it as a vindication of his policy, as well as the "door to peace through which later Egypt and Israel walked."[60] But not even the architect himself could have foreseen just how many years the walk would take—let alone the fearsome and murderous deserts into which it would wander. Immediately, however, in the first months of 1974 it would lead to his two famous expeditions of shuttle diplomacy between Egypt and Israel, and Israel and Syria.

CHAPTER 16

THE AWFUL GRACE OF GOD[1]

"Was there *anything* good about 1973? . . . A lousy year, and good
riddance to it."

—Jonathan Yardley[2]

"I think the airplane is God's punishment to mankind."
"No," replied Khaddam simply: "America is."

—Ambassador Richard Murphy, speaking to
Syrian Foreign Minister Abd al-Halim Khaddam[3]

"Détente is the mitigation of conflict among adversaries, not the
cultivation of friendship."

—Henry Kissinger[4]

I T WAS CHRISTMAS 1973, though a rather muted festive season
in Washington, D.C. The usual plethora of potted poinsettias
was somewhat reduced, because of greenhouse problems. On
White House instructions, the lights on the traditional tree had been
dimmed, to conform with provisions taken to meet the fuel crisis.
There was to be a national speed limit of 55 mph; a 25 percent reduction in jet fuel; a cut of 15 percent in heating oil for homes and 25
percent for business. The dimming of the Washington tree seemed

symbolic. Inside the White House the president lurked, beleaguered and miserable, like a Titan of yore, defiant but challenged. The wagons had been circled, but with the enemy closing in, the perimeter was getting ever smaller as the loyal were fired, or defected. Even Nixon by now must have known that his days were numbered. All depended on those elusive tapes, which the Supreme Court was now demanding, in totality.* Now a new front had been opened with the Internal Revenue Service asking questions about the president's taxes. Earlier in the month, the newly appointed vice president, Gerald Ford, had won the nation's heart with his gracious modesty, when he declared: "I am a Ford, not a Lincoln." Kissinger duly rang him to say "how moved I was by your speech." Ford, a man of simple words, told him it was "awful damn nice" of him to call; he added "It's pretty hard for me—I got emotional."[5] In nine months he would be president.

In sharp contrast to the previous election year, Nixon's own Gallup poll rating had slumped by 39 points, from its high of just a year ago, to 29 percent, the steepest decline since the poll had first started back in the 90s.† Even his good friend Senator Barry Goldwater told the *Christian Science Monitor* on December 19, "I have never known a man to be so much a loner in any field."[6]

At a Christmas dinner at the White House, Goldwater found that "His mind seemed to halt abruptly and wander aimlessly away—as if he were a tape with unexpected blank sections." Goldwater wondered if "the President was coming apart."[7] Pat Nixon, perhaps to liven up proceedings and distract her husband, faithfully criticized Kissinger for taking too much of the credit for her husband's foreign policy successes. Nixon reacted strongly, insisting that the initiatives to China and Russia had been his. He seemed, once more, to show signs of heavy drinking. After Christmas, the Nixons took off to San Clemente—which he had just decided to give to the ungrateful na-

---

* Commented his biographer, Stephen Ambrose, "His fate resided in the tapes, the tapes he had once counted on for his salvation. If he could hold on to them, he might survive. If he lost control, he was doomed" (*Nixon*, vol. 2, p. 288).

† Comparable to figures of President George W. Bush, between April and September 2007.

tion.* The trip was not a success; there was an unusual cold snap in California, and—in conformity with the rest of the nation—La Casa Pacifica was unheated. Late on New Year's Eve, he scribbled on his bedside notepad: "The basic question is: Do I fight all out or do I now begin the long process to prepare for a change, meaning, in effect, resignation." Predictably, Bebe Rebozo told him "You have to fight." Constantly reminded of his mother's deathbed words, "Don't let anybody tell you you are through!," Nixon began the new year pledging to the press "I am going to fight like hell."[8]

Meanwhile, the fighting in Vietnam had reached levels not seen since the signature of the peace accords the previous January. In the Middle East, the armistice was barely holding. In Israel, Golda Meir's Labor Party won the elections, and with only a 5 percent reduction in her vote. But she had been savagely mauled for Israel's unpreparedness less than three months previously. She would resign in three months' time, acceding to what she deemed as "the will of the people." She would be succeeded by Kissinger's good friend, and former ambassador to Washington, Yitzhak Rabin. As a consequence of the Yom Kippur War, Japan and Europe were howling with pain at the fuel shortage. The day after Christmas Nixon called in the Soviet ambassador, to confide, apologetically:

"Maybe we made a mistake in October."

"Maybe you did."

Perhaps rather undiplomatically, Dobrynin praised Kissinger for "bringing the parties [in the Middle East] together." Nixon then declared, in almost biblical terms: "I will deliver the Israelis. . . . It will be done."[9]

Returning from Geneva, spent with exhaustion, Kissinger passed the Christmas break quietly in Washington, having his hair cut, visiting the doctor, reporting to Nixon, conferring with Haig, Scowcroft, and other members of his entourage, and receiving a galaxy of ambassadors. His children, David and Elizabeth, came down to see him. On the 27th, he held a press conference about the Middle East situation, followed by a convocation of U.S. Jewish leaders. That evening Len

---

* In fact, six years later he would sell it for a hefty profit.

Garment, the White House insider, who had first tipped him off about the full significance of Watergate eight months previously, rang to compliment him on his performance that day, at the same time teasing Kissinger about the paintings in his office. It was coupled with a back-hander about his "abstract" style of operation.

> G: Henry, I think you ought to get those modern paintings out of your office. That abstraction is too much—evocative of your style.
>
> K: Not evocative of my style?
>
> G: No—evocative of your style. I think you ought to put in some Beaunards [sic—Bonnards?] and move to the Impressionists.

Defending his "style," Kissinger continued:

> K: . . . Well, you know I may fail, but so far we've gotten more than the situation permits.
>
> G: I can sense that.
>
> K: I think the Israelis have suddenly begun to realize. So—you don't like these paintings.
>
> G: I'm sick of modern art. It's symptomatic of the decline and fall of everything. You're a classical man with a classical style.
>
> K: Well, I happen to like it.
>
> G: I understand. I won't complain in the future.

On New Year's Eve Kissinger joined the president at San Clemente. He took New Year's Day off, and on the 2nd breakfasted with a group of journalists. The following night he was back in Washington, for the funeral of the legendary Charles Bohlen, the renowned Cold War expert on the Soviet Union. On the 4th, a chastened Moshe Dayan* visited him; while his social new year in Washington was

---

* Dayan was in political eclipse, no longer in charge of the ministry of Defense. Ariel Sharon once said of him: "He would wake up with a hundred ideas. Of them ninety-five were dangerous; three more were bad; the remaining two, however, were brilliant."

launched with an eggnog party given by the Marvin Kalbs out at Chevy Chase, followed by supper in town with his old friend Joe Alsop.[10]

To me, some thirty-two years later,[11] he described his mood that Christmas, contrasting with that of one year previously. We were sitting in his study at Kent, Connecticut, up the perilously steep stairway that always reminded me of an Aztec sacrificial pyramid, surrounded by photos and mementos of his life—the huge TV screen on which he would watch his favorite baseball teams, the shelves crammed with CDs of his chosen classical music, Bach. At Christmastime 1972, the prospects for the United States in the coming year had looked better than they had done at the same time twelve months previously. As he apostrophized the coming year of 1973 in his memoirs, following Nixon's landslide victory in November, it was to begin "with glittering promise; rarely had a Presidential term started with such bright foreign policy prospects."

He thought the nation then was "in a superb governmental position—everything seemed to be running well." He himself (so he asseverated) had made up his mind to leave government, at latest, by the end of 1973. He was thinking of going to Oxford, to All Souls College. "The international situation was very strong and I thought, personally my relations with Nixon could not go on much longer."[12] Then, Watergate—followed by his key appointment to be secretary of state—had intervened to keep him in Washington. But, a year later, at Christmas 1973, he recalled to me: "The situation was totally different from '72. I had had some big successes—in the Middle East, Egypt, but I had a terrible premonition. I was very uneasy about Nixon; I couldn't see how we could go on without paying a price—the Most Favored Nation, etc., had to be kept going—it was a period when the Soviet Union was sending missions to Vietnam, resuming weapons delivery. [Scoop] Jackson was absolutely reckless to press the U.S. against the Russians, at a time when we were so weak. I also felt they were weaker than they seemed. But you could never be sure. It was inconceivable to me to go harder at them. . . . Anyway I had a lot of successes ahead of me—though the disengagement on the canal hadn't happened, but I calculated that it would. In '72 I was on the verge of going to Paris negotiations with the Vietnamese—'73 on the verge of going to

Cairo—it looked like a better deal. . . . On the other hand, in '72, I thought we were strong from the international point of view; but I was personally weak. In 1973 it was quite the reverse." With Watergate, however, the authority of the American executive had been draining away daily.[13]

A few days later, in New York, Kissinger's analysis was adumbrated to me by Winston Lord. At the beginning of 1973, it had looked as if Nixon and Kissinger were poised to continue to build "a structure of peace. Nixon had been reelected in a landslide; Vietnam War was over. Opening to China, major progress with Soviet Union. Now they could continue progress on those fronts while turning to issues that needed more attention; shaping a new transatlantic partnership with Europe, and Japan (especially after China shocks), Middle East. A Republican Congress buoyed by an end to Vietnam War, dramatic summits, and progress with two Communist giants. Watergate only a small blip."

But, by the end of 1973, "The cracks were appearing on Watergate, and would gather steam. With it would come an impact of cynicism about presidency, powers, and secrecy; congressional reassertion of power; less respect and/or fear of U.S. abroad—because of weakened presidency; the backlash from Congress not fully apparent. It was easier in earlier years to deal with the Communists—with China and Russia. . . . We then had a small homogenous group at NSC. It became much bigger in the State Department . . . as HK took on State, he needed a wider structure to deal with. He would go from working with small staff, often in secrecy on issues primarily involving Communist regimes, to large State Department and foreign service, and a whole range of new issues and countries requiring much more public diplomacy. . . . Nineteen seventy-three began with Vietnam peace agreement, trip to Hanoi, and best trip ever to China. It would end with Yom Kippur War and the first shuttle, symbolizing new issues he would tackle. The end of 1973 was the beginning of a period when HK held foreign policy together under fading Nixon and interim Ford."[14]

The distinguished book critic of the *Washington Post*, Jonathan Yardley, questioned whether there "was *anything* good about 1973? . . . It was a time of deep paranoia in this country from which we show little evidence of recovering. The incredible damage that Watergate did

to the presidency and to popular confidence in governmental institu-
tions . . . the loss of Vietnam . . . the collapse of the economy and the
coming of the OPEC-induced gas lines . . . all of this combined to produce a mood of deep self-doubt, a belief that someone out there was
trying to 'get' us." It was "a lousy year, and good riddance to it." [15] It
had certainly been for Henry Kissinger one of the most promising, disappointing, challenging, and complex years in recent Western history.
But history won't adapt itself to pigeonholing, and, inconveniently for
us historians, insofar as it knows no temporal boundaries, has a habit
of spilling over into another year. No year is ever an island, entire of
itself. So events spilled over from 1973 into 1974; Watergate, starting—
almost unseen—in 1972, grew into a monster in 1973, to reach its
wretched climax in August 1974, with the supremely humiliating spectacle of a broken president climbing into a helicopter, to be lifted in
disgrace from the White House lawn. Eight months later, another helicopter, bringing even greater humiliation to America, would take off
from the embassy roof in Saigon—to mark the end of the Vietnam War.

Henry Kissinger, however, would go on through it all, and beyond,
as secretary of state—to the election of James Earl Carter Jr. in 1976. If
Kissinger had allowed himself the time, or was at all that way inclined,
over Christmas 1973 and the New Year he might have mused over a
profit-and-loss account for the year that was passed—and the
prospects to follow. Perhaps the main headings would have run somehow as follows:

- *The Middle East*: U.S. and Israel caught out; disaster narrowly averted, transformed into victory. Soviet influence
  eradicated. Kissinger triumphant. Negotiations for long- and
  short-term peace ongoing. Cause for optimism.

- *Energy crisis.* An unforeseen disaster, for Western economies
  as a whole. U.S. pressure on Arab oil producers heavy, and
  mounting. Cause for (limited) optimism.

- *Year of Europe.* Almost a total shipwreck, on rocks of in-
  ward-looking European leaders and heavy-handed Americans (notably Kissinger himself). The good news: three main

leaders in Europe, Heath, Pompidou, Brandt, about to disappear; need to propitiate America because of fuel reliance. Cause for modest optimism; a new semihoneymoon would lie ahead.

- *Chile*. Thorn-in-the-side Salvador Allende gone. Apart from the intractable, insufferable Castro, Nixon and the White House had no foes gnawing away from down below in Latin America. (Not yet registered just how nasty Pinochet would turn out to be.) Cause for optimism.

- *China*. Relations had cooled somewhat; China was not going to be helpful over Cambodia or Vietnam. But the great door which Nixon and Kissinger had heaved open in 1971 remained ajar. Soviet expansionism would be contained. Cause for (considerable) optimism.

- *Détente*. Definitely damaged since DEFCON 3. Moscow might be expected to exact revenge via Vietnam for bloody nose in the Middle East. But the mainstream of nuclear limitation agreements (SALT) seemed intact—despite increased sniping from the wings by Scoop Jackson and allies. Cause for (limited) optimism.

- *Vietnam*. North Vietnamese aggression mounting. Congress had now removed any possibility for U.S. intervention. No cause for optimism.

- *Watergate*. One sector where Kissinger had no input, except to continue to keep his distance. Future of Nixon grim. All foreign initiatives affected, if not hamstrung. No cause for optimism whatsoever.

To paraphrase the immortal lines of Charles Dickens in *A Tale of Two Cities*, 1973 might be seen as representing "the worst of times." It was certainly an "age of foolishness," a time of credulity, rather than "of incredulity" as the witch-doctors of the U.S. media took over; and a "season of Darkness." Possibly only in the breast of Henry Kissinger did the New Year offer any springs of hope.

On January 11, he set off on the 1974 shuttles to the Middle East that were to establish his reputation. As Wellington said of Waterloo, both of them would be "hard-slogging." The first, aboard the specially converted Boeing 707, took him to Aswan, Sadat's winter retreat in Upper Egypt. Once again Kissinger noted that the blackout was still in force. As part of the deal, Sadat agreed to withdraw from his reconquered area of Sinai all but a light covering force; a concession which caused his army chief, General Abdel al-Gamasy, to break down in tears.[16] Somehow Kissinger managed to fit in a trip to the stunning temples of Philae, which, by a miracle of modern technology, were being raised from the waters of the Nile that had been flooded by the new Soviet-built dam.* To a newsman, he remarked with an excess of pessimism, "Before we are through here we will see it all."[17] Yet, the next day he was off to Jerusalem, shuttling back and forth to Aswan within twenty-four hours of leaving it, with the latest Israeli input. In Israel, he encountered yet another hitch; Golda was suffering from shingles. (Kissinger wondered to himself, if the talks stumbled, would Sadat ever believe her illness had been genuine?) She was in pain, but "in fine sardonic form,"[18] full of distrust for all things Egyptian. Fortunately discussion of Sadat's position was carried on by her deputy, Yigal Allon, a former student of Kissinger's at Harvard, and a moderate with a scheme for withdrawal from the West Bank. The plan for the Israeli pull-back in Sinai finally came down to a matter of a kilometer or two. In Aswan, in Kissinger's words, Sadat—to the displeasure of his generals, "accomplished the spectacular by winnowing the essential from the tactical."[19]

Back to Israel, for more fine-tuning. Concealing exasperation, at one stage Kissinger commented wryly on obtaining "a great victory, to get Israel to accept its own proposal."[20] His third, and final, shuttle to Jerusalem was accompanied with twelve inches of snow; as he slithered

---

* One of the factors that lay behind the Suez dispute of 1956.

along perilous roads, again he wondered if Sadat basking in Aswan sun would comprehend the difficulties that might delay his next rendezvous. At the close of that last trip to get Sadat's signature, on Friday, January 18, he brought with him a personal message from Golda Meir, the unyielding foe. It reiterated words that Sadat had sent via Kissinger: "When I talk of permanent peace, between us, I mean it." She ended with a handsome tribute to Kissinger—"whom we both trust"—as architect of the peace agreement. Sadat responded: "I am today taking off my military uniform—I never expect to wear it again except for ceremonial occasions. Tell her that is the answer to her letter." * [21]

He then drove Kissinger down the Nile, to Luxor, to enjoy a few hours of repose and, as a historian, to drink in the glories of ancient Thebes. That night there was another dramatic moment of the kind Sadat reveled in; when a switch was thrown, the blackout ended, and suddenly the famous avenue of sphinxes was floodlit in all its glory. Twenty-five years of war between Israel and Egypt were over. It must have been an extraordinarily emotive moment for the historian-turned-statesman; it had required eleven separate flights within ten days, and an incalculable mental input.

In Washington the battered president received the news with "elation"; he had had "little enough to encourage him in recent weeks." Kissinger then flew home. He stopped in at Aqaba and Damascus (to report to King Hussein and President Asad—to whom the next, most delicate, and even trickier shuttle sequel would ensue), and then to Tel Aviv for a last session. Israel was still resistant to any withdrawal on the Golan Heights, or any participation in the peace process by the PLO.

But what had been achieved? The trapped Egyptian Third Army was freed; the Israelis pulled back twenty miles into Sinai, still short of the key Mitla and Gidi passes which had been fought over so bitterly in three consecutive wars. A United Nations force was to be interposed between the two armies. It was not much on the map, and it would take another five years (by which time Kissinger was out of office) be-

---

* It would, however, be at such a ceremony, in uniform, that the courageous Sadat would be assassinated by enemies of his peace process with Israel, in 1981.

fore the Camp David Accords would regain all Sinai for Egypt; but even then no final settlement materialized; no settlement over Jerusalem, or the West Bank. Nothing demonstrated more clearly the difficulties of finding any meaningful solution between Arabs and Jews; there was little advance on Kissinger's achievements in 1973–74. But this did lead to peace, of a kind, for the next thirty-five years; and the removal of the major anxiety for Israelis—a hostile Egypt, the most numerically powerful of all the Arab states, upon her southern flank.* Would they be able to build, positively, on this achievement of Kissinger's?

CHART OF FIRST KISSINGER (EGYPTIAN) SHUTTLE

January 11, 1974	HAK to Aswan
January 12	HAK to Jerusalem
January 13	HAK to Aswan again
January 14	HAK to Tel Aviv
	HAK back to Aswan
January 16	HAK to Jerusalem
January 18	HAK to Aswan, last time
January 19	HAK returns via Aqaba, Damascus, Tel Aviv
January 21	HAK returns to Washington

Returning home from the shuttle on Monday, January 21, to acclaim for his achievement in the Middle East, Kissinger was moved to find his boss "extraordinarily proud that even in the midst of domestic crisis his Administration had managed to play the decisive role in turning the Middle East toward peace."[22]

But the America he returned to was "not a happy place . . . ridden with suspicion, bitterness, cynicism." It was a relief to be out of it all on a shuttle, however tough the going. At home a "taste for sensational revelations had developed, much of it unhappily too justified, some of

---

* From the year of the peace agreement to 1997, Egypt received $1.3 billion U.S. military aid annually, Israel received $3 billion annually.

it pursued almost for its own sake." There seemed to be something approaching a semipornographic mood of self-flagellation among the media. For all his attempts to maintain distance, Kissinger found the Watergate-driven media closing in on him too. It was over a leakage of documents, in 1971, from his NSC office; then moved on to suggest he had lied about his declared ignorance, in May 1973, of the existence of the Plumbers unit. Swiftly the charges were dropped, but they had sufficed to send Kissinger off to Aswan angered and upset by such trivia when the whole Middle East policy "hung in the balance."[23] On his return they were followed by fresh attacks on his policy, from another foe, Senator Scoop Jackson and his allies. While there were many Americans who praised him for his achievement in Egypt and Israel, there were those—particularly in the pro-Israel lobby—who accused him of having been "too soft," and not gaining for Israel absolute assurance that the Yom Kippur War could not happen again. To Scowcroft he remarked bitterly they were: "as obnoxious as the Vietnamese," and "I'm going to be the first Jew accused of anti-Semitism!"[24]

A month later, February 26, Kissinger was back in Damascus, Israel, and Cairo, attempting to resolve the issue of Israeli POWs remaining in Syrian hands; and in Riyadh pressing for an end to the oil embargo. It was his fourth trip to the Middle East. What he was up against with the steely, unbending Asad was suggested by this somewhat brutal exchange between his minister of foreign affairs, Abd al-Halim Khaddam, regarded by Kissinger as "ferocious," and the future U.S. ambassador, Richard Murphy, as Kissinger's plane had been about to land on his January shuttle. "I think the airplane is God's punishment to mankind," observed the ambassador. "No," replied Khaddam simply: "America is."[25]

Asad had then followed up with an hour and a half's diatribe on the duplicity of his Arab "brother" and onetime ally, Sadat. While on this trip, Kissinger noted on the incidental hazards of Mideast shuttling (or could it have been Syrian psychological warfare?): having fallen into bed at 4 A.M., from 4:30 onward he was roused by the muezzin in the mosque adjacent to the state guesthouse beginning his calls to prayer—reinforced by a powerful amplifier. That day there was, apparently, a thwarted attempt to assassinate him by Palestinian terrorists. While on his return visit to Damascus he received news from Scowcroft in Washington that "the Watergate avalanche was moving relentlessly on"; a federal grand jury had indicted Haldeman, Ehrlichman, Mitchell, and four others. Kissinger was appalled at what was happening to those who only so recently had been his colleagues—and how close the net was now closing in on the president. His mind was concentrated by realization that the Administration could not afford to add a single foreign setback to its domestic debacles.

Following Nixon's personal plea, and threat, to King Faisal of December 3, Washington had indulged in some tough talking with the Arabs. If the oil embargo was not lifted, the secretary of state would cease his efforts to gain Israeli withdrawal from Sinai and the Golan, from Egyptian and Syrian territory. An international energy conference opened in Washington at the beginning of February, with the Europeans now showing a certain strength of unity (Lord Carrington, as Heath's minister for energy, recalled being astonished by a virtuoso performance by the damaged president, speaking without notes[26]). At the same time, rumors were rife in the city that the Pentagon was considering an operation to seize by force, and hold, the Saudi oilfields. Though finding no enthusiasm in Europe, combined with the support of Sadat, and heavy pressure from the White House, it had had its effect. On March 18, the Arab oil ministers (with the exception of Libya) lifted the oil embargo. But the damage, a great amount, had been done to the Western economies—damage that would be felt into the 1980s.

The peace process continued, with Kissinger in April and May now shuttling between Damascus and Tel Aviv, to achieve a settlement over the contentious Golan Heights. Meanwhile, a new and very special dimension for Kissinger had entered his life. On March 30, 1974, he and Nancy Maginnes were married. With engaging charm, and total veracity, he described it as "an act transcending all else in its effect on my life."[27] Anyone who ever met the enchanting Nancy, or saw them together, would never dispute this. She accompanied him, for the first time, on the shuttle to Damascus. But, preliminary to this, Kissinger first made a flying trip to Moscow, on March 24–28, to forestall the Soviets from intruding into the tricky negotiations, and wrecking them. "Caging the Bear" he called it in his memoirs.[28]

Much tougher than his dealings with Sadat were the arguments over the Golan Heights, considered by Golda Meir, and most other Israeli leaders as strategically essential to the nation's survival (as indeed seemed to have been proved during the first days of the Yom Kippur War). Negotiations came down to a matter of a few yards around the dusty, windblown, and ruined town of Quneitra, which had been taken from the Syrians in the Six Day War. In an Israel "in turmoil" over the talks, a vehement Golda (about to leave office as soon as the negotiations were concluded) exploded: "I don't know how to go to the people and explain to them that, after all, never mind, there was a war, there was another war, more dead, more wounded, but we had to give up Syrian territory. Why?"[29] In Damascus, Asad explained to Kissinger: "The Syrian difficulty is that people here who have been nurtured over twenty-six years on hatred, can't be swayed overnight by our changing our courses."[30] Finally a compromise peace deal of sorts, with U.N. backing, was hammered out.

Then, in the last stages of negotiations, there occurred an appalling atrocity of the sort all too familiar in the Middle East when an accord is about to be reached. On May 15, Palestinian terrorists attacked a town in the north of Israel, called Ma'alot, seizing the school and taking the children hostage. Israeli commandos stormed it; they killed the three terrorists, but in the siege sixteen children died and sixty-eight were wounded—all by Palestinian hand grenades. Israel was stunned; to Kissinger, Golda Meir remarked tragically that "Being victim seemed to be the destiny of the Jews, but the killing of children was too much."[31] Nevertheless, she would stick to what had been agreed. On June 2, she handed over the government to Yitzhak Rabin. It was almost the last time Kissinger would deal with Meir, the Iron Lady, in office. To this brave, intransigent "Mother of Her People" who had presented him with so many headaches, he offered an eloquent valedictory toast: "Madame Prime Minister, you represent a generation that came to this country when it was only a dream, and you have done what is given to very few—to bring a people to a country, to make the country a state, and turn the state into a home." The following day, as he set forth on his final mission to Damascus, was his

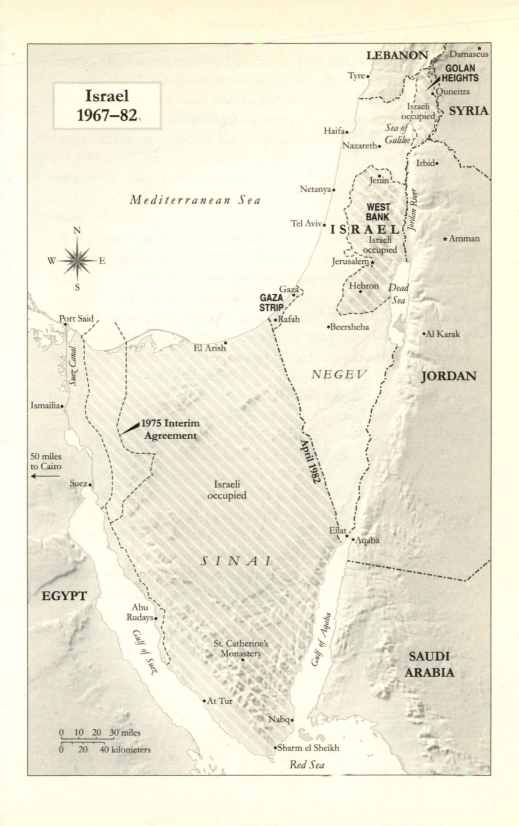

**Israel
1967–82**

LEBANON · Damascus ★
Tyre · GOLAN HEIGHTS
Quneitra
Israeli occupied · SYRIA

Haifa · Sea of Galilee
Nazareth · Irbid ·

Mediterranean Sea

Netanya · Jenin
Tel Aviv · WEST BANK
ISRAEL
Israeli occupied · ★ Amman
Jerusalem ★

Gaza · Hebron · *Dead Sea*
GAZA STRIP
· Rafah · Beersheba · Al Karak ·

Port Said · El Arish · *NEGEV* · **JORDAN**

Ismailia · **1975 Interim Agreement**

50 miles to Cairo
←

Suez ·

Israeli occupied

April 1982

S I N A I

Eilat · Aqaba ·

Abu Rudays ·

EGYPT

St. Catherine's Monastery

Gulf of Suez

Gulf of Aqaba

SAUDI ARABIA

At Tur ·

Nabq ·

0 10 20 30 miles
0 20 40 kilometers

· Sharm el Sheikh
Red Sea

fifty-first birthday. His staff presented him with a small slab of rock inscribed in Hebrew as a fake antiquity: "HAK was here—5683*— Quneitra." Certainly, by the end of that shuttle he must have felt that he knew every rock and stone on that dreary, forsaken landscape on the slopes of Mount Hermon, which mattered so much to both sides.

One more trip to and from Damascus, and—against all expectations (it was a cliffhanger right to the end)—the objections of both sides had been whittled down, and a deal was in the bag. The significance of the Golan Heights disengagement was, as he explains in his memoirs, not "primarily psychological. On the political plane, it marked a major breakthrough. If radical Syria could sign an agreement with Israel, there were no ideological obstacles to peace talks with any other Arab state." [32] Surely this should be so? Yet, with his residual pessimism, he could not help but foresee that the quest for "a durable peace" in the Middle East would "dwarf in complexity the disengagements that had required such massive labors." [33] This last shuttle had taken thirty-four days, and left Kissinger hoarse with fatigue, as well as "physically exhausted and emotionally drained." The stress of the trip hospitalized Nancy with two ulcers.

Returning to a Washington now plunged into the final agonies of Watergate, Kissinger found himself "experiencing the letdown that always follows great exertions." [34] The media was once again homing in on him. But what he had achieved on those shuttles had been—by any standard—historically monumental. With Israel's two main military threats, Egypt and Syria, divided from each other, and Soviet troublemaking excluded from the zone, there would be no full-scale Middle East war for the next generation and a half; the downside, from the American point of view, was that henceforth the United States would be taking on the burden as the sole arbiter of peace in the area—with all the responsibility that derived therefrom; a responsibility that would be driven home on September 11, 2001.

---

* The year of his birth, 1923, according to the Hebrew calendar. When, a year after the Six Day War, I visited Quneitra, a bleak locality under any circumstances, it was still as it had been abandoned by the retreating Syrians—deserted, shutters hanging off looted shops, curtains blowing in the incessant wind.

• • •

For Nixon, now mortally wounded, the Syrian settlement would be Kissinger's last offering, and a superlative one. "Elation" and "pride" would be diminutions for what Nixon felt on receiving the news. He needed whatever scrap of success his secretary of state could bring him. These outweighed any personal resentment, or jealousy, he might have felt. As Kissinger had observed, with becoming generosity, at the time of his award of the Nobel Prize, "Only those who knew Nixon well could perceive beneath the gallant congratulations the strain and hurt that I was being given all the credit for actions that had cost him so much."[35]

In terms of foreign affairs, the shuttles, and the lifting of the oil embargo, would be followed—and capitalized on—by what Kissinger would describe as Nixon's "Last Hurrah." In April, as he was being pilloried at home over his tax returns, Nixon visited Paris for Pompidou's funeral. A cartoon in *Le Figaro* depicted him as "Sovereign of the Western World," with an obeisant queen, representing Europe, kneeling before him. Less satirically, the more sedate *Le Monde* praised him for his continuing ability to dominate international politics. But back in Washington, that same month (April 18), the relentless Judge Sirica issued the all but lethal blow; a subpoena for the president to yield all his tapes. In response, Nixon read out the famous "expletives deleted," with all the "shits" and "fucks," as well as insulting references to senators, obliterated.* It would still not be enough to save him. His daughter Julie found "The tide engulfing the administration . . . almost unbearable."[36] Nevertheless, Nixon persisted in going on to a triumphant visit, in June, to Egypt where—even though suffering from phlebitis in his leg, and in considerable pain†—he was greeted with perhaps his greatest acclaim ever. Though he was truly the architect of that acclaim, Kissinger in his memoirs described the crowds being in a state of "delirium."[37] Wrote Nixon's biographer, Stephen Ambrose, with

---

* When Kissinger finally read the transcripts, he claims he was astonished by the language (*Years of Upheaval*, p. 1182).

† Nixon overruled his doctors, who had tried to prevent the trip on the grounds that it could be life-threatening, with the danger of a clot to the heart.

some eloquence: "Never had a President, not even Wilson, been so honored abroad, so hounded at home. Seldom had a President done more for world peace."[38] For his associates on the trip it was, however—so Kissinger thought, "an anguishing experience. We sensed in the exaggerated solicitude of our hosts the pity that is the one sentiment a head of state can never afford to evoke."[39]

Nixon ended that same month with a farewell trip to Moscow. If not actually delirious (given that he had made a point of going first to Cairo, and Brussels, to sign the new Atlantic Declaration formulated as one consequence of the Year of Europe—neither of which could exactly be construed as "Soviet-friendly"), Kissinger found that their hosts were uncharacteristically sensitive to Nixon's "human predicament." Yet they were no longer prepared to make long-term commitments to Nixon "or to pay a price for his good will." On the other hand, he judged that their gentle treatment of the "mortally wounded President was indeed one of the best testimonials to the impact of his policies."[40] But that was not the way it appeared in the U.S. media, now uniformly hostile to Nixon.

In his first few days back in Washington following the last shuttle, Kissinger found himself wondering how on earth the administration could launch itself in a quest of definitive peace in the Middle East while confronted by the "widening fissure of Watergate." By now it seemed to him that Nixon's impeachment was "inevitable,"[41] and from the notes he made one can deduce that—even with his immense reserves of energy—Kissinger's own batteries were running low. Battle fatigue was setting in; and the media was at him again. This time it was revival of old charges of wiretapping. While he was still away on the Syrian shuttle, a left-wing journal, *New Times,* wrote: "The honeymoon is over for Henry Kissinger. There are signs that the media is going after him for the first time."[42]

There was nasty talk about a perjury indictment. *Newsweek* came up with a lead of: "An Ugly Blot on Mr. Clean?" Always painfully sensitive to this sort of criticism, with which Washington was now steeped, Kissinger says he was "shattered."[43] Swiftly the dust settled, with the Senate Foreign Relations Committee fully absolving him by the beginning of August. It was not the same for Nixon, however. Surrender of his tapes—"the smoking gun," which made it plain that he had known about the Watergate cover-up—doomed him. Toward the end of July, the vote began on Capitol Hill for impeachment. Nixon decided that, rather than go through a trial in the Senate, he would resign. Although in the passage of time he would concede errors of judgment, he never admitted to any criminality. He explained in his memoirs that the country could "simply not afford to have a crippled President for six months."[44] At the beginning of August, Haig rang Vice President Ford, the former scoutmaster, and warned him to "be prepared."[45] He would become the only man to assume the vice presidency and then the presidency without having been voted into either office.

As he himself recognized, the final days of Richard Nixon did indeed contain all the ingredients of an Aristotelian tragedy: the superman fallen into the lowest pit, all through essential flaws in his own character. From his White House vantage point Kissinger could view it all happening, helpless to stem the tide of events. He could record with deep feeling how "Those of us who had worked with Nixon for five and a half years found it impossible to join in the wave of outrage sweeping through the media. We did not condone the shabby practices revealed by Watergate; we were as appalled as anyone. Nor did we have any illusion about the evasions and untruths unearthed. We had seen some of these tendencies at first hand. But we had a different perspective. We could see how they had helped to turn a serious error into a national disaster."[46] The scale of that disaster would be measured nine months later, in Vietnam.

During what would be the last days of the presidency, Kissinger had accompanied the stricken president once more to San Clemente, then on a poignant trip of nostalgia instigated by Nixon to his humble birthplace, Yorba Linda, and his college town of Whittier. On the way to California they inspected a Minuteman missile installation in bleak North Dakota; it was the first time Kissinger had seen one of the weapons of mass destruction over which he had negotiated so industriously all those months with Brezhnev. On his return home, breaking "an unspoken rule" over Watergate, Kissinger told Haig he thought the end of the presidency was now "inevitable."[47] Haig agreed.

In the course of the evening of August 7, Nixon called Kissinger in to tell him of his decision. Kissinger speaks in his memoirs of "a great tenderness" he felt for Nixon at that moment, seeing beneath that "almost inhuman self-containment" a glimpse of what the real man might be suffering: "To have striven so hard, to have molded a public personality out of so amorphous an identity, to have sustained that superhuman effort only to end with every weakness disclosed and every error compounding the downfall—that was a fate of biblical proportions. Evidently the Deity would not tolerate the presumption that all can be manipulated; an object lesson of the limits of human presumption was necessary."[48]

Later that same evening, Kissinger was dining at home with Nancy and Joe Alsop, when the telephone rang. It was Nixon, asking him to return. Kissinger found the president alone in the Lincoln sitting room of the White House, "sitting in a characteristic pose, slouched in the brown-covered chair, his legs on the settee, a yellow pad on his lap—a last crutch at the moment of despair."[49] It was a setting that brought many powerful memories flooding back. There then followed the bizarre scene when Nixon invited Kissinger, a Jew, to kneel down and pray with him, the Protestant. Kissinger's own recollections of the event were not so clear-cut as Nixon's. But he recalled, running through his mind, a verse of Aeschylus that had been a favorite of the late Robert Kennedy:

Pain that cannot forget
falls drop by drop
upon the heart
until in our despair
there comes wisdom
through the awful
grace of God.[50]

Certainly, at that dark moment, Kissinger might well have prayed for the future. For a "fleeting moment" in those last days, he recalled having an apocalyptic sense that "we might all be in danger."[51] There was some truth in his thought, at the time, that "In destroying himself, Nixon had wrecked the lives of almost all who had come in contact with him."[52]

Kissinger's own life was perhaps the sole exception; in fact it might even be said that Nixon's self-destruction had *made* Kissinger.

Two days later the helicopter came to lift the fallen president from the White House lawn. He climbed on board with upstretched arms in one last V sign of heroic defiance for the TV cameras. There were harrowingly emotional scenes. An honest man making an honest statement, Ford told his predecessor, "You have given us the finest foreign policy this country has ever had," while Kissinger murmured to Ford, "You know the whole world depends on you, Mr. Vice President," pledging that he "could count on me." As he watched Gerald Ford enter the White House that night, Kissinger, in the concluding words of his *Years of Upheaval*, recalled uttering the prayer that had eluded him two nights previously: "For the sake of us all, that fate will be kind to this good man, that his heart will be stout, that America under his leadership would find again its faith." [53]

"When Nixon resigned," wrote his biographer, Stephen Ambrose, in his epilogue: "we lost more than we gained." [54] In the opening sentence of his inaugural address Ford began: "Our long national nightmare is over." [55] But it was not strictly true, there was Vietnam, and there was the eternal problem of the Russian Bear still left for Kissinger to deal with. Telling Ford of his decision to resign (on August 8), Nixon had also stressed to him that the only man who was "absolutely indispensable" in foreign policy was Kissinger. He was "a genius . . . but you don't have to accept everything he recommends . . . you can't let him have a totally free hand." [56]

After Nixon's departure, relations with Moscow, and Beijing, took something of a nosedive. It wasn't just that Brezhnev and Mao both admired him—which they did (to Mao, according to Ted Heath, he was always "a man who knows what he stands for . . . and has the strength of mind to get it" [57]). The old dictator would not develop the same degree of respect for the well-meaning Ford. Like Mao, in the Kremlin the Bear recognized and respected power; Ford, and even more Carter, lacked these crude essentials. So Kissinger was left to keep the détente show on the road. In the Kremlin the DEFCON 3 crisis had, inevitably, left its mark. Perhaps a bit like the pregnant nun who confessed that her sin had "only been a little one," Kissinger and the White House had regarded DEFCON 3 as no more than a minor escalation. But this was not entirely how Brezhnev and his marshals had perceived it. Coupled with it came the humiliation suffered by Soviets in their expulsion from the Middle East, reversing a strategic policy of almost twenty years' standing. There seems to have been little or no reflection on whether pouring arms into so unstable a region could have resulted, inevitably, in a major eruption. Victor Israelyan was of the opinion that "perhaps the most important result of the war was that the Soviet-American détente did not blow up."[58] That may be, but certainly from the end of 1973 it did little more than limp along.

As 1973 turned into 1974, in the United States there was a shift in attitudes toward the Soviets. Events, and trends, were pushing each side further apart. Increased opposition to Kissinger's policy of détente came from two opposite poles. On the right there was mounting criticism that he had "given away" too much to Brezhnev. These included not only the neocons like Richard Perle[*] and the hard-liners of the Pentagon, but intellectuals like Zbigniew Brzezinski, later to succeed Kissinger as Jimmy Carter's head of the NSC. Brzezinski, who would never quite shrug off his proud Polish origins, would always criticize Kissinger for having accepted too readily the status quo in Eastern Europe, thereby perpetuating the subjection of his native country. Another influential thinker from Harvard, and also of Polish descent, but a conservative, Professor Richard Pipes, substantially agreed with him.[59] Brzezinski blamed Kissinger's attachment to realpolitik at the expense of human rights. He thought the 1970s were "overly dominated by a sense of historical gloom." In contrast to Kissinger, he had regarded his role as being "to undermine the positions of the Soviet bloc. I thought the Soviets were getting weaker internally; we were concentrating too much on their external strength."[60] Early on in my conversations with Kissinger, he expounded how "I differed with my conservative friends—I didn't think the Russians were as strong as they

---

[*] Ambassador Arthur Hartman, a leading Soviet expert on Kissinger's team, and subsequently ambassador to Moscow from 1981 to 1987, to me brusquely dismissed Perle's views of "having given away too much" as "absolute bullshit" (interview, 5/6/05).

did . . . in my view, the USSR was weaker than it looked, and not likely to engage us in a sustained confrontation—but they might have made a mistake. The neocons believed the USSR was designing WMDs to destroy us . . . every time I went to the USSR the machinery struck me as so cumbersome that they couldn't possibly launch this kind of surprise attack, first strike that would succeed. The CIA believed as I did; the military intelligence, as always, was pessimistic."[61]

At the other end of the spectrum was a coalition of members of the pro-Israel lobby, AIPAC, some of whom felt Kissinger had leaned too heavily on Israel to make concessions during the Yom Kippur War, and others—like the neocons—that he had been too soft on the Soviets on this issue. He had, they declared, gotten back no "linkage" on the issue of emigration for Jews wanting to leave the country. Hence "the left-wing Jews all rallied around Israel—so they gave Russia (and me!) a bad time."[62] By the close of 1973, Kissinger saw Senator Scoop Jackson as having assumed the mantle of his principal opponent. In fact, there was the U.S. secretary of state, even confiding to Soviet foreign minister Gromyko (in a moment of what seems like amazing openness) that "We have a common enemy—Senator Jackson. I speak frankly with you."[63] Much of it stemmed from Watergate, and the president's ever-growing weakness. Says Kissinger, with some bitterness, in his memoirs: "The blood feud with Nixon ran too deep. If Nixon was for détente, so the subconscious thinking seemed to run, perhaps the Cold War wasn't all bad!"[64]

With the redoubtable Richard Perle and his unyielding hostility to the Soviets, and all things Russian, at his side—or at his back might perhaps be more appropriate—Jackson now emerged as a "fundamental" opponent of Kissinger's détente. He "sought to destroy our policy, not to ameliorate it," claims Kissinger.[65] Representing the state of Washington, Jackson, a mainstream Democrat, was neither Jewish nor had a substantial Jewish electorate; yet he had been captured by the thorny human rights issue of Jewish emigration from the USSR. His view, in sum, was—if Moscow would not let the Jews leave, then it should not get from the United States Most Favored Nation status in East–West trade benefits. A major component of Kissinger's "linkage" was negotiations, the quid pro quo deal to get a reduction in the missiles inventory. Jackson's demand for a written Soviet guarantee of

100,000 exit visas—or three times the existing number—was, Kissinger held, totally "unrealistic." Kissinger thought Scoop was being unfair. He claimed that under Nixon in fact the numbers of permits granted had risen nearly a hundredfold, from 400 a year to nearly 35,000 in 1973. "He did not want a compromise," thought Kissinger, regarding Jackson's whole approach as flawed, and counterproductive. His attempts to resolve the issue with Jackson by March "made me long for the relative tranquility of the Middle East."[66]

By the cataclysmic summer of 1974, because of the Jackson-Vanik Amendment,* détente had lost the carrot it had proffered Moscow. Eventually the trade agreement with the USSR collapsed; meanwhile, on Kissinger's figures, emigration actually sank by more than twenty thousand from its peak in 1973. Then, on top of Jackson and his allies, SALT and the attempts to set limits on the Soviet nuclear threat began falling apart in a welter of high-tech discord. He was up against James Schlesinger and the men in the Pentagon, and, as explained earlier, this was not Kissinger's domain. (But then, Kissinger might respond, would Metternich or Castlereagh have been conversant in calibers of cannon, ranges, and ball weights?) The visit to Moscow in March 1974 met with a wide and growing gulf; while the Vladivostok summit of that November proved to be little short of "a disaster," Kissinger admitted.[67] Throughout the rest of the 1970s both sides went on increasing their nuclear inventories, with superpower tensions intensifying under the Ford presidency, when America was in a state of rehab, and the even feebler administration of Carter. In 1976, Kissinger was gone; was it any surprise that Brezhnev risked the fatal plunge into Afghanistan in 1978? By then détente was all but dead.

On September 26, 1973, Kissinger had held a significant meeting in New York, with the acting foreign minister from the government

---

* Named for its major co-sponsors, Washington Democratic senator Scoop Jackson and Representative Charles Vanik, Ohio Democrat, the amendment denied Most Favored Nation privileges to countries that restricted emigration rights. This of course targeted principally the Soviet Union.

of South Vietnam, Nguyen Phu Duc (no relation of "Ducky"), and his ambassador, Tran Kim Phuong. Duc began by congratulating Kissinger on his appointment as secretary of state, then immediately expressed his fears sparked by reports that there was about to be "another Communist offensive this year." He claimed the North had "infiltrated 70,000 since January and 400 tanks." Disagreeing, Kissinger said he saw no possibility of any pending offensive until next March or April, and "no evidence of a massive infiltration effort." Seventy thousand was not enough to start an offensive. Playing down the importance of Congress's recent decision to ban military support to Indochina as a whole, Kissinger continued on a remarkably upbeat note: "There is no evidence that they [the Communists] can defeat you. They are exhausted and in difficulty. If there is a massive offensive, we will do our best to overcome Congressional difficulties and do something. Our Congress has acted most irresponsibly, and I consider the bombing cut-off disastrous. This clearly changes the attitude of the North Vietnamese. . . . It is important that you show confidence and behave strongly."[68]

It was a surprising exhortation. Did Kissinger entirely believe what he was saying—or how much was he simply trying to keep up the spirits of the South Vietnamese? It was surely improbable that the North failed to understand the fateful import of Congress's actions; equally Kissinger's interlocutors from the South must by then have appreciated that they were now, in effect, on their own. In the earliest days of the peace talks, Vernon Walters, for one, had noted Kissinger's constant fear that the Democratic majority in Congress would "give the farm away."[69]

From the very beginning to the very end, the hardest blows in the Vietnam War would be struck, not in the jungles and paddy fields, but at home in the United States. Early on in the opening to China, the shrewd Mao had told the North Vietnamese encouragingly that, once the U.S. troops had left, they would be unlikely to return. So, "After rest and reorganisation, you can fight again to reach the final victory."[70] Certainly the Yom Kippur War, breaking out just ten days after Kissinger's pep talk to the Saigon delegation, would change things, and to the advantage of the North. Would it be unfair to suggest, although there is no hard evidence to back this up, that in Vietnam the Kremlin would seek its revenge for humiliation in the Middle East? I put it to Kissinger that the Soviet tanks awaiting delivery to Syria and Egypt after October 1973 would almost inevitably have been shipped to Hanoi instead. He did not disagree. Yet, unmistakably when the final catastrophe occurred in spring 1975, with the Communist forces slicing down through the south like General Heinz Guderian in France in May 1940, they were led—not by Viet Cong guerrillas clad in black track suits—but by a main-army force headed by masses of the latest Soviet tanks. Meanwhile, Congress would celebrate the end of 1973 with legislation depriving Vietnam shipments of fuel to keep even their own tanks and aircraft in business. As Kissinger's trips to Beijing and Moscow in November 1973 and 1974 respectively would evince, what possible enticement could there now be for the two dictatorships to come to the aid of a broken president—in a situation favorable to their interests, when both Cambodia and all Vietnam could be had for the plucking—thanks to Congress?

While Kissinger was actually in China with Zhou Enlai, attempting in vain to get intercession on behalf of Cambodia, in the Oval Office on November 15, 1973, Nixon was giving Cambodia's minister for foreign affairs, Long Boret, warnings comparable to those Kissinger had dealt out to the Vietnamese in late September. Boret too was expecting a new offensive shortly—by the Khmer Rouge. Nixon could give him even less real comfort: "You have this government's support and my support personally. Our problem is a drastic one of support from the Congress. They made us stop the bombing, which made it difficult. . . . Our help is not decisive in your struggle. Without it you would lose; with it you have some chance to win. Basically, it is up to you."[71] In other words, you too are on your own now. Only days before North Vietnam marched into Saigon, on April 17, 1975, the Khmer Rouge captured Phnom Penh. In the Killing Fields subsequently an estimated one in five of the country's population, 1.5 million, would die at the hands of Pol Pot's henchmen.

Throughout 1974 and into 1975, Kissinger watched the unraveling of his hard-fought peace accords in distress, and indeed agony. "It was," he wrote in *Crisis,* "the first time that the United States had deprived itself of the ability to enforce an agreement for which American forces had fought and died"[72]—55,000 in total. He blamed Watergate—noting how, historically, no other nation "defended by the United States through the Cold War had ever been asked to stand entirely on its own."[73] In March 1975 the long-awaited Hanoi onslaught began, with eleven of their twelve divisions thrusting down into South Vietnam. Kissinger, on one more shuttle mission to the Middle East, impotently "observed the unfolding of the tragedy, unable to affect events."[74] In vain did Thieu appeal desperately to the Ford administration for help; in the two years since the signature of the peace accords his forces had lost 26,000 men in combat deaths, while they had received no replacement equipment or spare parts. As Kissinger returned to the United States on March 23*, invasion had turned into a rout, with the South running out of fuel even for their trucks, thanks to Congress's legislation, and without air support. The once vast U.S. base at Da Nang, linchpin to the defense of the northern third of the rump state, was lost. General Giap's men were advancing swiftly toward the suburbs of Saigon. The Senate turned its back on President Thieu's last desperate appeals for aid. On April 2, he resigned, bitterly castigating the United States for failing to enforce the Paris accords, or to provide the material support that had been promised him. Thieu then fled to Taiwan; he would die, in Massachusetts, twenty-five years later.

Kissinger felt that Thieu, whom he had pushed relentlessly over acceptance of the peace terms, "had every reason to resent America's conduct."[75]

On April 29, the world's TV screens showed those final humiliating moments atop the U.S. embassy in Saigon, as desperate Vietnamese who had remained loyal to America clawed their way onto the last small helicopters (run by the CIA) that lifted off from the roof. That day, there took place an anguished brief exchange between Kissinger and William Clements, deputy secretary of defense:

---

* It was a bad month for U.S. foreign policy; on the 25th, King Faisal of Saudi Arabia, an anchor of U.S. policy, was assassinated.

C: We finally got those people out.

K: Is that absolutely certain now?[76]

By way of celebrating the end in Vietnam, the *New York Times* ran a heartless headline: "Indo-China Without Americans; For Most a Better Life."[77]

Speaking, however, for the dormant conscience of America, the "silent minority," one among few on Capitol Hill, the Conservative senator for New York, James Buckley, expressed a sense of "shame" that day, which he would never forget.[78] Kissinger himself recalled, sitting alone in the NSC office in the West Wing of the White House, "enveloped by the eerie solitude that sometimes attends momentous events . . . what did torment me in these hours was my own role in the next-to-last act: the acceleration of negotiations after Le Duc Tho's breakthrough offer on October 8, 1972."[79]

Many times over the course of my various interviews with Henry Kissinger, over four long years, he would return to the theme that the only major regret he had in his life was the failure in Vietnam. It haunted, and plagued him relentlessly. It "still evokes a sinking feeling in me," he wrote in *Years of Renewal*.[80] In his writings he noted that neither the Nixon nor Ford administrations had a *"legal obligation"* to assist the South; but it was "something deeper—a moral obligation. We owed such assistance to the peoples who had stood with us, to the casualties we had left, and to the common efforts in which we had been involved—in short, to ourselves."[81] Had he and Nixon, he questioned himself, pressed South Vietnam too hard and too fast in that winter of 1972–73? In that "mystical stillness" in his NSC office as Saigon surrendered, he had felt "too drained"[82] to analyze the various decisions that had led to it. "What has torn at me ever since," however, he wrote in *Years of Renewal*, "is whether such an outcome might not have been better. Did the demoralizations of the Saigon structure which led to its collapse in 1975 start with the pace of negotiations we imposed back in 1972? Did Nixon and I assume too much?"[83]

In fact, could Vietnam possibly have ended differently? As indicated earlier, when he signed the peace accords, Kissinger was never overly optimistic. But he thought there was a chance, provided certain conditions were met. His associate, Winston Lord, put to me succinctly the vital two conditions which were not met:

"1. If truce violations by the North were massive, we thought the American electorate would support air strikes.

"2. China and Russia would have incentives to see that Hanoi did not break the cease-fire."[84]

For reasons that we have seen, neither of these conditions was fulfilled.

AFTERMATH

"Then, as suddenly as I had been catapulted to public service, it was over."

—Henry Kissinger[1]

"In destroying himself, Nixon had wrecked the lives of almost all who had come in contact with him."

—Henry Kissinger[2]

IN SEPTEMBER 1974, declaring his intent to bring an end to "an American tragedy in which we all have played a part," the new president, Gerald Ford, declared "a full, free, and absolute pardon unto Richard Nixon for all offenses against the United States." It was, he had concluded, "only I [who] can do that, and if I can, I must."[3] For many Americans it was a just and generous way of drawing a line under a wretched episode which had divided the country. To others, it represented a deplorable whitewashing; and it might well have cost Ford and the Republicans the election in 1976.

Kissinger developed considerable respect for Ford, but it was a very different relationship from the one he had had with Nixon over five years (in his homily on the death of Ford in 2006, Kissinger declared that "in his understated way he did his duty as a leader, not as a performer playing to the gallery," but with "the virtues of small-town America").[4] There would be no exciting new initiatives. It was a time of recuperation, of rehab—of domestic tidying up. Compared with 1974, and its predecessor, under Ford the year of 1975 was neither an eventful nor an encouraging one. In January, Ford—under strong congressional pressure—appointed his vice president, Nelson Rockefeller, to head a special commission looking into alleged abuses by the CIA. A few months later, a joint congressional committee on intelligence operations, eventually to become known as the Church Committee, under Idaho Democratic senator Frank Church would be set up. It had been sparked by the overthrow of Chile's President Allende. In matters related to the Watergate scandal, in February, former United States Attorney General John Mitchell, and former White House aides H. R. Haldeman and John Ehrlichman, were sentenced to between thirty months and eight years in prison. There would be no pardon for the lesser minions involved in Watergate. The same month, Turkey invaded the Turkish-speaking area of Cyprus. In some of the media, Kissinger was accused of supporting the Turks; once again the indefatigable Joseph Sisco was sent into the breach. In Britain, Margaret Thatcher defeated Edward Heath for the leadership of the Conservative Party, now in opposition. In the United States, because of the energy crisis, Daylight Saving Time began nearly two months early.

Two months later, in April, came the degrading surrender of South Vietnam. The following month brought the *Mayagüez* incident, another humiliation for the United States when Khmer Rouge forces in Cambodia seized a U.S. merchant ship, the *Mayagüez,* in international waters. Eventually it was rescued by the U.S. Navy, but thirty-eight Americans were killed. Offering more comfort to Kissinger, as a spin-off from détente, in July an American Apollo and a Soviet Soyuz spacecraft docked in orbit, marking the first such linkup between spacecraft from the two nations; while in August came signature of the Helsinki Accords, which officially recognized Europe's national borders and respect for human rights. In September there were two separate abortive attempts to assassinate President Gerald Ford, both in California. In October, Ford asked Kissinger to relinquish his role as national security adviser to his deputy, Brent Scowcroft. There ended a unique duality in U.S. affairs of state.

On May 31, 1976, Syria intervened in the Lebanese civil war, opposing the PLO, which it had previously supported. July 4 brought the United States its Bicentennial celebrations. On this milestone anniversary of the Declaration of Independence, there were many sober-

ing reflections on past American triumphs—and on a much less glori-
ous present. That same month, Indonesia moved into East Timor, a
former colony of the collapsed Portuguese empire. Once again, there
were questions about Kissinger's involvement. September brought
more unpleasant innuendos, following the murder in Washington of
former Chilean minister of foreign affairs Orlando Letelier by agents
of General Pinochet's DINA secret service. Two weeks earlier, the
Viking 2 spacecraft landed on Mars. On the 9th, Chairman Mao died.
Meanwhile America was amid election turmoil. On November 2, at
the presidential election, Gerald Ford was defeated by Jimmy Carter,
who became the first candidate from the Deep South to win the presidency since the Civil War.

Kissinger packed up his papers in the State Department, to make
way for Cyrus Vance. Into his former post at the NSC would move his
old adversary from Harvard days, Zbigniew Kazimierz Brzezinski.
"As suddenly as I had been catapulted to public service," he wrote in
his memoirs, "it was over."[5]

But that is how it happens in public life.

Back in 1974, there had been talk[6] of amending the requirement
that a U.S. president be born in America so that Kissinger could have
a chance to run; but nothing further came of it. About his role in office, the sniping, however, continued. He returned to writing and
teaching, but not to his alma mater, Harvard—preferring to remain
nearer the seats of power he knew so well. That same year he joined the
faculty of Georgetown University. In 1980 when the Republicans returned to power under Ronald Reagan, Kissinger was bitterly disappointed to find there would be no room for him in the new,
California-oriented, conservative administration. He was still only
fifty-seven, and charged with energy. He waited, but the telephone
never rang. Starting with *White House Years*, published in 1979, and
spanning twenty years of writing, he began recording, in Churchillian
scope, his account of events during the time of his stewardship. There
would be three weighty—but extremely readable—volumes, *Years of
Upheaval* in 1982 and *Years of Renewal* in 2000, each of over a thousand pages, laced frequently with enticing vignettes of personalities.
Huge sales made him a rich man. There followed other distinguished
books.

Kissinger was, nevertheless, unable to keep away from contemporary foreign affairs, nor resist his temptation to get on every airplane. Unlike most modern human beings, ever since the days of his shuttle diplomacy the thought of air travel provided him constant exhilaration. He watched with gloom as, under the weak Carter regime, America's stock plunged when the shah fell and members of the U.S. embassy staff in Tehran were taken hostage for humiliating months on end. Then, taking advantage of Washington's debility, the Soviets invaded Afghanistan. One positive achievement in the Carter years came in 1978, with the Camp David Accords, whereby Kissinger's old partner Sadat and Prime Minister Menachem Begin of Israel, a former terrorist, shook hands at last. They agreed on Israel's withdrawal from Sinai, in return for a definitive ending to the thirty years of enmity with Egypt. (Yet, since it was he who had laid the foundations which made the historic handshake possible, he might have been excused had he watched it with a certain pang of exclusion, of not being prime party to such a historic moment.)

In 1982, Kissinger founded a consulting firm, Kissinger Associates, advising the powerful and the influential across the globe on the intricacies of dealing with foreign regimes, based on his own copious experience derived from his White House years. Post-Mao China in particular formed a focus of his attention. Kissinger Associates too proved highly profitable; and he had many bidders for his lectures at approximately $100,000 each, sometimes delivering more than a hundred in a year.[7] At the same time, while living in style in a Manhattan apartment overlooking the East River, with Nancy—a born gardener and hostess without peer—he delighted in the existence of a country squire in a Shangri-la carved out of the woodlands of upstate Connecticut. He would entertain friends and scholars from all walks of life, yet at the same time unable to cease fretting at the deficiencies of statecraft in the contemporary world. Fresh honors, as well as slings and arrows, came pouring in. Through his close personal friendship with the German (Socialist) chancellor Helmut Schmidt, he formed new bonds with the country which had driven out the Kissingers, revisiting it often, and becoming honorary president of his old hometown soccer team in Fürth, Bavaria.

It was all a long way from those childhood memories.

As far as life in the corridors of power was concerned, the years from Carter through Clinton were lean ones. There must have been times when he missed bitterly that "ultimate aphrodisiac" of power. Then the younger Bush came to office and with him almost immediately the dread, unprecedented challenge of 9/11. With it Kissinger, renowned for his expertise on Middle East affairs, was called in for what would become regular, monthly visits to the White House, followed by a parallel relationship with the new national security adviser and subsequent secretary of state, Condoleezza Rice. Though he fought shy of providing any input on strategy for Iraq, it was not a policy to which he was intrinsically opposed, and he would come to be regarded as a valued adviser, and elder statesman, by President Bush. His reach would later be extended to embrace frequent visits to Vladimir Putin's Kremlin. There, as the man who could once claim to have been "kissed on the mouth by Brezhnev," his linkage with the new, perhaps frightening, world of a resurgent Russia could claim a unique currency. (On a visit to the Oval Office in May 2007, the author was bid farewell with the words: "Please thank Henry for all the good work he's doing for us with Putin—though I think maybe he's a bit too kind on the guy!")[8]

When Kissinger left office, it could almost be said of him, in the words Shakespeare once used of Julius Caesar, that he had been a colossus to "bestride the narrow world." In fact, was there not something of Classical connotation in the twin-colossi of the two men, Nixon and Kissinger, especially in the year of 1973? Parallels are frequently drawn between Imperial America and Rome, and the suggestion has already been made here of Nixon fulfilling the requirements of Greek tragedy: the man of huge stature who falls from a great height to the depths, through a fault of his own making. Kissinger, however, conveys more of the Roman image. Certainly there was something Roman in the scale of the drama and the world panorama over which he was called upon to assume a dominant role in 1973. On account of the extraordinary circumstances prevailing (i.e., Watergate), Kissinger found himself projected into a position of unprecedented authority in 1973—and power—more than he could have bargained for, and certainly unprecedented for any secretary of state in the history of the United States. Of course, there are dangers in extending the Classical parallels too far; Rome was a far less forgiving society than twentieth-century America, and would hardly have countenanced the way in which the disgraced and fallen president was allowed, in his old age, to rehabilitate himself—almost to the extent of becoming a respected elder.

Peculiar to America (though also to an extent in ancient Rome) was the possibility that an impoverished refugee from another part of the world could rise, as did Kissinger, to all but the very pinnacle of power.* One may recall the sense of deep gratitude for all America had done for him, of all that it had signified for the uprooted, as he expressed it in his confirmation address of September 1973; perhaps it took a refugee from Hitler, endowed with a keen awareness of America's imperial destiny—as well as all its faults and blemishes—to achieve what it was granted to Kissinger to achieve. Certainly when it comes to attempting to assess those achievements on so great a scale, by so complex a human being, one is enticed to contemplate them somewhat by the standards of ancient Rome.

To this day, these achievements are bound to give rise to argument and controversy, with violent pros and cons. When, in 2004, I first took on the task of writing the story of Kissinger in 1973, I nervously inquired of my U.S. editor, Michael Korda, "Do I have to play the role of defense attorney, prosecutor—and, as well, judge and jury?" over all those thirty-three tons of archive material? Great Heavens! Korda, with the wisdom of a veteran editor (and himself no mean writer), replied: "No; leave the verdict to the reader!" So be it; I accepted his instruction with relief. Yet, nevertheless, some brief commentary on the affairs of 1973 over which Kissinger had stewardship may be permitted.

Over the whole scene of 1973 loomed the shadow of Watergate. What Kissinger might have achieved but for that lowering cloud we cannot know with any certainty. Equally, as the one major figure of the Nixon administration who remained outside it all, had Kissinger allowed Watergate to embrace and destroy him, as it had destroyed Nixon and others, the consequences—both for the United States and the Western world as a whole—would have been unimaginable.

---

* Only in Rome could foreigners like Diocletian or Trajan achieve the ultimate rank of emperor.

Of his various initiatives, the Year of Europe ended as an almost unqualified failure, shipwrecked (not for the last time) on the rocks of European self-interest and American arrogance. Détente with the Soviet Union, a brave and farsighted enterprise, was weakened partly by the unanticipated war in the Middle East, and partly by the effects of the Watergate crisis on the Nixon administration; yet, how much more dangerous might the world have become without that initiative? Nixon's inspired China gambit undoubtedly made the world a safer place; but it too would drift into the doldrums because of the wind that Watergate had taken out of the American sail. In the Middle East, in common with the Kremlin and all the intelligence agencies outside the Arab world, Kissinger was caught napping; but his recovery through the Yom Kippur War, and the shuttle diplomacy that followed, was to prove a lasting monument to his stewardship. Might he have been more deserving of Nobel recognition for that, than for Vietnam? Then, at the other end of the spectrum from the Middle East shuttles of 1973–74, came the collapse of U.S. hopes in Indochina. To this day, Kissinger regards the failure of all his labors to achieve "peace with honor" in Vietnam as the outstanding disappointment of his life—a source of never-ending regret. As he wrote in the concluding words of *Crisis*, when the last U.S. helicopters took off from the embassy roof in Saigon, "only a feeling of emptiness remained."[9]

It is an emptiness that has remained with him ever since. But could he have done better? There, once again, the shadow of Watergate, and the unremitting hatred for Nixon, hung heavy. By 1973 the unsilent minority of American opinion, so much more raucous than the voice of the so-called silent majority, was pledged to the liquidation of all U.S. responsibilities in Vietnam. Could Kissinger, thwarted as he was in his hopes of some degree of neutrality, if not complicity, from Beijing and Moscow, possibly have fought against the overwhelming tide of the Watergate mood and what it had done to the American will at home?

As I have noted, few people (certainly not Americans) can be neutral about Henry Kissinger, they either hate him, or love him. Some critics endeavor, not always with success, to divide the image of the statesman from his persona. I met those who would eagerly have liked to see him arraigned for crimes against humanity. Walter Isaacson, a not unfriendly earlier biographer of Kissinger, stressed to me the final paragraphs of his book, where he deemed that Kissinger's morality had "faltered" over issues such as Cambodia and Chile. In conclusion, where he found him strong on realpolitik he judged him weak on issues of human rights.[10] Others, such as Brzezinski, the diehard Pole, might have agreed. Where Kissinger would have pleaded that the ends justify the means, Isaacson judged his diplomacy "ill-suited to an open and democratic society" like America.

When Kissinger questioned me at lunch later that same day about my meeting with Isaacson, he instantly rebutted his remark about realpolitik with a laugh: "Well, America has to be the only country where reality isn't a virtue!"[11] It was a critique he had heard before, and one that will long linger. Yet, if it implied heartlessness on a personal level, as I got to know him progressively from many hours of conversations, including visits to his home at Kent, Connecticut, I realized how little validity it held. There were repeated displays of concern, of heart, for former colleagues, old staffers. Most—like his archivist, Rosemary Niehuss, "Miss Moneypenny," who had remained with him the best part of three decades—seemed bound with deep bonds of loyalty, indeed affection, and regardless of how brusquely they might have been treated during the office years. That well-known hypersensitivity was not just directed subjectively toward himself. There was deep concern over the plight of sick friends, like Bill Buckley in his declining months. On one occasion at Kent, I found him in deep gloom over the scandal, with implications of a replay in miniature of Watergate 1973, which was currently embracing a senior aide to Vice President Dick Cheney—Lewis I. "Scooter" Libby. "That poor man; I know what will happen. He'll be ruined. He won't get another job, he may go to prison, he'll be crushed by legal fees." I asked him if he knew Scooter? "No, he was not a personal friend; but I'm going to ring him, to offer him sympathy." And he did just that.*

Kissinger's view of the world, a profoundly pessimistic one, strongly influenced by his German provenance, was always that of the

---

* In June 2007, Libby was sentenced to thirty months in federal prison, and a fine of $250,000, on counts of perjury. President Bush commuted Libby's prison sentence, but left the other parts of his sentence intact.

historian, concerned predominantly with statecraft. If it was realpolitik that overruled human rights, it was that sense—again, essentially Roman, if not of the eighteenth-century Age of Enlightenment—of the overriding importance of order in an essentially anarchic world; an order that held as its objective the maximum well-being of the majority of citizens. In this context alone Kissinger surely stands out as belonging to the tradition, probably the last of the line, of the great European diplomatists, of the Metternichs and Castlereaghs about whom he wrote with such enthusiasm those many years ago.

Repeatedly in the course of writing this book, I have been asked, "Do you consider Henry Kissinger a *great man*?" A distinguished British biographer, Philip Ziegler, closes his monumental official biography *Mountbatten* with the admission that, when "enraged" by his (posthumous) subject he would have to set in front of him a notice reminding himself: "REMEMBER, IN SPITE OF EVERYTHING, HE WAS A GREAT MAN." [12] He seems to have had occasional doubts (though Mountbatten himself certainly never did).

With Kissinger, I never felt a need for this reminder. (In the first place, while I may have infuriated *him*, he never "enraged" me!) The tribute, in his case, should surely read not "in spite of," but "because of" circumstances: Watergate, Nixon, the Yom Kippur War, and Vietnam. When, in 2005, I was working on the Kissinger papers at the Library of Congress, the librarian, Dr. James Billington, a scholar seldom given to hyperbole, and with long experience of Washington, mused to me how leaders tended to be always either "show horses" or "work horses": "But," he added, "Henry was both, and he deserves full credit." Himself a distinguished expert on the Soviet Union, speaking of détente against that backdrop of Kissinger working under the shadow of Watergate and a mortally impaired president, Billington summed up how "The period which Henry had to deal with was an extraordinarily difficult one—because of the cards that were dealt him." [13] To me it was, if anything, a major understatement.

One thing that seems indisputable about Henry Kissinger in office: he was surely one of the very few statesmen of our era to try to do *something* positive to break the logjam of the Cold War; to try to end the war in Vietnam; to bring a halt to the cycle of war in the Middle East. His was a role of not just *reacting*—or of rolling with the punches. If circumstances were indeed "extraordinarily difficult," with Watergate frustrating him from attainment of his ultimate objectives, such as "peace with honor" in Vietnam, then it could be said that, at least, because of the straitjacket it imposed on his president, Kissinger was granted opportunities and powers never given to other mere secretaries of state before—or after.

As I pen the last words of this book, I am hearing in my ears the inspirational words of Barack Obama's acceptance speech in Chicago. Like hundreds of millions across the globe, I was as moved as any American: "If there is anyone out there who still doubts that America is a place where all things are possible . . ." It brought back to me the whole tremendous cavalcade of America's enthralling history, which first grabbed me as a refugee schoolboy from Britain in wartime Millbrook, New York. But it also made me reflect on the career of Henry Kissinger. Only in America! A first African-American president; and the first Jewish secretary of state. In Britain we once had a Jewish prime minister, Benjamin Disraeli; but he did not come to our shores as an impoverished refugee, and I doubt if Disraeli ever faced anything comparable to the challenges which I tracked in one year of Kissinger's career.

And what an opportunity, exciting beyond belief, for a professor of history to find himself uniquely in a position to be able to DO SOMETHING—instead of just writing and lecturing to students about where statesmen had gone wrong in the past.

To how many would such a challenge ever be given?

In another era deeply challenging to a young America, a fellow Briton wrote memorably: "THESE are the times that try men's souls. The summer soldier and the sunshine patriot will, in this crisis, shrink from the service of their country; but he that stands by it now, deserves the love and thanks of man and woman." As in 1776, a Tom Paine might well have deemed the year of 1973 one that was sent to "try men's souls." It was one in which Henry Kissinger certainly proved himself to be neither "summer soldier" nor "sunshine patriot."

Acknowledgments

I N ADDITION TO Dr. Kissinger, the following were generous with their time given in interview or conversation:

Professor Christopher Andrew, Dr. Alan Angell, Dr. Walter Armbrust, Ms. Elizabeth Becker, Dr. James Billington, Ms. Joan Bingham, Conrad Black, Ms. Gill Brett, the Hon. Zbigniew Brzezinski, Judge James Buckley, William F. Buckley Jr., Lord Carrington, Ray Close, Dominic Coldwell, Arnaud de Borchgrave, Paul Delaney, Tony Dolan, Lawrence Eagleburger, Son Excellence Gérard Errera, Mark Falcoff, Stanley Flink, the Rt. Hon. John Freeman, Sir David Frost, Ms. Georgie-Anne Geyer, Ambassador Ashraf Ghorbal, General Vo Nguyen Giap, Sir Ronald Grierson, Kristian C. Gustafson, General Lord Guthrie, Alexander Haig, Ms. Catherine Hansen, Ambassador Arthur Hartman, Mohamed Heikal, Mrs. Richard Helms, Sir Nicholas Henderson, Walter Isaacson, Ms. Jung Chang and Jon Halliday, Don Kendall, Ambassador Jean Kennedy-Smith, Peter Kornbluh, Miss Victoria Legge-Bourke, Jan Lodal, Winston Lord, Professor Margaret MacMillan, John Newhouse, Señora Nena Ossa, Peter G. Peterson, Professor Richard Pipes, Professor William Quandt, Hon. Stanley Resor, Peter Rodman, Dr. Eugene Rogan, Ambassador William D. Rogers, Ambassador S. Roosevelt, Dr. Harold Saunders, Professor Arthur Schlesinger, James Schlesinger, General Brent Scowcroft, William Shawcross, Professor A. Shlaim, Hani Shukrallah, Helmut Sonnenfeldt, Dr. Jonathan Spence, Ambassador Stapleton Roy, Ambassador Michael Sterner, Strobe Talbott, Ambassador W. Vanden

Heuvel, Sir Robert Wade-Gery, Judge William H. Webster, Stanley Weiss, Dr. Sam Wells.

I am beholden to the Library of Congress, and to Dr. James Billington and Dr. Prosser Gifford for the award of a fellowship in 2005 to the John W. Kluge Center, and especially—in subsequent months—to a similar fellowship at my alma mater in Washington, the Woodrow Wilson Center, coupled with the names of Director Lee Hamilton, Dr. Sam Wells, and Michael van Dusen. Without the support of both these admirable foundations it would have been impossible for me to pursue, or fund, my essential researches. I am also much indebted to the friendly and efficient team at Dr. Kissinger's K Street office in Washington, and particularly to his painstaking archivist of many years standing, Rosemary Niehuss. It was never their job to point me toward any smoking gun, but to lead me to locate all the documents I felt I needed.

As ever my oldest, and much lamented, friend Bill Buckley and his late wife, Pat, provided never failing hospitality in Connecticut, as well as constant support. Equally generous hosts, on frequent occasions, were Nancy and Henry Kissinger up at Kent. All helped make it a happy, as well as fruitful, time for me.

But this book would never have gotten off the ground but for the initial, and continued, encouragement and expertise of Michael Korda of Simon & Schuster, New York—surely one of the legendary editors of our times, as well as being a most distinguished author in his own right. In England I am also indebted to another editor of legend, Ion Trewin of Orion, and especially to the indefatigable efforts of transcription by his assistant, Bea Hemming. At Simon & Schuster, New York, I also owe a significant debt to the editorial input of Dedi Felman. Prior to submission of the manuscript I had no conception of the problems, or pitfalls, of editing at three thousand miles distance. I must have driven them all mad with my vagaries, delays, and inconsistencies— plus the additional hazard of three major illnesses. I cannot overstate my gratitude to all the above in preparation of the finished product; it needs hardly be emphasized that any surviving errors or lacunae rest with the author alone.

At home in England, I was loyally and indefatigably aided by Janet

Robjohn; but above all I remain the perpetual debtor to my long-suffering and adorable consort, Sheelin.

In Majorca, once again, I am indebted to Sheila Pecznik for providing a summer haven in which to think, read, write, and relax. Finally, within the family, I cannot forget my grandson, Kipper Berven, and his ten-year-old classmates in Grade 4 of Town School, San Francisco, who helped significantly in my quest for a title.

Turville, Oxon., 2004–2009

Notes

ABBREVIATIONS

AH: Author
EVW: *Ending the Vietnam War*
HAK: Henry Kissinger
MM: Margaret MacMillan
NSA: National Security Archives
RN: *RN: The Memoirs of Richard Nixon*
WHY: *White House Years*
YOR: *Years of Renewal*
YOU: *Years of Upheaval*
1800 K St. and HAK Misc. boxes: AH notes from Kissinger files

1: A Very Odd Couple

1 HAK int., 10/29/05.
2 Walter Isaacson, *Kissinger: A Biography* (New York, 1992), 479.
3 See *WHY*, 1409–10.
4 Isaacson, 479.
5 David Frost, *"I Gave Them a Sword": Behind The Scenes of the Nixon Interviews* (New York, 1978), 137.
6 *WHY*, 1457–58.
7 Isaacson, 461–80; Theodore White, xi-xiii.
8 *YOU*, 5.
9 Lord int., 10/31/05.
10 *YOU*, xix, 3–8.
11 HAK int., 29–30, 2005.
12 See Stephen Ambrose, *Nixon* (3 vols.) (New York, 1987–91), III, 30.
13 *YOU*, 7.
14 From HAK archives.
15 Andreas Killen, *1973 Nervous Breakdown: Watergate, Warhol, and the Birth of Post-Sixties America* (New York, 2006), 2.
16 Ibid., 67.
17 See ibid., 57 ff.
18 Ibid., 62.
19 AH, H. Macmillan notes.
20 HAK int., 8/15/04.
21 HAK int., 4/24/08.
22 Isaacson, 40.
23 HAK, eulogy, 10/8/03.
24 HAK int.

25 Isaacson, 45.
26 HAK int., 10/28/05.
27 Isaacson, 56–57.
28 Marvin Kalb and Bernard Kalb, *Kissinger* (Boston, 1974), 42.
29 *A World Restored* (1957) and *Diplomacy* (1994).
30 Isaacson, 75.
31 Sir Ronald Grieson int., 9/22/04.
32 Brzezinski int., 10/05.
33 Isaacson, 127.
34 Ibid., 137.
35 *WHY*, 12.
36 Richard Nixon, *RN: The Memoirs of Richard Nixon* (New York, 1990) 341.
37 Ibid., 340.
38 MM, 95, Strobe Talbott int., 5/23/05.
39 MM, 92, ref. 70.
40 HAK, Fritz Kraemer eulogy, 10/8/03.
41 *RN*, 341.
42 Isaacson 128. (MM, 78.)
43 *A World Restored* (1957, republished in 2000), 4–5.
44 Ibid., p. 12.
45 Ibid., 20.
46 Ibid., 43.
47 Ibid., 326.
48 Sir Robert Wade-Gery int.
49 *Foreign Affairs*, January 1969, *211*.
50 Isaacson, 160.
51 Schlesinger int., 5/16/05.
52 Eagleburger int., 10/26/05.
53 Freeman int., 1/19/06.
54 Ambrose, I, 14.
55 HAK int., 5/06.
56 Haig int., 5/19/05.
57 Scowcroft int., 5/26/05.
58 Rodman int., 5/13/05.
59 Ambrose, II, 19, 49.
60 Frost, *"I Gave Them a Sword"* (New York, 1978), 11.
61 Haig int., 5/19/05.
62 Carrington int., 6/9/04.
63 Op. cit. 1.
64 Garry Wills, *Nixon Agonistes* (New York, 1970); Killen, 65.
65 *WHY*, 11.
66 Ambrose, I, 624–25.
67 *RN*, 711.
68 Frost, 65, 284.
69 *RN*, 341.
70 Leonard Garment, *In Search of Deep Throat* (New York, 2000), 186–87 (MM, 84).
71 Ambrose, I, 641.
72 Frost int., 9/23/05.
73 MM, 89.
74 Hartmann int., 5/6/06.
75 MM, 86.

76 *Sunday Telegraph*, 2/14/81.
77 *Times*, 7/23/04.
78 Isaacson, 140.
79 Ibid., 140.
80 HAK int., Paris, 5/13/06.
81 Haig int., 5/19/05.
82 Scowcroft int., 5/26/05.
83 Eagleburger int., 10/26/05.
84 Hartmann int., 5/6/05.
85 Lodal int., 5/13/06.
86 Niehuss int., 10/7/05.
87 Lodal int., 10/21/05.
88 Lord int., 10/31/05.
89 Eagleburger conv., 10/26/05.
90 Isaacson, 140.
91 Scowcroft int., 5/26/05.
92 Victoria Legge-Bourke int.
93 *NYT*, 1/30/72.
94 Ibid., 11/26/72.
95 Ibid., 10/22/04.
96 Ibid.
97 Newhouse int., 12/04.
98 Isaacson, 149, 218–27.
99 HAK int., 10/28/05.

2: The Black Hole: Vietnam

1 *EVW*, 11.
2 Vo Nguyen Giap int., 3/2/98.
3 HAK int., 12/7/07.
4 *EVW,* 13.
5 Ibid., 13.
6 Ibid., 31, 1.
7 Westmoreland, *Foreign Affairs*, 11/67, 1.
8 *EVW*, 41.
9 Ibid., 166.
10 Ibid., 9.
11 Ibid., 7.
12 *A Savage War of Peace,* 226
13 Isaacson, 265.
14 Ibid., 269.
15 *Sideshow* (New York, 1979).
16 Margaret Becker conv., 5/14/05.
17 *EVW*, 192.
18 Ibid., 198.
19 Ibid., 123.
20 Ibid., 191.
21 Ibid., 233–36.
22 *WHY*, 272.
23 Ibid., 272–74.

24 HAK conv., 7/11/06.

25 HAK int., 5/13/06.

26 Walters, *The Mighty and the Meek*, 91.

27 Muir and Wilkinson (Lexington, VA, 2005), 233; HAK int., 5/13/06.

28 HAK int; Muir and Wilkinson, 233.

29 Walters, I, 515, 509.

30 *EVW*, 220.

31 *WHY*, 279.

32 *EVW*, 113.

33 HAK int., 5/13/06.

34 *EVW*, 113.

35 To author, 4/15/05.

36 Giap int., 3/2/98.

37 Isaacson, 252.

38 *EVW*, 114; HAK int., 5/13/06.

39 Walters, I, 518.

40 Ibid., II, 89.

41 Ibid., II, 91–94.

42 HAK int., 5/13/06.

43 *EVW*, 301.

44 *NYT*, 7/17/72.

45 *NYT*, 10/1/72.

46 *EVW*, 338.

47 Isaacson, 439–41; *EVW*, 329.

48 *EVW*, 329–30; *WHY*, 1345–46.

49 *EVW*, 338.

50 *RN*, 691.

51 Ibid., 690.

52 *EVW*, 375.

53 *RN*, 705.

54 Haig int., 5/19/05; Lord int., 10/30/05; Isaacson, 255.

55 Kalb and Kalb, 375.

56 *RN*, 722.

57 Ibid., 725.

58 Ibid., 733, 755.

59 *EVW*, 395.

60 Ibid., 418.

61 *RN*, 726–27, 739.

62 Kalb and Kalb, 399.

63 Ibid., 101.

64 *RN*, 734.

65 Rodman int., 4/15/05.

66 Kalb and Kalb, 416.

67 Ibid.

68 *WHY*, 1453.

69 Ibid., 1460–61.

70 Isaacson, 468.

71 Isaacson, 475–81; Fallaci, in *New Republic*, 12/16/72.

72 To Admiral Zumwalt, in Isaacson, 474.

73 Ibid., 479; John Ehrlichman, *Witness to Power* (New York, 1982), 313–16.

74 *NYT*, 12/30/73.

75 HAK int., 5/13–14/06.
76 HAK int., 5/13/06.
77 *EVW*, 421.
78 *RN*, 753–54.
79 *YOU*, 23.
80 Ibid., 29.
81 *WHY*, 1472.
82 *EVW*, 430.
83 Ibid.
84 *WHY*, 1476.
85 Ibid., 428.
86 *EVW*, 428.
87 Memcon, 1/25/73.
88 Memcon, 2/15/73.
89 Killen, 95.
90 Ibid., 94.
91 Pilgrims luncheon, 9/30/08.
92 *RN*, 866–68.
93 Ibid., 867–68.
94 *EVW*, 460.
95 HAK to author, 12/7/06.

3: The Opening to China

 1 MM, 246.
 2 Ibid., 245.
 3 *RN*, 497.
 4 Ibid., 508.
 5 Isaacson, 335; *Foreign Affairs*, October 1967.
 6 Isaacson, 336.
 7 MM, 122.
 8 Isaacson, 336.
 9 *WHY*, 694.
10 *WHY*, 688.
11 Walters, I, 527.
12 Ibid., 521.
13 *WHY*, 187.
14 Isaacson, 339.
15 Ibid.
16 *WHY*, 711 (*RN*, 550–53).
17 *RN*, 550.
18 MM, 183.
19 Ibid., 552.
20 *WHY*, 718.
21 MM, 161.
22 Isaacson, 343; *NYT*, 7/10/71.
23 *WHY*, 775; MM, 147.
24 *WHY*, 744.
25 *Mao*, Jung Chang.
26 Jung Chang int., 9/23/05; *WHY*, 745.

27 *WHY*, 747.
28 MM, 191.
29 *WHY*, 746.
30 Ibid., 748.
31 Ibid., 755.
32 MM, 200.
33 *RN*, 554.
34 *WHY*, 756.
35 Ibid., 760; *RN*, 553.
36 Isaacson, 349.
37 Ibid., 349.
38 Nixon archives, released 2005; HAK ints.
39 *YOU*, 7.
40 *WHY*, 739.
41 *RN*, 553–55; MM; *WHY*, 776, 782.
42 *RN*, 555.
43 *WHY*, 783.
44 Ibid.
45 *RN*, 559.
46 *WHY*, 1051.
47 Ibid., 1054.
48 MM, 283.
49 Ibid., 45ff.
50 *RN*, 560.
51 *WHY*, 1059.
52 *WHY*, 1053–96ff.
53 AH notes.
54 *Mao*, 606.
55 Martin Gilbert, *Finest Hour* (London, 1983), 1119.
56 Halliday int., 9/13/05.
57 Jussi Hanhimaki, *The Flawed Architect: Henry Kissinger and American Foreign Policy* (New York, 2004), 192.
58 *WHY*, 1061.
59 *WHY*, 1068.
60 Ibid., 1082.
61 MM, 305.
62 Ibid., 307.
63 Ibid., 308–9.
64 *WHY*, 1057.
65 Hanhimaki, 193.
66 *WHY*, 1057; MM, 60–63.
67 MM, 246.
68 Ibid., 258.
69 *WHY*, 1079.
70 MM, 311–12.
71 *WHY*, 1086.
72 *WHY*, 1092.
73 *Mao*, 603–5, 608–9.
74 Halliday int., 9/13/05.
75 HAK letter of 6/28/05.
76 MM, 26.

77 HAK int., 10/28/05.
78 MM, 321.
79 MM, 318.
80 MM, p. 287; William J. Galloway int., 9/28/99.
81 Edward Heath, *The Course of My Life* (London, 1998), 495.
82 MM, 287.
83 MM, 289; *WHY*, 766.
84 MM, 321.
85 MM, 336.
86 Ibid., 338; memcon, 10/20/71.
87 *YOU*, 44–45.
88 Ibid., 45.
89 Lord int., 10/30/05.
90 *YOU*, 47; MM, 210; Lord int., 5/30/10.
91 *Mao*, 610.
92 Ibid., 612; meeting of 7/6/73.
93 Lord int., 10/30/05.
94 Ibid.
95 *Mao*, 613; Spence conv., 10/28/05.
96 *YOU*, 53.
97 Ibid., 53–54.
98 Ibid., 56.
99 Ibid., 64–65.
100 MM, 245.
101 Ibid., 273–4.
102 Memcon, 5/15/73; "1800 St.files."
103 *YOU*, 71.

4: A Feather-Brained Crime

1 Richard Helms, *A Look Over My Shoulder* (New York: Random House, 2003), 7.
2 MM, 333.
3 *YOU*, 72ff.
4 Ibid., 73.
5 Ibid., 75.
6 Ibid., 76; HAK int., 4/21/05.
7 Memcon, 3/21/73.
8 *YOU*, 76.
9 *RN*, 625–27.
10 Ambrose, I, 577, 606.
11 Adrian Havill, "*Deep Truth: The Lives of Bob Woodward and Carl Bernstein* (Secaucus, 1993).
12 HAK int., May 05.
13 See Bob Woodward and Carl Bernstein, *All the President's Men* (New York, 1974), 163.
14 *Washington Post*, 4/24/85.
15 Woodward and Bernstein, 275.
16 Helms, 9.
17 Ibid., 10.
18 Walters II, 38–39; Helms, 3–13.
19 Walters, *Silent Mission*, 39.

20 *YOU*, 78; HAK ints.
21 *YOU*, 77–78.
22 HAK int., 5/13–14/06.
23 Ibid.
24 *YOU*, 79.
25 HAK int., 4/21/05.
26 *YOU*, 81.
27 *Public Papers of the Presidents* 298, April 17, 1973.
28 Ibid., 299.
29 *YOU*, 90.
30 Ibid., 94.
31 Ibid., 95–97.
32 Ibid., 99.
33 HAK int., 5/13–14/06.
34 *RN*, p. 814; Ambrose, II, 99.
35 *YOU*, 77.
36 Ibid., 98.
37 Ibid., 81, 102; 100, 123; 122–23; 122; 124–26.
38 Ibid., 99.
39 HAK ints., 4/21/05, 5/13–14/06.
40 *YOU*, 102.
42 *YOU*, 107–10.
43 Isaacson, 492–93.
44 *YOU*, 109.
45 Ibid., 110.
46 Rodman int., 4/15/05.
47 Isaacson, p. 500–502; Isaacson int., 4/20/05.
48 Isaacson, 501.
49 *RN*, 851.
50 Ibid., 874.

5: The Year of Europe

 1 *YOU*, 191.
 2 Ibid., 152–53.
 3 Ibid., 153.
 4 Legge-Bourke conv., 8/25/06.
 5 *YOU*, 130.
 6 Ibid., 131.
 7 Ibid., 30
 8 Memcon, 4/13/17.
 9 Alistair Horne, *Harold Macmillan: Volume II, 1957–1986* (London, 1988), 242.
10 MM, 287.
11 *YOU*, 140.
12 Ibid., 141.
13 Talbott int., 5/23/05.
14 HAK int., 4/21/05.
15 *YOU*, 148.
16 Sonnenfeldt int., 5/18/05.
17 Ibid.; *YOU*, 164.

18 Press conf. minutes, 5/29/73.
19 *YOU*, 172.
20 Ibid., 171.
21 Ibid., 179.
22 Ibid., 181.
23 Ibid., 184.
24 Ibid., 187.
25 Ibid., 188.
26 Ibid., 189.
27 Ibid., 190–91.
28 Ibid., 191.
29 Ibid., 192.
30 NSC memcon, 9/25/73.
31 Ibid.
32 Errera int., 10/18/06.
33 Schlesinger int., 5/16/05.
34 Scowcroft int.
35 Memcon, 11/12/74.

6: Storm Clouds over the Middle East

1 Elinor Burkett, *Golda: The Iron Lady of the Middle East* (New York, 2008), 312.
 2 NSCAE, 4.
 3 William Quandt, *Decade of Decision* (Berkeley, 1977), 98–104.
 4 *YOU*, 202.
 5 *YOU*, 203.
 6 Ibid.
 7 HAK int., 10/28/05.
 8 HAK ints.
 9 Michael Sterner int., 10/27/07.
10 Christopher Andrews and Vasili Mitrokhin, *Mitrokhin Archive* (2004), II, 146.
11 NSCAE, 5.
12 *YOU*, 200.
13 In an interview with Barbara Walters of NBC News, 2/23/73.
14 *YOU*, 214.
15 HAK int., 10/28/05.
16 *YOU*, 214.
17 Ibid.
18 Kendall int., 10/15/05.
19 *YOU*, 212.
20 Ibid., 211–12; Ambrose, II, 167.
21 Ibid., 220.
22 F. Huré to author, 1969.
23 *NYT*, 12/9/78.
24 Ambrose, II, 167.
25 HAK ints., 5/05.
26 *Newsweek*, 4/9/73.
27 *YOU*, 225.
28 Close int., 11/18/05.
29 Ibid.

30 *YOU*, 225–26.
31 Donald Neff int.; *Washington Report on Middle East Affairs*, 10–11/97.
32 Close int., 11/18/05.
33 From *Dado*, Hanoch Bartov, quoted in *Ha'aretz*, 9/6/02.
34 Walter J. Boyne, *The 2 O'Clock War* (New York, 2002), 19.
35 From Avi Shlaim, *The Iron Wall* (New York, 2000), 316.
36 Amir Oren, *Ha'aretz*, 8/14/03; Shlaim, *The Iron Wall*, 306–18.
37 See Robert Lacey, *The Kingdom: Arabia and the House of Sa'ud* (New York, 1982), 400–402; State Dept. Middle East Task Force, "Situation Report §51," 10/21/73.
38 *YOU*, 227.
39 Quandt, 101.
40 AH Cairo ints., 2005.

7: Coming to Grips with the Polar Bear

1 Michael Korda to author.
2 *YOU*, 242.
3 Ibid., 243.
4 HAK int.
5 HAK int., 8/15/04.
6 *Diplomacy*, 742.
7 NSA telcons, rel 5/26/04.
8 Henderson conv.
9 Ibid.
10 Ibid.
11 To CNN, 10/1/79.
12 Henderson, *NYT*, 9/10/95.
13 Anatoly Dobrynin, *In Confidence: Moscow's Ambassador to America's Six Cold War Presidents* (New York, 1995), 688.
14 Billington int., 5/12/05.
15 Hartman int., 5/6/05.
16 Lodal int., 10/14/05.
17 MM, 246.
18 *Diplomacy*, 733.
19 *WHY*, 1127–28.
20 Isaacson, 429.
21 *YOU*, 232.
22 Ibid., 229–35.
23 Hartman int., 5/6/05.
24 Kendall int., 10/17/05.
25 Peterson int., 4/27/05.
26 HAK int., 8/15/04; Schlesinger int., 5/16/05.
27 *WHY*, 1138–39; *Diplomacy*, 727.
28 HAK int., 8/15/04.
29 Frost, 305; MM, 287.
30 *YOU*, 229–31.
31 Henderson int., 1/11/07.
32 Isaacson, 317.
33 See Isaacson, 322; Kissinger briefing, 12/3/74.

34 John Newhouse, *War and Peace in the Nuclear Age* (New York, 1989), 216.
35 Ibid., 231.
36 *WHY*, 1234.
37 Isaacson, 430–31; Jan Lodal ints., 5/13/05, 10/14/05; Schlesinger int., 5/16/05; *WHY*, 1234; Newhouse int.; Newhouse, 234; Ambrose, I, 546–48, q. Garthoff, Hersh, 535; Gerard C. Smith, *Doubletalk: The Untold Story of SALT* (Lanham, Md., 1985), 376.
38 Newhouse, 234.
39 *WHY*, 1235.
40 Ibid., 1233.
41 *RN*, 615.
42 HAK int.
43 Kalb and Kalb, 328.
44 Isaacson, 437.
45 Newhouse, 233.
46 Isaacson, 436.
47 Ambrose, I, 548.
48 *Mitrokhin Archive*, 15–16.
49 *YOU*, 239.
50 Ibid., 237.
51 Ibid., 242.
52 Ibid., 238.
53 Ibid., 243.
54 Newhouse, 214.
55 *YOU*, 247–56; Isaacson, 428, 607–13; Ambrose, II, 478, 616.
56 Newhouse, 235.
57 *YOU*, 259; *Diplomacy*, 752–58; Ambrose, I, 478, 583, 616; II, 170.
58 *YOU*, 25.
59 Ibid., 253.
60 Ibid., 255.
61 *YOU*, 274–75.
62 Ibid., 281–82.
63 Ibid., 282.
64 *YOU*, 283–85.
65 Ibid., 289–90; HAK int.
66 *YOU*, 290–92.
67 Ibid., 291.
68 Ibid., 288–89, 292.
69 Ibid., 287–89.
70 Ibid., 293–94.
71 Ibid., 294–95.
72 Ibid., 297–99.
73 HAK int., 8/04.
74 Dobrynin, 276.
75 Ambrose, II, 368; quoted in Raymond Garthoff, *Detente and Confrontation* (Washington, D.C., 1985), 409.
76 Newhouse, 240 n. 445.
77 Newhouse, 238.
78 Ibid., 238; *YOU*, 286.
79 *YOU*, 300 301.
80 Ibid., 300–301.

8: A Long Hot Summer

1 Ambrose, II, 178; *YOU*, 359.
2 *YOU*, 110; HAK int. 12/04.
3 *YOU*, 127.
4 HAK ints., 5/05.
5 Erréra int., 10/18/06.
6 *RN*, 851.
7 HAK ints., 10/28–30/05.
8 *RN*, 874.
9 G. Brett int., 5/6/05.
10 Ambrose, II, 178; *YOU*, 359.
11 Ambrose, II, 178; *YOU*, 359.
12 *Diplomacy*, 667–68.
13 Ambrose, II, 115, 138.
14 Ibid., 156.
15 Ibid., 163.
16 *YOU*, 105–6.
17 *YOU*, 110; HAK int., 12/04.
18 Telcon, 6/29/73.
19 Killen, 55.
20 Ambrose, II, 202, 232.
21 Ibid., II, 205.
22 Ibid., II, 208–9.
23 *RN*, 905.
24 Ambrose, II, 220.
25 *YOU*, 124–27.
26 Ibid., 122–24.
27 Ibid., 153, 161–62.
28 Ibid., 193–94.
29 Ibid., 229, 253–55.
30 Ibid., 253.
31 Ibid., 255.
32 HAK int., 8/2–3/04.
33 *YOU*, 300.
34 Schlesinger int., 5/16/05.
35 *YOU*, 353, 363.
36 Ibid., 363–64.
37 Ibid., 302.
38 Ibid., 322.
39 Ibid., 318.
40 *Newsweek*, 3/26/73.
41 *YOU*, 369.
42 Ibid., 311.
43 Ibid., 325.
44 Ibid., 326.
45 Ibid., 327.
46 Office of the White House Press Secretary, 6/13/73.
47 *YOU*, 337–39.
48 François Ponchaud, *Cambodia: Year Zero* (New York, 1978), xvi, 21, 135–36, 192.

49 *YOU*, 337–55.
50 Ibid., 356.
51 Ibid., 361.
52 Ibid., 369.
53 HAK int., 10/28–30/05.
54 Ambrose II, 61.
55 *Diplomacy*, 677.
56 Ibid., 731.
57 Ibid., 741.
58 Ibid., 756.
59 Haig int., 5/19/07.
60 Lord int. and notes, 4–5, 10/3/05, 12/30/05.
61 Memcon, 7/10/07; *FD*, p. 200.
62 *YOU*, 416.

9: To Secretary of State

1 Arthur Schlesinger to author.
2 HAK int., 5/13–14/06.
3 *YOU*, 422–23.
4 Ibid., 422.
5 Ibid., 423.
6 HAK int., 5/13–14/06.
7 Kalb and Kalb, 425.
8 HAK int., 5/13–14/06.
9 Ambrose, II, 108.
10 HAK ints., 10/28/05, 5/13–14/06; Haldeman, *The Haldeman Diaries*, 634.
11 HAK int., 8/15/04.
12 HAK; Dobrynin telcoms "1800 K. St.," Box 28, 7–8/73.
13 Ambrose, II, 214–15.
14 *YOU*, 431.
15 Ibid., 432.
16 Ambrose, II, 108, 214–15; *YOU*, 418–32; HAK ints., 8/15/04, 10/28/05, 5/13/06, 3/2/04; Haldeman, 634; *A World Restored*, 43; Dobrynin, 2.
17 *YOU*, 425.
18 *YOU*, 439–41.
19 *YOU*, 412–14.
20 Lodal int., 5/13/05.
21 Ibid.
22 HAK int., 2/28/05.
23 HAK, memcons, 9/12/07, 1–2.
24 HAK, memcons, 9/13/07, 2.
25 *YOU*, 447.
26 Ibid., 449.
27 Ibid., 447.
28 Ambrose, II, 235.
29 Ibid., 370–73.
30 Ibid., 371.
31 *NYT* and *Washington Post*, 10/17/73; *Hartford Times*, 10/22/73; *Richmond Times-Dispatch*, 10/23/73.

10: A Dagger Pointing at the Heart of Antarctica

1 WSAG meeting, 6/27/70.
2 *YOU*, 383.
3 *YOU*, 403, 406–8.
4 Christopher Hitchens, *The Trial of Henry Kissinger* (New York, 2002), 67.
5 *YOU*, 410–11.
6 Korry ints. 1971; *SEC; WHY*, 665–71.
7 *Helms*, n.p.
8 *WHY*, 671.
9 Memorandum to author, 7/11/08.
10 Thomas Powers, *The Man Who Kept the Secrets: Richard Helms and the CIA* (London, 1980), 234; *New York Times*, 5/26/77.
11 Helms, 604.
12 Powers, 230.
13 *WHY*, 673; *SEC*, 21ff.
14 HAK int., 10/28/05.
15 Helms, 404.
16 Ibid.
17 To the author, note of 7/11/08.
18 *WHY*, 676.
19 Powers, 362 n. 33.
20 Memorandum to author, 11/5/08.
21 HAK int., 10/28/05.
22 HAK int., 10/28/05.
23 Régis Debray, *The Chilean Revolution: Conversations with Allende* (New York, 1971), 82.
24 J. Haslam, *The Nixon Administration and the Death of Allende's Chile* (London, 2005), 25.
25 *SEC*, 137.
26 *YOU*, 374.
27 Ibid., 400.
28 Ibid., 382–83.
29 Mark Falcoff, "Kissinger and Chile: The Myth That Will Not Die," *Commentary*, 11/03, 46; Kristian C. Gustafson, Cambridge thesis, "The Coup Against Allende and Events to September 11, 1973"; *Mitrokhin Archive*, II, 59ff.
30 Nathaniel Davis, *The Last Two Years of Salvador Allende* (London, 1975), 171.
31 Telcon, 2/4/73; Kornbluh files.
32 Christopher Hitchens, "The Case Against Henry Kissinger," Part II, *Harper's*, March 2001.
33 11/12/71.
34 Cable, C/WHD to COS Santiago, 12/1/71. I am indebted to Dr. Kristian C. Gustafson, formerly of Corpus Christi College, Cambridge, for bringing this exchange to my attention.
35 Memorandum, "Proposed Covert Financial Support of Chilean Private Sector," quoted in Gustafson, p. 91.
36 Mark Falcoff, *Modern Chile, 1970–1989: A Critical History* (New Brunswick, N.J., 1989), 238.
37 *YOU*, 413.
38 Davis, 255.
39 *YOU*, 403–4.

40 Telcons; Falcoff, 48; Kornbluh files.

41 *YOU*, 409.

42 Quoted in Haslam, 200.

43 *Times Literary Supplement*, 5/28/08.

44 *Mitrokhin Archive*, II, 59ff.

45 WSAG meeting, 6/27/70.

46 Falcoff, 306.

47 Davis, 342.

48 HAK, note to AH, 7/11/08.

49 Ibid.

50 See AH, *Macmillan*, I, 252–85, and the *Aldington v. Tolstoy* case. Lord Aldington won £1.5 million in a 1991 libel case against Nikolai Tolstoy, for being accused of having been a "war criminal," but died without ever collecting a penny of the record damages — London's highest ever.

11: *The War of Atonement*

1 Boyne, 274.

2 *YOU*, 450–84; Henry Kissinger, *Crisis: The Anatomy of Two Major Foreign Policy Crises* (New York, 2003), 13–112 (10/6–7).

3 *Crisis*, 13.

4 Ibid., 16.

5 *Crisis*, 17–18.

6 Ibid., 32.

7 Ibid., 27.

8 Ibid., 35.

9 Ibid., 37.

10 Ibid., 45.

11 Ibid., 34–57.

12 Ibid., 57.

13 Telcon, 10/6/73.

14 *Crisis*, 68.

15 Ibid., 71.

16 From AH telcons.

17 Memcon, 10/6/73, from HAK Misc. box, p. 11.

18 AH diaries, 1968–69.

19 Boyne, 274. (see n. 53, below).

20 Geoffrey Lewis, *The Turkish Language Reform: A Catastrophic Success* (Oxford, 1999).

21 Memcon, Gromyko, 9/28/73.

22 *Crisis*, 84–85.

23 *Crisis*, 86–87.

24 *YOU*, 477.

25 *Crisis*, 89.

26 Ibid., 93.

27 Ibid., 94.

28 Ibid., 90.

29 Ibid., 96.

30 Ibid., 97.

31 *YOU*, 480.

32 *Crisis*, 108.
33 Ibid., 109.
34 *YOU*, 482.
35 *Crisis*, 110–12.
36 *YOU*, 483.
37 Ibid., 138–141.
38 Ibid., 143.
39 AH notes, 1973.
40 *YOU*, 493.
41 *Crisis*, 147.
42 Ibid., 160.
43 Ibid., 165–66.
44 Ibid., 165–66, 176–77.
45 *YOU*, 497.
46 Ibid., 503.
47 *Crisis*, 188–89. Telcon, 10/11/73, 7:55 P.M.
48 *YOU*, 514.
49 *Crisis*, 249.
50 HAK conv., 3/3/08.
51 *Crisis*, 249–52.
52 Ibid., 273–81.
53 Additional notes; Horne *Times*, Oct. 2003; *Haaretz*, 9/02, 8/03; Avi Shlaim, *The Iron Wall*; Walter J. Boyne, *The 2 O'Clock War* (New York, 2002); Chaim Herzog, *The War of Atonement* (1975); General Saad el-Shazly, *The Crossing of Suez: The October War, 1973* (Beirut, 1980); Mohamed Heikal, *The Ramadan War*; Coldwell notes.
54 *YOU*, 498.
55 Ibid., 516, 721 passim.
56 *YOU*, 497; *Crisis*, 216.
57 *YOU*, 513.
58 *Crisis*, 201–3, 228.
59 *YOU*, 499; Telcons.
60 *YOU*, 515.
61 *Crisis*, 252.
62 Telcons, 10/12/73.
63 *Crisis*, 223.
64 Ibid., 230.
65 Ibid., 238.
66 *YOU*, 510.
67 *Crisis*, 243–44.
68 Ibid., 257.
69 Ibid., 255.
70 Ibid., 258.
71 Ibid.
72 Ibid., 282.

12: The Crisis: DEFCON 3

1 *YOU*, 535.
2 *Crisis*, 260.
3 Ibid., 110–11; *YOU*, 481–82; NSA, 20; Doc 20.

4 *YOU*, 482.

5 *Crisis*, 265.

6 *YOU*, 527.

7 Memcons, 10/17/73.

8 Ibid., 535.

9 Ibid., 535.

10 *Crisis*, 281.

11 Ibid., 290–91.

12 Ibid., 292.

13 Ibid., 283–95.

14 Memcon, 10/19/73, 7:17–7:28.

15 *Crisis*, 295–96.

16 Ibid., 295–98.

17 Ibid., 285, 302; *YOU*, 544.

18 Victor Israelyan, *Inside the Kremlin During the Yom Kippur War* (University Park, Pa., 1995), xix.

19 Ibid., xiii.

20 Ibid., 25.

21 Ibid., 1–2.

22 Ibid., 16.

23 Ibid., 37.

24 Ibid., 31.

25 Ibid., 56.

26 Ibid., 55.

27 Ibid., 66.

28 Ibid., 49.

29 Ibid., 50.

30 Ibid., 76.

31 Ibid., 79.

32 See *YOU*, 519.

33 Israelyan, 83.

34 Ibid., 94.

35 Ibid., 96–98; 106–7.

36 Ibid., 112.

37 Ibid., 116.

38 *Crisis*, 303–4; *YOU*, 547–49.

39 *YOU*, 551; NSA, §46–9, p. 35–37.

40 *YOU*, 551: Isaacson, 525.

41 *Crisis*, 303.

42 *YOU*, 550.

43 Israelyan, 121.

44 Ibid., 123.

45 Ibid., 124.

46 *Crisis*, 304.

47 Israelyan, 124, 129.

48 Ibid., 130–31.

49 *YOU*, 553.

50 Crisis, 304.

51 Israelyan, 138.

52 Ibid., 136; *YOU*, 559.

53 Israelyan, 148.

54 *YOU*, 557–7.
55 Israelyan, 143–44.
56 *Crisis*, 305.
57 HAK int., 4/26/08.
58 Israelyan, 149.
59 *YOU*, 555.
60 Ibid., 559.
61 Telcons, 10/19/73.
62 *YOU*, 560–61.
63 Ibid., 563.
64 Ibid., 562.
65 Ibid., 564–65.
66 Shlaim, *The Iron Wall*, 316.
67 Heikal, *Ramadan War*, 233.
68 Kalb and Kalb, 525.
69 HAK ints., 8/04, 10/28/05.
70 HAK ints., esp. 4/5/08.
71 Ibid.
72 Kalb and Kalb, 527.
73 HAK ints.
74 Memcon, 10/22/73, 1:35–2:15 P.M.; *see NSA, §54; Burr p. 39.*
75 Isaacson, 527; and AH int.
76 *YOU*, 565.
77 Memcon, 10/22/73, 2:30–4:00 P.M.
78 Ibid., 4:15–4:57 P.M.
79 *YOU*, 565–67.
80 Quandt, 118, 120, 461.
81 *YOU*, 567.
82 Ibid., 569, 571; NSA docs., §59 "Sit rep" (Burr, 42).
83 NSA docs., §61A-B; messages from Brezhnev (Burr, 43).
84 *Crisis*, 313–14.
85 *YOU*, 573.
86 NSA Burr, 44.
87 *Crisis*, 314–15.
88 Ibid., 322–32.
89 Ibid., 325.
90 *YOU*, 575.
91 Ibid., 576.
92 Ibid., 569.
93 *Crisis*, 337.
94 *YOU*, 581–83.
95 *Crisis*, 342.
96 *YOU*, 581.
97 *Crisis*, 336.
98 *Crisis*, 336–43; telcons; *YOU*, 585.
99 *Crisis*, 345.
100 *RN*, 938; HAK int., 4/5/08, and see *Crisis*, 347.
101 Schlesinger int., 5/16/05.
102 *Crisis*, 349–55.
103 Arthur Schlesinger int., 5/16/05.
104 *YOU*, 589; *Crisis*, 351.

105 *Crisis*, 351–53.
106 Ibid., 353; *YOU*, 591.
107 Haig int. 5/19/05; Richard Parker, ed., *The October War: A Retrospective* (Gainesville, Fl., 2001), 247, 480 n. 122.
108 Alexander M. Haig, with Charles McCarry, *Inner Circles: How America Changed the World, A Memoir* (New York, 1992), 415–16; Lebow and Stein, 481.
109 Schlesinger int., 5/16/05.
110 Scowcroft int., 5/26/05.
111 Rodman int., 5/13/05.
112 Ambrose, II, 252–56.
113 Isaacson, 532.
114 *YOU*, 593; *Crisis*, 355.
115 HAK ints., 10/28–30/05.
116 Roger Morris, *Haig: The General's Progress* (New York, 1982), 257–59.
117 Isaacson, 532.
118 *Crisis*, 354.
119 Ibid., 355.
120 Dobrynin, 296–97.
121 *Crisis*, 360–61.
122 Dobrynin, 297.
123 Israelyan, 161.
124 Ibid., 160–63.
125 Ibid., 171–73.
126 Ibid., 179–80.
127 Ibid., 188–89.
128 Ibid., 192.
129 Ibid., 183.

13: To Sadat

1 Telcons, 10/26/73.
2 *YOU*, 236; C. W. Wells, 21.
3 *YOU*, 648–47.
4 State Dept. press release, 10/25/73.
5 Ambrose, II, 256.
6 *YOU*, 596.
7 Telcons; *Crisis*, 363–65.
8 See http://www.wagingpeace.org/articles/1998/01/00_phillips_20-mishaps.htm.
9 Isaacson, 532–33.
10 Ambrose, II, 256.
11 British Cabinet memcon, 10/25/73, released 1/2/04.
12 Adm. E. R., Zumwalt, Jr., *On Watch: A Memoir* (New York, 1976), 446.
13 *YOU*, 585.
14 Lebow and Stein, 251–60.
15 *YOU*, 980; Lebow and Stein, 265–68.
16 Scowcroft int., 5/26/05; Schlesinger int., 5/16/05; Parker, 175.
17 Lodal int., 10/05.
18 Rodman ints., 4/15/05; Parker, 168–77.
19 Parker, 168, 176–81, 201–3, 213; Rodman ints.
20 HAK ints., esp. 4/5/08.

21 Telcons, 10/26/73.

22 Ambrose, II, 258.

23 *YOU*, 606–7; *Crisis*, 390; Isaacson, 534–36.

24 *Crisis*, 234–36.

25 Ibid., 390–91.

26 Ibid., 370–71.

27 Ibid., 379.

28 Ibid., 379–88.

29 Ibid., 394–94.

30 Ibid., 398.

31 *YOU*, 610.

32 *Crisis*, 413.

33 Ibid., 416.

34 Ibid., 612.

35 Ibid., 611.

36 Ibid., 616.

37 *YOU*, 617.

38 Ibid., 619–23.

39 Ibid., 621.

40 *Crisis*, 393.

41 *YOU*, 631.

42 Ibid., 633.

43 Anwar El Sadat, *In Search of Identity: An Autobiography* (New York, 1977).

44 HAK int., 10/28/05.

45 *YOU*, 636.

46 C. W. Wells, "Kissinger and Sadat, Improbable Partners for Peace," doctoral thesis, Yale University, 1004, 20. I am indebted to Dr. Wells for his doctoral thesis, which I found tallied greatly with my own sense of this historic meeting, and Kissinger's own account.

47 *YOU*, 236; Wells, 21.

48 Mohamed Heikal, *Autumn of Fury* (London, 1983), 67.

49 Heikal, *The Road to Ramadan*, (London, 1975), 40.

50 HAK int., etc 4/5/08; *YOU*, 638–46.

51 *YOU*, 561.

52 *YOU*, 640.

53 Ibid., 643.

54 Ibid., 646.

55 Ibid., 651.

56 Sadat, 291–92; Wells, 29.

57 White House memcon, 11/7/73.

58 Memcon, 11/12/73; State Dept. staff mtg., 11/19/73; HAK memcon, 11/19/73; Wells, 30.

59 Heikal int., 2/19/05.

60 *YOU*, 645.

61 Heikal, *Autumn of Fury*, 67.

62 Heikal ints., Cairo, 2/05.

63 Heikal, *Autumn of Fury*, 5–6.

64 AH notes, 2/17–18/08.

65 *YOU*, 654.

66 Shlaim conv.; Avi Shlaim, *Lion of Jordan: The Life of King Hussein in War and Peace* (London, 2007), 356–73.

67 YOU, 661–65.
68 Ibid., 673.

14: On to China

1 Memcon, 10/23/73.
2 *YOU*, 693.
3 *YOU*, 678.
4 Message, 7/18/73; Kissinger misc., boxes 9.
5 Memcon, 7/19/73.
6 Memcon, 9/28/73.
7 Memcons, 10/25/73 and 10/6/73.
8 *YOU*, 684.
9 Lord int., 10/30/05; *YOU*, 686–87.
10 Jung Chang and Jon Halliday, *Mao*, 614; J. Spence conv., 10/28/05.
11 *YOU*, 688.
12 Ibid., 689.
13 Ibid., 693–94.
14 Report of 11/19/73; from Kissinger misc. boxes p. 13.
15 HAK int., 10/28/05.
16 *Mao*, 617–21.
17 HAK int., 10/28–29/05.
18 Ints. of 10/3, 10/21 (S. Roy), and 10/30/05 (Lord).
19 HAK letter of 6/28/05.
20 Lord int., 10/30/05.
21 *Mao*, 618.
22 HAK letter of 6/28/05.
23 *YOU*, 699.

15: To Geneva and Shuttle

1 *YOU*, 755.
2 Memcon, 12/22/73.
3 Crisis, 411.
4 Ibid., 237.
5 Ibid., 390–91.
6 Memcons, 11/30/73.
7 Heikal, *Road to Ramadan*, 255; NSA docs. §81, 10/27/73, 55.
8 NSA docs., §81, 10/27/73, 55.
9 *YOU*, 709.
10 W. Buell conv., 4/30/05.
11 PRO, 2/1/04.
12 *YOU*, 704.
13 Ibid., 710.
14 NSA doc. 51, §75.
15 *YOU*, 728.
16 Ibid., 745–46.
17 White House memcon, 12/11/73.
18 NSA docs., §90, 60.

19 *Crisis*, 239.
20 Close int., 11/18/05.
21 Heikal, *Road to Ramadan*, 268.
22 Quandt, 126.
23 *YOU*, 872–73.
24 Ibid., 715; NSA docs., §81 State Dept. cable to U.S. Embassy, Germany, 10/27/73.
25 HAK memcons, 10/26/73.
26 NSA doc., §82, memcon, 10/26/73.
27 *YOU*, 714, 717.
28 Ibid.
29 Israelyan, 97–98.
30 Quandt, 172.
31 *YOU*, 819–21.
32 Harold Saunders int., 5/13/05.
33 Ibid., 755.
34 Rodman int., 5/13/05.
35 *YOU*, 762–65; memcon, 12/13/73.
36 Memcon, 12/13/73; HAK misc. boxes, '73, p. 15.
37 *YOU*, 770.
38 Ibid., 771–72.
39 Nixon to Faisal, 12/3/73; R. Close int.
40 *YOU*, 775.
41 Ibid., 779–82.
42 Memcon, 12/15/73.
43 HAK misc, boxes, '73; memcon, 12/16/73.
44 *YOU*, 786.
45 Memcon, 12/17/73; HAK misc. boxes.
46 *YOU*, 790–92.
47 Ibid., app. 1249–50.
48 Ibid., 791.
49 Saunders int., 5/13/08.
50 Shlaim conv., 4/10/08.
51 Memcon, 12/21/73, via Scowcroft.
52 *YOU*, 792.
53 Memcons, 12/19/73.
54 Ibid.; HAK misc boxes.
55 *YOU*, 793.
56 Memcons, 12/22/73.
57 Parker, 249; *YOU*, 767, 795.
58 Memcons, 12/17/73, 12/21/73; HAK misc. boxes; M. Sterner notes, AH int., 10/27/05.
59 *YOU*, 797–98.
60 Ibid., 798.

16: *The Awful Grace of God*

1 As quoted from Aeschylus, *YOU*, 1210.
2 Jonathan Yardley, *Washington Post* review of Killen, *1973 Nervous Breakdown*.
3 *YOU*, 849.
4 Ibid., 753.

5 Telcon, 12/7/73.

6 Ambrose, II, 279–93.

7 Barry M. Goldwater, *Goldwater* (New York, 1988), 267–70.

8 Ambrose, II, 286.

9 HAK memcon, 12/26/08; misc. boxes.

10 Record of Sec. Kissinger's schedule.

11 HAK ints., 12/28–30/05.

12 *YOU*, 5.

13 HAK ints., 12/28–30/05.

14 Lord int., 10/31/05.

15 Yardley, *Washington Post* review of Killen, *1973 Nervous Breakdown.*

16 Note from H. Shukrallah to Heikal, 2/17/08.

17 *YOU*, 812.

18 Ibid., 815–16.

19 Ibid., 825.

20 Ibid., 831.

21 Ibid., 844.

22 Ibid., 852.

23 Ibid., 805–9.

24 Quoted by Jeremi Suri, *Henry Kissinger and the American Century*, 265; telcons, 10/18/73; 11/2/73.

25 *YOU*, 849.

26 P. Carrington int., 5/08.

27 *YOU*, 1032.

28 Ibid., 1033.

29 Ibid., 1054.

30 Ibid., 1067.

31 Ibid., 1079.

32 Ibid., 1109.

33 Ibid., 1112.

34 Ibid., 1111.

35 Ambrose, II, 294; *YOU*, 371.

36 Ambrose, II, 336.

37 *YOU*, 1128.

38 Ambrose, II, 357.

39 *YOU*, 1140.

40 *YOU*, 1177.

41 Ibid., 1112.

42 Ibid., 1117.

43 Ibid., 1117.

44 *RN*, 1054–55.

45 Ambrose, II, 406.

46 *YOU*, 1181.

47 Ibid., 1196.

48 Ibid., 107–8.

49 Ibid., 1207.

50 Ibid., 1210.

51 Ibid., 1201.

52 Ibid., 1198.

53 Ibid., 1211–14.

54 Ambrose, II, 597.

55 Ibid., 445.
56 Ambrose, II, 432.
57 Heath, 495.
58 Israelyan, 213.
59 Pipes convs., 12/07.
60 Brzezinski int., 10/26/05.
61 HAK ints., 8/13–15/04.
62 HAK int., 4/21/05.
63 At Geneva, 12/22/73; noted down by P. Rodman; HAK misc. boxes.
64 *YOU*, 983.
65 Ibid., 984–87.
66 Ibid., 991.
67 HAK int., 3/3/08.
68 Memcon, 9/26/73.
69 Walters, II, 89.
70 MM, 269.
71 White House memcon, 11/15/73.
72 *Crisis*, 422.
73 *YOR*, 476.
74 *Crisis*, 424.
75 Ibid., 534.
76 *Crisis*, 427.
77 4/13/75; quoted in *EVW*, 530.
78 Buckley conv., 5/05; James Buckley, *If Men Were Angels: A View from the Senate* (New York, 1975).
79 *YOR*, 541.
80 Ibid., 463.
81 Ibid., 471; HAK ints., 4/26/04, 8/12/05, 10/28/05, 4/26/08, etc.
82 *EVW*, 555.
83 *YOR*, 542.
84 Lord int., 10/30/05; Stanley Resor int., 10/19/05.

Aftermath

1 *YOR*, 1059.
2 *YOU*, 1198.
3 Presidential Proclamation, 9/8/74.
4 HAK, eulogy for President Gerald Ford, 1/2/07.
5 *YOR*, 1059.
6 *Time*, 3/74.
7 Isaacson, 744–45.
8 Pres. G. W. Bush int., 5/3/07.
9 *Crisis*, 544.
10 See Isaacson, 761–67; Isaacson int., 4/20/05.
11 HAK int., 4/20/05.
12 Philip Ziegler, *Mountbatten: The Official Biography* (London, 1985), 701.
13 Billington int., 5/12/05.

BIBLIOGRAPHY

Ambrose, Stephen E. *Nixon: Ruin and Recovery, 1973–1990.* New York: Simon & Schuster, 1991.

——. *Nixon: The Triumph of a Politician, 1962–1972.* New York: Simon & Schuster, 1989.

Andrew, Christopher M., and Vasili Mitrokhin. *The Mitrokhin Archive: The KGB and the World,* vol. II. London: Allen Lane, 2005.

Billington, James H. *Fire in the Minds of Men.* New York: Basic Books, 1980.

——. *Russia Transformed: Breakthrough to Hope.* New York: Free Press, 1992.

Black, Conrad. *Richard Milhous Nixon: The Invincible Quest.* London: Quercus, 2007.

Blum, John Morton. *Years of Discord: American Politics and Society, 1961–1974.* New York: W. W. Norton, 1991.

Boyne, Walter J. *The 2 O'Clock War.* New York: Thomas Dunne Books, 2002.

Burkett, Elinor. *Golda Meir: The Iron Lady of the Middle East.* London: Gibson Square Books, 2008.

Burr, William, ed. *The Kissinger Transcripts: The Top Secret Talks with Beijing and Moscow.* New York: New Press, 1999.

Chang, Jung, and Jon Halliday. *Mao: The Unknown Story.* London, 2005.

Colson, Charles. *Born Again.* Old Tappan, N.J.: Chosen Books, 1976.

Dallek, Robert. *Nixon and Kissinger: Partners in Power.* London: HarperCollins, 2007.

Dean, John. *Blind Ambition: The White House Years.* New York: Simon & Schuster, 1976.

Dobrynin, Anatoly. *In Confidence: Moscow's Ambassador to America's Six Cold War Presidents.* New York: Times Books, 1995.

Eban, Abba. *Personal Witness: Israel Through My Eyes.* New York: G. P. Putnam's Sons, 1992.

Ehrlichman, John. *Witness to Power: The Nixon Years.* New York: Simon & Schuster, 1982.

Ellsberg, Daniel. *Secrets: A Memoir of Vietnam and the Pentagon Papers.* New York: Viking Press, 2002.

Ervin, Jr., Sam J. *The Whole Truth: The Watergate Conspiracy.* New York: Random House, 1980.

Falcoff, Mark. *Modern Chile, 1970–1989: A Critical History.* New Brunswick, N.J.: Transaction Publishers, 1989.

Ford, Gerald R. *A Time to Heal.* New York: Harper & Row, 1979.

Frost, David. *"I Gave Them a Sword": Behind the Scenes of the Nixon Interviews.* New York: William Morrow, 1978.

Garment, Leonard. *In Search of Deep Throat: The Greatest Political Mystery of Our Time.* New York: Basic Books, 2000.

Garthoff, Raymond L. *Détente and Confrontation: American-Soviet Relations from Nixon to Reagan.* Washington, D.C.: Brookings Institution Press, 1985.

Geyer, Georgie Anne. *Buying the Night Flight: The Autobiography of a Woman Foreign Correspondent.* Chicago: University of Chicago Press, 2001.

Ghanayem, Ishaq I., and V. Alden. *The Kissinger Legacy: American-Middle East Policy.* New York: Praeger, 1984.

Goldwater, Barry M., with Jack Casserly. *Goldwater.* New York: Doubleday, 1988.

Gromyko, Andrei. *Memoirs.* New York: Doubleday, 1989.

Haig, Jr., Alexander M., with Charles McCarry. *Inner Circles: How America Changed the World.* New York: Warner Books, 1992.

Halberstam, David. *The Best and the Brightest.* New York: Random House, 1992.

Haldeman, H. R. *The Haldeman Diaries: Inside the Nixon White House.* New York: G. P. Putnam's Sons, 1994.

Hanhimaki, Jusi M. *The Flawed Architect: Henry Kissinger and American Foreign Policy.* New York: Oxford University Press, 2004.

Heath, Edward. *The Course of My Life.* London: Hodder & Stoughton, 1998.

Heikal, Mohamed. *Autumn of Fury: The Assassination of Sadat.* London: Corgi, 1984.

———. *The Road to Ramadan.* London: Collins, 1975.

Helms, Richard, with William Hood. *A Look Over My Shoulder.* New York: Random House, 2003.

Hersh, Seymour M. *The Price of Power: Kissinger in the Nixon White House.* New York: Summit, 1983.

Herzog, Chaim. *The War of Atonement.* London: Weidenfeld and Nicholson, 1975.

Hitchens, Christopher. *The Trial of Henry Kissinger.* New York: Verso, 2001.

Horne, Alistair. *A Bundle from Britain.* London: Picador, 1992.

———. *Macmillan,* vol. II. London: Macmillan, 1988.

———. *Small Earthquake in Chile.* New York and London: Macmillan, 1972.

Isaacson, Walter. *Kissinger.* New York: Simon & Schuster, 1992.

Israelyan, Viktor. *Inside the Kremlin During the Yom Kippur War.* University Park, Penn.: Pennsylvania State University Press, 1995.

Kalb, Marvin L., and Bernard Kalb. *Kissinger.* Boston: Little, Brown, 1974.

Killen, Andreas. *1973 Nervous Breakdown.* New York: Bloomsbury, 2006.

Kissinger, Henry A. *Crisis: The Anatomy of Two Major Foreign Policy Crises.* New York: Simon & Schuster, 2003.

———. *Diplomacy.* New York: Simon & Schuster, 1994.

———. *Does America Need a Foreign Policy?* New York: Simon & Schuster, 2001.

———. *Ending the Vietnam War.* New York: Simon & Schuster, 2003.

———. *White House Years.* Boston: Little, Brown, 1979.

———. *A World Restored: Metternich, Castlereagh and the Problems of Peace, 1812–1822.* Boston: Houghton Mifflin, 1957.

———. *Years of Renewal.* New York: Simon & Schuster, 1999.

———. *Years of Upheaval.* Boston: Little, Brown, 1982.

Kornbluh, Peter. *The Pinochet File.* New York: New Press, 2003.

Kutler, Stanley I. *The Wars of Watergate: The Last Crisis of Richard Nixon.* New York: W. W. Norton, 1992.

Lebow, Richard Ned, and Janice Gross Stein. *We All Lost the Cold War.* Princeton: Princeton University Press, 1994.

Litwak, Robert. *Détente and the Nixon Doctrine.* New York: Cambridge University Press, 1984.

MacMillan, Margaret. *Nixon and Mao: The Week That Changed the World.* New York: Random House, 2007.

Mollenhoff, Clark R. *Game Plan for Disaster: An Ombudsman's Report on the Nixon Years.* New York: W. W. Norton, 1976.

Morris, Roger. *Uncertain Greatness: Henry Kissinger and American Foreign Policy.* New York: Harper & Row, 1977.

Muir, M., and M. F. Wilkinson. *The Most Dangerous Years: The Cold War, 1953–1975.* Lexington, Va.: Virginia Military Institute, 2005.

Newhouse, John. *Cold Dawn: The Story of SALT.* New York: Holt, Rinehart & Winston, 1973.

———. *War and Peace in the Nuclear Age.* New York: Alfred A. Knopf, 1989.

Nixon, Richard M. *RN: The Memoirs of Richard Nixon.* New York: Touchstone, 1990.

Oren, Michael B. *Power, Faith, and Fantasy: America in the Middle East, 1776 to the Present.* New York: W. W. Norton, 2007.

———. *Six Days of War: June 1967 and the Making of the Modern Middle East.* New York: Oxford University Press, 2002.

Parker, Richard B. *The October War.* Gainesville, Fl.: University Press of Florida, 2001.

Powers, Thomas. *The Man Who Kept the Secrets: Richard Helms and the CIA.* New York: Alfred A. Knopf, 1979.

Quandt, William B. *Peace Process: American Diplomacy and the Arab-Israeli Conflict Since 1967.* Washington, D.C.: Brookings Institution Press, 2005.

Rabin, Yitzhak. *The Rabin Memoirs.* Berkeley, Calif.: University of California Press, 1996.

Reeves, Richard. *President Nixon: Alone in the White House.* New York: Simon & Schuster, 2001.

Sadat, Anwar. *In Search of Identity: An Autobiography.* New York: Harper & Row, 1978.

Safire, William. *Before the Fall: An Inside View of the Pre-Watergate White House.* Garden City, N.Y.: Doubleday, 1975.

Schlesinger, James R. *America at Century's End.* New York: Columbia University Press, 1989.

Schulzinger, Robert D. *Henry Kissinger: Doctor of Diplomacy.* New York: Columbia University Press, 1989.

———. *A Time for War: The United States and Vietnam, 1941–1975.* New York: Oxford University Press, 1997.

Shawcross, William. *Sideshow: Kissinger, Nixon, and the Destruction of Cambodia.* New York: Simon & Schuster, 1979.

Shazly, Saad el, *The Crossing of Suez: The October War, 1973.* San Francisco: American Mideast Research, 1980.

Sherill, Robert. *The Oil Follies of 1970–1980.* Garden City, N.Y.: Anchor Press, 1983.

Shlaim, Avi. *The Iron Wall: Israel and the Arab World.* New York: W. W. Norton, 2000.

———. *Lion of Jordan: The Life of King Hussein in War and Peace.* London: Allen Lane, 2007.

Sirica, John J. *To Set the Record Straight: The Break-in, the Tapes, the Conspirators, the Pardon.* New York: W. W. Norton, 1979.

Smith, Gerard C. *Doubletalk: The Story of SALT I.* Lanham, Md., University Press of America, 1985.

Spence, Jonathan D. *Mao Zedong.* New York: Viking Press, 1999.

Suri, Jeremi. *Henry Kissinger and the American Century.* Cambridge, Mass.: Belknap Press, 2007.

Szulc, Tad. *The Illusion of Peace: Foreign Policy in the Nixon Years.* New York: Viking Press, 1978.

Talbott, Strobe. *The Russia Hand: A Memoir of Presidential Diplomacy.* New York: Random House, 2002.

Walters, Vernon A. *The Mighty and the Meek.* London: St. Ermin's Press, 2001.

——. *Silent Missions.* Garden City, N.Y.: Doubleday, 1978.

Wells, Christopher W. *Kissinger and Sadat: Improbable Partners for Peace.* New Haven, Conn.: Yale, 2004.

White, Theodore H. *Breach of Faith: The Fall of Richard Nixon.* New York: Atheneum, 1975.

Wicker, Tom. *One of Us: Richard Nixon and the American Dream.* New York: Random House, 1991.

Wills, Garry. *Nixon Agonistes.* Boston: Houghton Mifflin, 1970.

Woodward, Bob, and Carl Bernstein. *All the President's Men.* New York: Simon & Schuster, 1974.

——. *The Final Days.* New York: Simon & Schuster, 1976.

Ziegler, Philip. *Mountbatten: The Official Biography.* London: William Collins, 1985.

Zumwalt, Jr., Elmo. *On Watch: A Memoir.* New York: Quadrangle, 1976.

INDEX